ARTIFACTS™

volume **5**

published by
Top Cow Productions, Inc.
Los Angeles

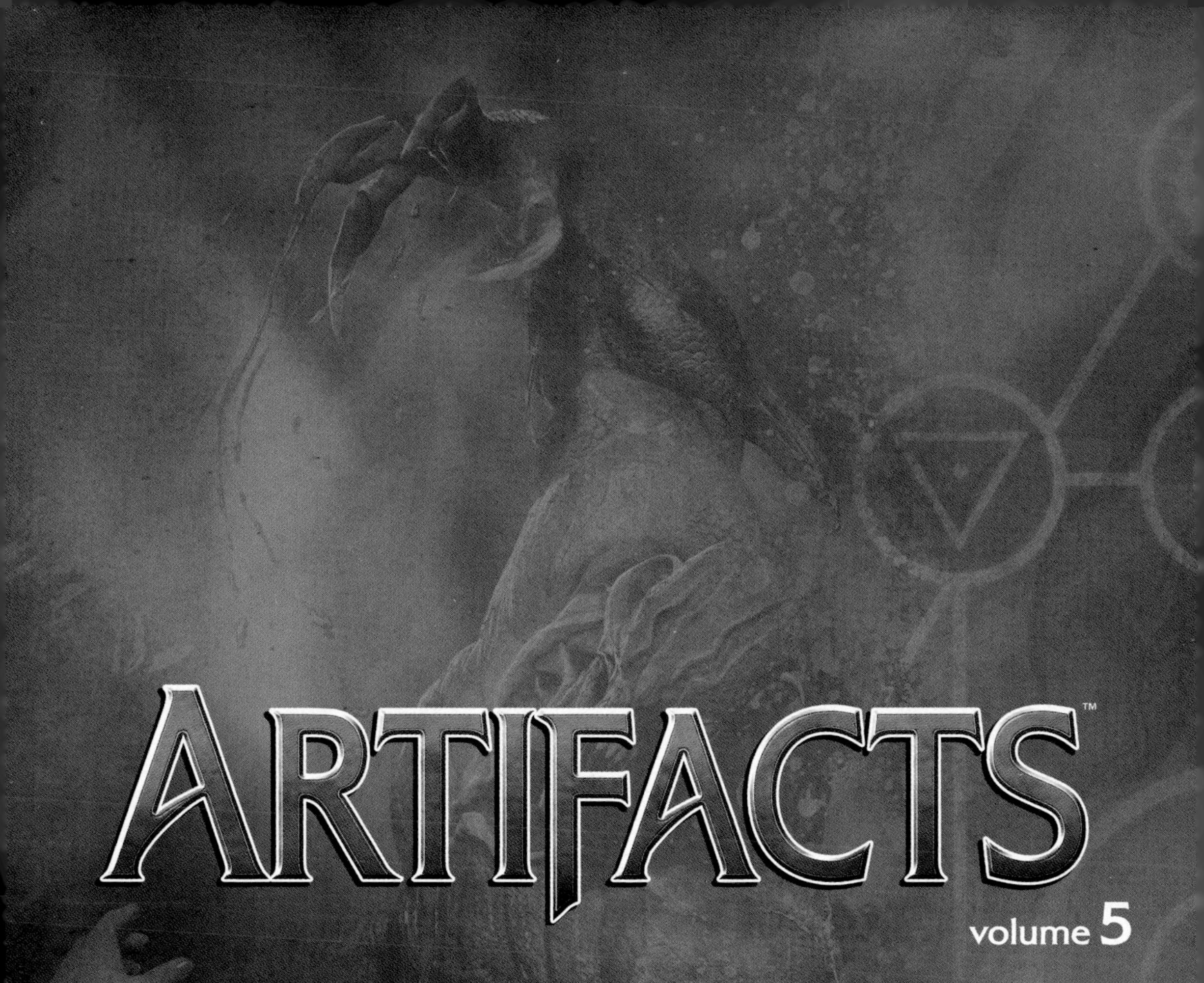

ARTIFACTS™

volume 5

WRITTEN BY:
RON MARZ

ART BY:
STJEPAN SEJIC

LETTERS BY:
TROY PETERI

The Darkness created by:
Marc Silvestri, Garth Ennis, & David Wohl

Top Cow Universe architects:
Marc Silvestri, Matt Hawkins, Filip Sablik, & Ron Marz

For this edition Cover Art by:
Stjepan Sejic

For this edition
Book Design and Layout by:
Vincent Kukua

Original editions edited by:
Bryan Rountree & Matt Hawkins

for Top Cow Productions Inc.
Marc Silvestri - CEO
Matt Hawkins - President & COO
Bryan Rountree - Managing Editor
Elena Salcedo - Operations Manager
Betsy Gonia - Production Assistant

Want more info? check out:
www.topcow.com
for news and exclusive
Top Cow merchandise!

IMAGE COMICS, INC.
Robert Kirkman - chief operating officer
Erik Larsen - chief financial officer
Todd McFarlane - president
Marc Silvestri - chief executive officer
Jim Valentino - vice-president
Eric Stephenson - publisher
Ron Richards - director of business development
Jennifer de Guzman - pr & marketing director
Branwyn Bigglestone - accounts manager
Emily Miller - accounting assistant
Jamie Parreno - marketing assistant
Jenna Savage - administrative assistant
Kevin Yuen - digital rights coordinator
Jonathan Chan - production manager
Drew Gill - art director
Tyler Shainline - print manager
Monica Garcia - production artist
Vincent Kukua - production artist
Jana Cook - production artist
www.imagecomics.com

ARTIFACTS Volume 5 Trade Paperback May 2013. FIRST PRINTING. ISBN: 978-1-60706-664-4, $16.99 U.S.D..
Published by Image Comics Inc. Office of Publication: 2001 Center St., 6th Floor, Berkeley, CA 94704. Originally published in single magazine form as ARTIFACTS 19-24.

TABLE OF CONTENTS

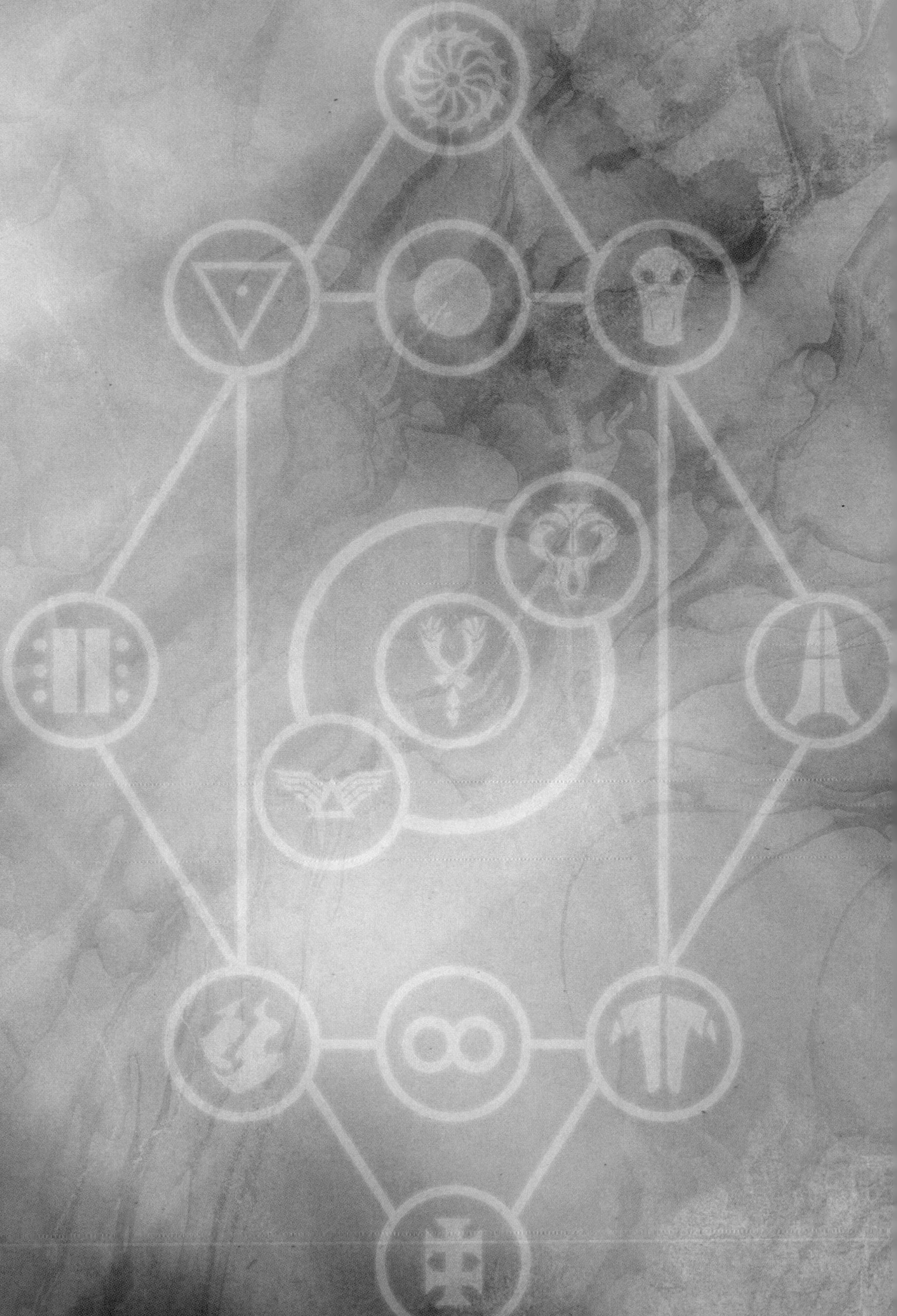

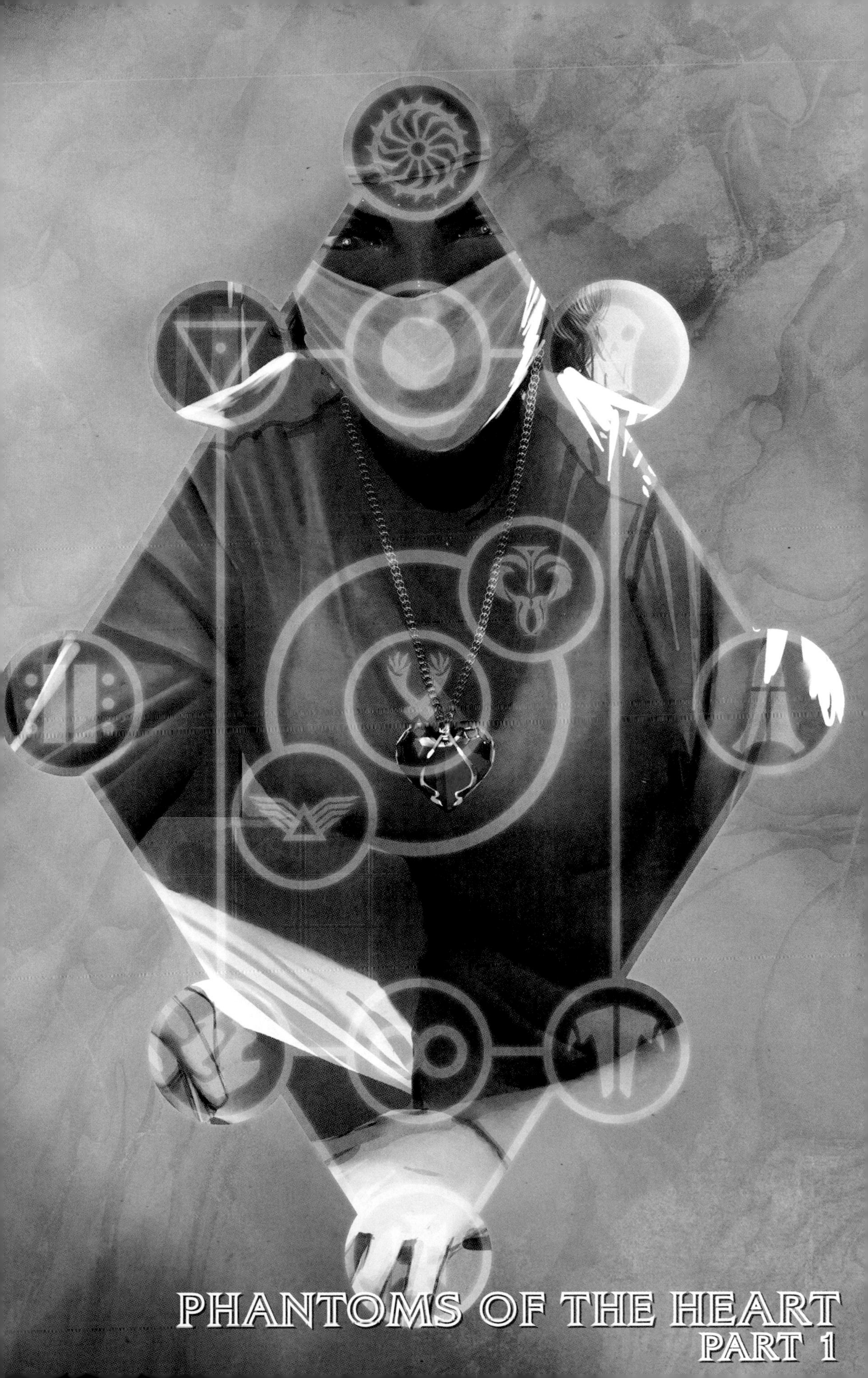
PHANTOMS OF THE HEART
PART 1

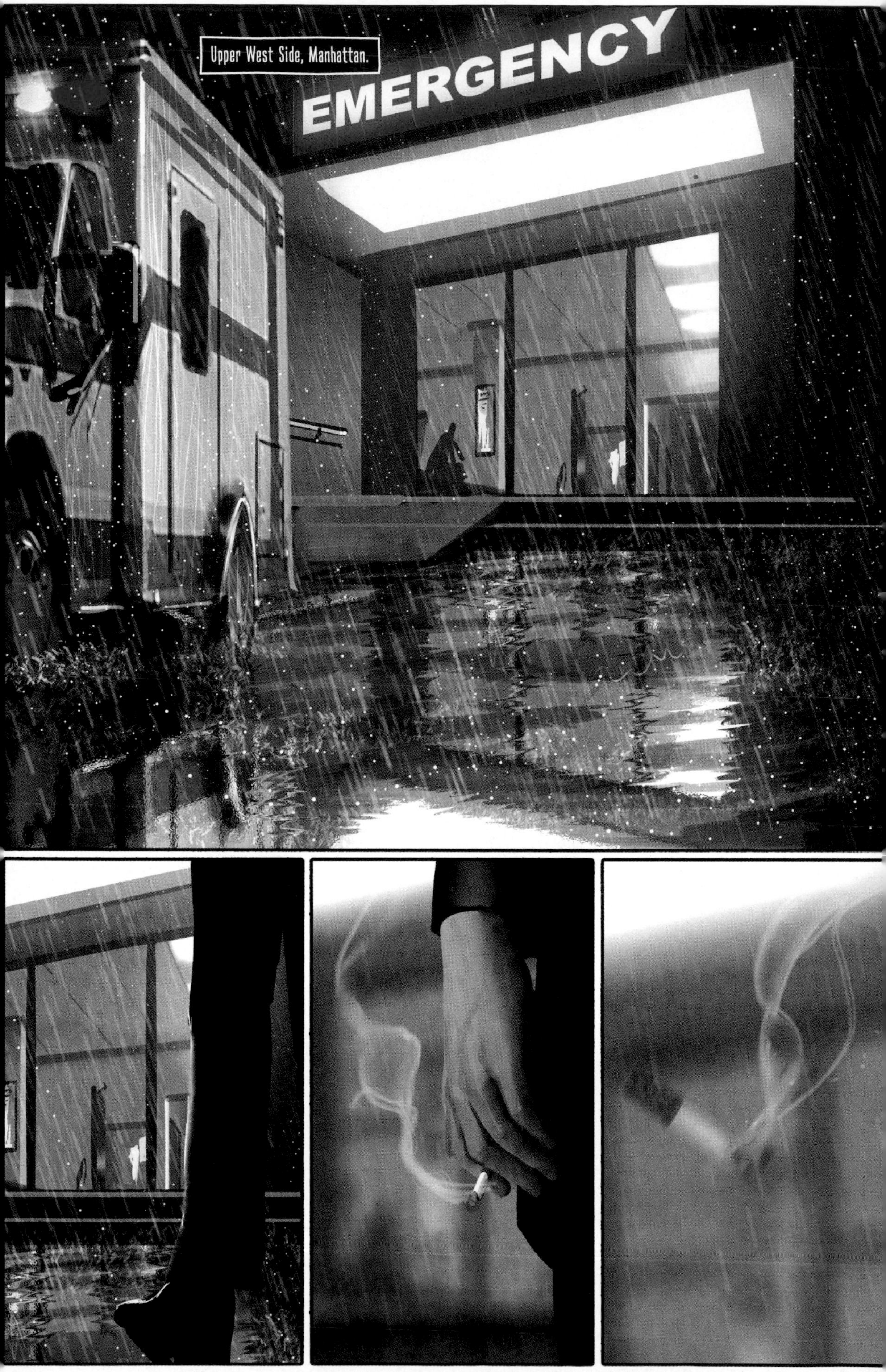
Upper West Side, Manhattan.
EMERGENCY

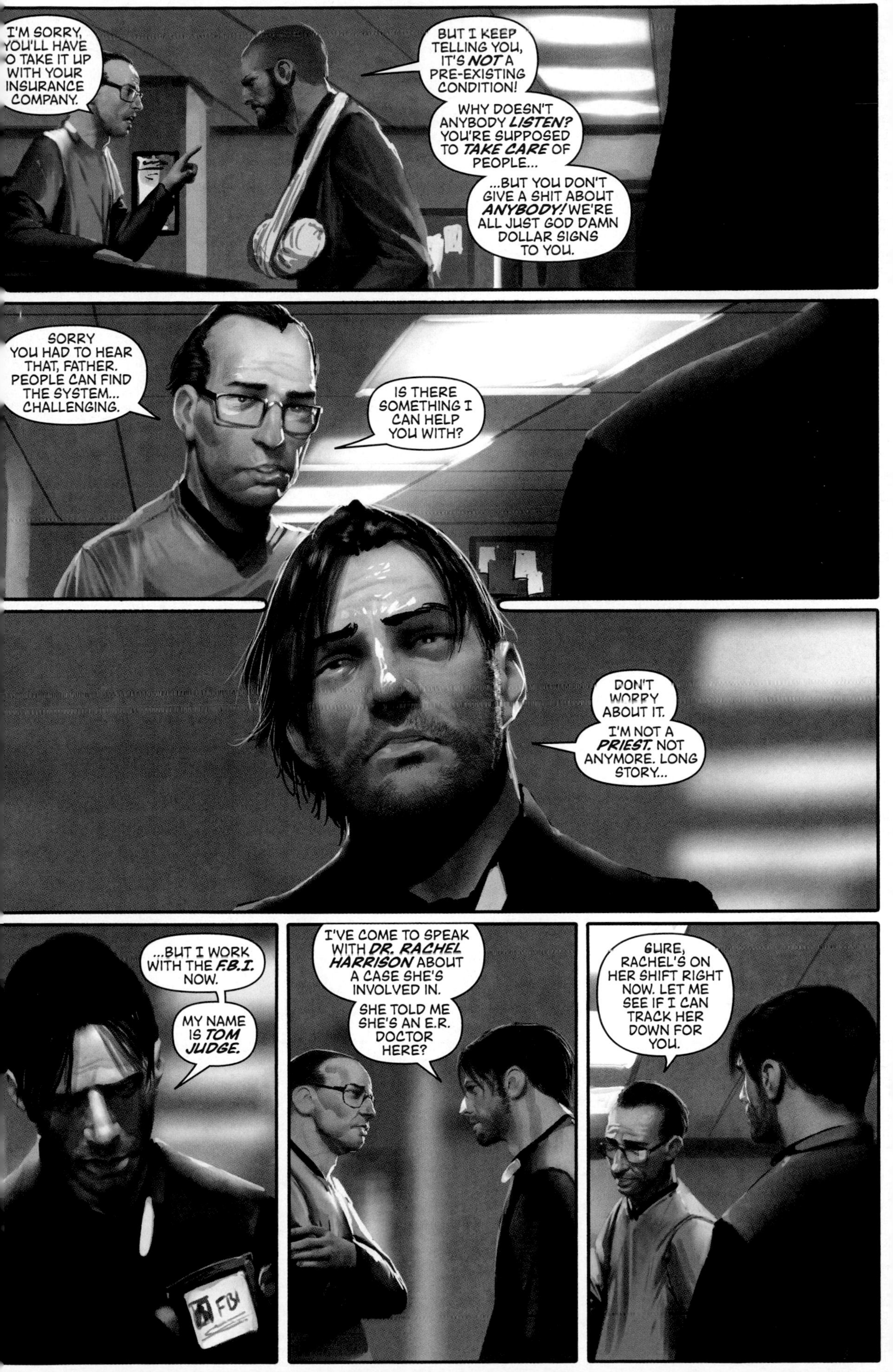
I'M SORRY, YOU'LL HAVE TO TAKE IT UP WITH YOUR INSURANCE COMPANY.
BUT I KEEP TELLING YOU, IT'S NOT A PRE-EXISTING CONDITION!
WHY DOESN'T ANYBODY LISTEN? YOU'RE SUPPOSED TO TAKE CARE OF PEOPLE...
...BUT YOU DON'T GIVE A SHIT ABOUT ANYBODY! WE'RE ALL JUST GOD DAMN DOLLAR SIGNS TO YOU.
SORRY YOU HAD TO HEAR THAT, FATHER. PEOPLE CAN FIND THE SYSTEM... CHALLENGING.
IS THERE SOMETHING I CAN HELP YOU WITH?
DON'T WORRY ABOUT IT.
I'M NOT A PRIEST. NOT ANYMORE. LONG STORY...
...BUT I WORK WITH THE F.B.I. NOW.
MY NAME IS TOM JUDGE.
FBI
I'VE COME TO SPEAK WITH DR. RACHEL HARRISON ABOUT A CASE SHE'S INVOLVED IN.
SHE TOLD ME SHE'S AN E.R. DOCTOR HERE?
SURE, RACHEL'S ON HER SHIFT RIGHT NOW. LET ME SEE IF I CAN TRACK HER DOWN FOR YOU.

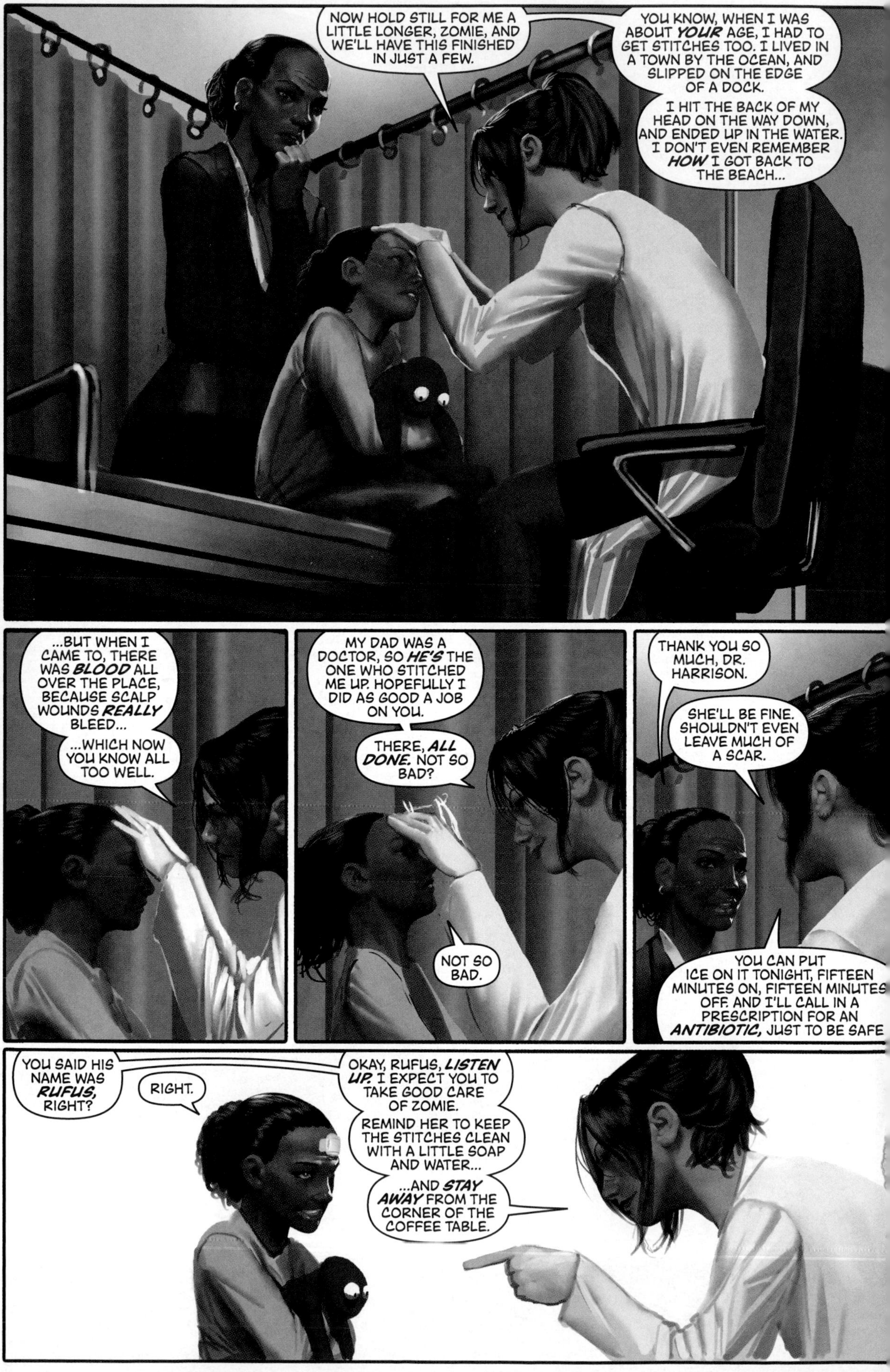
NOW HOLD STILL FOR ME A LITTLE LONGER, ZOMIE, AND WE'LL HAVE THIS FINISHED IN JUST A FEW.
YOU KNOW, WHEN I WAS ABOUT YOUR AGE, I HAD TO GET STITCHES TOO. I LIVED IN A TOWN BY THE OCEAN, AND SLIPPED ON THE EDGE OF A DOCK.
I HIT THE BACK OF MY HEAD ON THE WAY DOWN, AND ENDED UP IN THE WATER. I DON'T EVEN REMEMBER HOW I GOT BACK TO THE BEACH...
...BUT WHEN I CAME TO, THERE WAS BLOOD ALL OVER THE PLACE, BECAUSE SCALP WOUNDS REALLY BLEED...
...WHICH NOW YOU KNOW ALL TOO WELL.
MY DAD WAS A DOCTOR, SO HE'S THE ONE WHO STITCHED ME UP. HOPEFULLY I DID AS GOOD A JOB ON YOU.
THERE, ALL DONE. NOT SO BAD?
NOT SO BAD.
THANK YOU SO MUCH, DR. HARRISON.
SHE'LL BE FINE. SHOULDN'T EVEN LEAVE MUCH OF A SCAR.
YOU CAN PUT ICE ON IT TONIGHT, FIFTEEN MINUTES ON, FIFTEEN MINUTES OFF. AND I'LL CALL IN A PRESCRIPTION FOR AN ANTIBIOTIC, JUST TO BE SAFE
YOU SAID HIS NAME WAS RUFUS, RIGHT?
RIGHT.
OKAY, RUFUS, LISTEN UP. I EXPECT YOU TO TAKE GOOD CARE OF ZOMIE.
REMIND HER TO KEEP THE STITCHES CLEAN WITH A LITTLE SOAP AND WATER...
...AND STAY AWAY FROM THE CORNER OF THE COFFEE TABLE.

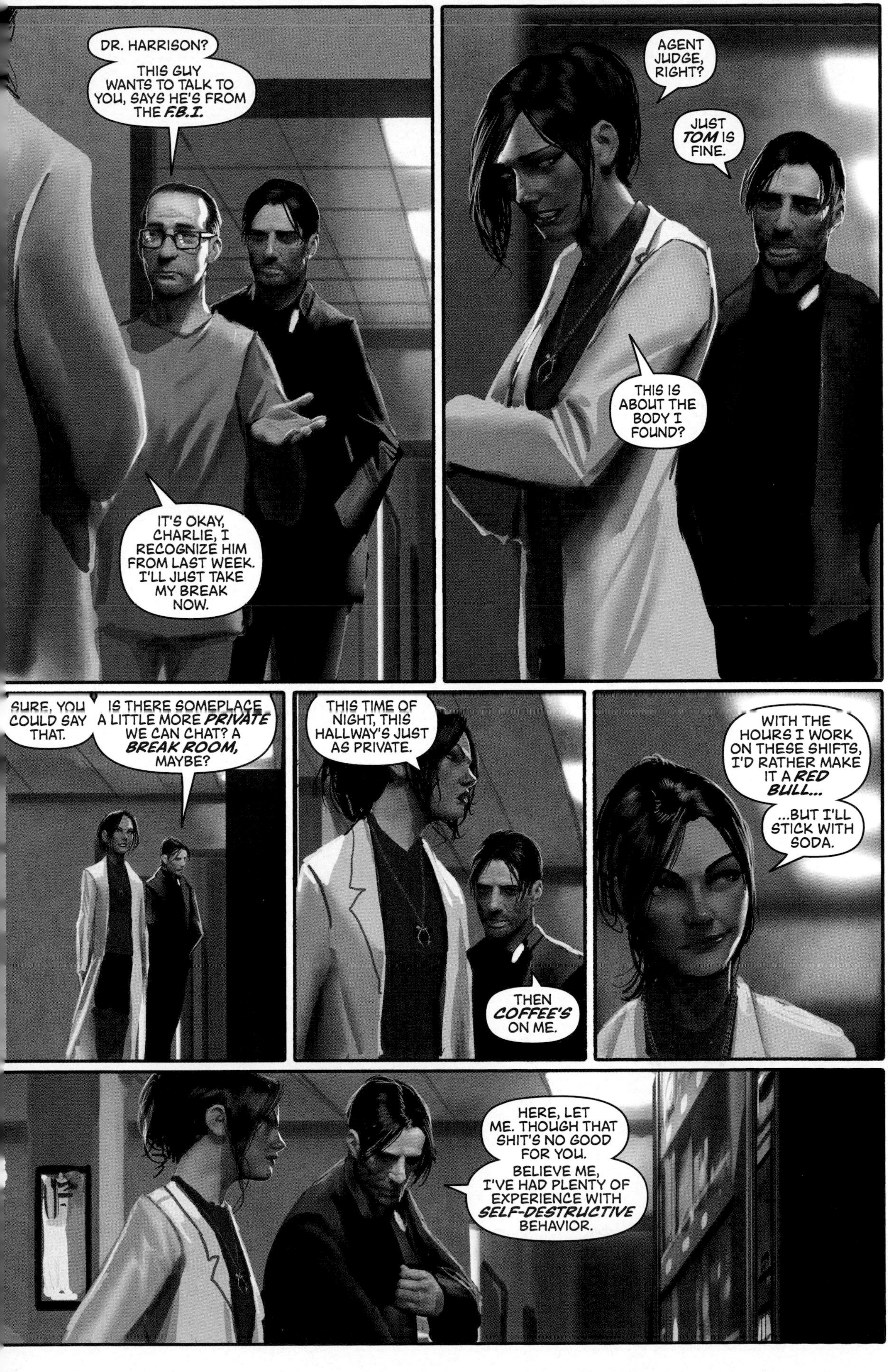

DR. HARRISON?
THIS GUY WANTS TO TALK TO YOU, SAYS HE'S FROM THE F.B.I.
IT'S OKAY, CHARLIE, I RECOGNIZE HIM FROM LAST WEEK. I'LL JUST TAKE MY BREAK NOW.
AGENT JUDGE, RIGHT?
JUST TOM IS FINE.
THIS IS ABOUT THE BODY I FOUND?
SURE, YOU COULD SAY THAT.
IS THERE SOMEPLACE A LITTLE MORE PRIVATE WE CAN CHAT? A BREAK ROOM, MAYBE?
THIS TIME OF NIGHT, THIS HALLWAY'S JUST AS PRIVATE.
THEN COFFEE'S ON ME.
WITH THE HOURS I WORK ON THESE SHIFTS, I'D RATHER MAKE IT A RED BULL...
...BUT I'LL STICK WITH SODA.
HERE, LET ME. THOUGH THAT SHIT'S NO GOOD FOR YOU.
BELIEVE ME, I'VE HAD PLENTY OF EXPERIENCE WITH SELF-DESTRUCTIVE BEHAVIOR.

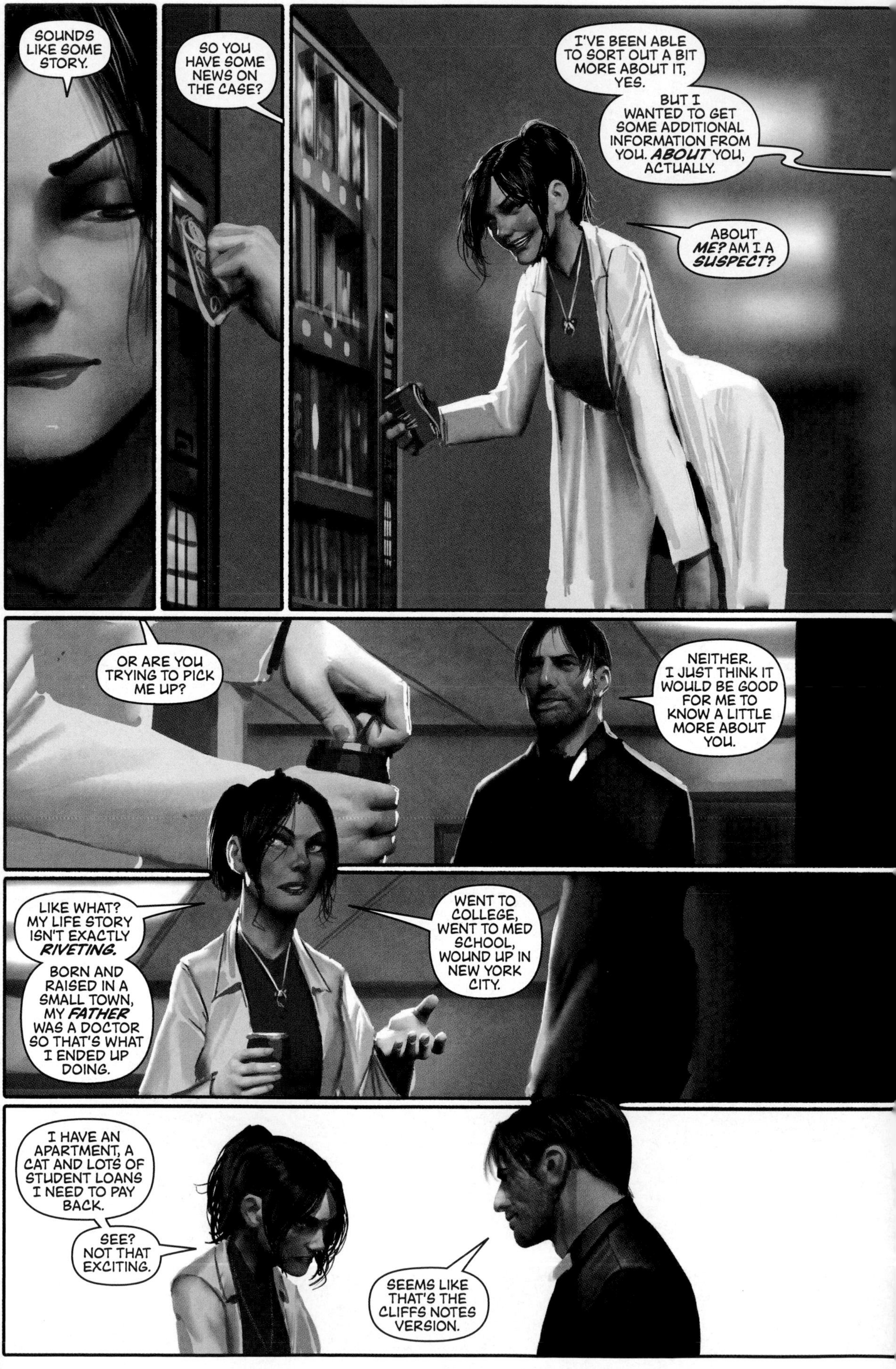
SOUNDS LIKE SOME STORY.
SO YOU HAVE SOME NEWS ON THE CASE?
I'VE BEEN ABLE TO SORT OUT A BIT MORE ABOUT IT, YES.
BUT I WANTED TO GET SOME ADDITIONAL INFORMATION FROM YOU. *ABOUT* YOU, ACTUALLY.
ABOUT *ME?* AM I A *SUSPECT?*
OR ARE YOU TRYING TO PICK ME UP?
NEITHER. I JUST THINK IT WOULD BE GOOD FOR ME TO KNOW A LITTLE MORE ABOUT YOU.
LIKE WHAT? MY LIFE STORY ISN'T EXACTLY *RIVETING.*
BORN AND RAISED IN A SMALL TOWN, MY *FATHER* WAS A DOCTOR SO THAT'S WHAT I ENDED UP DOING.
WENT TO COLLEGE, WENT TO MED SCHOOL, WOUND UP IN NEW YORK CITY.
I HAVE AN APARTMENT, A CAT AND LOTS OF STUDENT LOANS I NEED TO PAY BACK.
SEE? NOT THAT EXCITING.
SEEMS LIKE THAT'S THE CLIFFS NOTES VERSION.

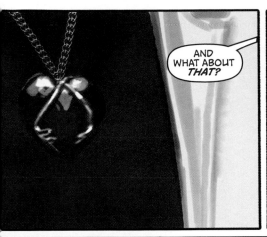

AND WHAT ABOUT *THAT?*

LIKE I SAID AT THE CRIME SCENE, IT'S AN *HEIRLOOM.*

IT'S BEEN IN MY FAMILY FOR YEARS. MY *GRANDMOTHER* GAVE IT TO ME.

HAVE YOU EVER NOTICED ANYTHING... *UNUSUAL...* ABOUT IT?

WHY... WOULD YOU ASK THAT?

RACHEL, WHAT I DO FOR THE F.B.I. IS INVESTIGATE THE THINGS THAT DON'T HAVE AN *OBVIOUS* EXPLANATION.

THE *WEIRD SHIT,* FOR LACK OF A BETTER DESCRIPTION. DOES THAT GIVE YOU A BETTER IDEA OF WHAT I'M LOOKING FOR?

WELL, HONESTLY THERE *ARE* SOME THINGS ABOUT THE PENDANT THAT...AREN'T NORMAL. I'VE JUST COME TO *ACCEPT* IT...

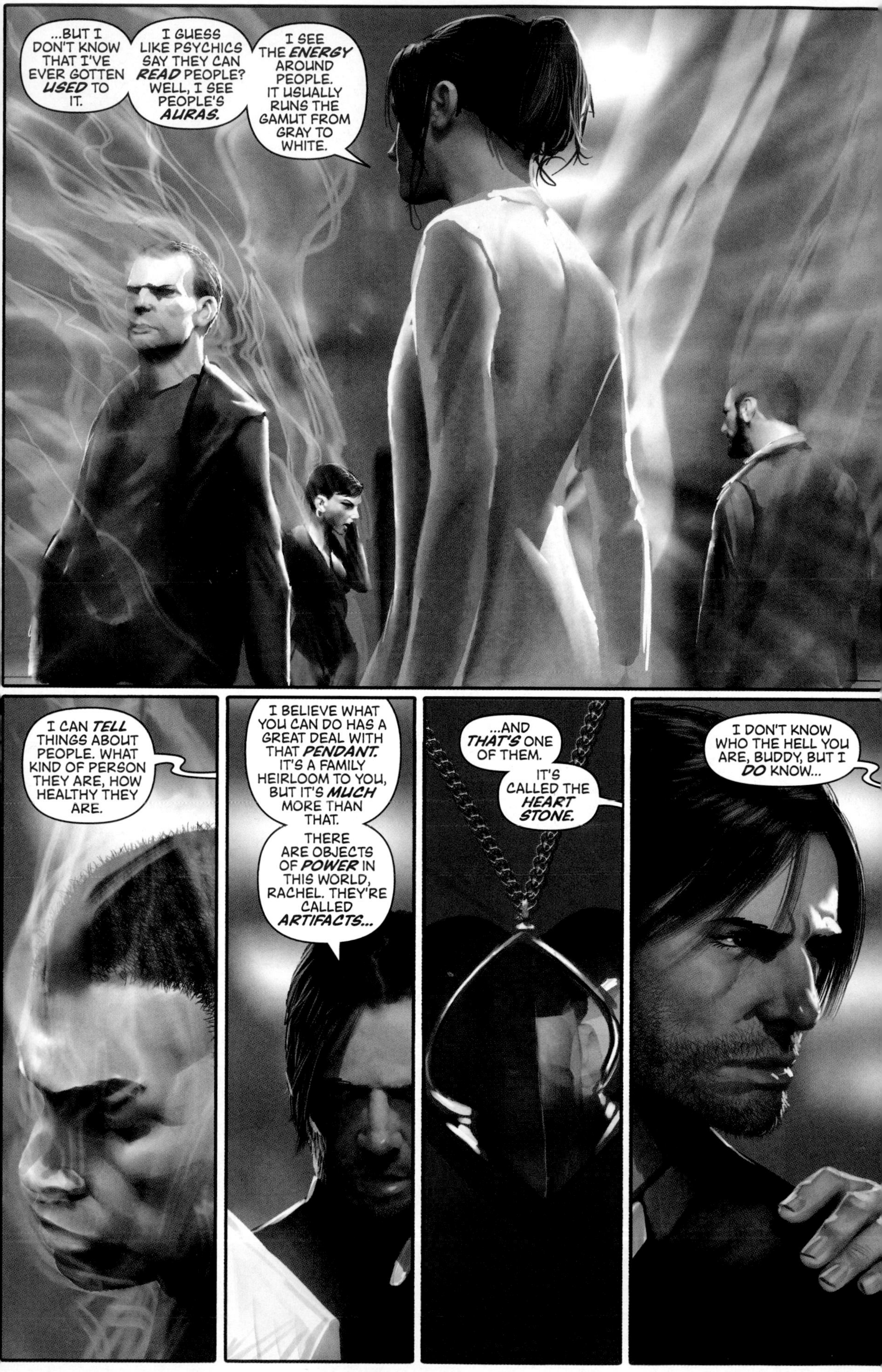
...BUT I DON'T KNOW THAT I'VE EVER GOTTEN USED TO IT.
I GUESS LIKE PSYCHICS SAY THEY CAN READ PEOPLE? WELL, I SEE PEOPLE'S AURAS.
I SEE THE ENERGY AROUND PEOPLE. IT USUALLY RUNS THE GAMUT FROM GRAY TO WHITE.
I CAN TELL THINGS ABOUT PEOPLE. WHAT KIND OF PERSON THEY ARE, HOW HEALTHY THEY ARE.
I BELIEVE WHAT YOU CAN DO HAS A GREAT DEAL WITH THAT PENDANT. IT'S A FAMILY HEIRLOOM TO YOU, BUT IT'S MUCH MORE THAN THAT.
THERE ARE OBJECTS OF POWER IN THIS WORLD, RACHEL. THEY'RE CALLED ARTIFACTS...
...AND THAT'S ONE OF THEM.
IT'S CALLED THE HEART STONE.
I DON'T KNOW WHO THE HELL YOU ARE, BUDDY, BUT I DO KNOW...

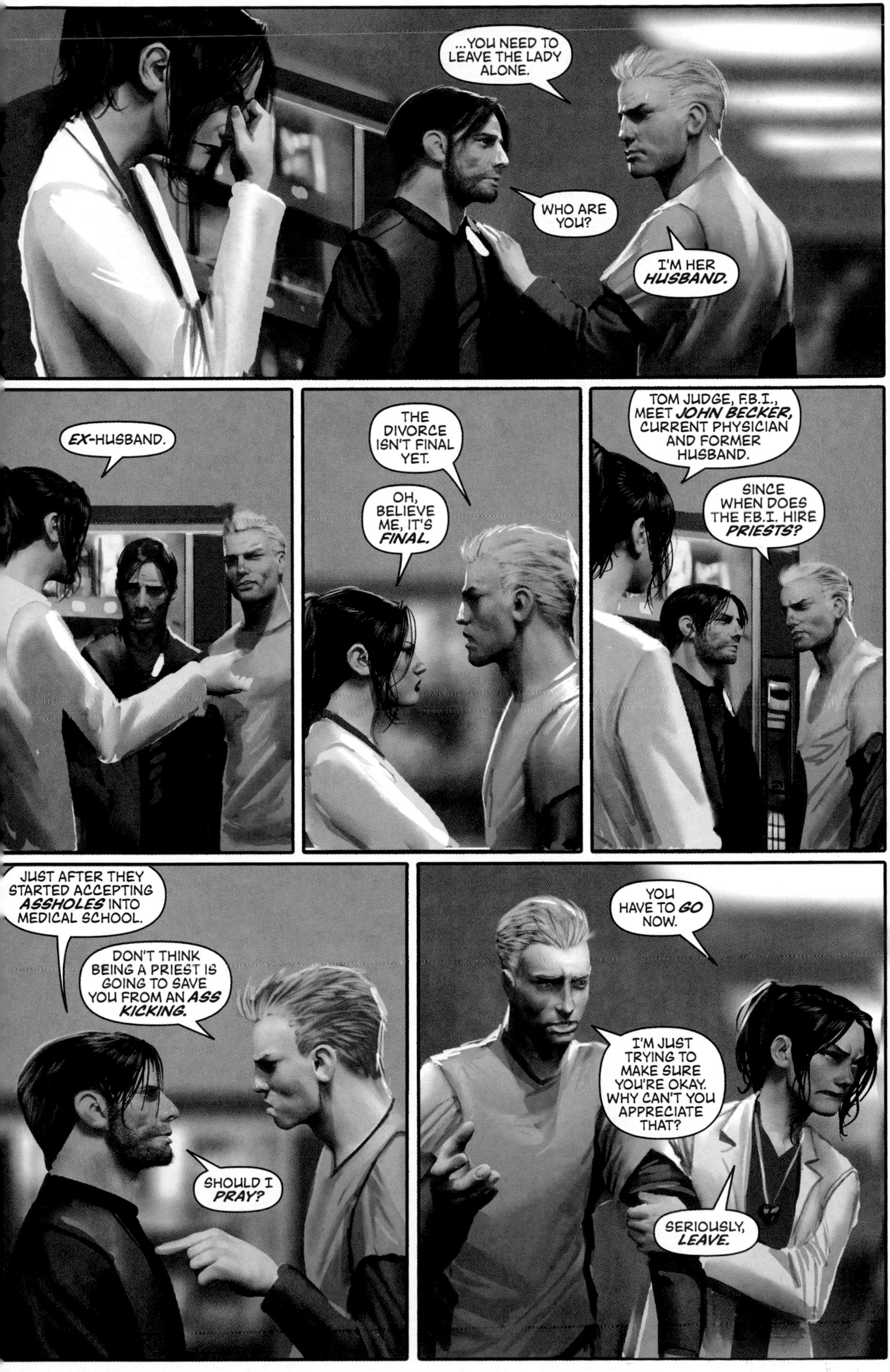
...YOU NEED TO LEAVE THE LADY ALONE.
WHO ARE YOU?
I'M HER HUSBAND.
EX-HUSBAND.
THE DIVORCE ISN'T FINAL YET.
OH, BELIEVE ME, IT'S FINAL.
TOM JUDGE, F.B.I., MEET JOHN BECKER, CURRENT PHYSICIAN AND FORMER HUSBAND.
SINCE WHEN DOES THE F.B.I. HIRE PRIESTS?
JUST AFTER THEY STARTED ACCEPTING ASSHOLES INTO MEDICAL SCHOOL.
DON'T THINK BEING A PRIEST IS GOING TO SAVE YOU FROM AN ASS KICKING.
SHOULD I PRAY?
YOU HAVE TO GO NOW.
I'M JUST TRYING TO MAKE SURE YOU'RE OKAY. WHY CAN'T YOU APPRECIATE THAT?
SERIOUSLY, LEAVE.

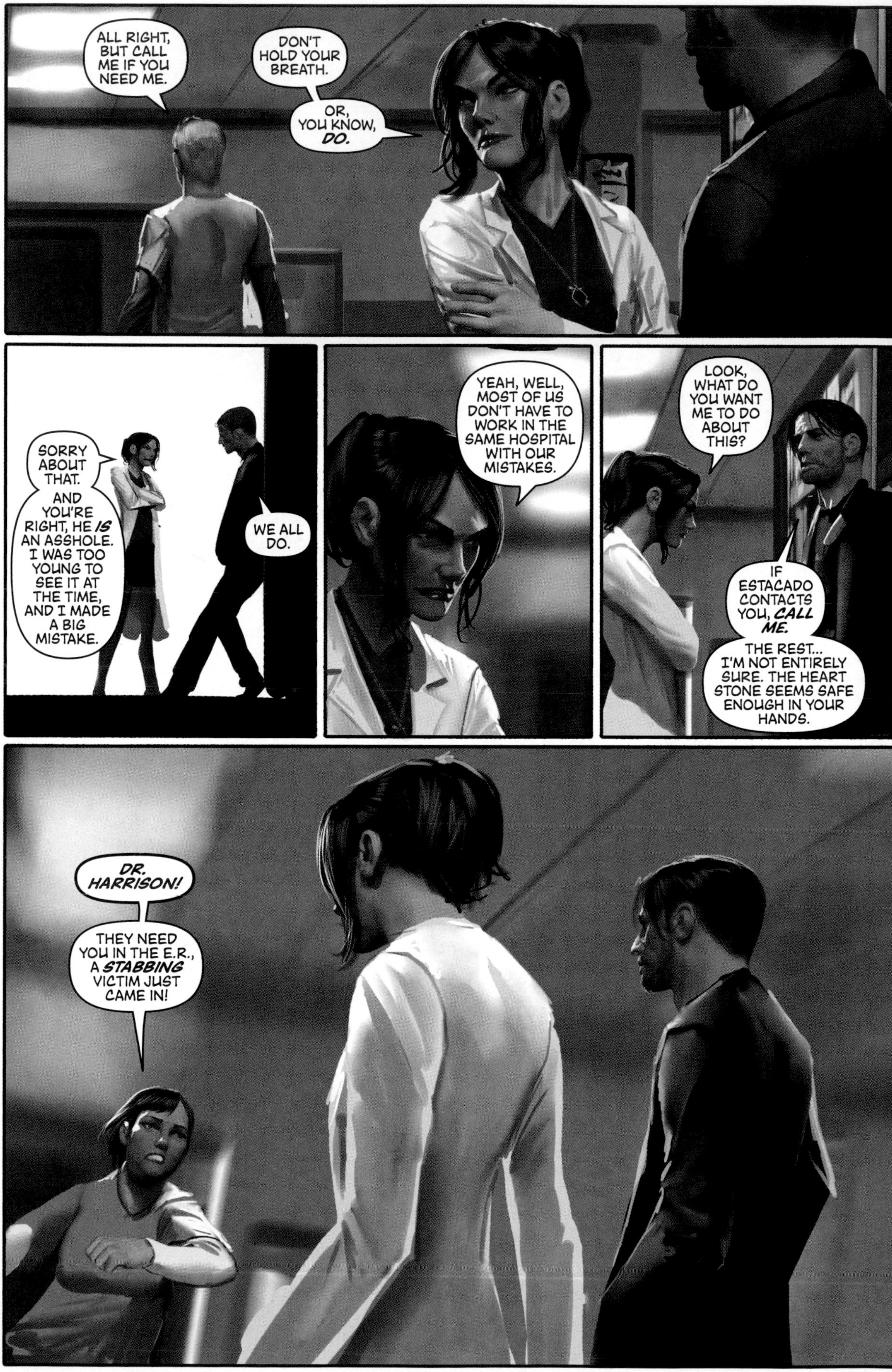

ALL RIGHT, BUT CALL ME IF YOU NEED ME.
DON'T HOLD YOUR BREATH.
OR, YOU KNOW, *DO.*
SORRY ABOUT THAT.
AND YOU'RE RIGHT, HE *IS* AN ASSHOLE. I WAS TOO YOUNG TO SEE IT AT THE TIME, AND I MADE A BIG MISTAKE.
WE ALL DO.
YEAH, WELL, MOST OF US DON'T HAVE TO WORK IN THE SAME HOSPITAL WITH OUR MISTAKES.
LOOK, WHAT DO YOU WANT ME TO DO ABOUT THIS?
IF ESTACADO CONTACTS YOU, *CALL ME.*
THE REST... I'M NOT ENTIRELY SURE. THE HEART STONE SEEMS SAFE ENOUGH IN YOUR HANDS.
DR. HARRISON!
THEY NEED YOU IN THE E.R., A *STABBING* VICTIM JUST CAME IN!

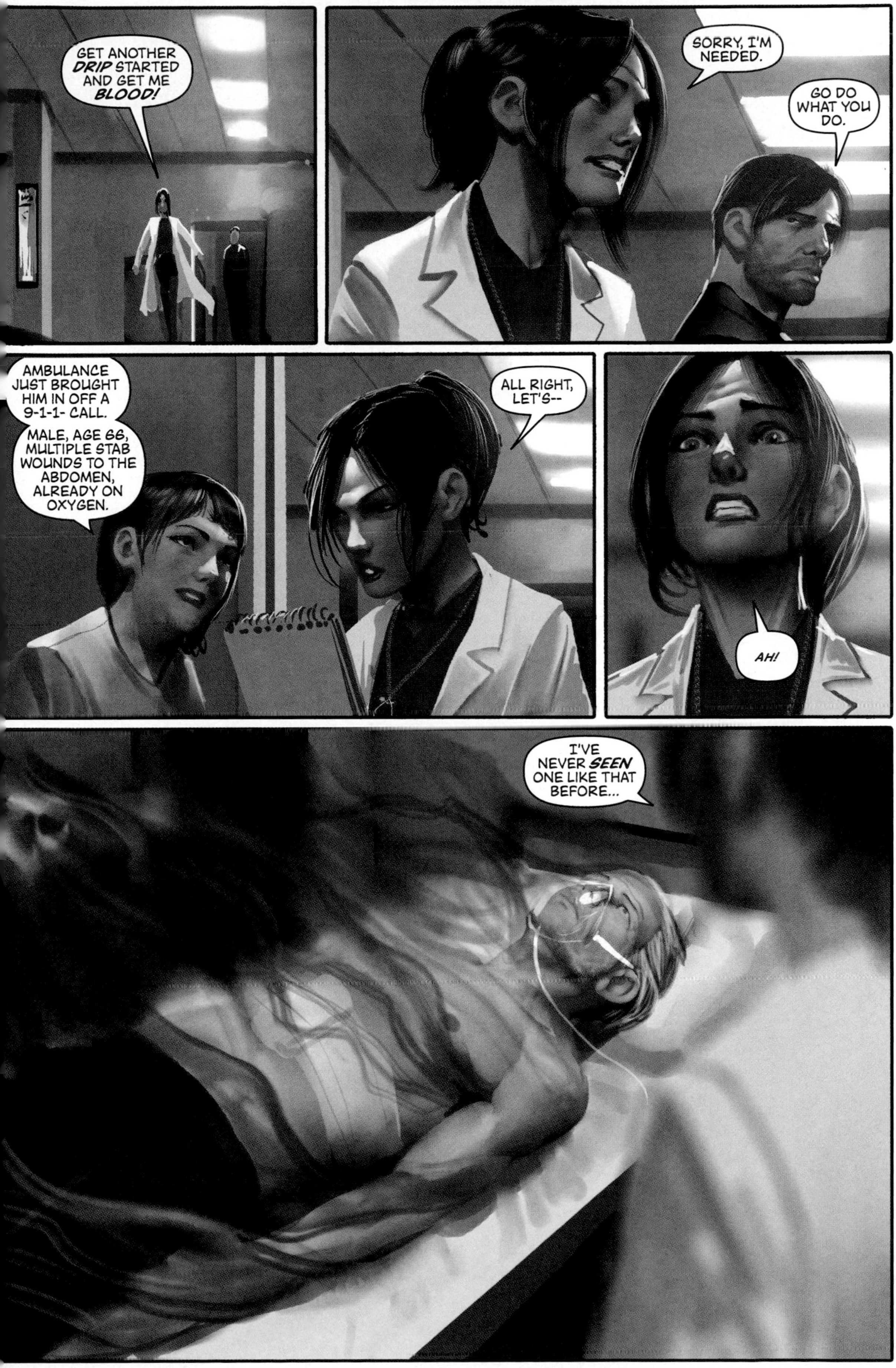
GET ANOTHER DRIP STARTED AND GET ME BLOOD!
SORRY, I'M NEEDED.
GO DO WHAT YOU DO.
AMBULANCE JUST BROUGHT HIM IN OFF A 9-1-1- CALL.
MALE, AGE 66, MULTIPLE STAB WOUNDS TO THE ABDOMEN, ALREADY ON OXYGEN.
ALL RIGHT, LET'S--
AH!
I'VE NEVER SEEN ONE LIKE THAT BEFORE...

DOCTOR HARRISON? YOU'VE NEVER SEEN A *STAB* WOUND?

UH... SORRY, SOMETHING ELSE.

HOW MUCH BLOOD HAS HE LOST? PULL THE *EMT* IN HERE SO I CAN GET A SENSE OF WHAT...

...WHAT...

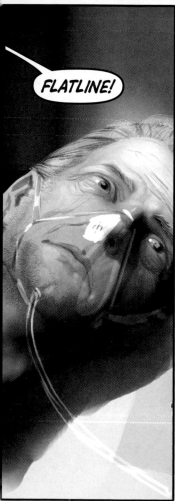

FLATLINE!

DAMN IT! CRASH CART, NOW!

CART'S CHARGING!

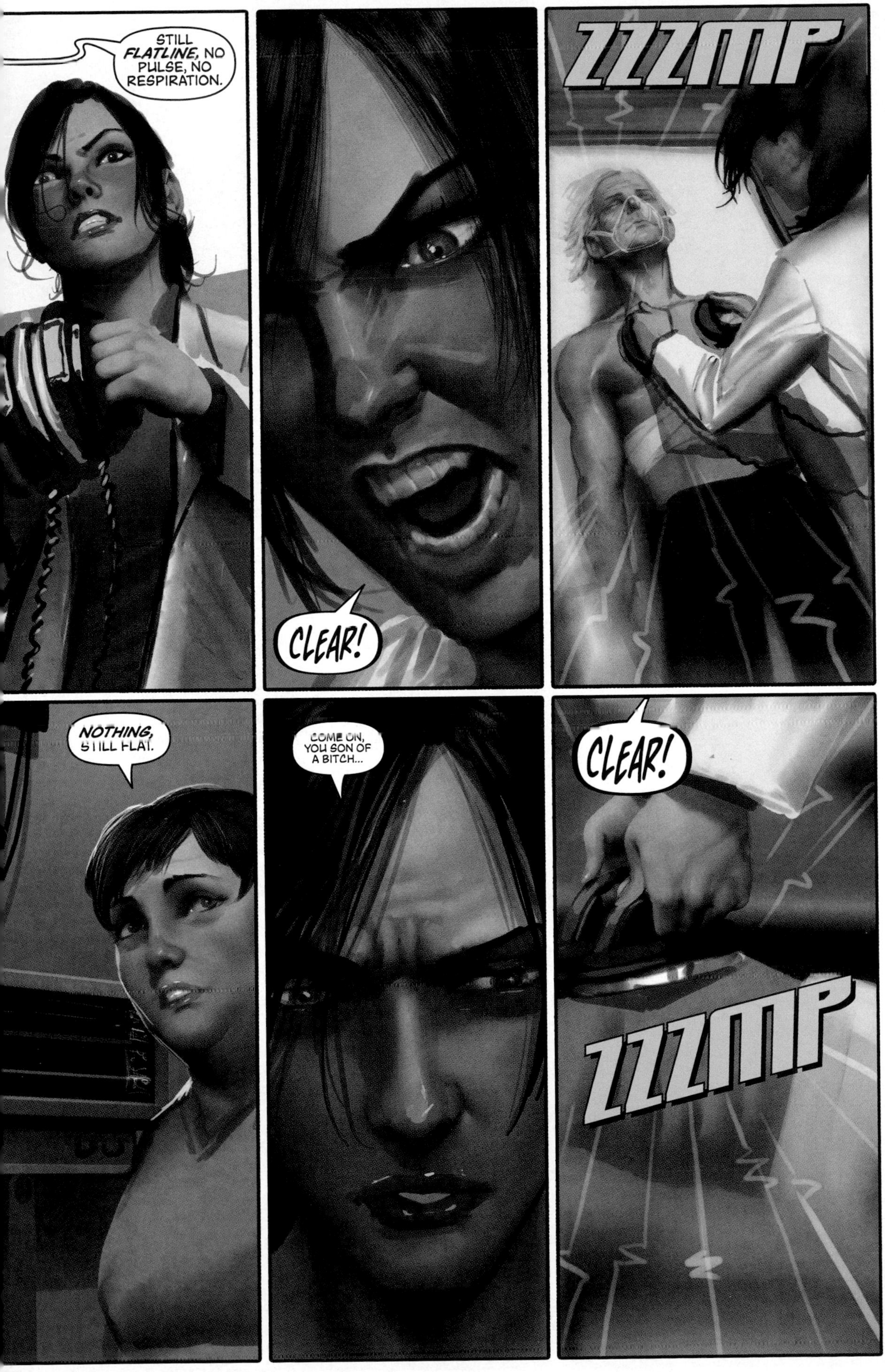
STILL FLATLINE, NO PULSE, NO RESPIRATION.
CLEAR!
ZZZMP
NOTHING, STILL FLAT.
COME ON, YOU SON OF A BITCH...
CLEAR!
ZZZMP

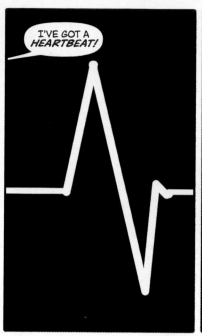

I'VE GOT A *HEARTBEAT!*

HEARTBEAT'S STEADY. YOU PULLED THIS MAN BACK FROM THE OTHER SIDE, DOCTOR.

LET'S GET HIM STABILIZED AND DEAL WITH THESE PUNCTURE WOUNDS.

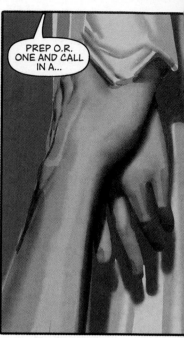

PREP O.R. ONE AND CALL IN A...

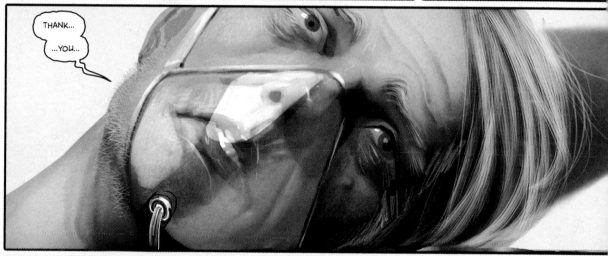

THANK... ...YOU...

UH... SURE THING...

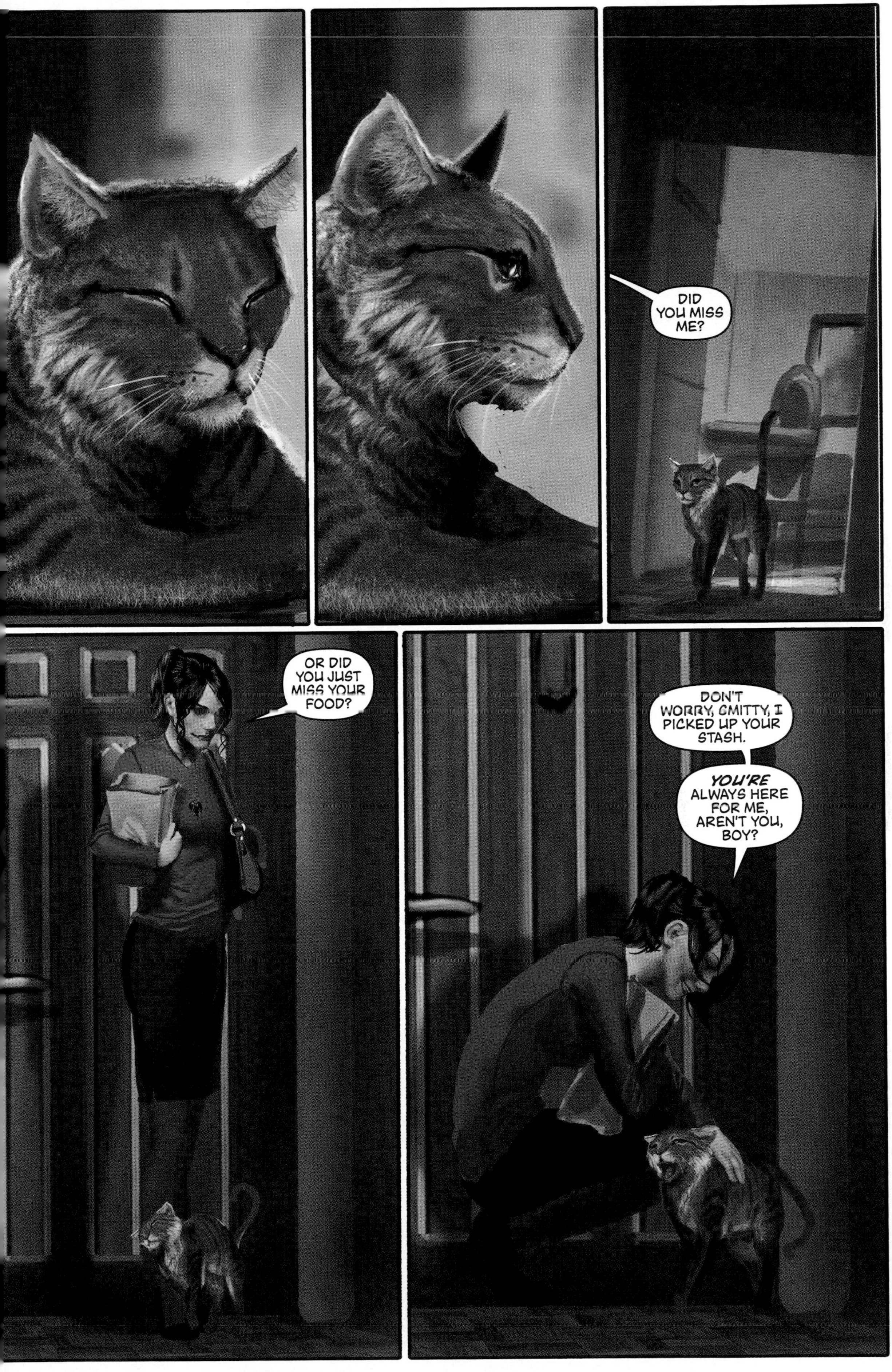
DID YOU MISS ME?
OR DID YOU JUST MISS YOUR FOOD?
DON'T WORRY, SMITTY, I PICKED UP YOUR STASH.
YOU'RE ALWAYS HERE FOR ME, AREN'T YOU, BOY?

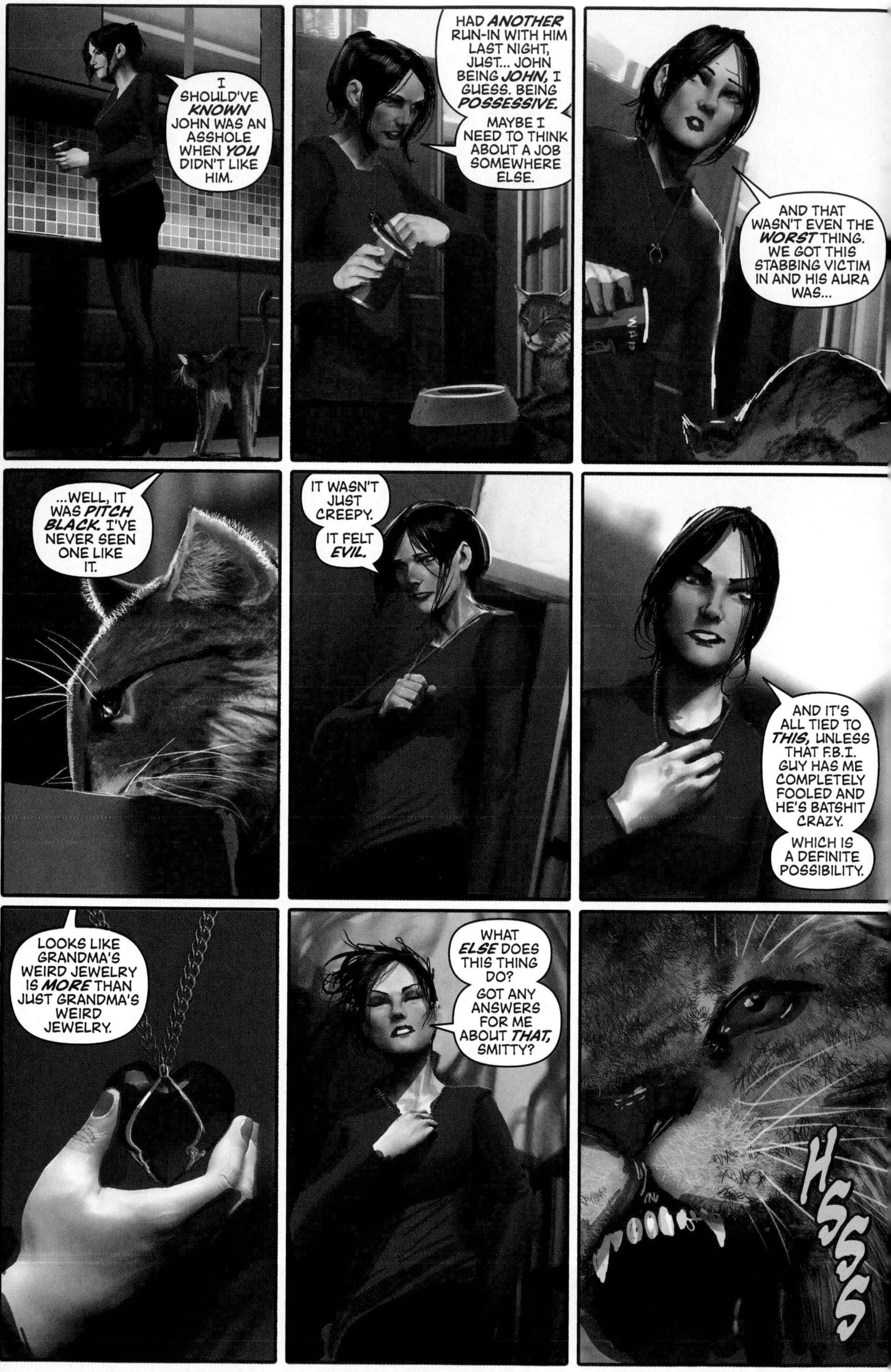
I SHOULD'VE KNOWN JOHN WAS AN ASSHOLE WHEN YOU DIDN'T LIKE HIM.
HAD ANOTHER RUN-IN WITH HIM LAST NIGHT, JUST... JOHN BEING JOHN, I GUESS. BEING POSSESSIVE.
MAYBE I NEED TO THINK ABOUT A JOB SOMEWHERE ELSE.
AND THAT WASN'T EVEN THE WORST THING. WE GOT THIS STABBING VICTIM IN AND HIS AURA WAS...
...WELL, IT WAS PITCH BLACK. I'VE NEVER SEEN ONE LIKE IT.
IT WASN'T JUST CREEPY.
IT FELT EVIL.
AND IT'S ALL TIED TO THIS, UNLESS THAT F.B.I. GUY HAS ME COMPLETELY FOOLED AND HE'S BATSHIT CRAZY.
WHICH IS A DEFINITE POSSIBILITY.
LOOKS LIKE GRANDMA'S WEIRD JEWELRY IS MORE THAN JUST GRANDMA'S WEIRD JEWELRY.
WHAT ELSE DOES THIS THING DO?
GOT ANY ANSWERS FOR ME ABOUT THAT, SMITTY?
HSSS

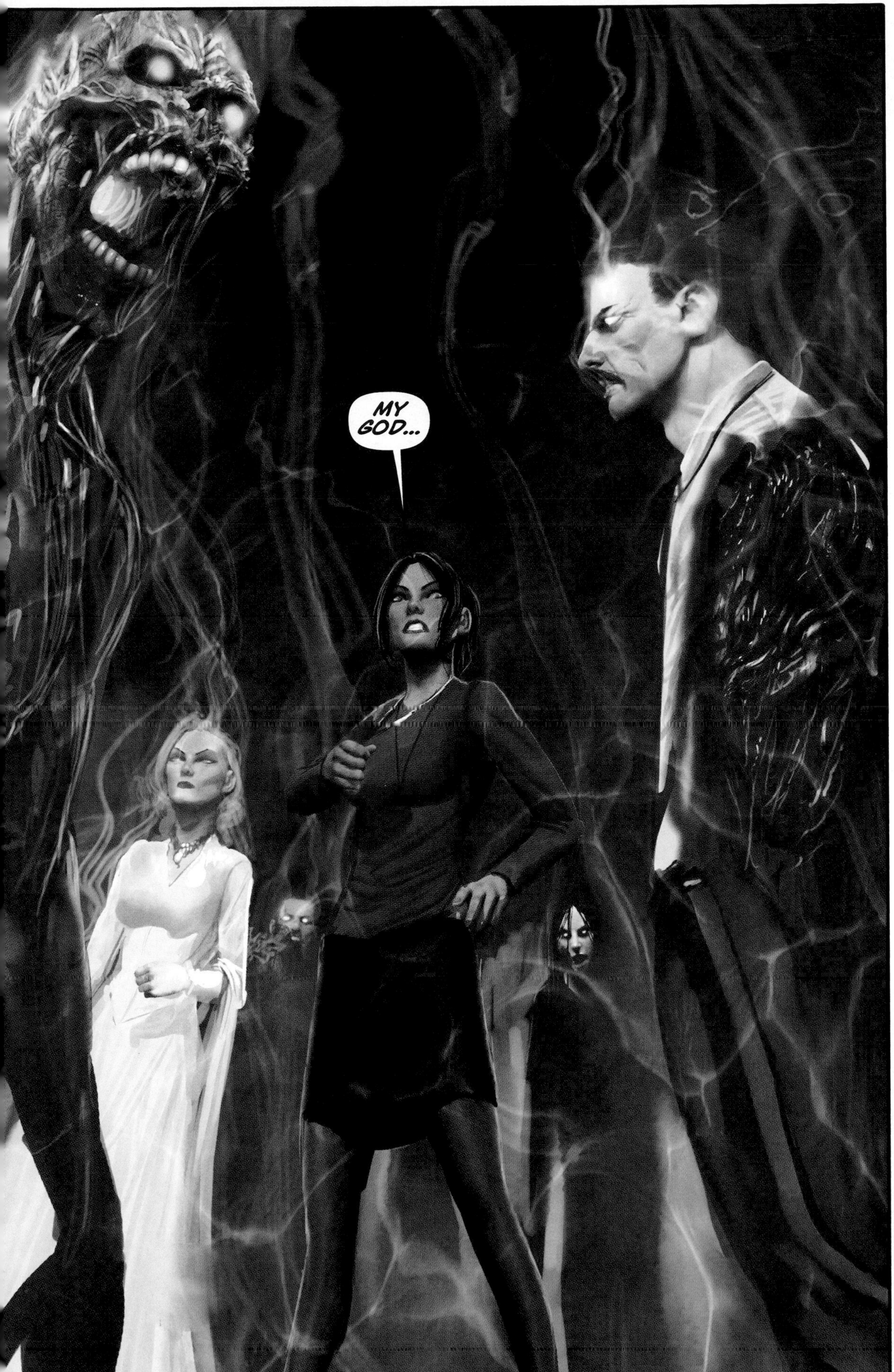
MY GOD...

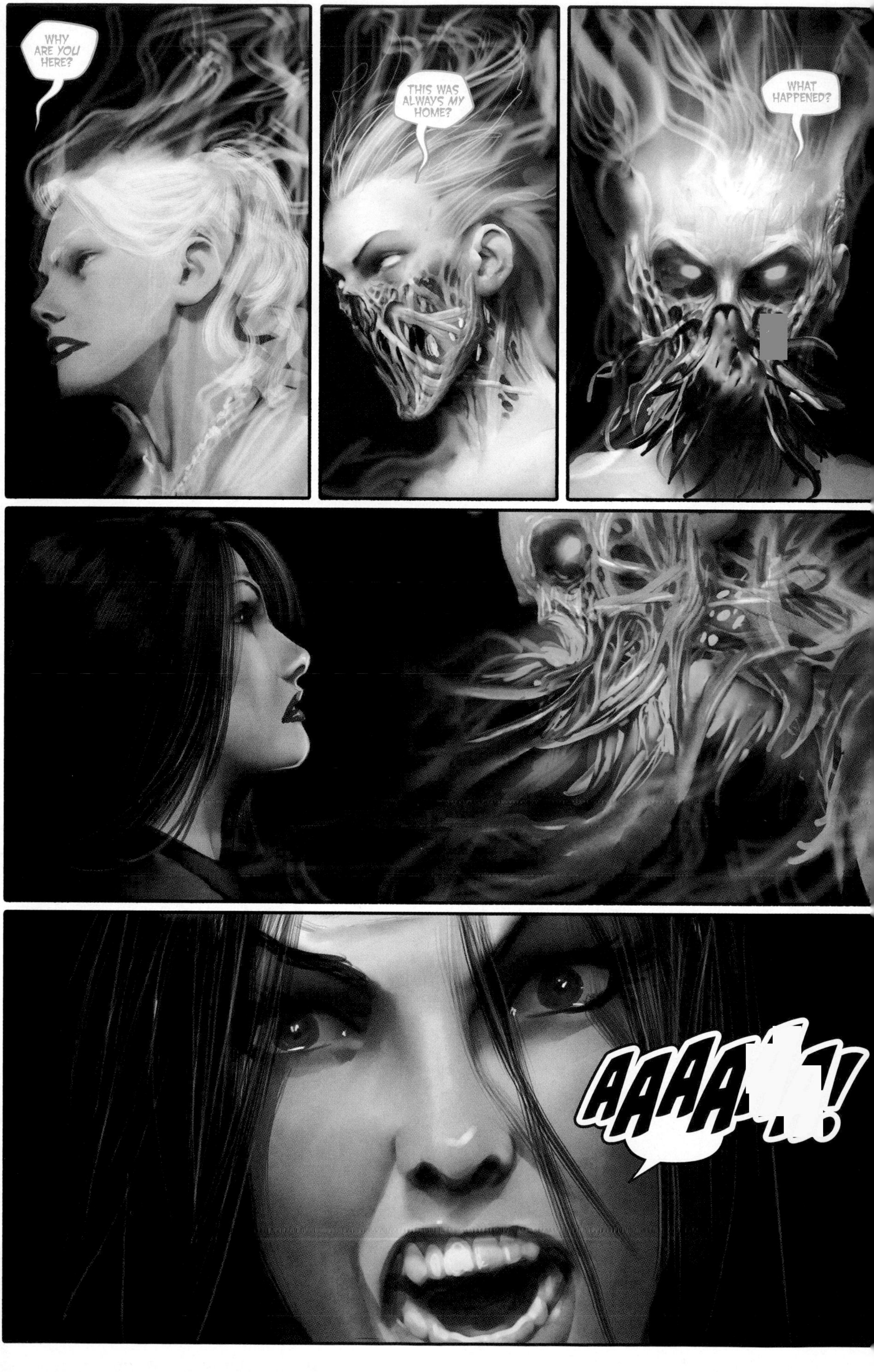
WHY ARE YOU HERE?
THIS WAS ALWAYS MY HOME?
WHAT HAPPENED?
AAAA!

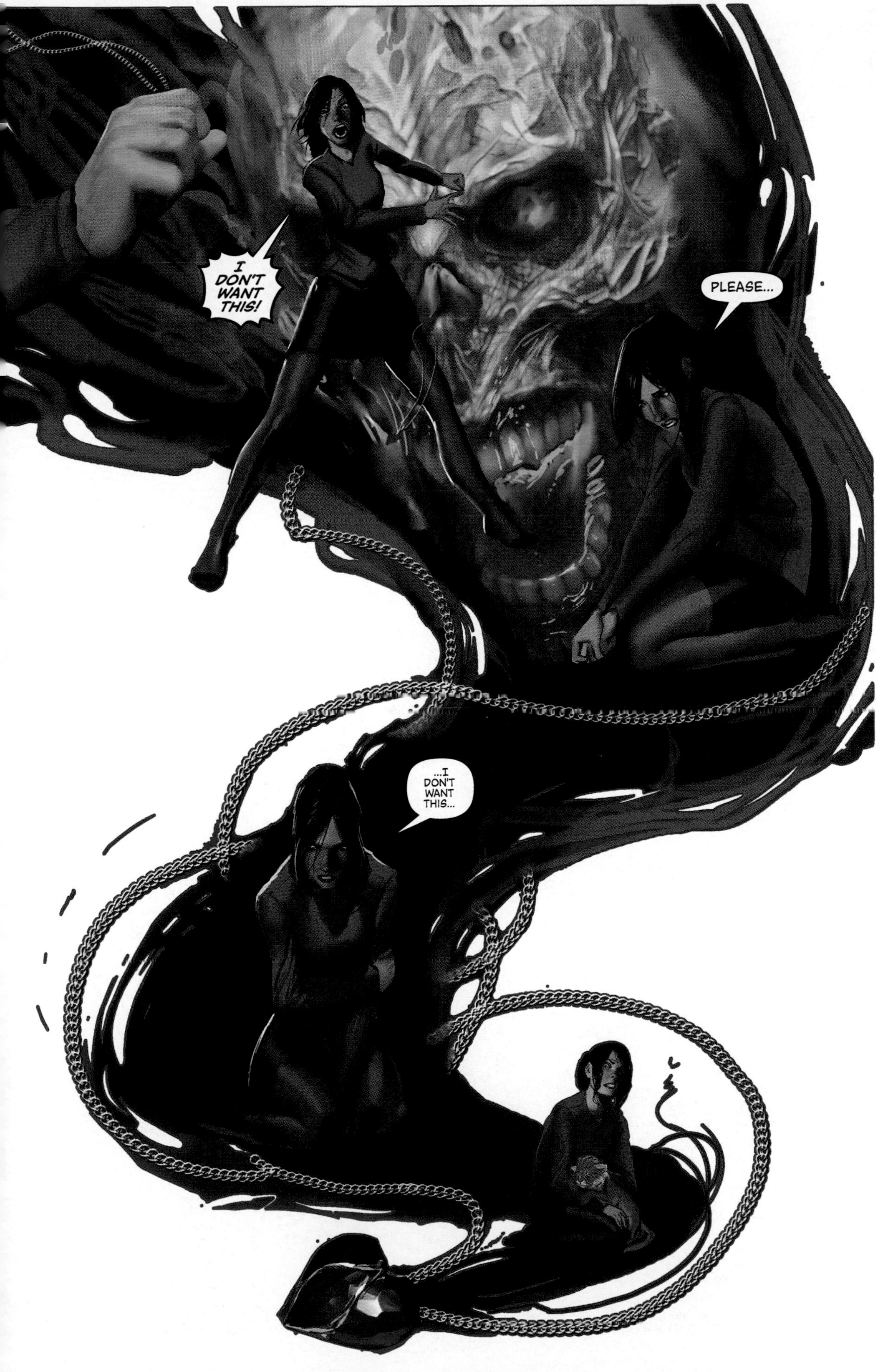
I DON'T WANT THIS!
PLEASE...
...I DON'T WANT THIS...

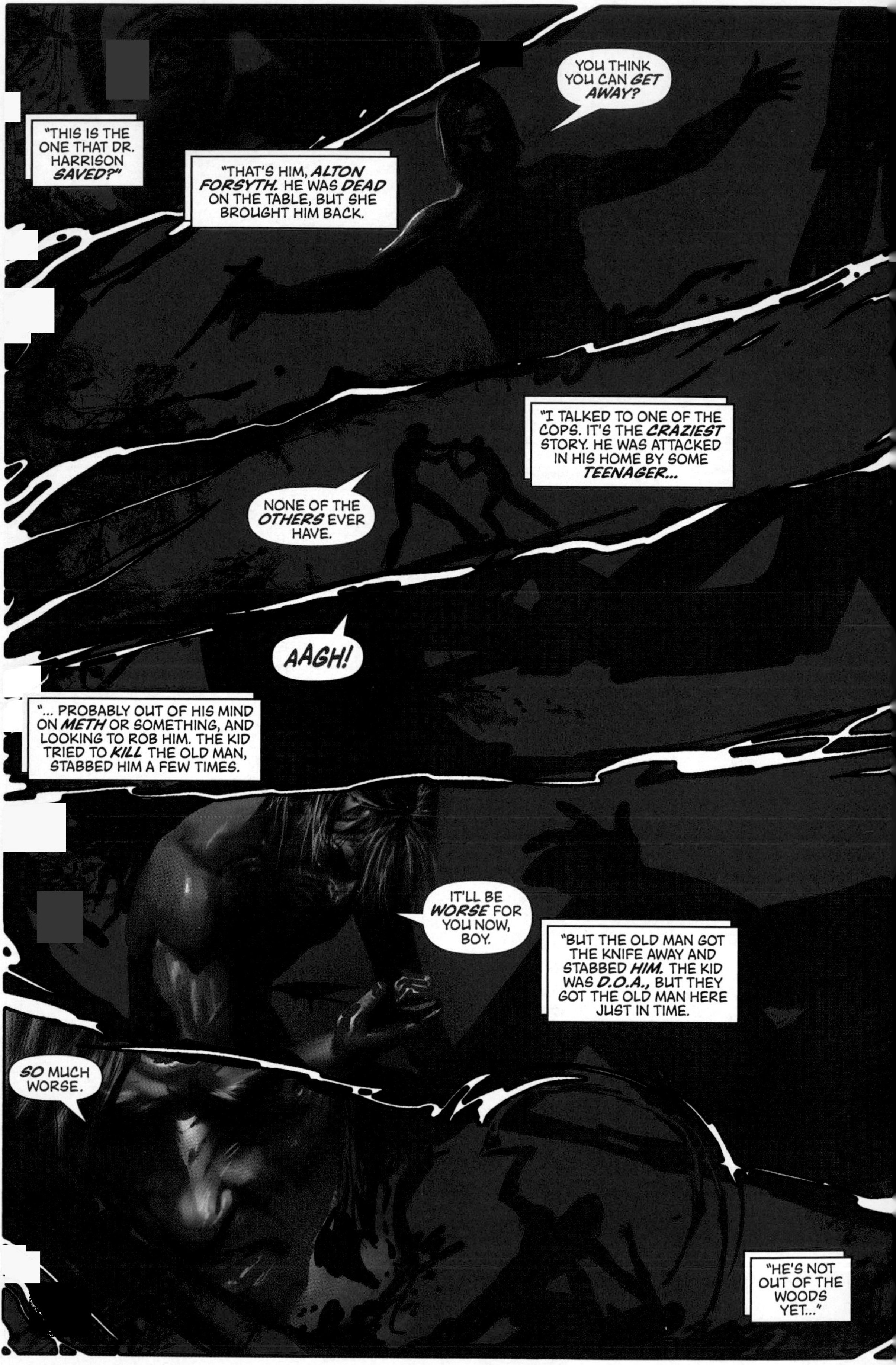
"THIS IS THE ONE THAT DR. HARRISON SAVED?"
"THAT'S HIM, ALTON FORSYTH. HE WAS DEAD ON THE TABLE, BUT SHE BROUGHT HIM BACK.
YOU THINK YOU CAN GET AWAY?
"I TALKED TO ONE OF THE COPS. IT'S THE CRAZIEST STORY. HE WAS ATTACKED IN HIS HOME BY SOME TEENAGER...
NONE OF THE OTHERS EVER HAVE.
AAGH!
"... PROBABLY OUT OF HIS MIND ON METH OR SOMETHING, AND LOOKING TO ROB HIM. THE KID TRIED TO KILL THE OLD MAN, STABBED HIM A FEW TIMES.
IT'LL BE WORSE FOR YOU NOW, BOY.
"BUT THE OLD MAN GOT THE KNIFE AWAY AND STABBED HIM. THE KID WAS D.O.A., BUT THEY GOT THE OLD MAN HERE JUST IN TIME.
SO MUCH WORSE.
"HE'S NOT OUT OF THE WOODS YET..."

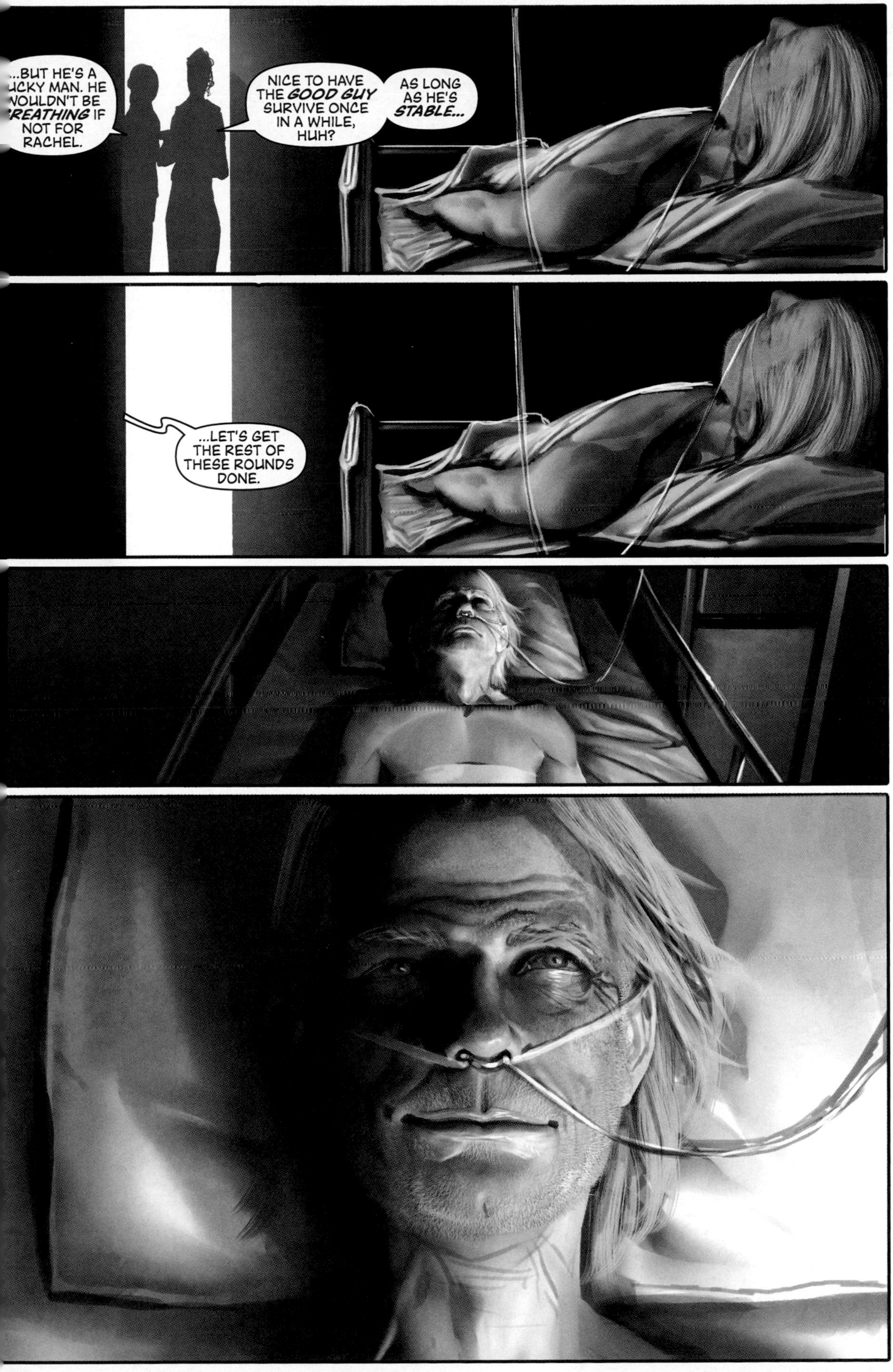
...BUT HE'S A
UCKY MAN. HE
WOULDN'T BE
REATHING IF
NOT FOR
RACHEL.
NICE TO HAVE THE GOOD GUY SURVIVE ONCE IN A WHILE, HUH?
AS LONG AS HE'S STABLE...
...LET'S GET THE REST OF THESE ROUNDS DONE.

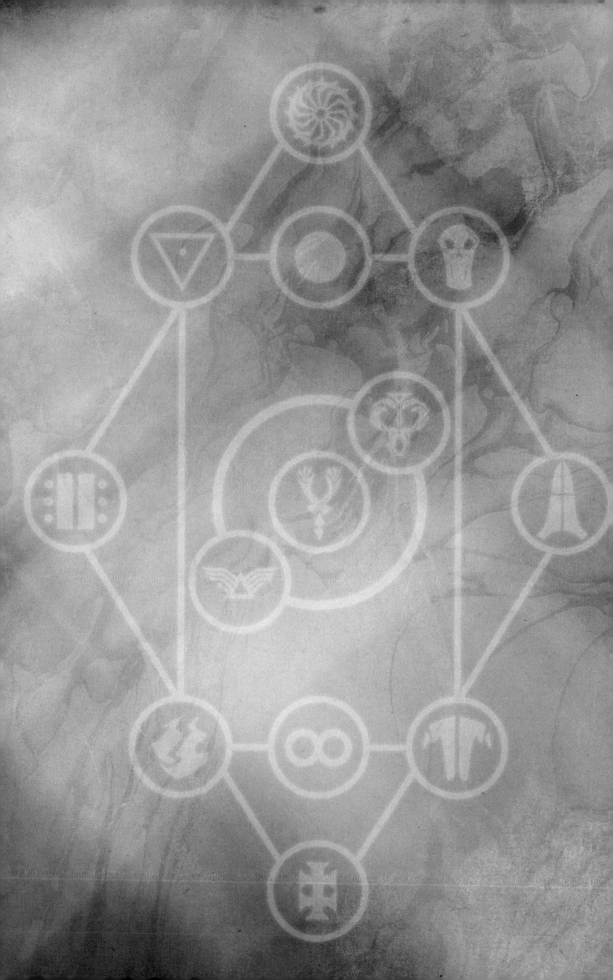

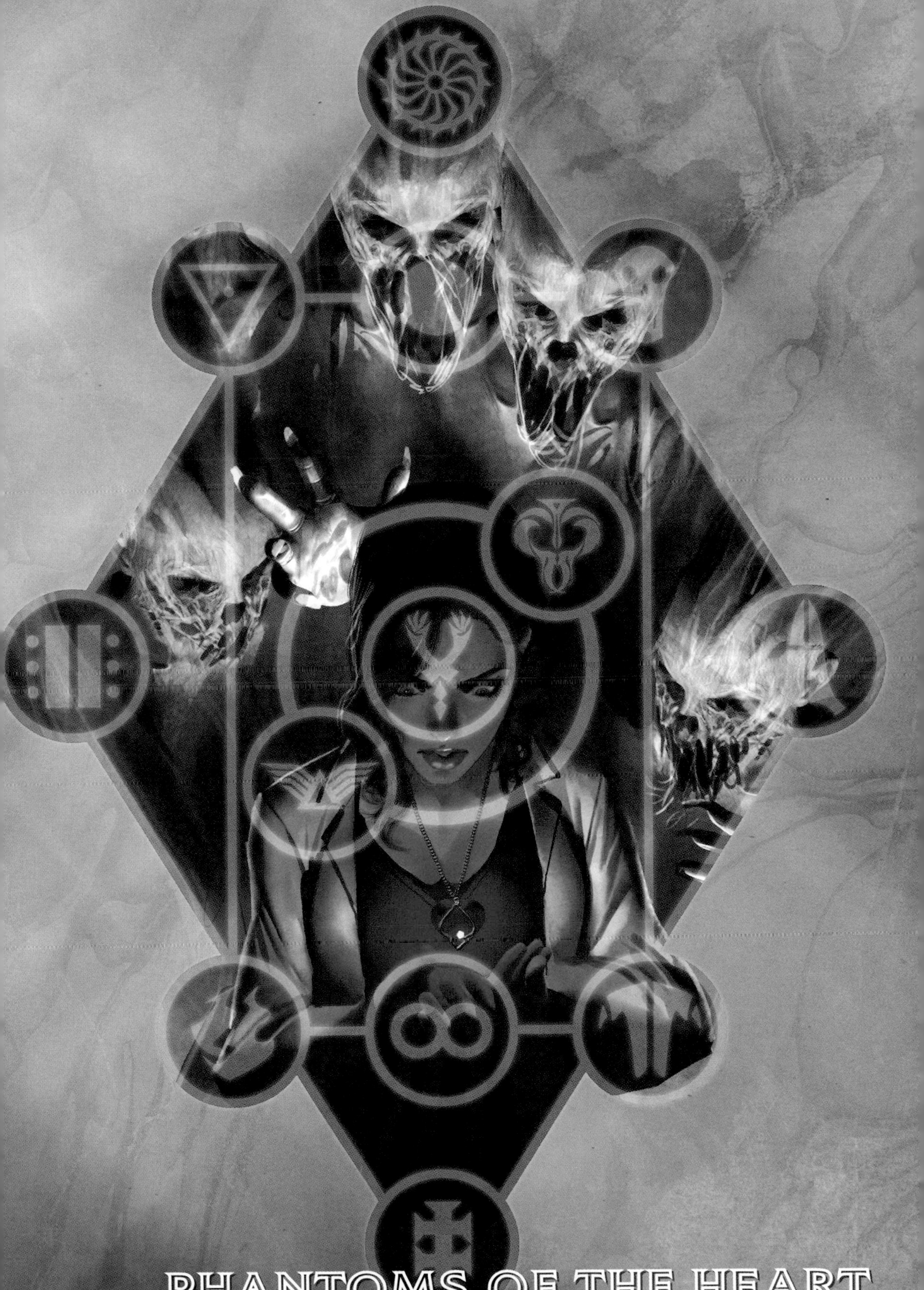

PHANTOMS OF THE HEART
PART 2

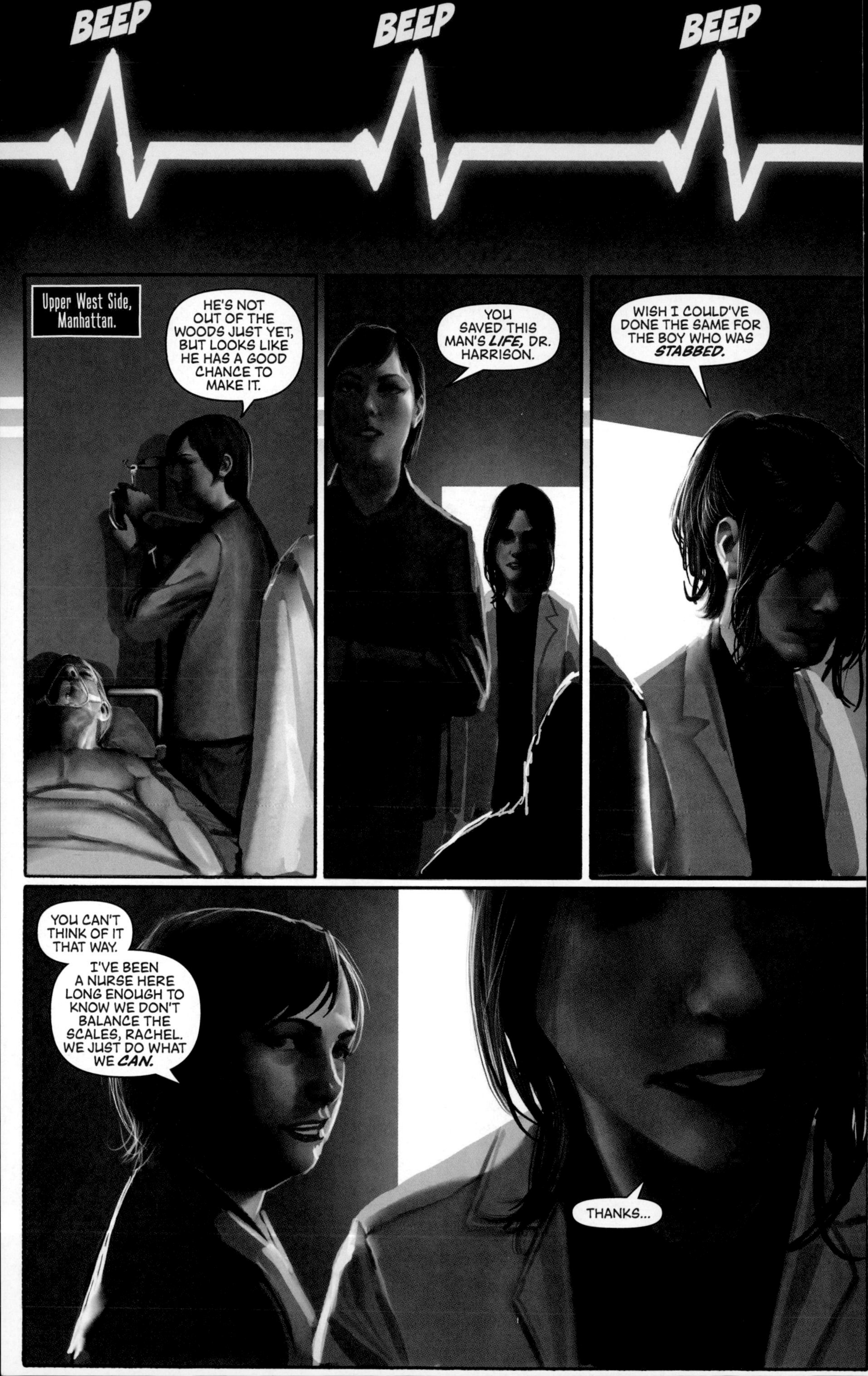
BEEP
BEEP
BEEP
Upper West Side, Manhattan.
HE'S NOT OUT OF THE WOODS JUST YET, BUT LOOKS LIKE HE HAS A GOOD CHANCE TO MAKE IT.
YOU SAVED THIS MAN'S LIFE, DR. HARRISON.
WISH I COULD'VE DONE THE SAME FOR THE BOY WHO WAS STABBED.
YOU CAN'T THINK OF IT THAT WAY.
I'VE BEEN A NURSE HERE LONG ENOUGH TO KNOW WE DON'T BALANCE THE SCALES, RACHEL. WE JUST DO WHAT WE CAN.
THANKS...

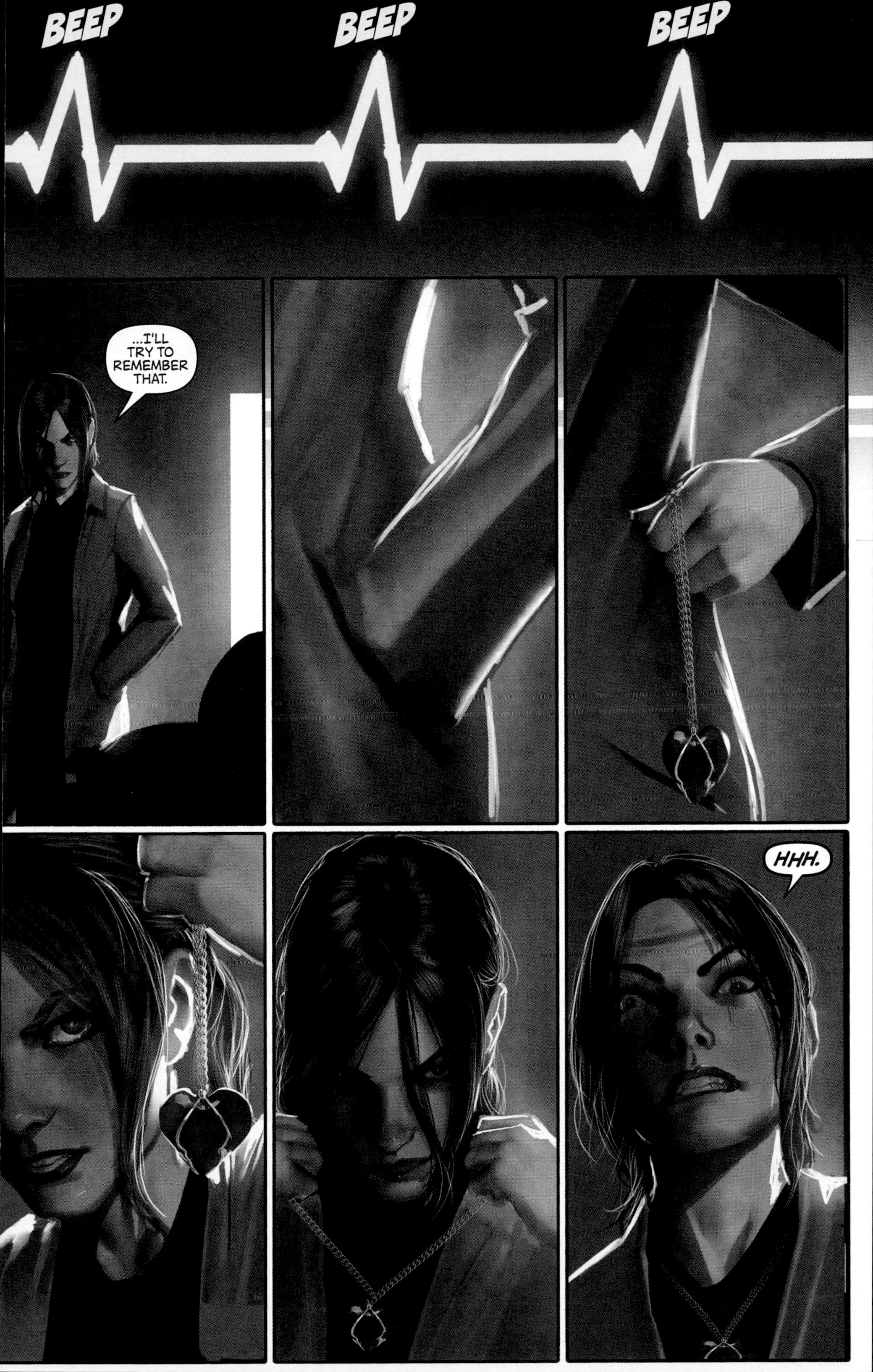
BEEP
BEEP
BEEP
...I'LL TRY TO REMEMBER THAT.
HHH.

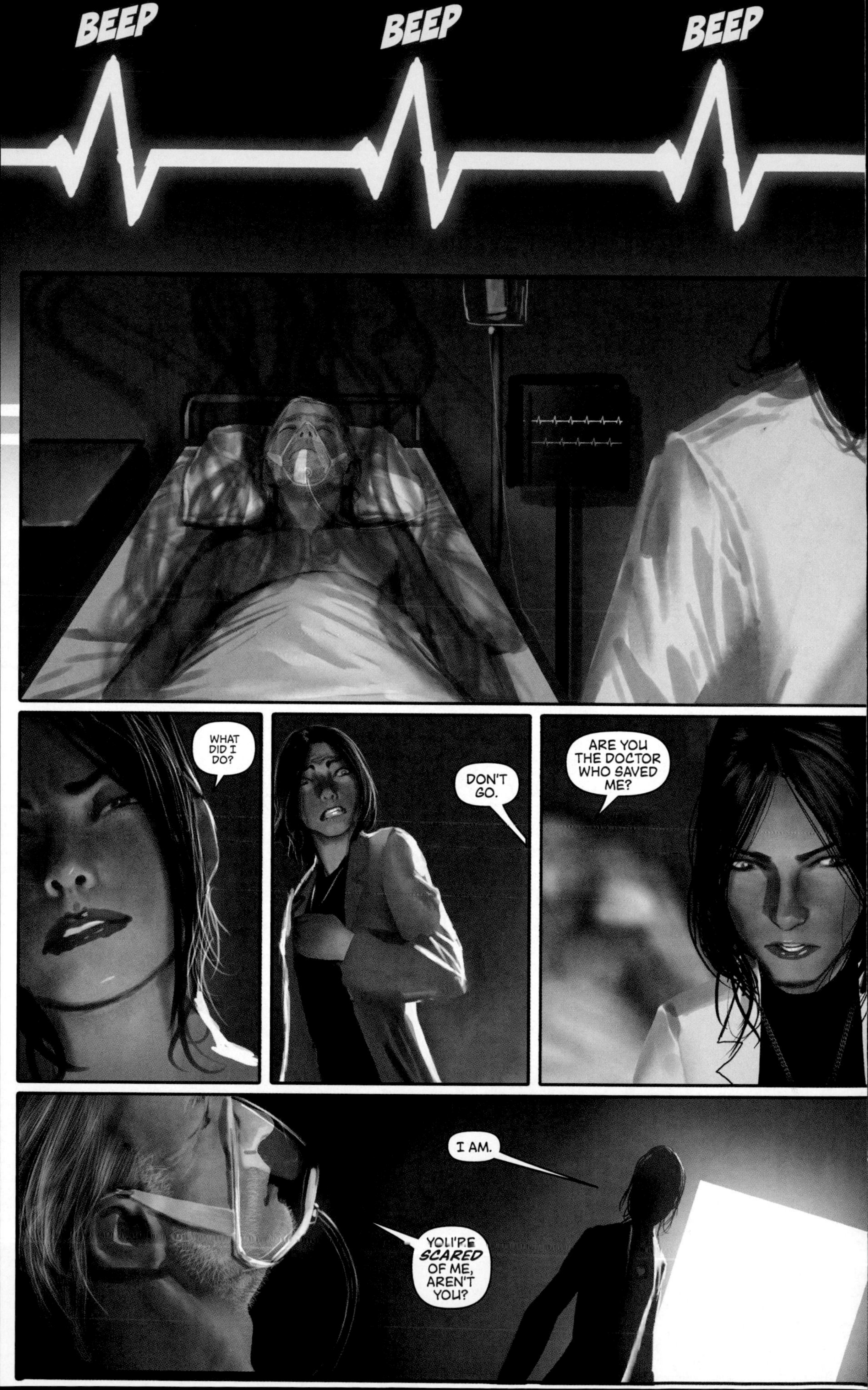
BEEP
BEEP
BEEP
WHAT DID I DO?
DON'T GO.
ARE YOU THE DOCTOR WHO SAVED ME?
I AM.
YOU'RE *SCARED* OF ME, AREN'T YOU?

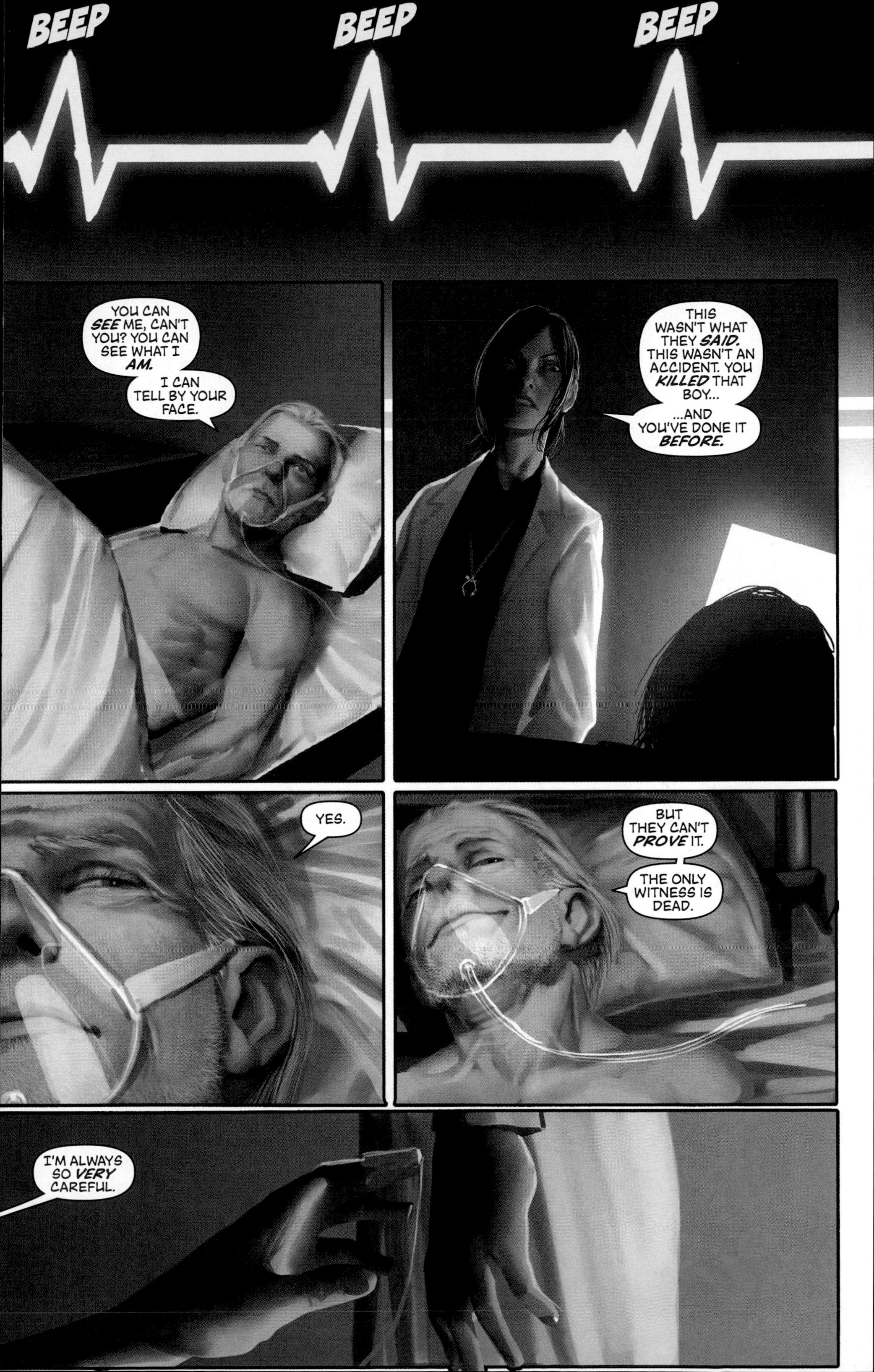
BEEP
BEEP
BEEP
YOU CAN SEE ME, CAN'T YOU? YOU CAN SEE WHAT I AM.
I CAN TELL BY YOUR FACE.
THIS WASN'T WHAT THEY SAID. THIS WASN'T AN ACCIDENT. YOU KILLED THAT BOY...
...AND YOU'VE DONE IT BEFORE.
YES.
BUT THEY CAN'T PROVE IT.
THE ONLY WITNESS IS DEAD.
I'M ALWAYS SO VERY CAREFUL.

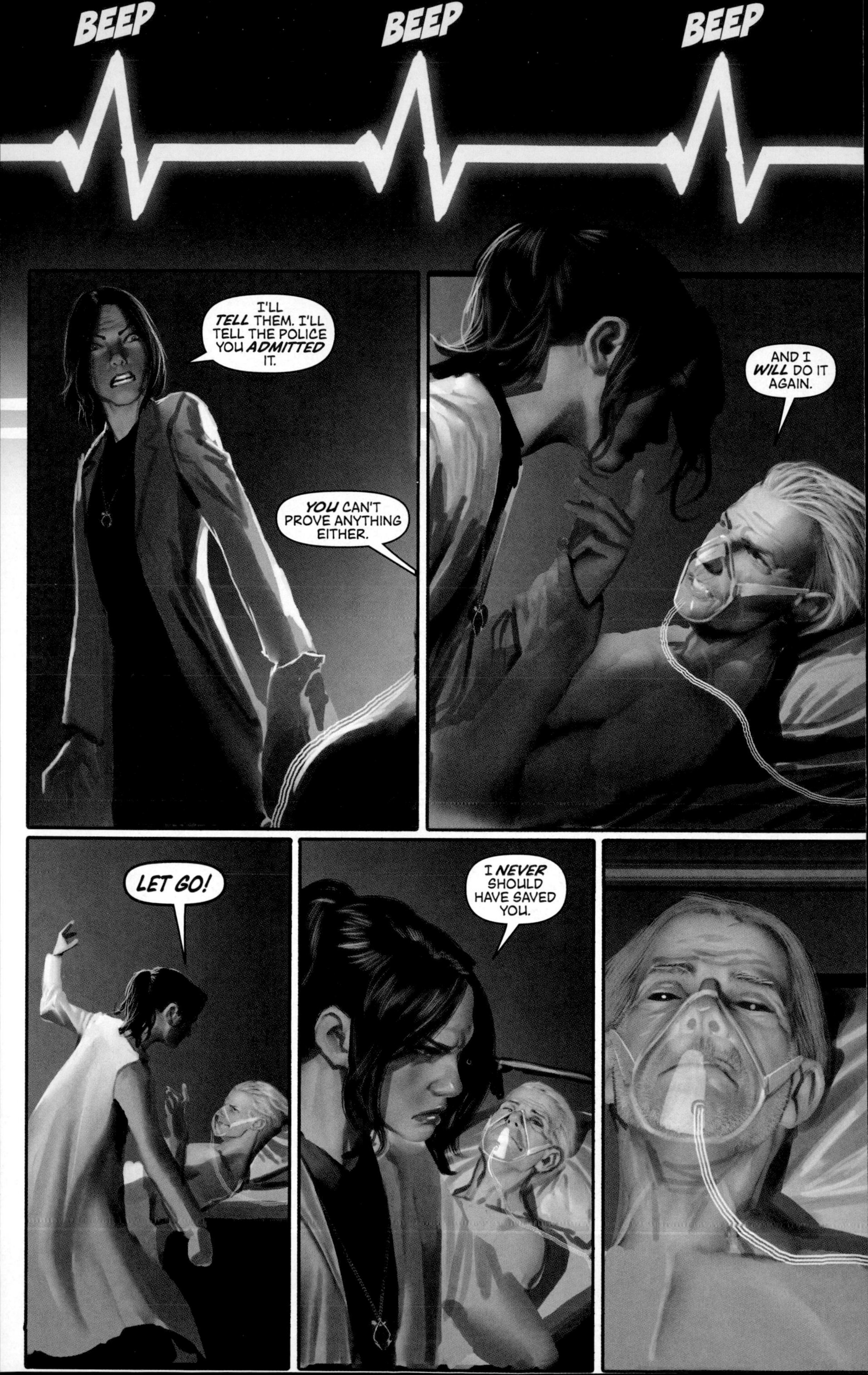
BEEP
BEEP
BEEP
I'LL TELL THEM. I'LL TELL THE POLICE YOU ADMITTED IT.
YOU CAN'T PROVE ANYTHING EITHER.
AND I WILL DO IT AGAIN.
LET GO!
I NEVER SHOULD HAVE SAVED YOU.

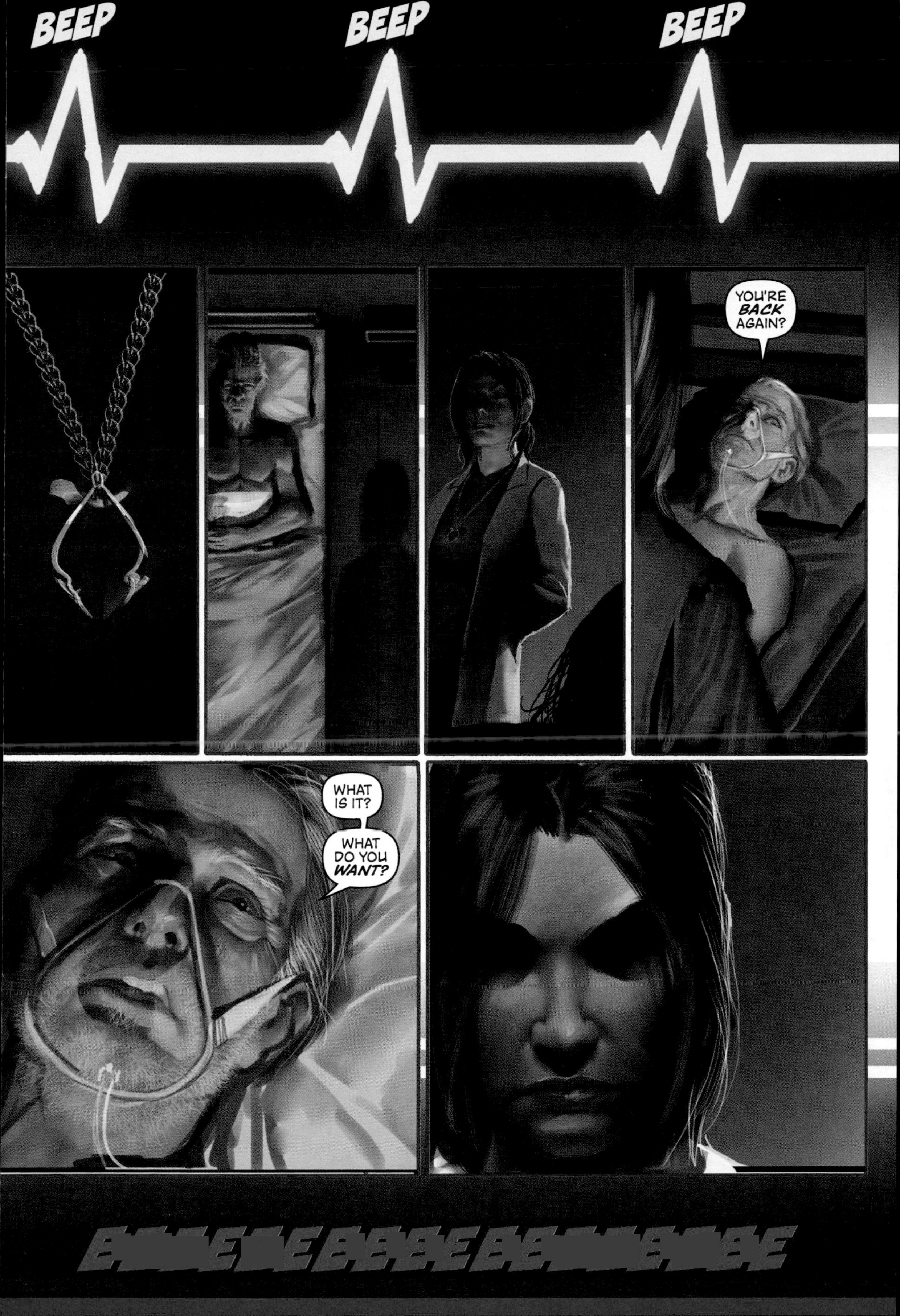
BEEP
BEEP
BEEP
YOU'RE *BACK* AGAIN?
WHAT IS IT?
WHAT DO YOU *WANT?*

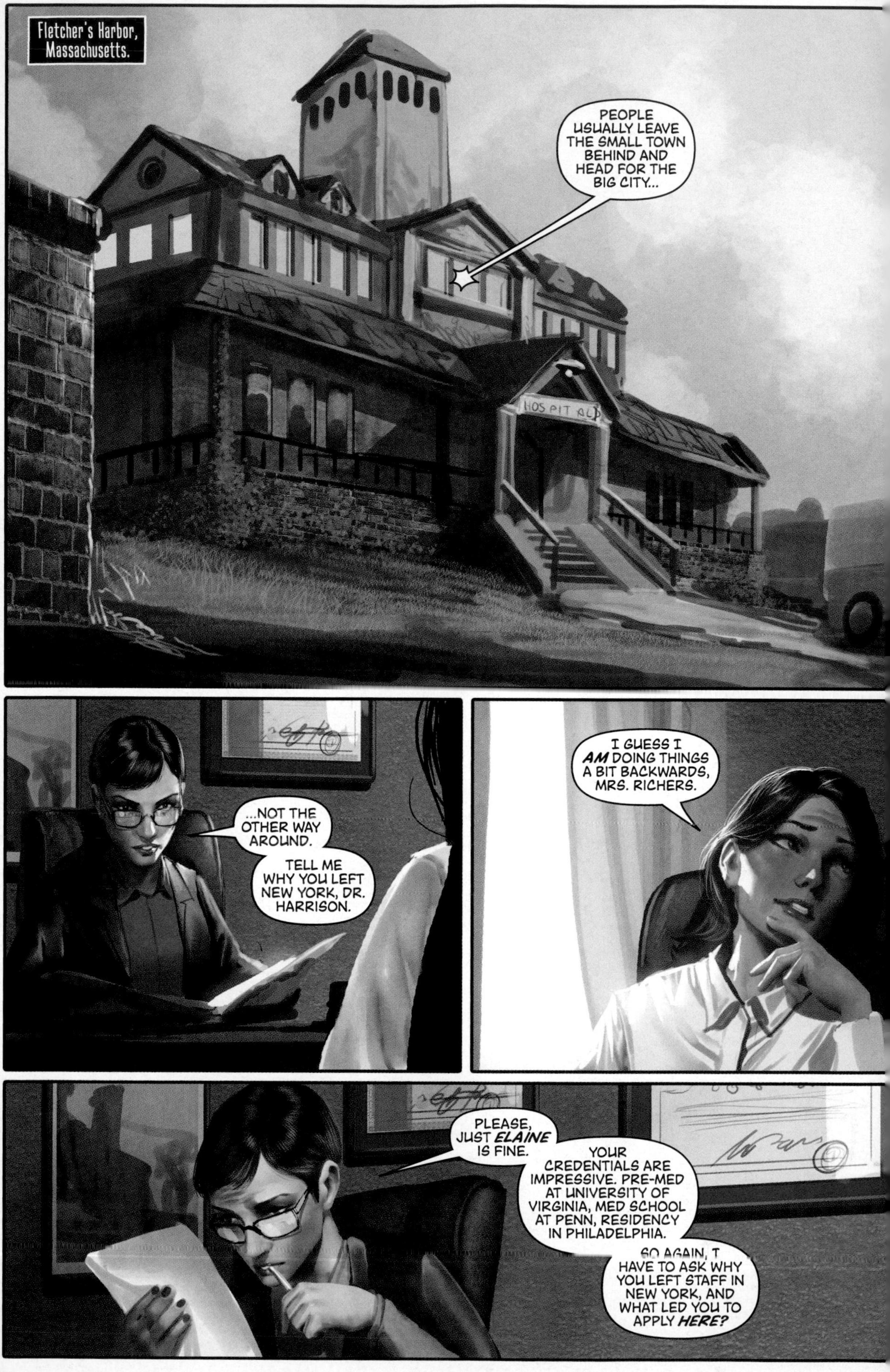
Fletcher's Harbor, Massachusetts.
PEOPLE USUALLY LEAVE THE SMALL TOWN BEHIND AND HEAD FOR THE BIG CITY...
HOS PIT AL
...NOT THE OTHER WAY AROUND.
TELL ME WHY YOU LEFT NEW YORK, DR. HARRISON.
I GUESS I AM DOING THINGS A BIT BACKWARDS, MRS. RICHERS.
PLEASE, JUST ELAINE IS FINE.
YOUR CREDENTIALS ARE IMPRESSIVE. PRE-MED AT UNIVERSITY OF VIRGINIA, MED SCHOOL AT PENN, RESIDENCY IN PHILADELPHIA.
SO AGAIN, I HAVE TO ASK WHY YOU LEFT STAFF IN NEW YORK, AND WHAT LED YOU TO APPLY HERE?

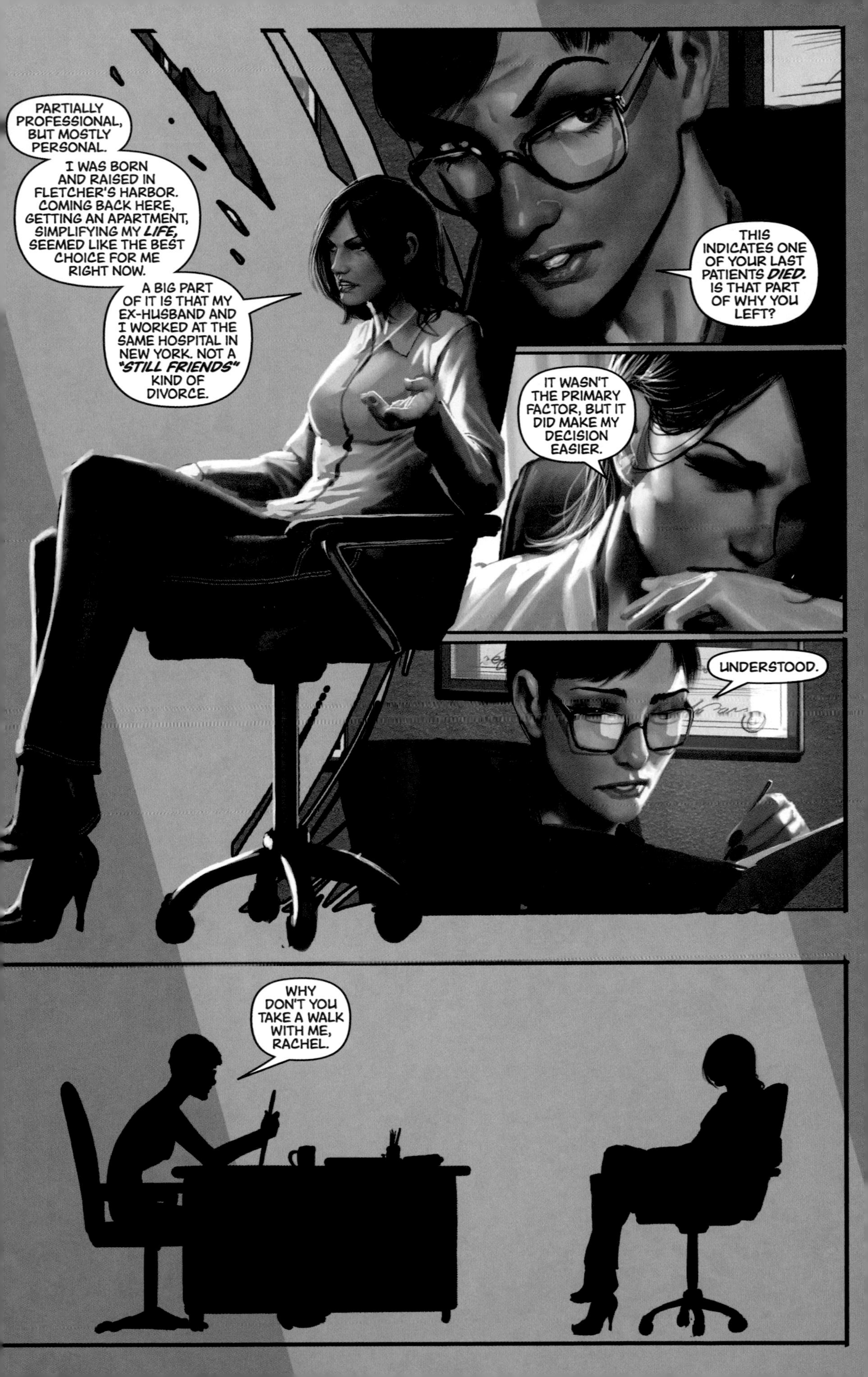

PARTIALLY PROFESSIONAL, BUT MOSTLY PERSONAL.
I WAS BORN AND RAISED IN FLETCHER'S HARBOR. COMING BACK HERE, GETTING AN APARTMENT, SIMPLIFYING MY *LIFE,* SEEMED LIKE THE BEST CHOICE FOR ME RIGHT NOW.
A BIG PART OF IT IS THAT MY EX-HUSBAND AND I WORKED AT THE SAME HOSPITAL IN NEW YORK. NOT A *"STILL FRIENDS"* KIND OF DIVORCE.
THIS INDICATES ONE OF YOUR LAST PATIENTS *DIED.* IS THAT PART OF WHY YOU LEFT?
IT WASN'T THE PRIMARY FACTOR, BUT IT DID MAKE MY DECISION EASIER.
UNDERSTOOD.
WHY DON'T YOU TAKE A WALK WITH ME, RACHEL.

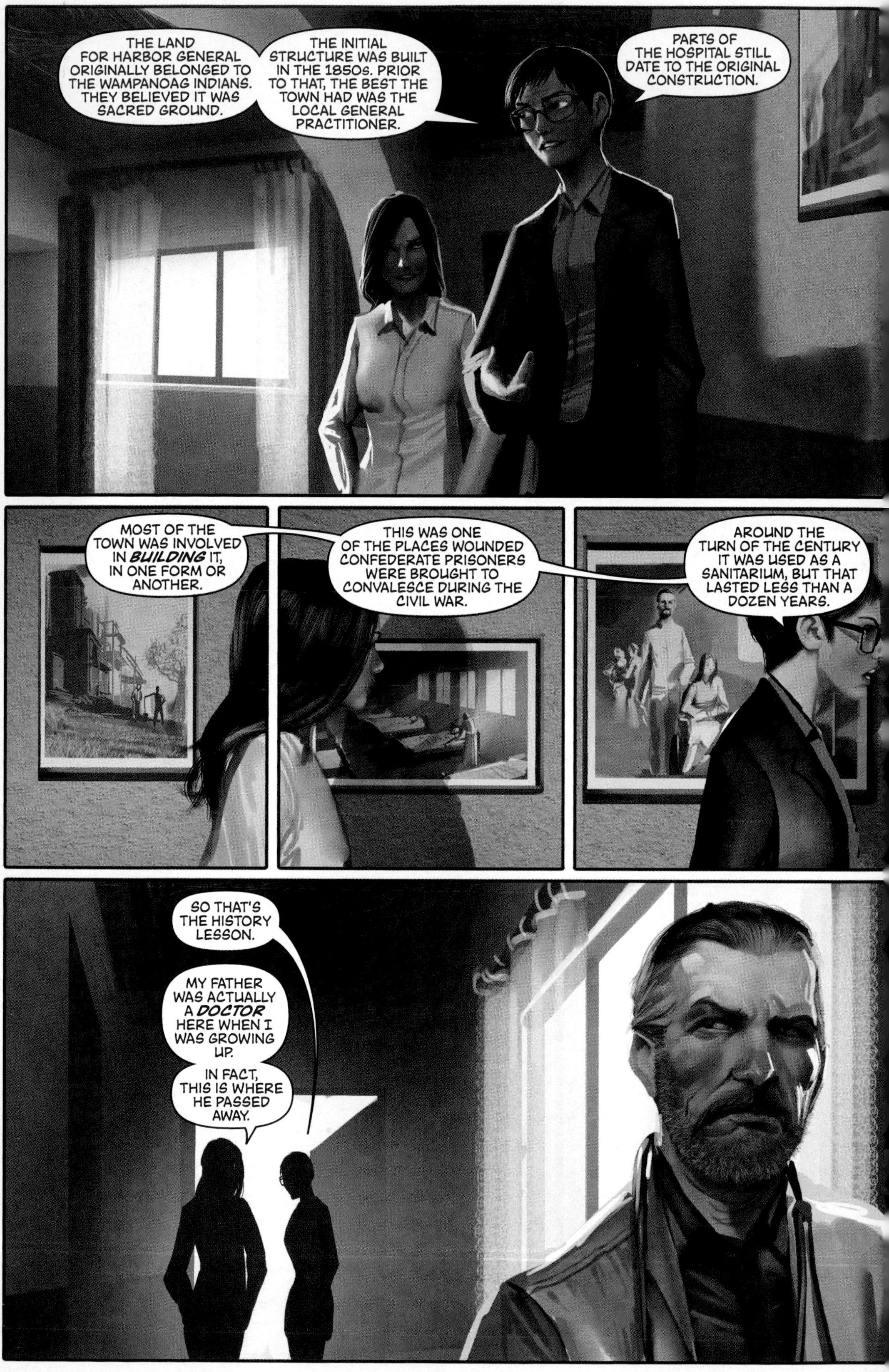
THE LAND FOR HARBOR GENERAL ORIGINALLY BELONGED TO THE WAMPANOAG INDIANS. THEY BELIEVED IT WAS SACRED GROUND.
THE INITIAL STRUCTURE WAS BUILT IN THE 1850s. PRIOR TO THAT, THE BEST THE TOWN HAD WAS THE LOCAL GENERAL PRACTITIONER.
PARTS OF THE HOSPITAL STILL DATE TO THE ORIGINAL CONSTRUCTION.
MOST OF THE TOWN WAS INVOLVED IN *BUILDING* IT, IN ONE FORM OR ANOTHER.
THIS WAS ONE OF THE PLACES WOUNDED CONFEDERATE PRISONERS WERE BROUGHT TO CONVALESCE DURING THE CIVIL WAR.
AROUND THE TURN OF THE CENTURY IT WAS USED AS A SANITARIUM, BUT THAT LASTED LESS THAN A DOZEN YEARS.
SO THAT'S THE HISTORY LESSON.
MY FATHER WAS ACTUALLY A *DOCTOR* HERE WHEN I WAS GROWING UP.
IN FACT, THIS IS WHERE HE PASSED AWAY.

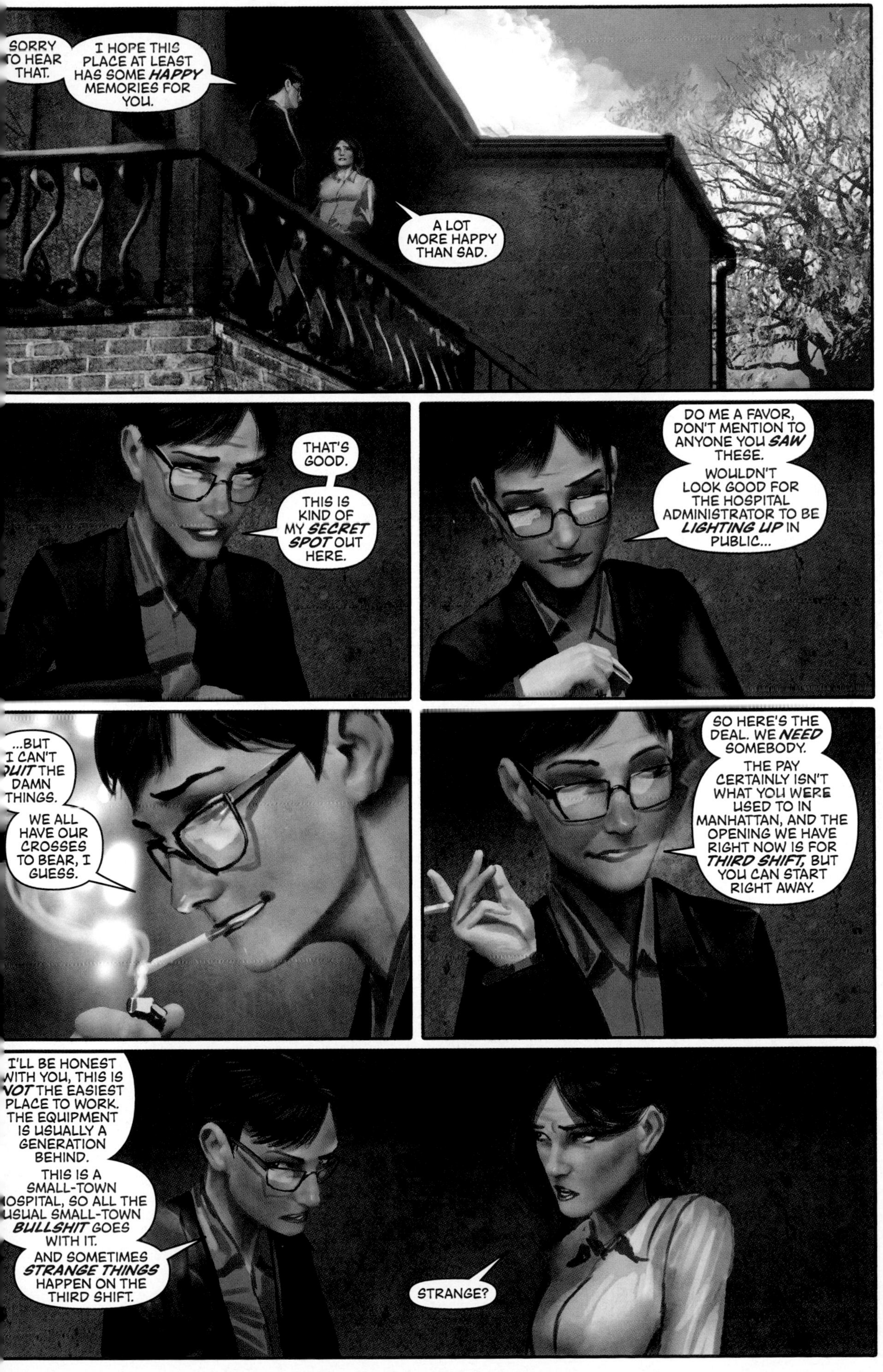

SORRY TO HEAR THAT.
I HOPE THIS PLACE AT LEAST HAS SOME HAPPY MEMORIES FOR YOU.
A LOT MORE HAPPY THAN SAD.
THAT'S GOOD.
THIS IS KIND OF MY SECRET SPOT OUT HERE.
DO ME A FAVOR, DON'T MENTION TO ANYONE YOU SAW THESE.
WOULDN'T LOOK GOOD FOR THE HOSPITAL ADMINISTRATOR TO BE LIGHTING UP IN PUBLIC...
...BUT I CAN'T QUIT THE DAMN THINGS.
WE ALL HAVE OUR CROSSES TO BEAR, I GUESS.
SO HERE'S THE DEAL. WE NEED SOMEBODY.
THE PAY CERTAINLY ISN'T WHAT YOU WERE USED TO IN MANHATTAN, AND THE OPENING WE HAVE RIGHT NOW IS FOR THIRD SHIFT, BUT YOU CAN START RIGHT AWAY.
I'LL BE HONEST WITH YOU, THIS IS NOT THE EASIEST PLACE TO WORK. THE EQUIPMENT IS USUALLY A GENERATION BEHIND.
THIS IS A SMALL-TOWN HOSPITAL, SO ALL THE USUAL SMALL-TOWN BULLSHIT GOES WITH IT.
AND SOMETIMES STRANGE THINGS HAPPEN ON THE THIRD SHIFT.
STRANGE?

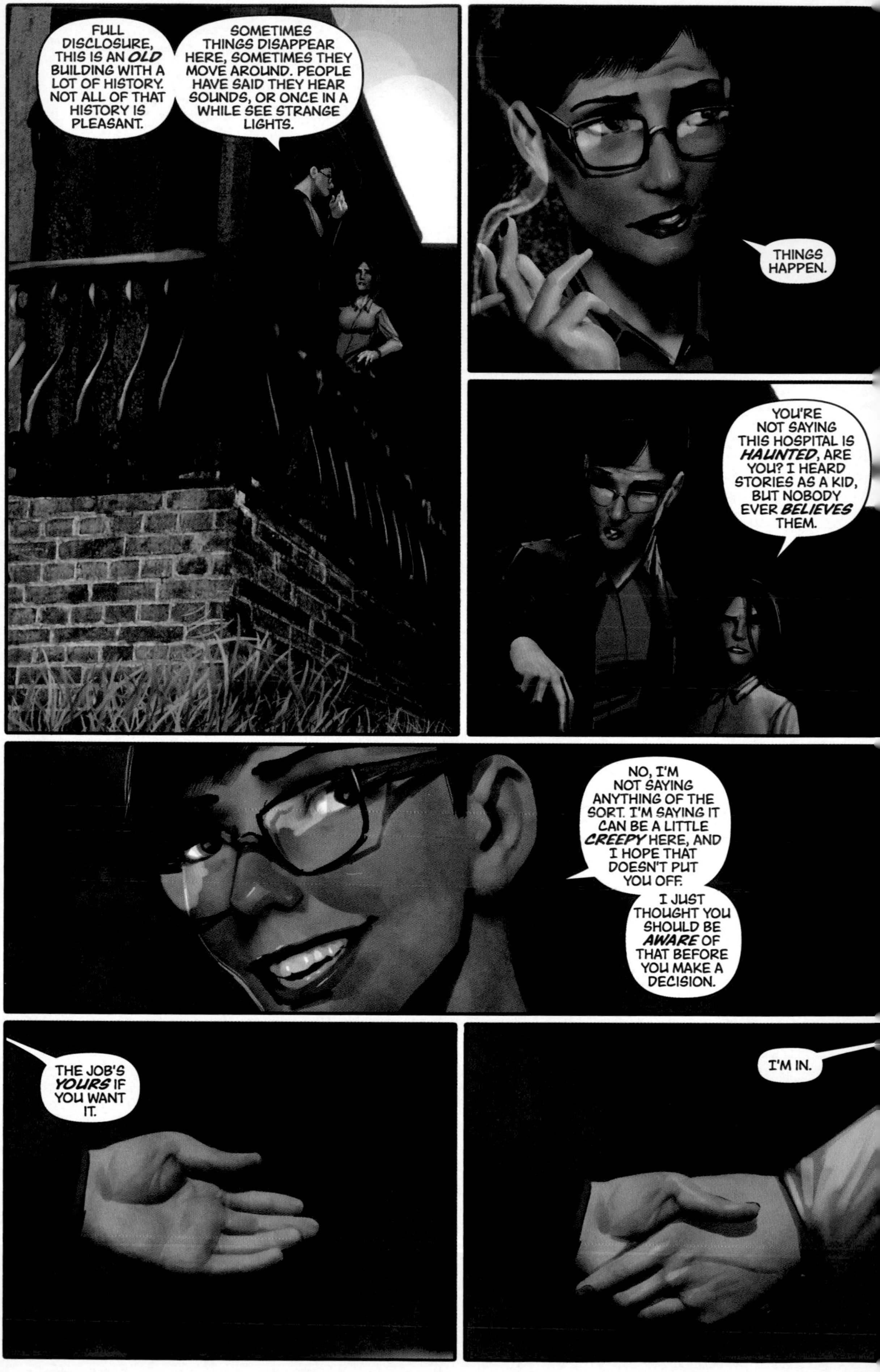

FULL DISCLOSURE, THIS IS AN OLD BUILDING WITH A LOT OF HISTORY. NOT ALL OF THAT HISTORY IS PLEASANT.
SOMETIMES THINGS DISAPPEAR HERE, SOMETIMES THEY MOVE AROUND. PEOPLE HAVE SAID THEY HEAR SOUNDS, OR ONCE IN A WHILE SEE STRANGE LIGHTS.
THINGS HAPPEN.
YOU'RE NOT SAYING THIS HOSPITAL IS HAUNTED, ARE YOU? I HEARD STORIES AS A KID, BUT NOBODY EVER BELIEVES THEM.
NO, I'M NOT SAYING ANYTHING OF THE SORT. I'M SAYING IT CAN BE A LITTLE CREEPY HERE, AND I HOPE THAT DOESN'T PUT YOU OFF.
I JUST THOUGHT YOU SHOULD BE AWARE OF THAT BEFORE YOU MAKE A DECISION.
THE JOB'S YOURS IF YOU WANT IT.
I'M IN.

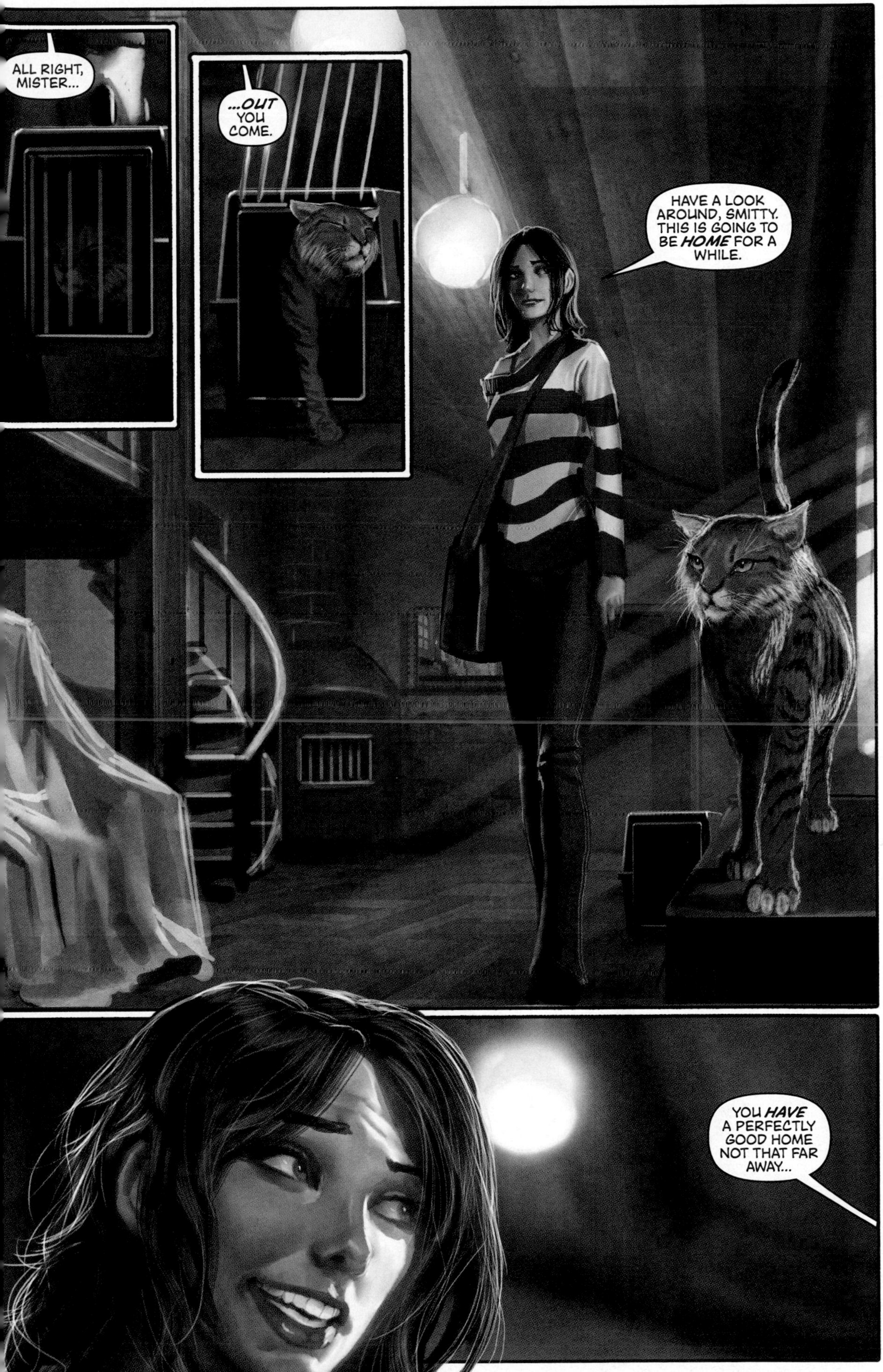
ALL RIGHT, MISTER...
...OUT YOU COME.
HAVE A LOOK AROUND, SMITTY. THIS IS GOING TO BE HOME FOR A WHILE.
YOU HAVE A PERFECTLY GOOD HOME NOT THAT FAR AWAY...

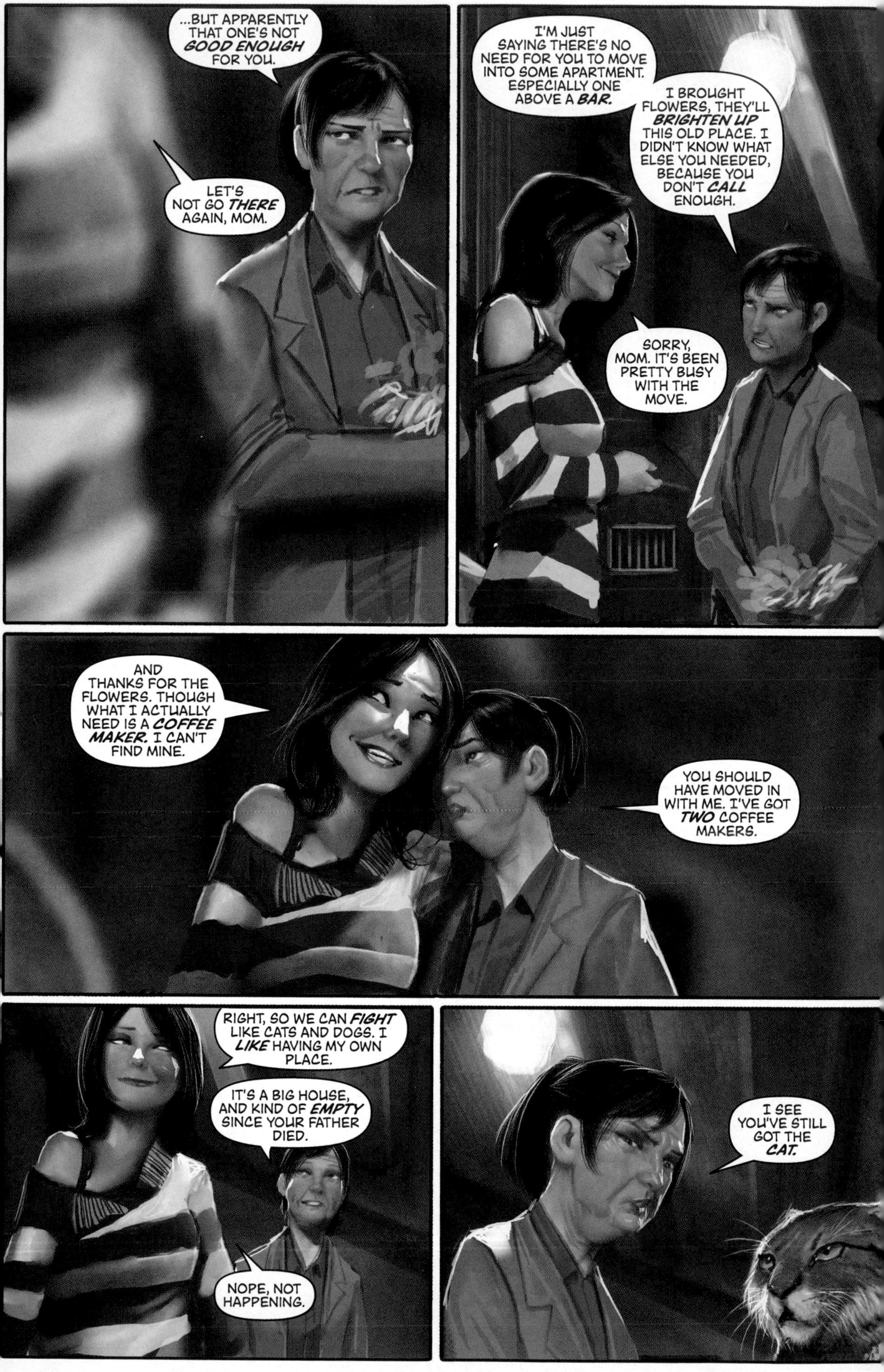
...BUT APPARENTLY THAT ONE'S NOT GOOD ENOUGH FOR YOU.
LET'S NOT GO THERE AGAIN, MOM.
I'M JUST SAYING THERE'S NO NEED FOR YOU TO MOVE INTO SOME APARTMENT. ESPECIALLY ONE ABOVE A BAR.
I BROUGHT FLOWERS, THEY'LL BRIGHTEN UP THIS OLD PLACE. I DIDN'T KNOW WHAT ELSE YOU NEEDED, BECAUSE YOU DON'T CALL ENOUGH.
SORRY, MOM. IT'S BEEN PRETTY BUSY WITH THE MOVE.
AND THANKS FOR THE FLOWERS. THOUGH WHAT I ACTUALLY NEED IS A COFFEE MAKER. I CAN'T FIND MINE.
YOU SHOULD HAVE MOVED IN WITH ME. I'VE GOT TWO COFFEE MAKERS.
RIGHT, SO WE CAN FIGHT LIKE CATS AND DOGS. I LIKE HAVING MY OWN PLACE.
IT'S A BIG HOUSE, AND KIND OF EMPTY SINCE YOUR FATHER DIED.
NOPE, NOT HAPPENING.
I SEE YOU'VE STILL GOT THE CAT.

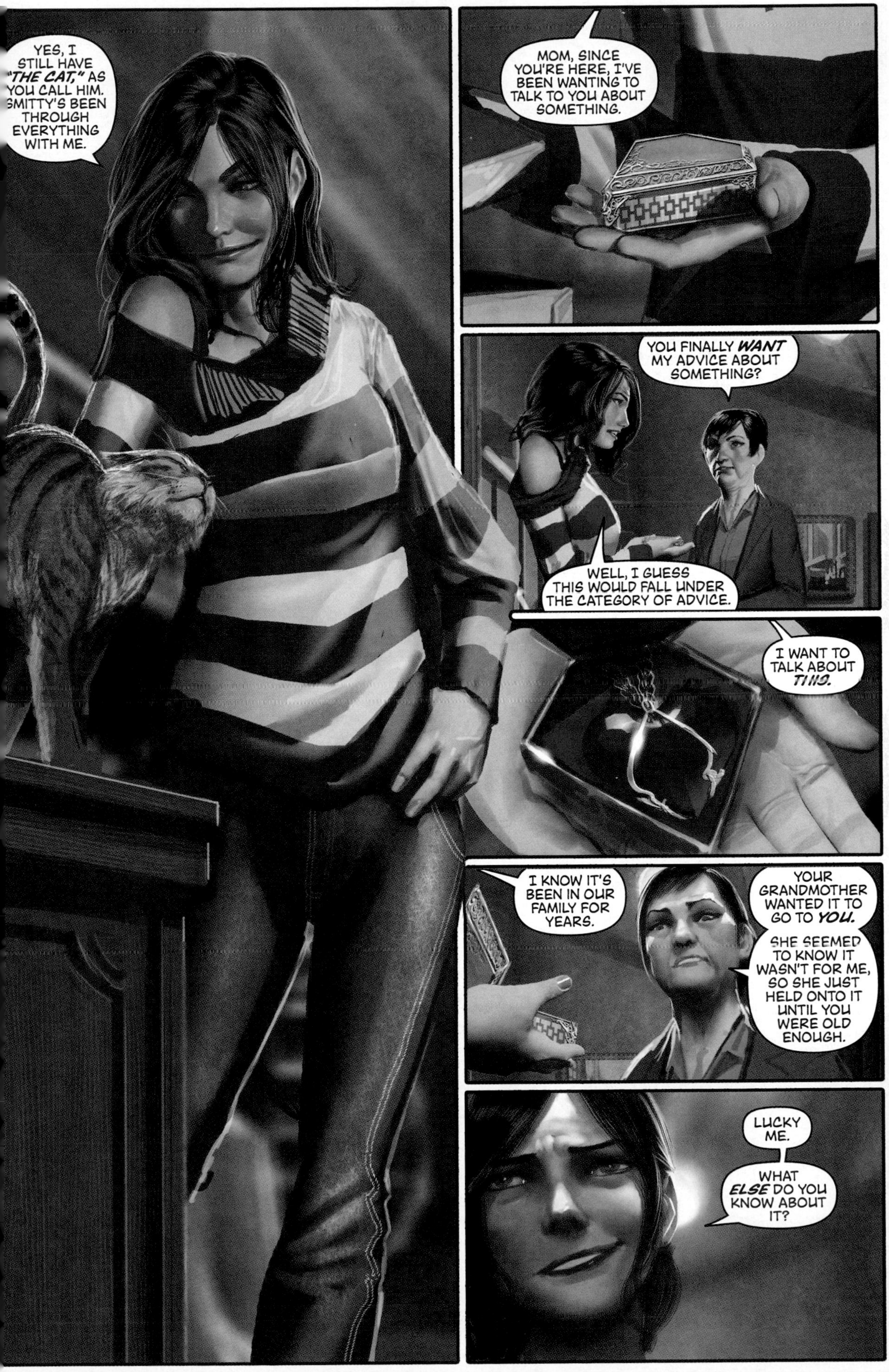
YES, I STILL HAVE *"THE CAT,"* AS YOU CALL HIM. SMITTY'S BEEN THROUGH EVERYTHING WITH ME.
MOM, SINCE YOU'RE HERE, I'VE BEEN WANTING TO TALK TO YOU ABOUT SOMETHING.
YOU FINALLY ***WANT*** MY ADVICE ABOUT SOMETHING?
WELL, I GUESS THIS WOULD FALL UNDER THE CATEGORY OF ADVICE.
I WANT TO TALK ABOUT ***THIS.***
I KNOW IT'S BEEN IN OUR FAMILY FOR YEARS.
YOUR GRANDMOTHER WANTED IT TO GO TO ***YOU.***
SHE SEEMED TO KNOW IT WASN'T FOR ME, SO SHE JUST HELD ONTO IT UNTIL YOU WERE OLD ENOUGH.
LUCKY ME.
WHAT ***ELSE*** DO YOU KNOW ABOUT IT?

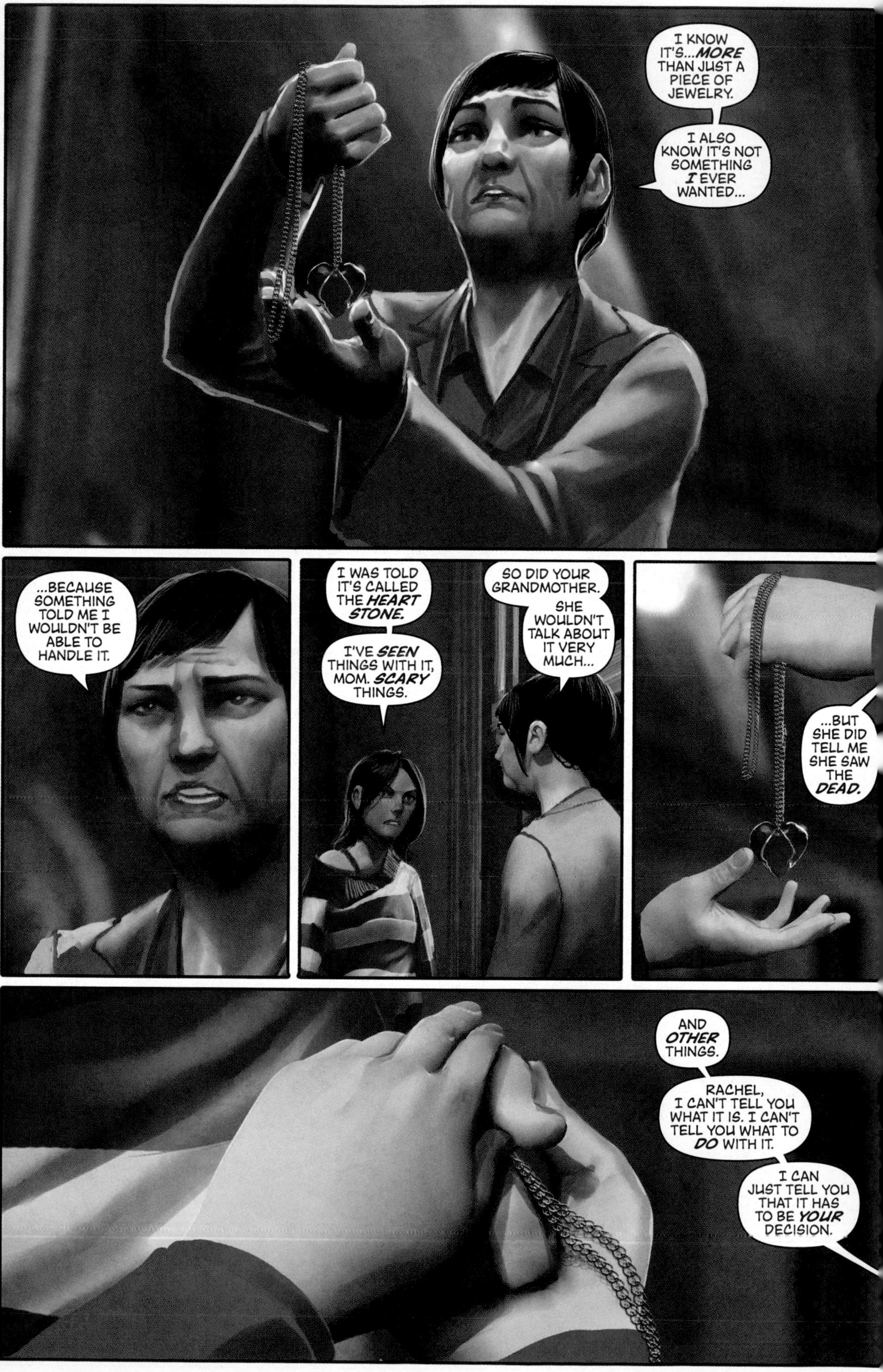
I KNOW IT'S...MORE THAN JUST A PIECE OF JEWELRY.
I ALSO KNOW IT'S NOT SOMETHING I EVER WANTED...
...BECAUSE SOMETHING TOLD ME I WOULDN'T BE ABLE TO HANDLE IT.
I WAS TOLD IT'S CALLED THE HEART STONE.
I'VE SEEN THINGS WITH IT, MOM. SCARY THINGS.
SO DID YOUR GRANDMOTHER.
SHE WOULDN'T TALK ABOUT IT VERY MUCH...
...BUT SHE DID TELL ME SHE SAW THE DEAD.
AND OTHER THINGS.
RACHEL, I CAN'T TELL YOU WHAT IT IS. I CAN'T TELL YOU WHAT TO DO WITH IT.
I CAN JUST TELL YOU THAT IT HAS TO BE YOUR DECISION.

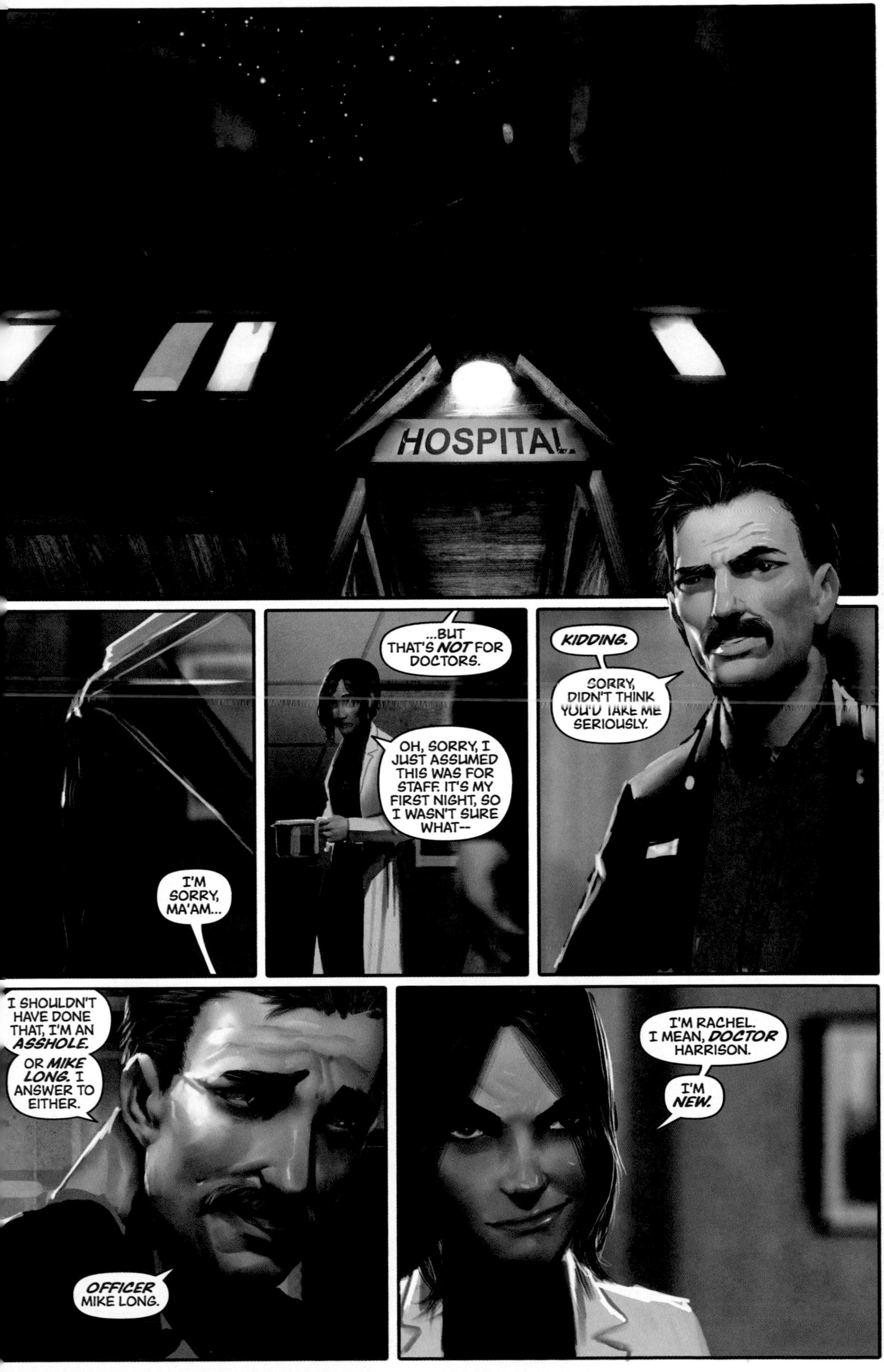
HOSPITAL
I'M SORRY, MA'AM...
...BUT THAT'S NOT FOR DOCTORS.
OH, SORRY, I JUST ASSUMED THIS WAS FOR STAFF. IT'S MY FIRST NIGHT, SO I WASN'T SURE WHAT--
KIDDING.
SORRY, DIDN'T THINK YOU'D TAKE ME SERIOUSLY.
I SHOULDN'T HAVE DONE THAT, I'M AN ASSHOLE.
OR MIKE LONG. I ANSWER TO EITHER.
OFFICER MIKE LONG.
I'M RACHEL. I MEAN, DOCTOR HARRISON.
I'M NEW.

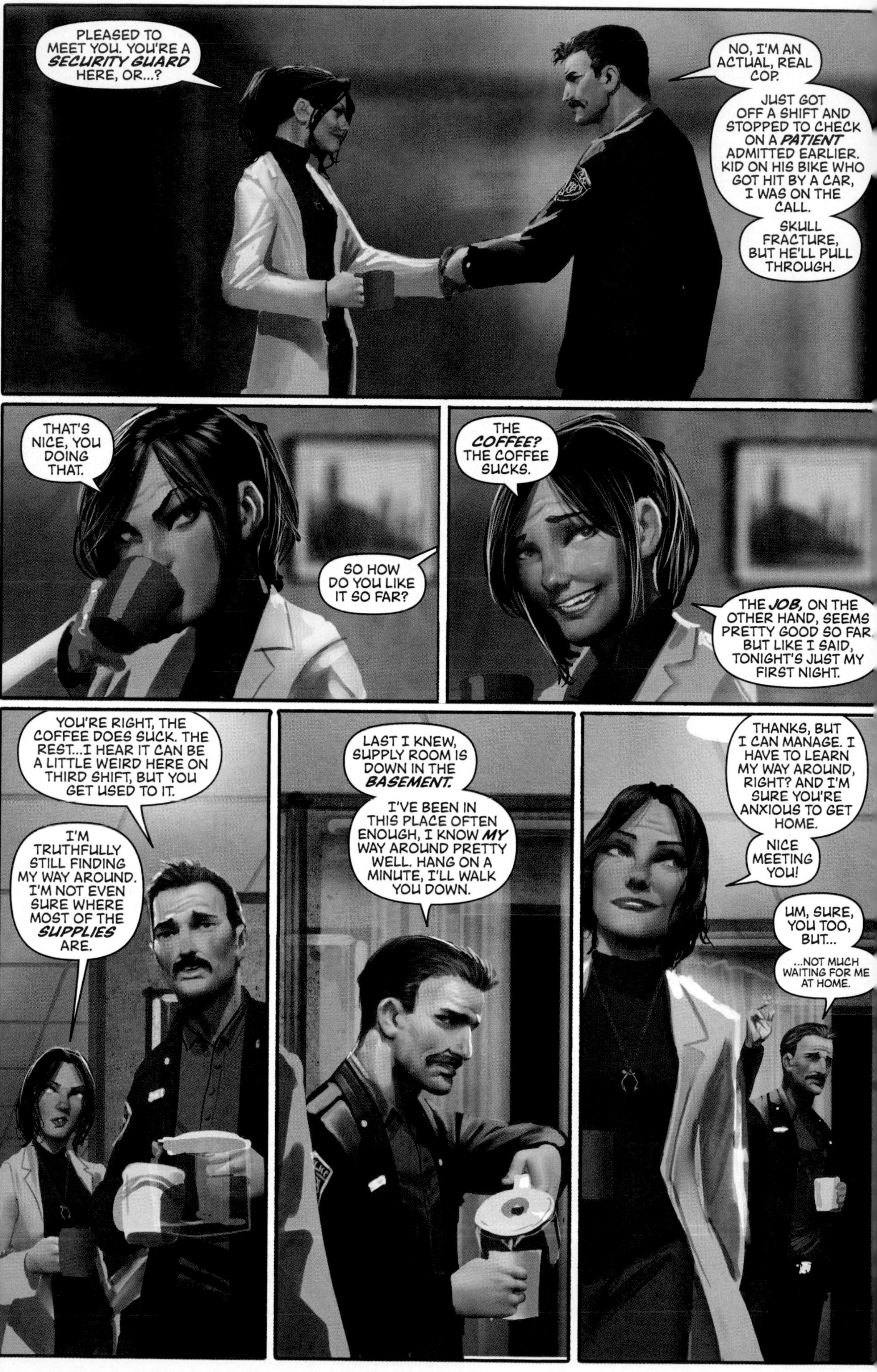
PLEASED TO MEET YOU. YOU'RE A *SECURITY GUARD* HERE, OR...?
NO, I'M AN ACTUAL, REAL COP.
JUST GOT OFF A SHIFT AND STOPPED TO CHECK ON A *PATIENT* ADMITTED EARLIER. KID ON HIS BIKE WHO GOT HIT BY A CAR, I WAS ON THE CALL.
SKULL FRACTURE, BUT HE'LL PULL THROUGH.
THAT'S NICE, YOU DOING THAT.
SO HOW DO YOU LIKE IT SO FAR?
THE *COFFEE?* THE COFFEE SUCKS.
THE *JOB,* ON THE OTHER HAND, SEEMS PRETTY GOOD SO FAR. BUT LIKE I SAID, TONIGHT'S JUST MY FIRST NIGHT.
YOU'RE RIGHT, THE COFFEE DOES SUCK. THE REST...I HEAR IT CAN BE A LITTLE WEIRD HERE ON THIRD SHIFT, BUT YOU GET USED TO IT.
I'M TRUTHFULLY STILL FINDING MY WAY AROUND. I'M NOT EVEN SURE WHERE MOST OF THE *SUPPLIES* ARE.
LAST I KNEW, SUPPLY ROOM IS DOWN IN THE *BASEMENT.*
I'VE BEEN IN THIS PLACE OFTEN ENOUGH, I KNOW *MY* WAY AROUND PRETTY WELL. HANG ON A MINUTE, I'LL WALK YOU DOWN.
THANKS, BUT I CAN MANAGE. I HAVE TO LEARN MY WAY AROUND, RIGHT? AND I'M SURE YOU'RE ANXIOUS TO GET HOME.
NICE MEETING YOU!
UM, SURE, YOU TOO, BUT...
...NOT MUCH WAITING FOR ME AT HOME.

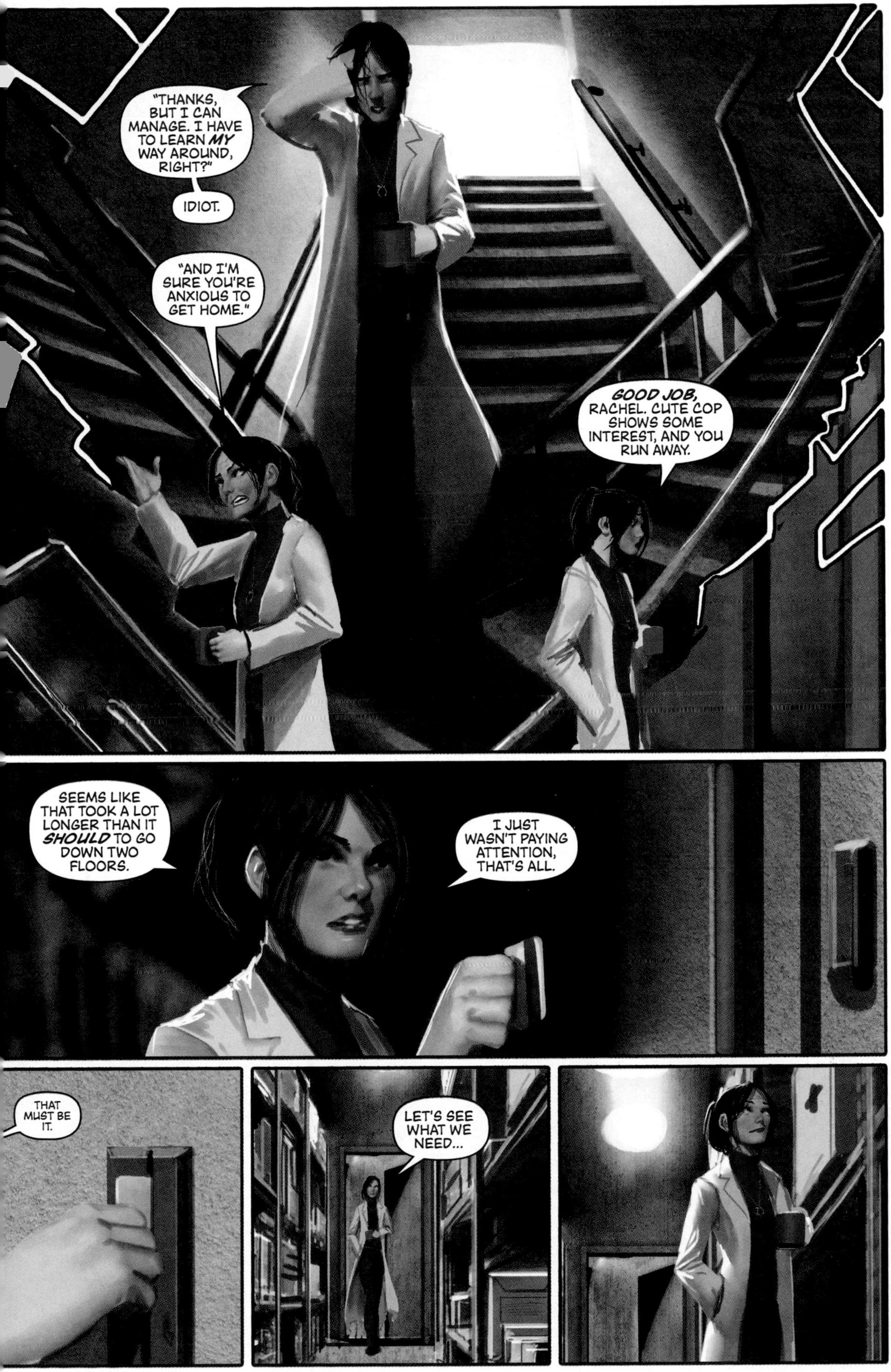
"THANKS, BUT I CAN MANAGE. I HAVE TO LEARN *MY* WAY AROUND, RIGHT?"
IDIOT.
"AND I'M SURE YOU'RE ANXIOUS TO GET HOME."
GOOD JOB, RACHEL. CUTE COP SHOWS SOME INTEREST, AND YOU RUN AWAY.
SEEMS LIKE THAT TOOK A LOT LONGER THAN IT *SHOULD* TO GO DOWN TWO FLOORS.
I JUST WASN'T PAYING ATTENTION, THAT'S ALL.
THAT MUST BE IT.
LET'S SEE WHAT WE NEED...

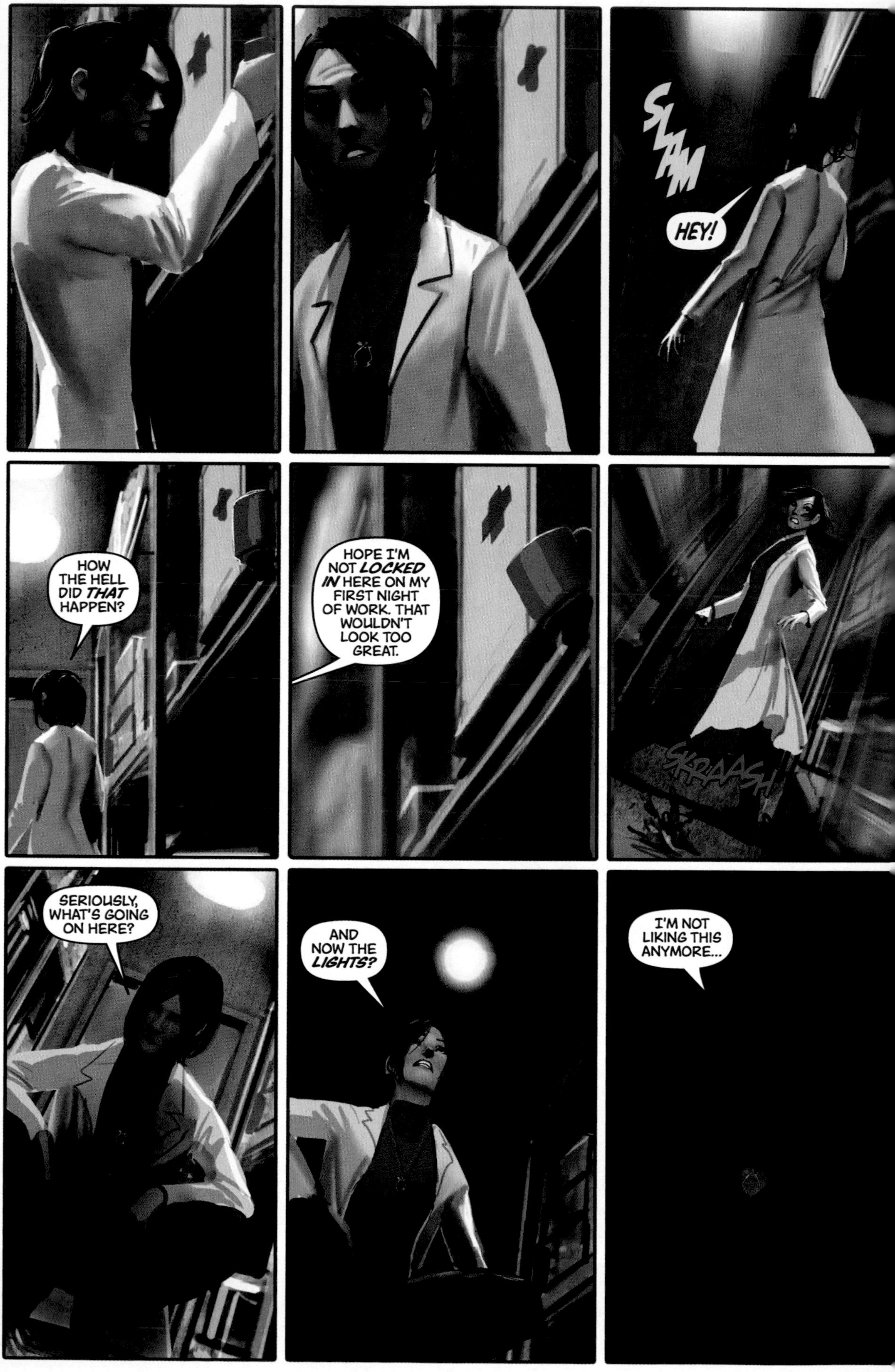

SLAM
HEY!
HOW THE HELL DID THAT HAPPEN?
HOPE I'M NOT LOCKED IN HERE ON MY FIRST NIGHT OF WORK. THAT WOULDN'T LOOK TOO GREAT.
SKRAASH
SERIOUSLY, WHAT'S GOING ON HERE?
AND NOW THE LIGHTS?
I'M NOT LIKING THIS ANYMORE...

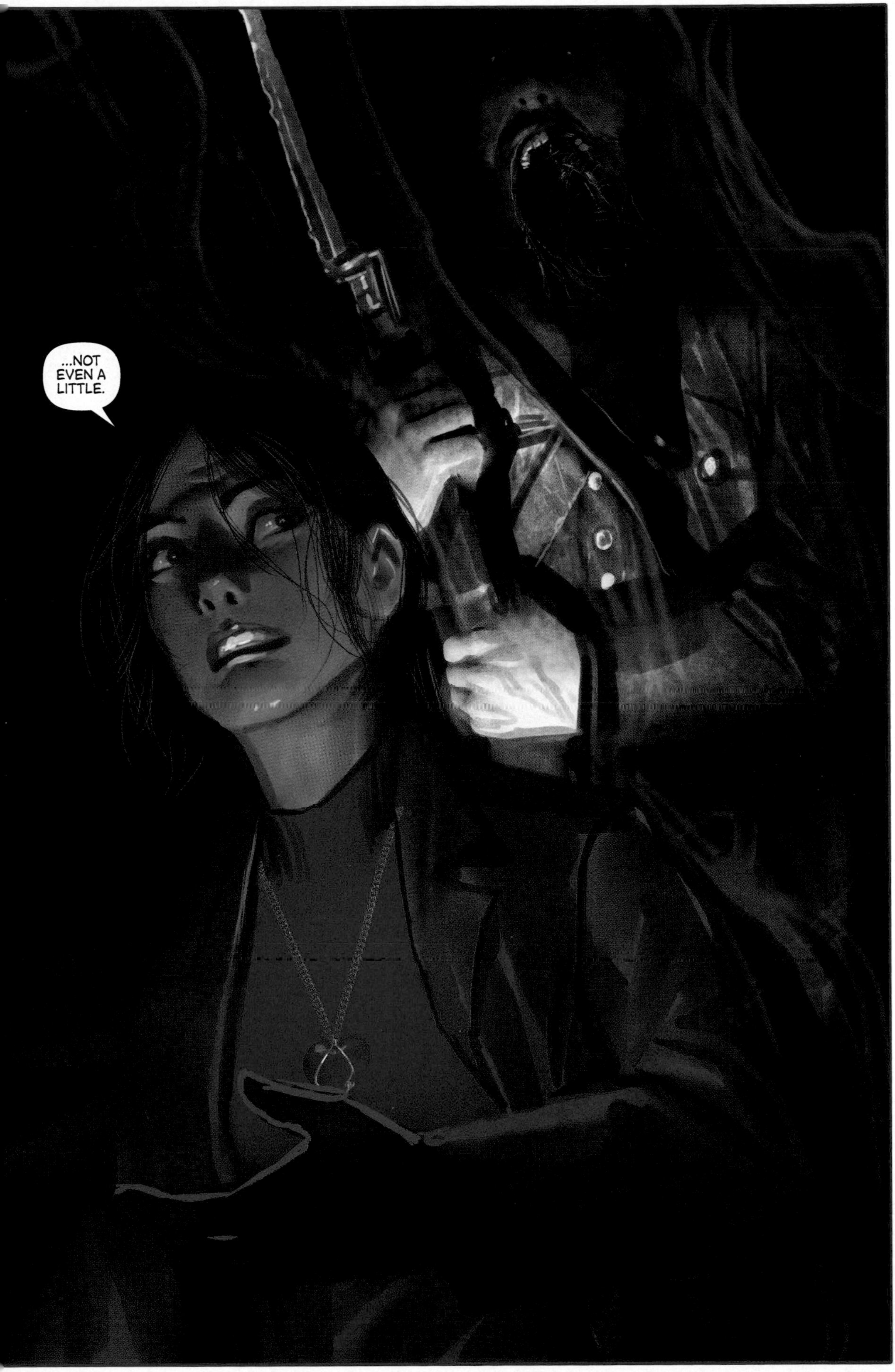
...NOT EVEN A LITTLE.

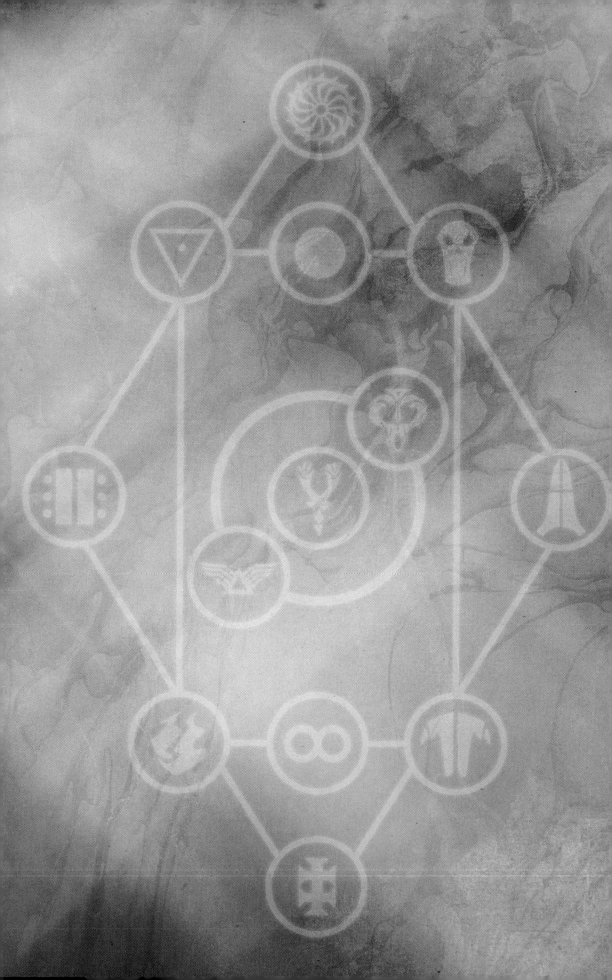

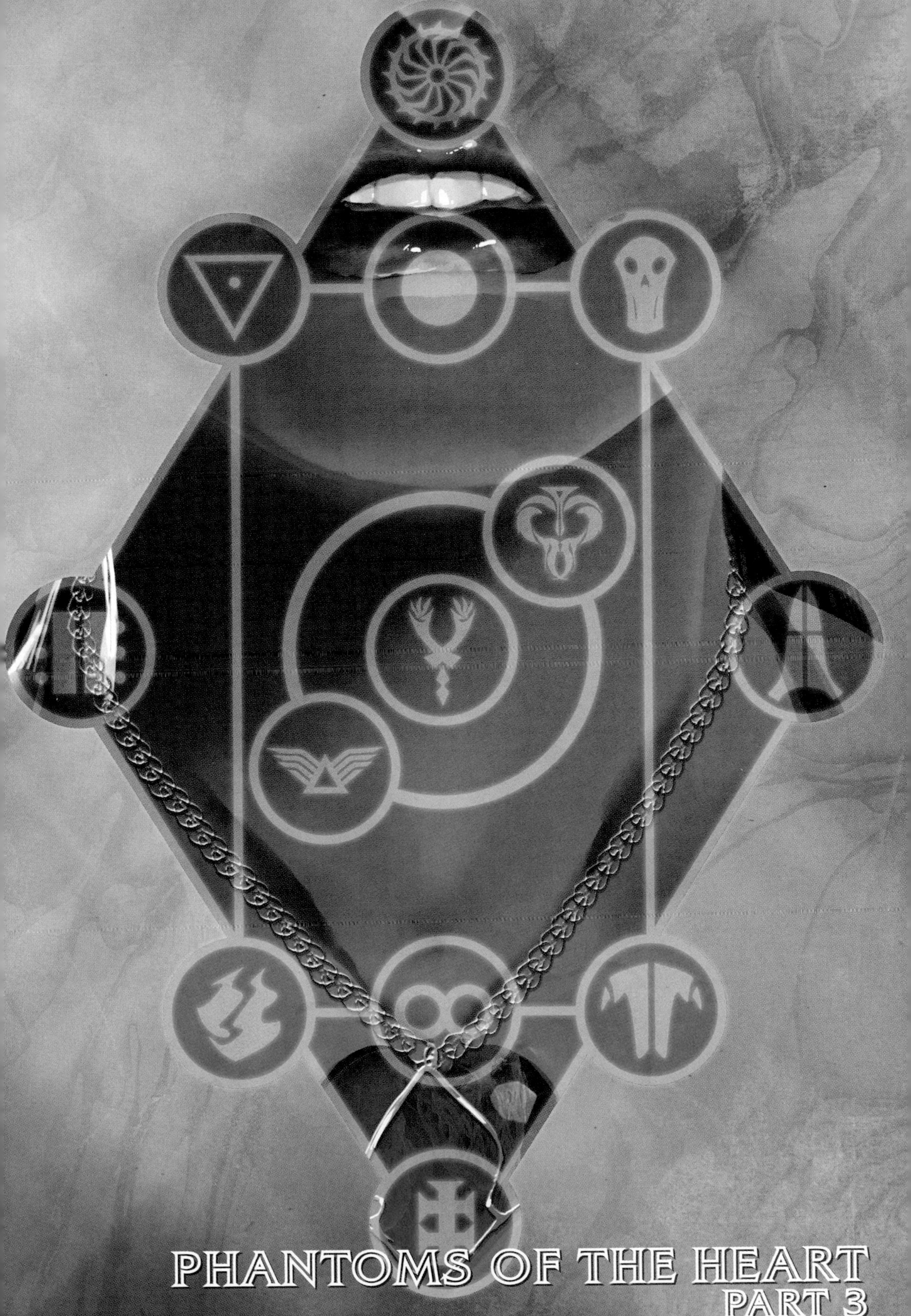

PHANTOMS OF THE HEART
PART 3

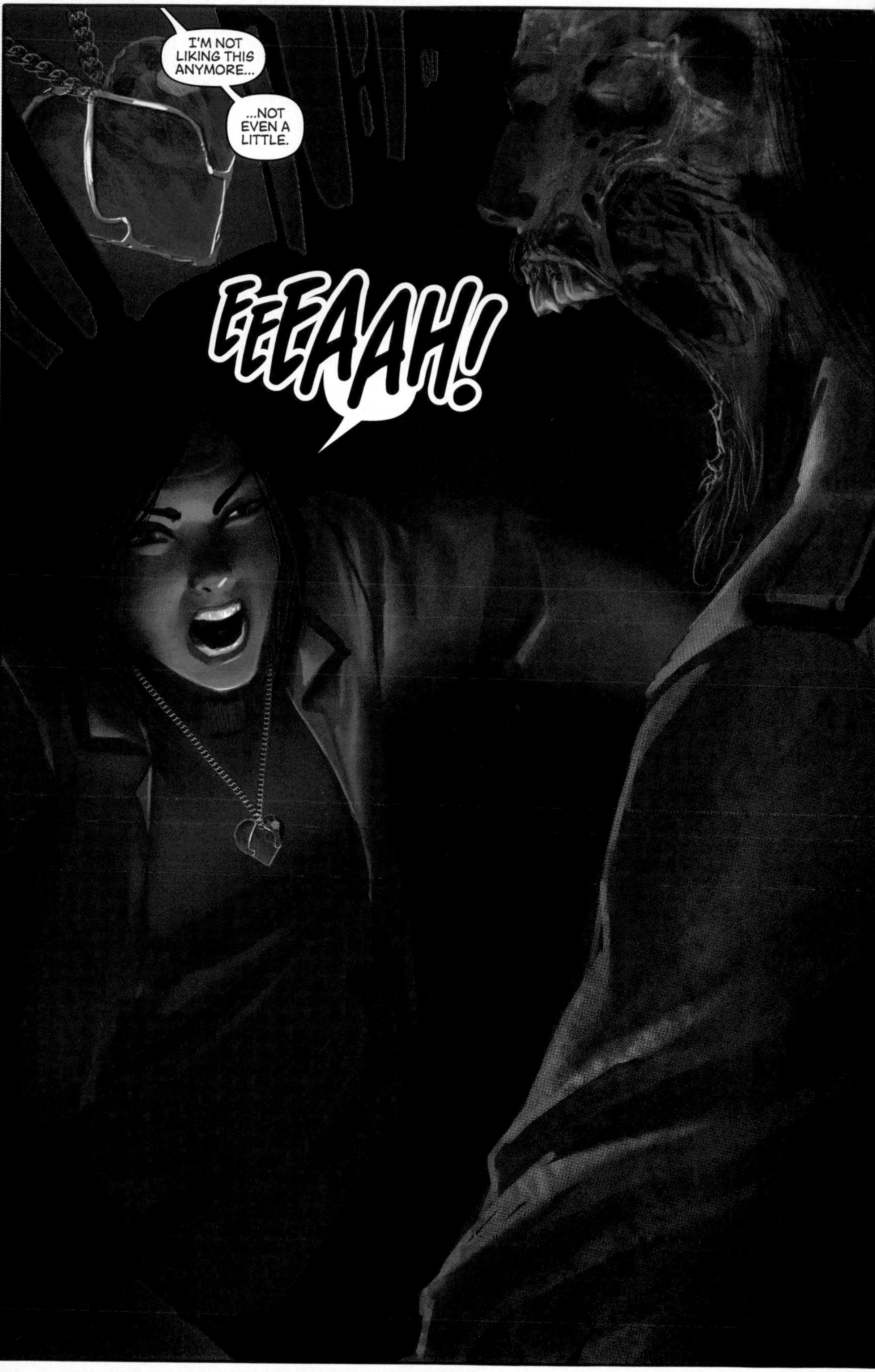
I'M NOT LIKING THIS ANYMORE...
...NOT EVEN A LITTLE.
EEEAAH!

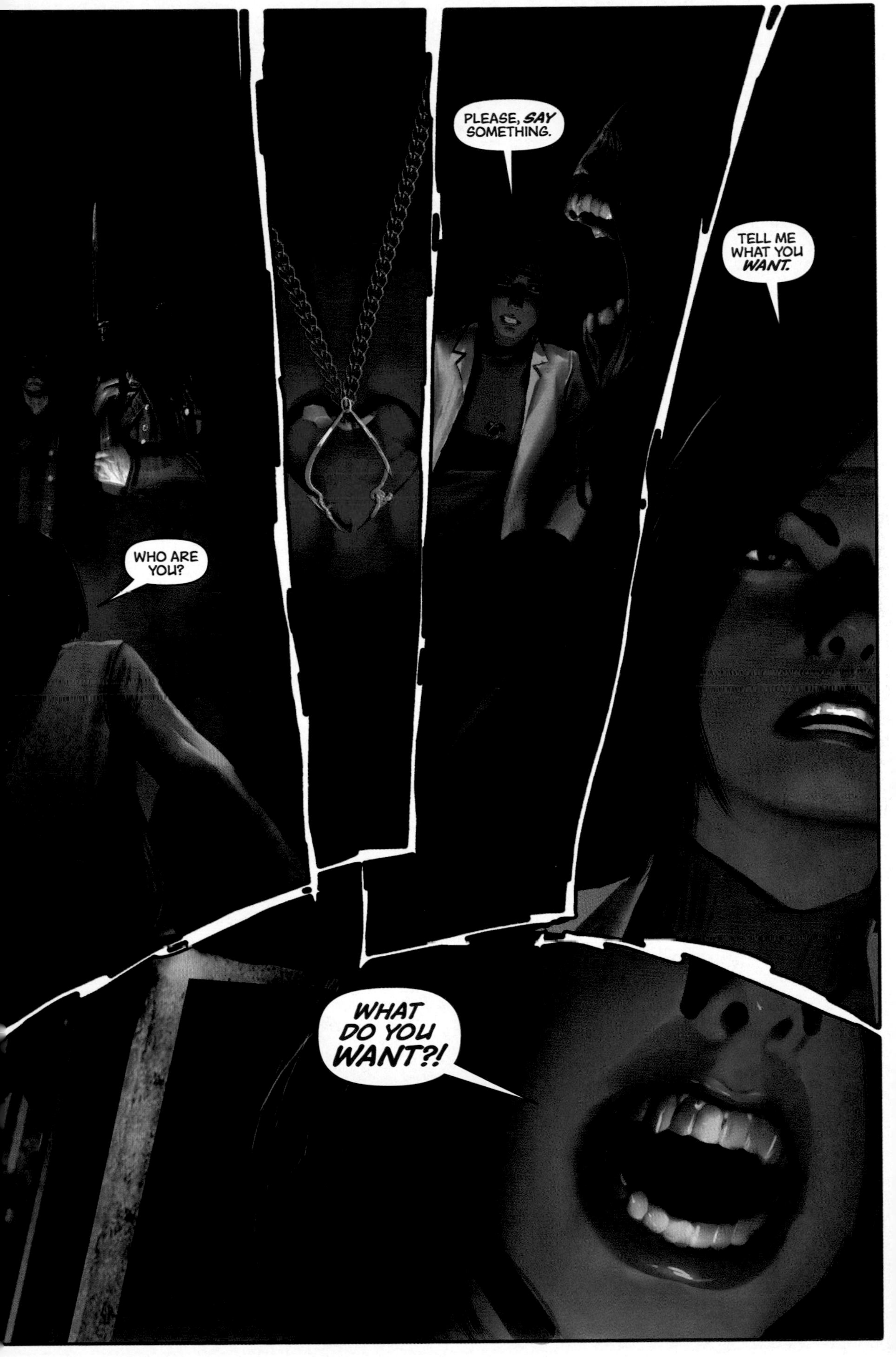
WHO ARE YOU?
PLEASE, SAY SOMETHING.
TELL ME WHAT YOU WANT.
WHAT DO YOU WANT?!

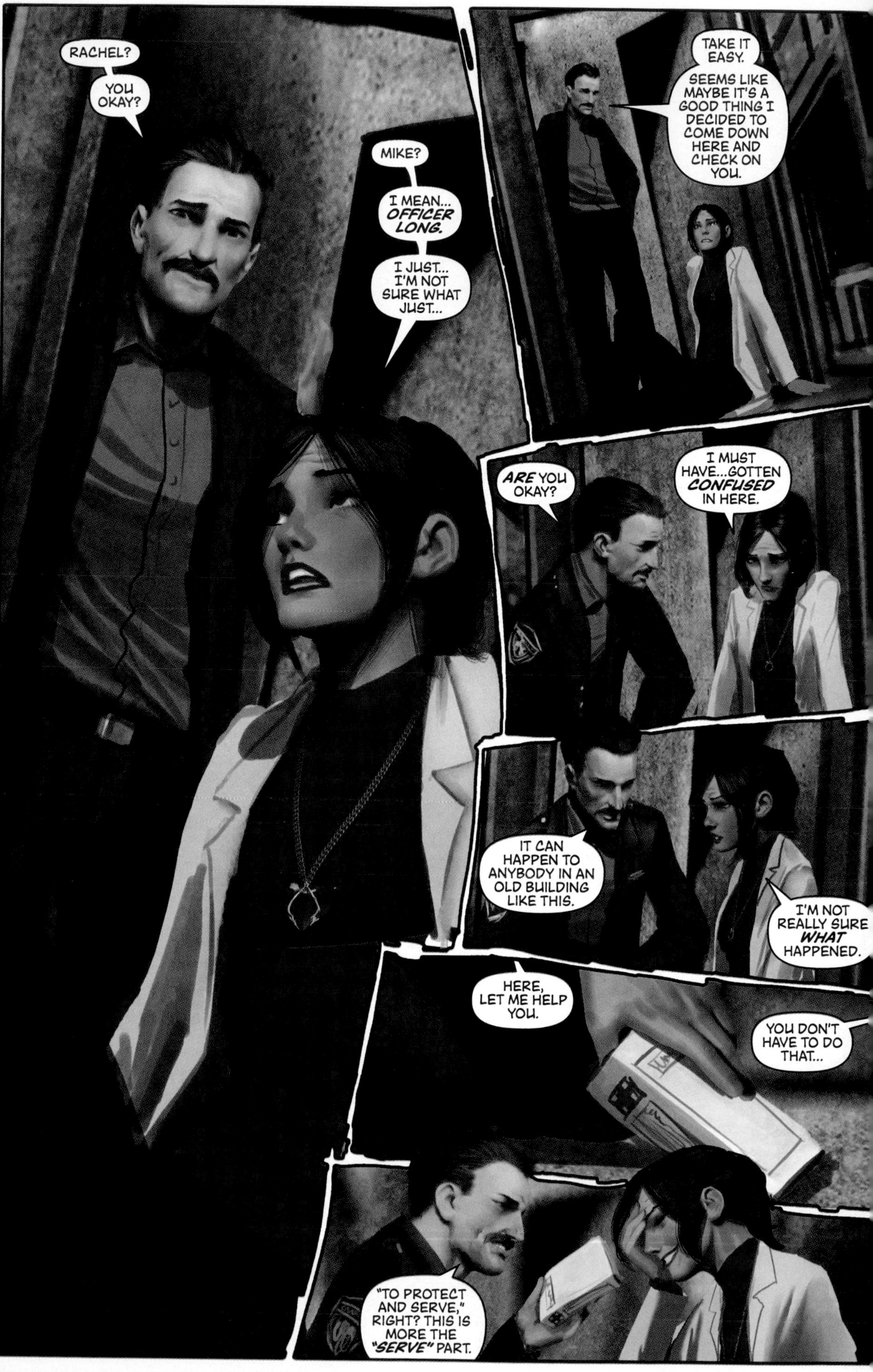

RACHEL?
YOU OKAY?
MIKE?
I MEAN... OFFICER LONG.
I JUST... I'M NOT SURE WHAT JUST...
TAKE IT EASY.
SEEMS LIKE MAYBE IT'S A GOOD THING I DECIDED TO COME DOWN HERE AND CHECK ON YOU.
ARE YOU OKAY?
I MUST HAVE...GOTTEN CONFUSED IN HERE.
IT CAN HAPPEN TO ANYBODY IN AN OLD BUILDING LIKE THIS.
I'M NOT REALLY SURE WHAT HAPPENED.
HERE, LET ME HELP YOU.
YOU DON'T HAVE TO DO THAT...
"TO PROTECT AND SERVE," RIGHT? THIS IS MORE THE "SERVE" PART.

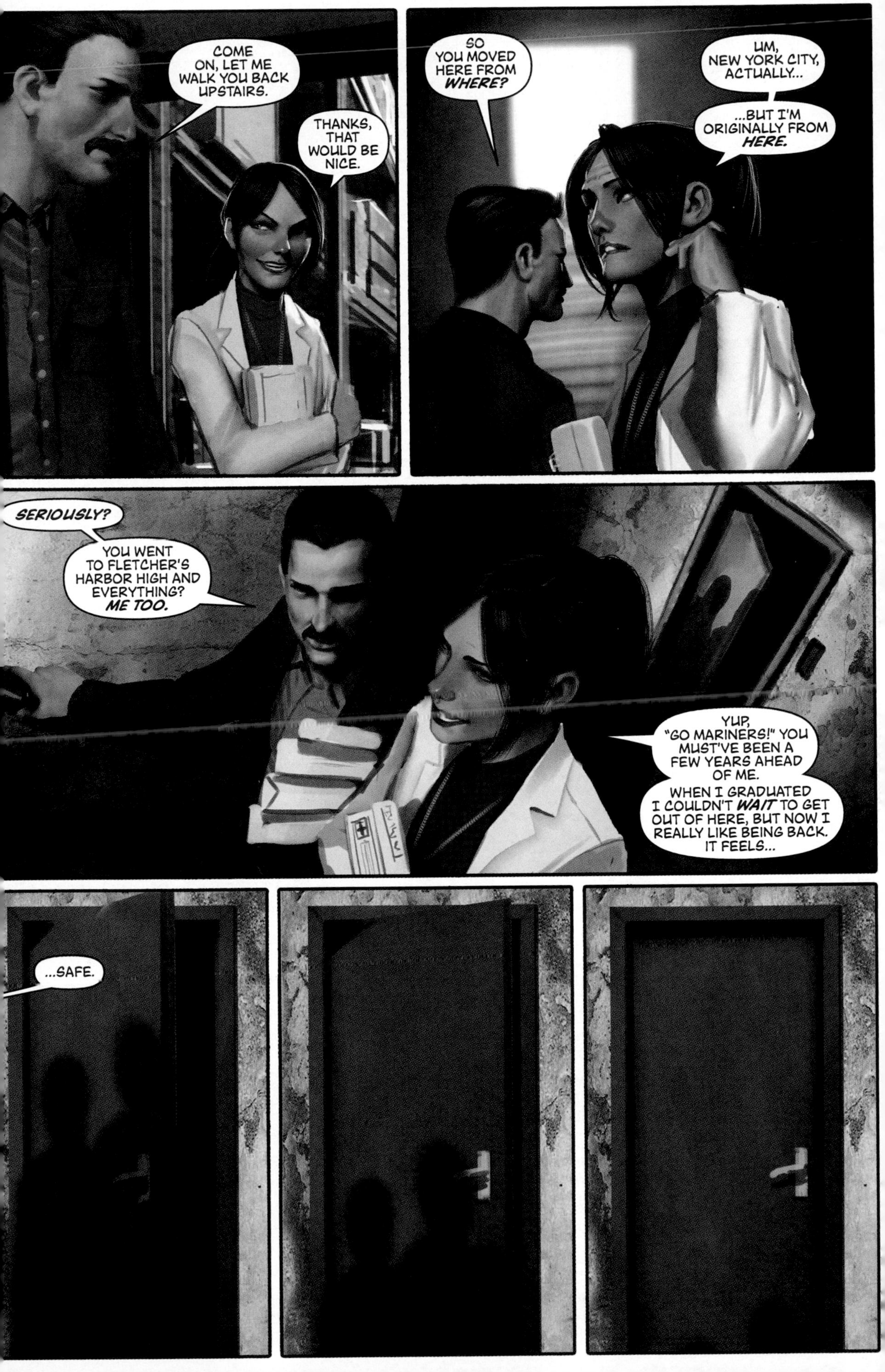
COME ON, LET ME WALK YOU BACK UPSTAIRS.
THANKS, THAT WOULD BE NICE.
SO YOU MOVED HERE FROM *WHERE?*
UM, NEW YORK CITY, ACTUALLY...
...BUT I'M ORIGINALLY FROM *HERE.*
SERIOUSLY?
YOU WENT TO FLETCHER'S HARBOR HIGH AND EVERYTHING? *ME TOO.*
YUP, "GO MARINERS!" YOU MUST'VE BEEN A FEW YEARS AHEAD OF ME.
WHEN I GRADUATED I COULDN'T *WAIT* TO GET OUT OF HERE, BUT NOW I REALLY LIKE BEING BACK. IT FEELS...
...SAFE.

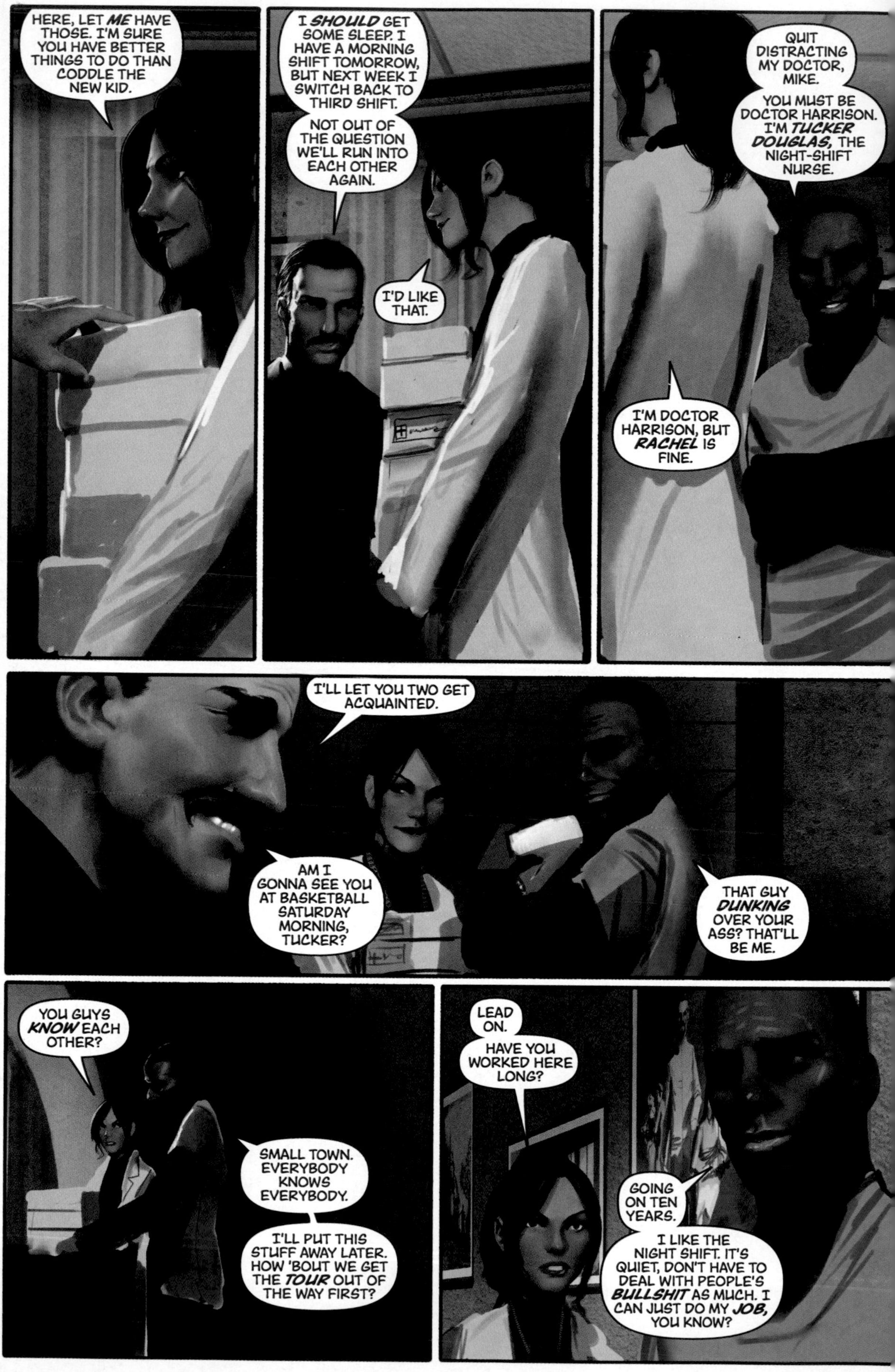
HERE, LET ME HAVE THOSE. I'M SURE YOU HAVE BETTER THINGS TO DO THAN CODDLE THE NEW KID.
I SHOULD GET SOME SLEEP. I HAVE A MORNING SHIFT TOMORROW, BUT NEXT WEEK I SWITCH BACK TO THIRD SHIFT.
NOT OUT OF THE QUESTION WE'LL RUN INTO EACH OTHER AGAIN.
I'D LIKE THAT.
QUIT DISTRACTING MY DOCTOR, MIKE.
YOU MUST BE DOCTOR HARRISON. I'M TUCKER DOUGLAS, THE NIGHT-SHIFT NURSE.
I'M DOCTOR HARRISON, BUT RACHEL IS FINE.
I'LL LET YOU TWO GET ACQUAINTED.
AM I GONNA SEE YOU AT BASKETBALL SATURDAY MORNING, TUCKER?
THAT GUY DUNKING OVER YOUR ASS? THAT'LL BE ME.
YOU GUYS KNOW EACH OTHER?
SMALL TOWN. EVERYBODY KNOWS EVERYBODY.
I'LL PUT THIS STUFF AWAY LATER. HOW 'BOUT WE GET THE TOUR OUT OF THE WAY FIRST?
LEAD ON.
HAVE YOU WORKED HERE LONG?
GOING ON TEN YEARS.
I LIKE THE NIGHT SHIFT. IT'S QUIET, DON'T HAVE TO DEAL WITH PEOPLE'S BULLSHIT AS MUCH. I CAN JUST DO MY JOB, YOU KNOW?

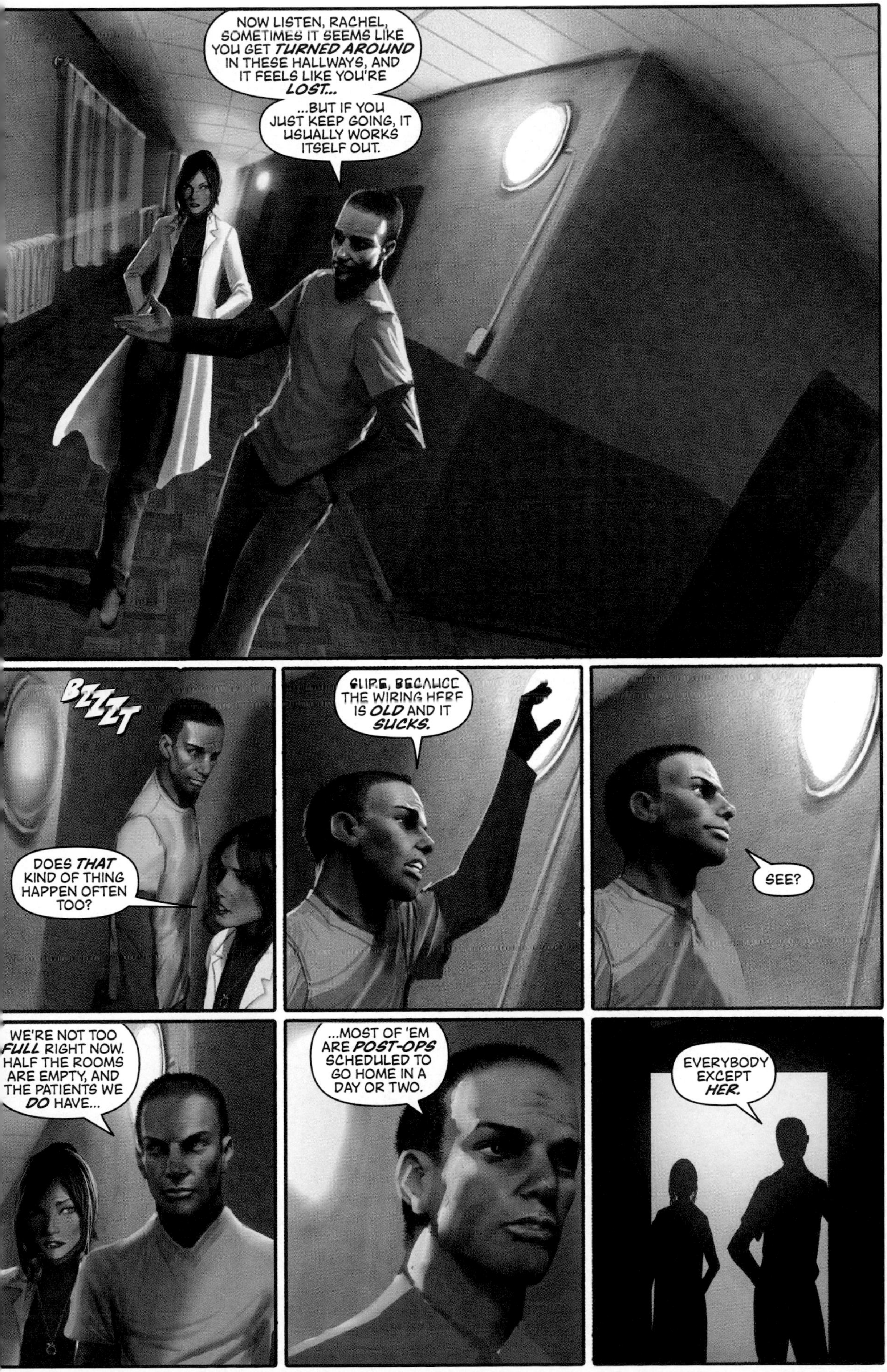
NOW LISTEN, RACHEL, SOMETIMES IT SEEMS LIKE YOU GET *TURNED AROUND* IN THESE HALLWAYS, AND IT FEELS LIKE YOU'RE *LOST...*
...BUT IF YOU JUST KEEP GOING, IT USUALLY WORKS ITSELF OUT.
BZZZT
DOES *THAT* KIND OF THING HAPPEN OFTEN TOO?
SURE, BECAUSE THE WIRING HERE IS *OLD* AND IT *SUCKS.*
SEE?
WE'RE NOT TOO *FULL* RIGHT NOW. HALF THE ROOMS ARE EMPTY, AND THE PATIENTS WE *DO* HAVE...
...MOST OF 'EM ARE *POST-OPS* SCHEDULED TO GO HOME IN A DAY OR TWO.
EVERYBODY EXCEPT *HER.*

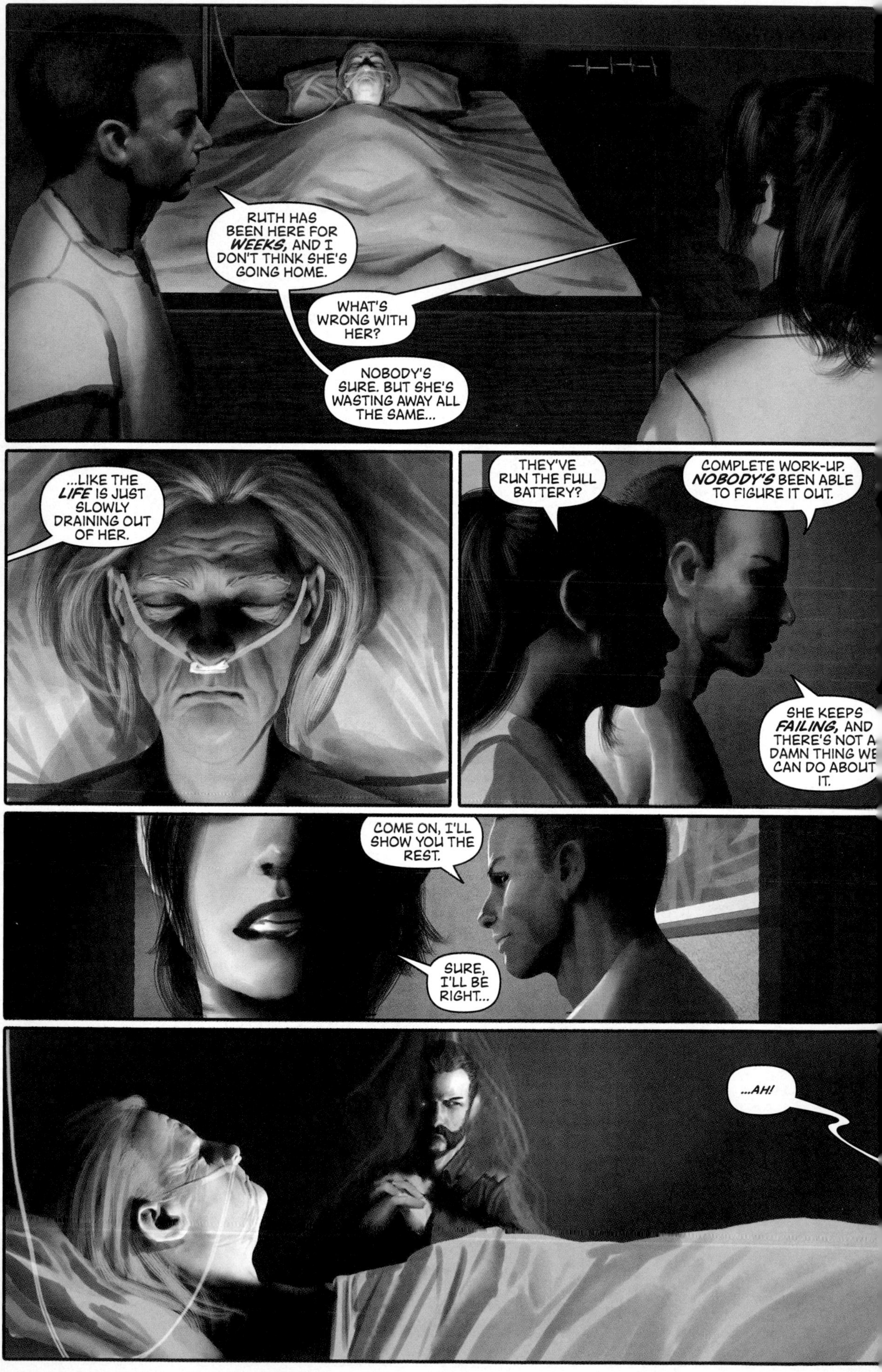
RUTH HAS BEEN HERE FOR WEEKS, AND I DON'T THINK SHE'S GOING HOME.
WHAT'S WRONG WITH HER?
NOBODY'S SURE. BUT SHE'S WASTING AWAY ALL THE SAME...
...LIKE THE LIFE IS JUST SLOWLY DRAINING OUT OF HER.
THEY'VE RUN THE FULL BATTERY?
COMPLETE WORK-UP. NOBODY'S BEEN ABLE TO FIGURE IT OUT.
SHE KEEPS FAILING, AND THERE'S NOT A DAMN THING WE CAN DO ABOUT IT.
COME ON, I'LL SHOW YOU THE REST.
SURE, I'LL BE RIGHT...
...AH!

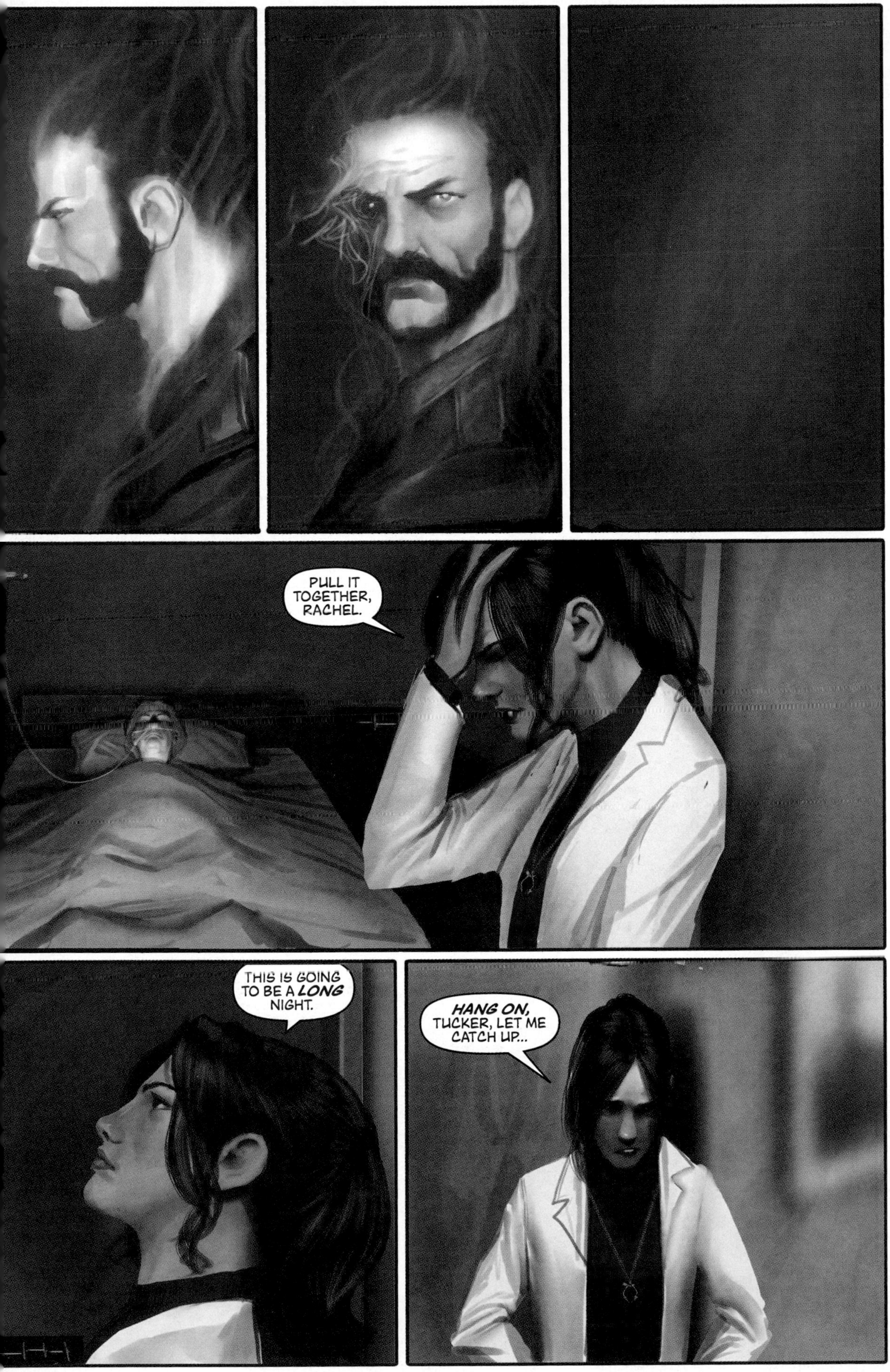
PULL IT TOGETHER, RACHEL.
THIS IS GOING TO BE A *LONG* NIGHT.
HANG ON, TUCKER, LET ME CATCH UP...

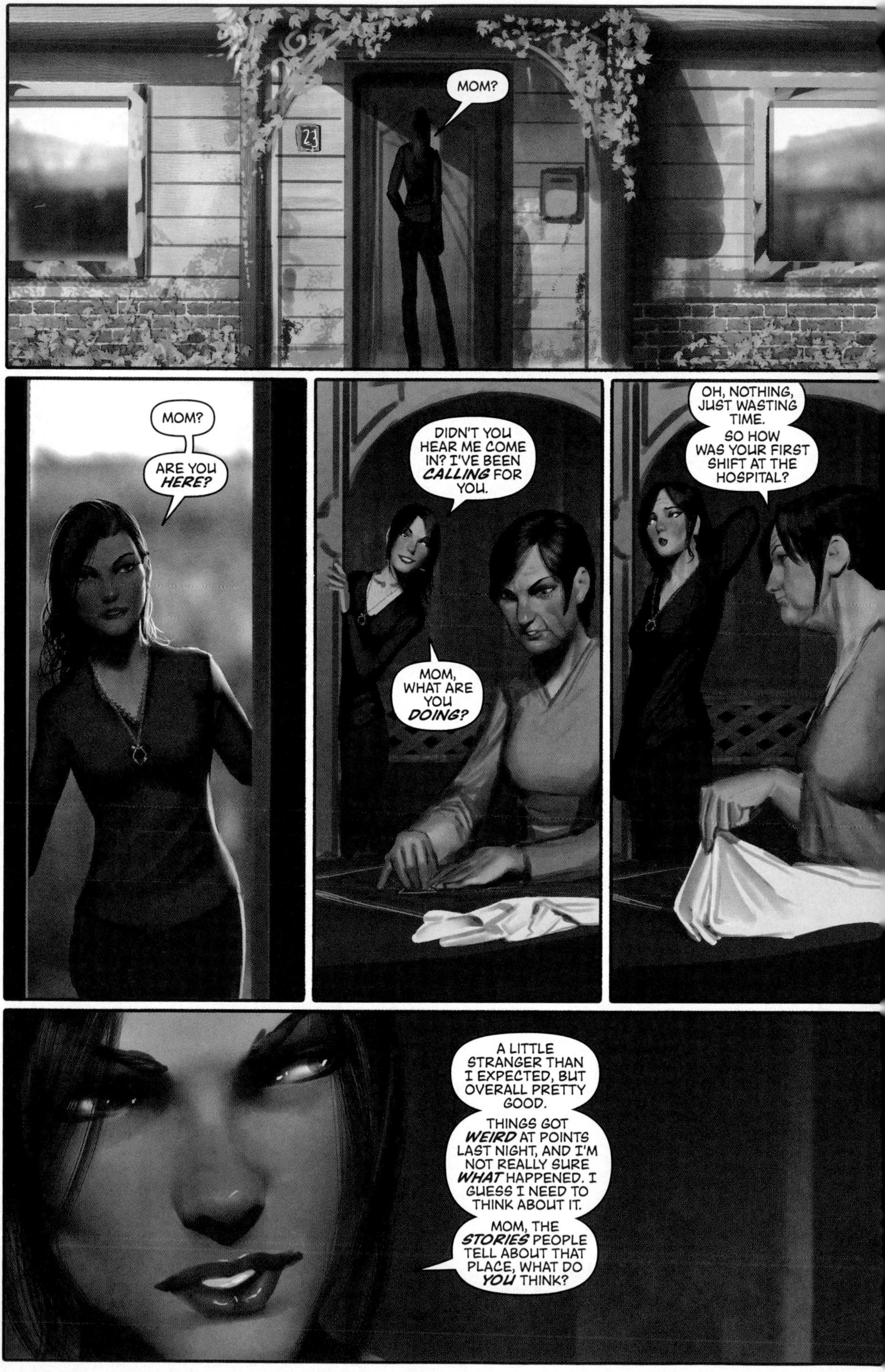

MOM?
MOM?
ARE YOU HERE?
DIDN'T YOU HEAR ME COME IN? I'VE BEEN CALLING FOR YOU.
MOM, WHAT ARE YOU DOING?
OH, NOTHING, JUST WASTING TIME.
SO HOW WAS YOUR FIRST SHIFT AT THE HOSPITAL?
A LITTLE STRANGER THAN I EXPECTED, BUT OVERALL PRETTY GOOD.
THINGS GOT WEIRD AT POINTS LAST NIGHT, AND I'M NOT REALLY SURE WHAT HAPPENED. I GUESS I NEED TO THINK ABOUT IT.
MOM, THE STORIES PEOPLE TELL ABOUT THAT PLACE, WHAT DO YOU THINK?

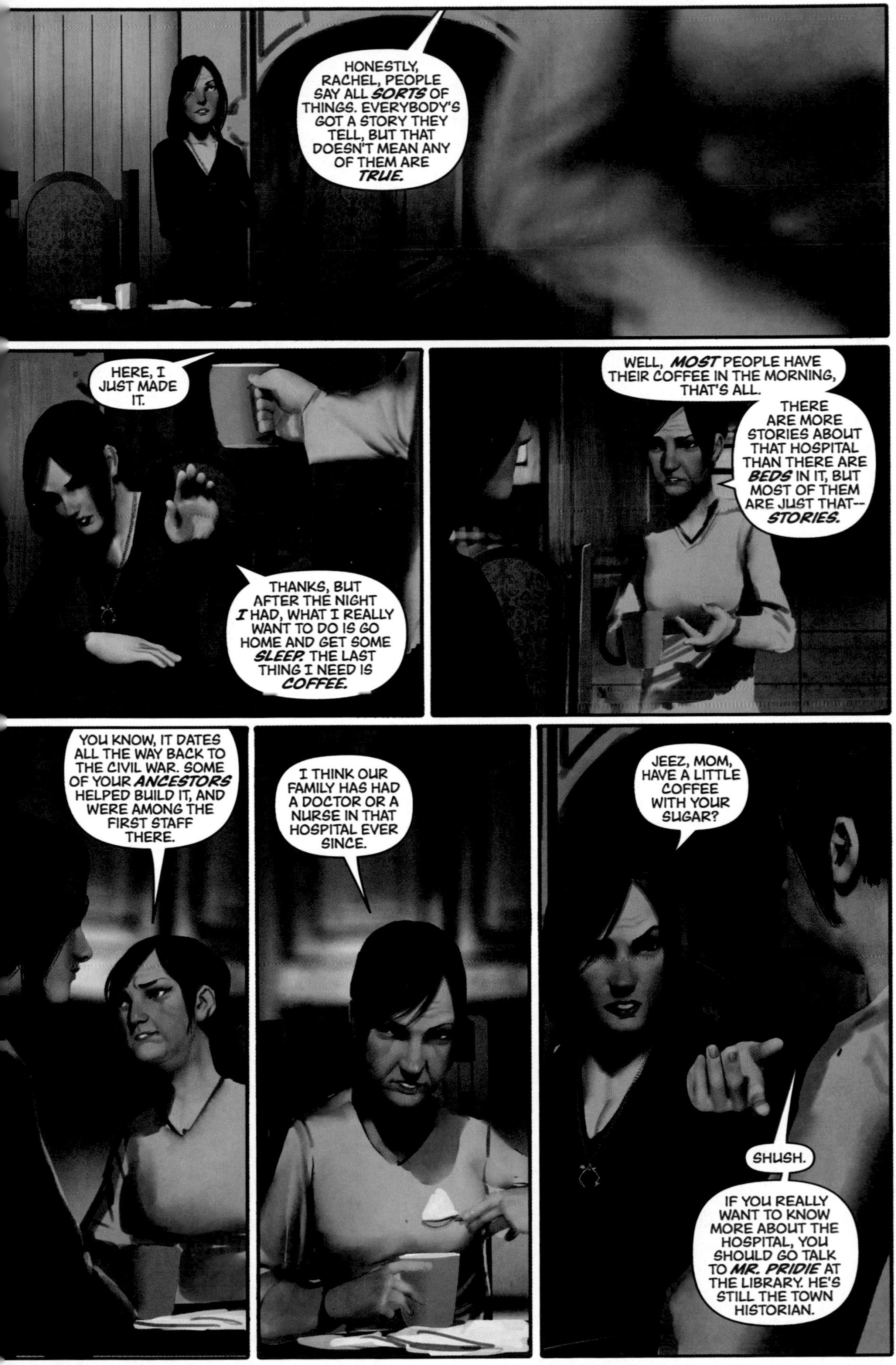
HONESTLY, RACHEL, PEOPLE SAY ALL *SORTS* OF THINGS. EVERYBODY'S GOT A STORY THEY TELL, BUT THAT DOESN'T MEAN ANY OF THEM ARE *TRUE.*
HERE, I JUST MADE IT.
THANKS, BUT AFTER THE NIGHT *I* HAD, WHAT I REALLY WANT TO DO IS GO HOME AND GET SOME *SLEEP.* THE LAST THING I NEED IS *COFFEE.*
WELL, *MOST* PEOPLE HAVE THEIR COFFEE IN THE MORNING, THAT'S ALL.
THERE ARE MORE STORIES ABOUT THAT HOSPITAL THAN THERE ARE *BEDS* IN IT, BUT MOST OF THEM ARE JUST THAT-- *STORIES.*
YOU KNOW, IT DATES ALL THE WAY BACK TO THE CIVIL WAR. SOME OF YOUR *ANCESTORS* HELPED BUILD IT, AND WERE AMONG THE FIRST STAFF THERE.
I THINK OUR FAMILY HAS HAD A DOCTOR OR A NURSE IN THAT HOSPITAL EVER SINCE.
JEEZ, MOM, HAVE A LITTLE COFFEE WITH YOUR SUGAR?
SHUSH.
IF YOU REALLY WANT TO KNOW MORE ABOUT THE HOSPITAL, YOU SHOULD GO TALK TO *MR. PRIDIE* AT THE LIBRARY. HE'S STILL THE TOWN HISTORIAN.

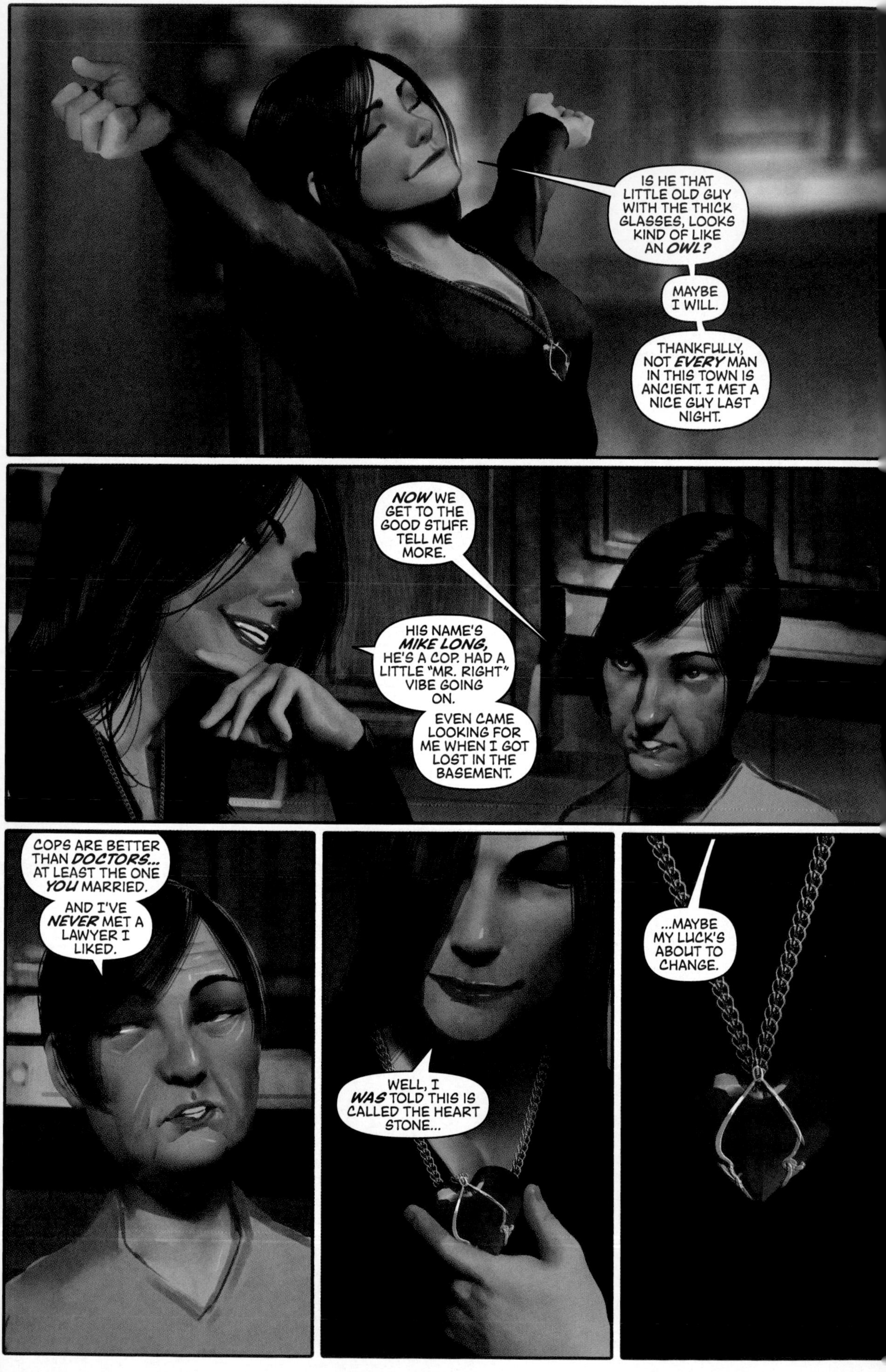
IS HE THAT LITTLE OLD GUY WITH THE THICK GLASSES, LOOKS KIND OF LIKE AN OWL?
MAYBE I WILL.
THANKFULLY, NOT EVERY MAN IN THIS TOWN IS ANCIENT. I MET A NICE GUY LAST NIGHT.
NOW WE GET TO THE GOOD STUFF. TELL ME MORE.
HIS NAME'S MIKE LONG, HE'S A COP. HAD A LITTLE "MR. RIGHT" VIBE GOING ON.
EVEN CAME LOOKING FOR ME WHEN I GOT LOST IN THE BASEMENT.
COPS ARE BETTER THAN DOCTORS... AT LEAST THE ONE YOU MARRIED.
AND I'VE NEVER MET A LAWYER I LIKED.
WELL, I WAS TOLD THIS IS CALLED THE HEART STONE...
...MAYBE MY LUCK'S ABOUT TO CHANGE.

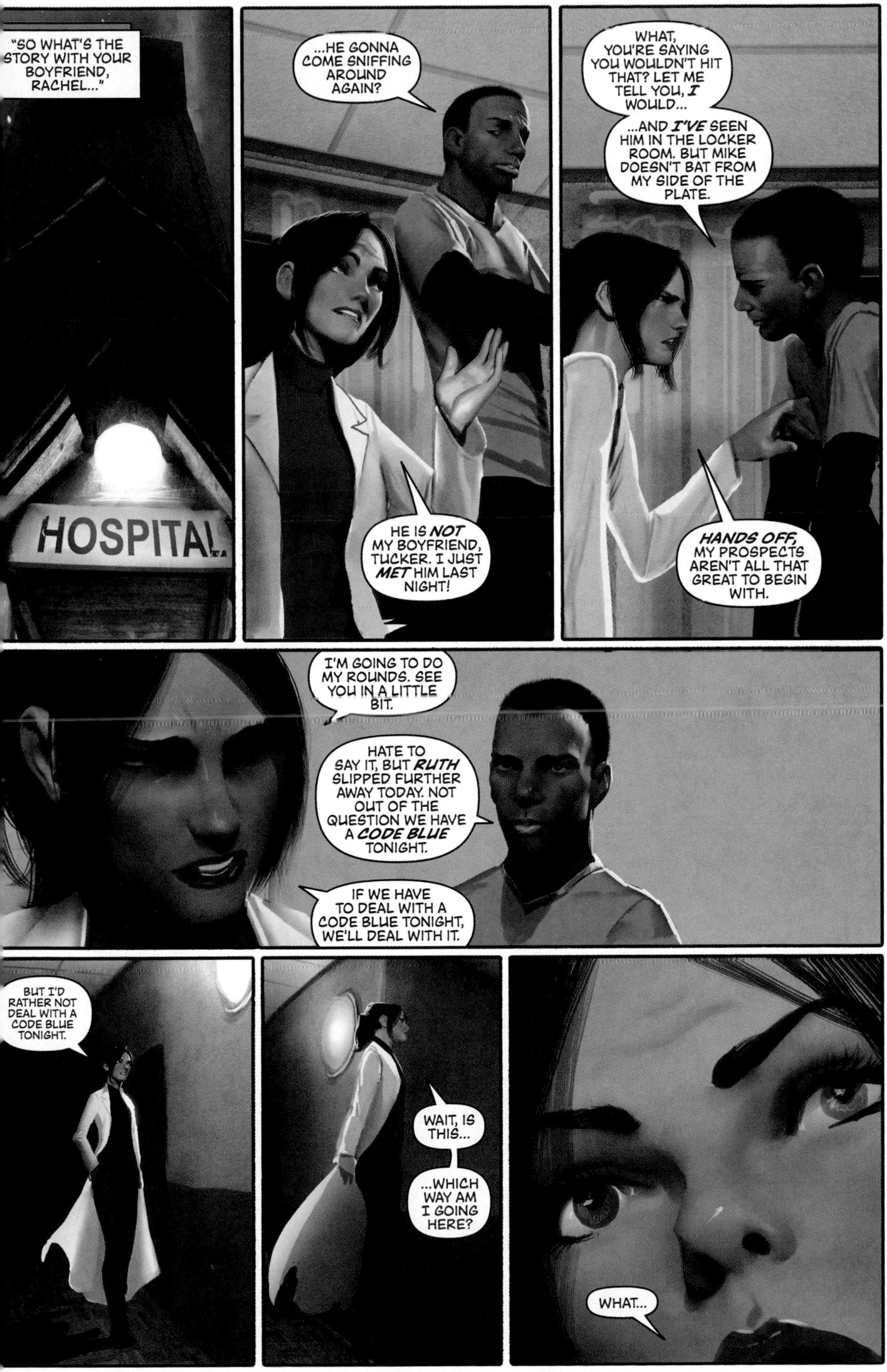
"SO WHAT'S THE STORY WITH YOUR BOYFRIEND, RACHEL..."
HOSPITAL
...HE GONNA COME SNIFFING AROUND AGAIN?
HE IS *NOT* MY BOYFRIEND, TUCKER. I JUST *MET* HIM LAST NIGHT!
WHAT, YOU'RE SAYING YOU WOULDN'T HIT THAT? LET ME TELL YOU, *I* WOULD...
...AND *I'VE* SEEN HIM IN THE LOCKER ROOM. BUT MIKE DOESN'T BAT FROM MY SIDE OF THE PLATE.
HANDS OFF, MY PROSPECTS AREN'T ALL THAT GREAT TO BEGIN WITH.
I'M GOING TO DO MY ROUNDS. SEE YOU IN A LITTLE BIT.
HATE TO SAY IT, BUT *RUTH* SLIPPED FURTHER AWAY TODAY. NOT OUT OF THE QUESTION WE HAVE A *CODE BLUE* TONIGHT.
IF WE HAVE TO DEAL WITH A CODE BLUE TONIGHT, WE'LL DEAL WITH IT.
BUT I'D RATHER NOT DEAL WITH A CODE BLUE TONIGHT.
WAIT, IS THIS...
...WHICH WAY AM I GOING HERE?
WHAT...

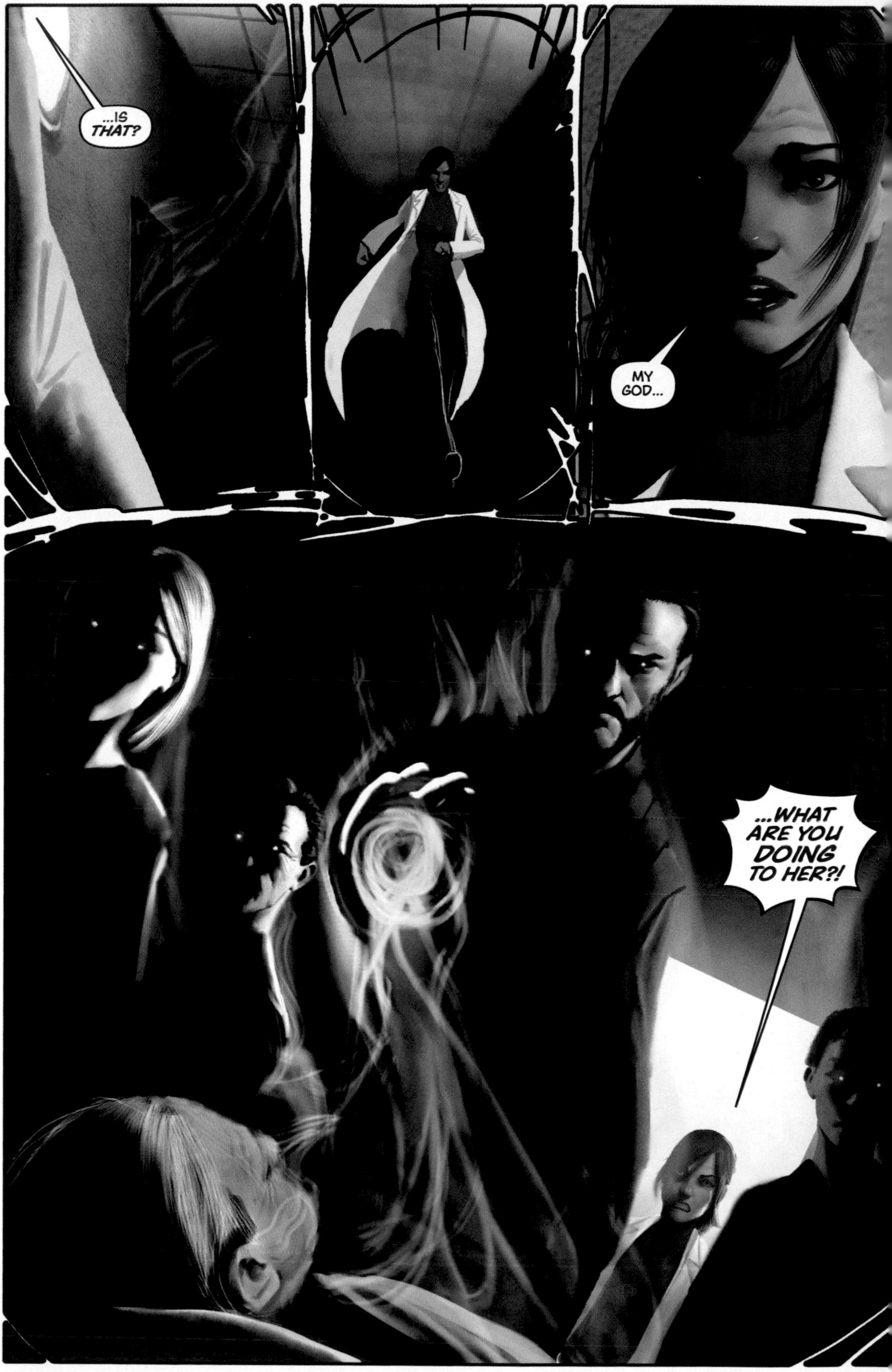
...IS THAT?
MY GOD...
...WHAT ARE YOU DOING TO HER?!

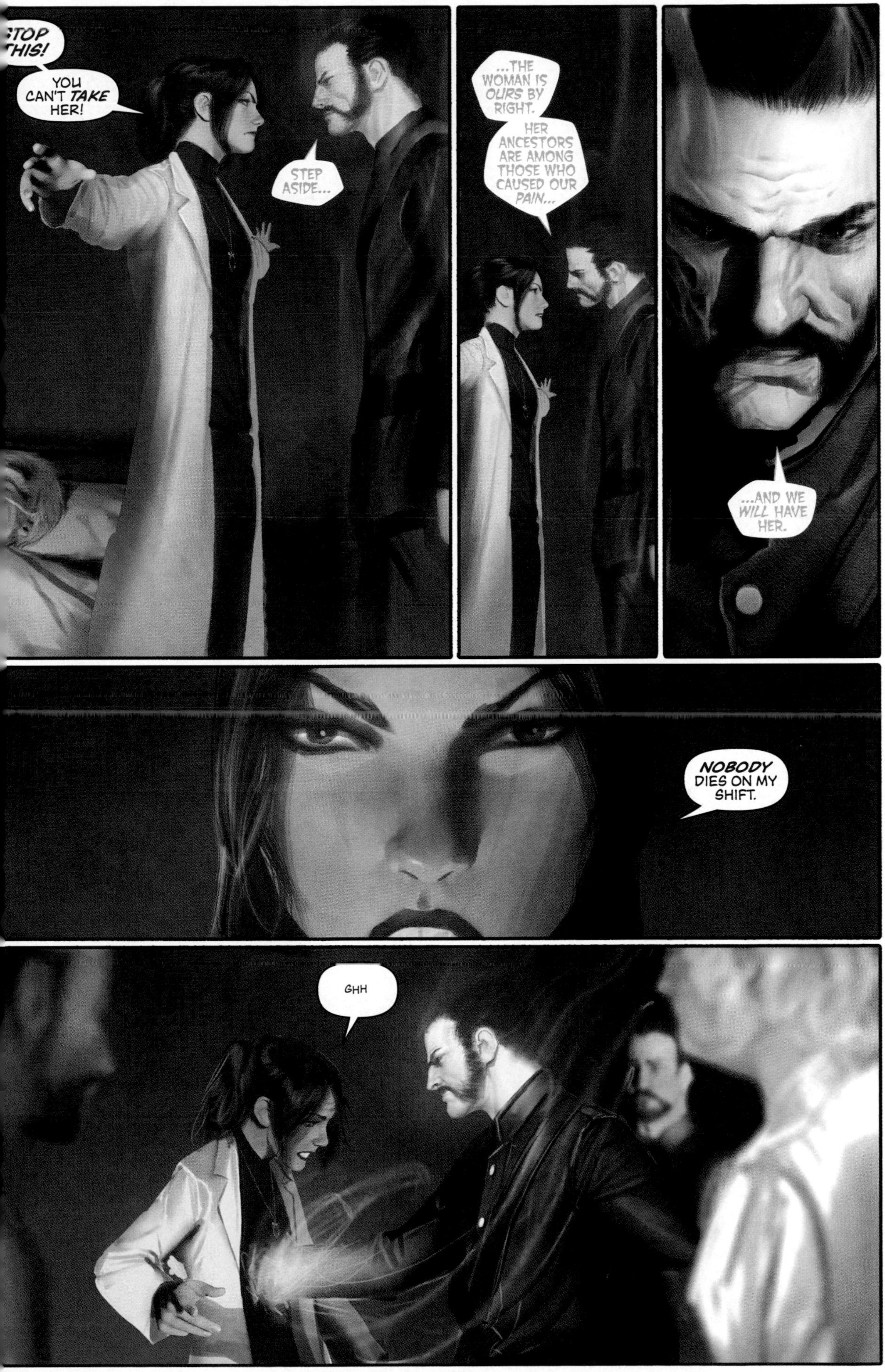
STOP THIS!
YOU CAN'T TAKE HER!
STEP ASIDE...
...THE WOMAN IS OURS BY RIGHT.
HER ANCESTORS ARE AMONG THOSE WHO CAUSED OUR PAIN...
...AND WE WILL HAVE HER.
NOBODY DIES ON MY SHIFT.
GHH

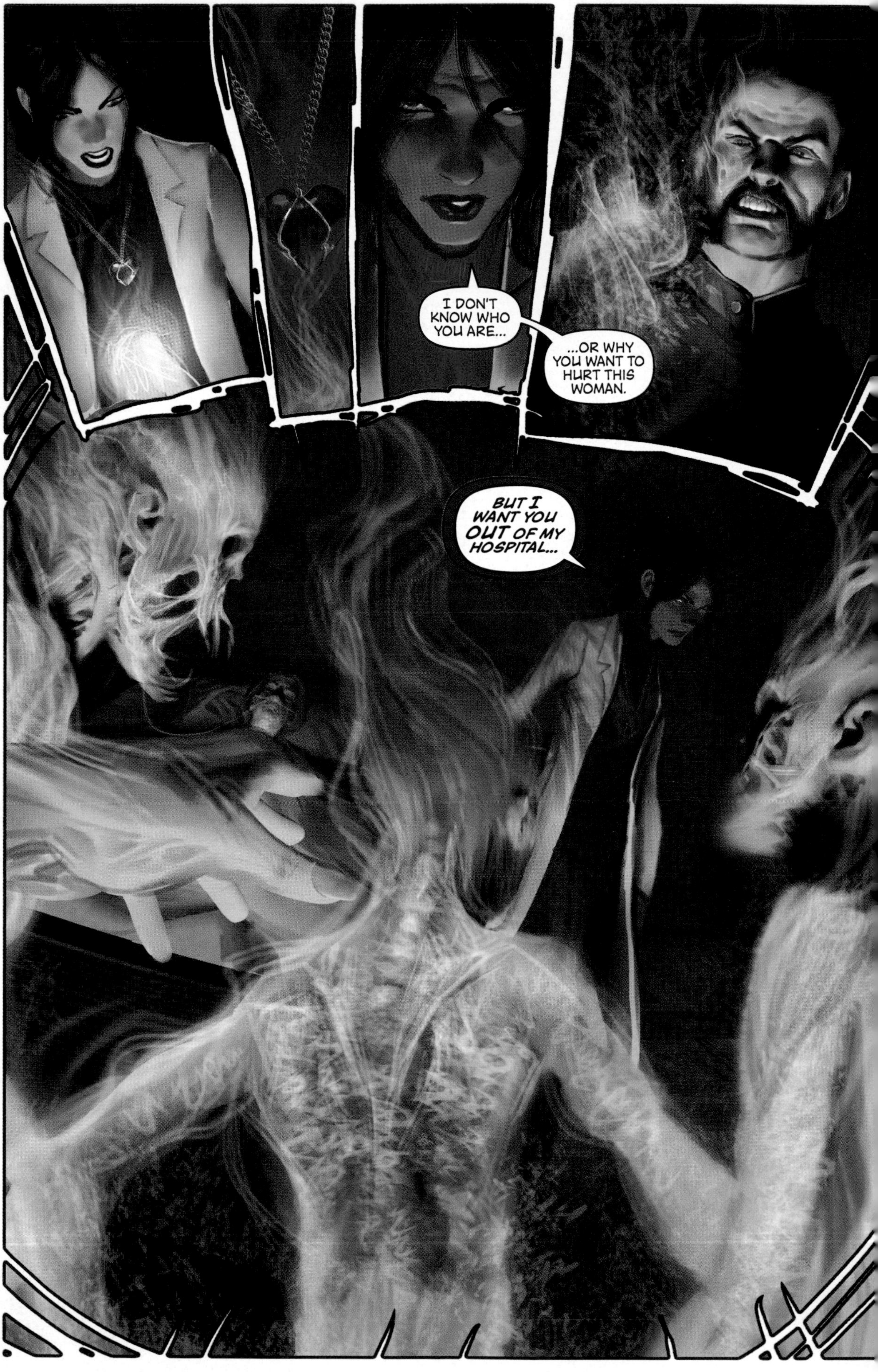
I DON'T KNOW WHO YOU ARE...
...OR WHY YOU WANT TO HURT THIS WOMAN.
BUT I WANT YOU OUT OF MY HOSPITAL...

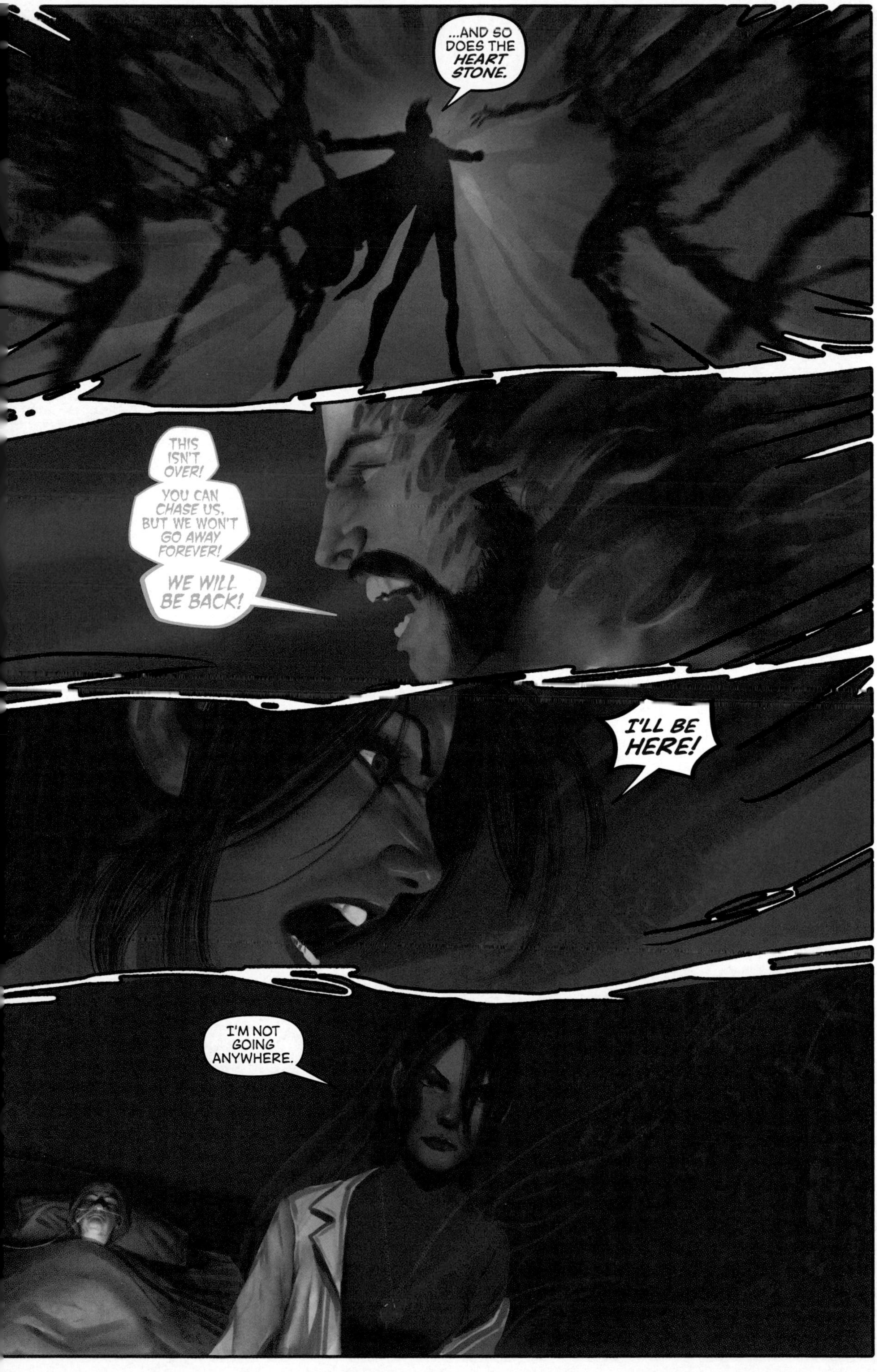
...AND SO DOES THE HEART STONE.
THIS ISN'T OVER!
YOU CAN CHASE US, BUT WE WON'T GO AWAY FOREVER!
WE WILL BE BACK!
I'LL BE HERE!
I'M NOT GOING ANYWHERE.

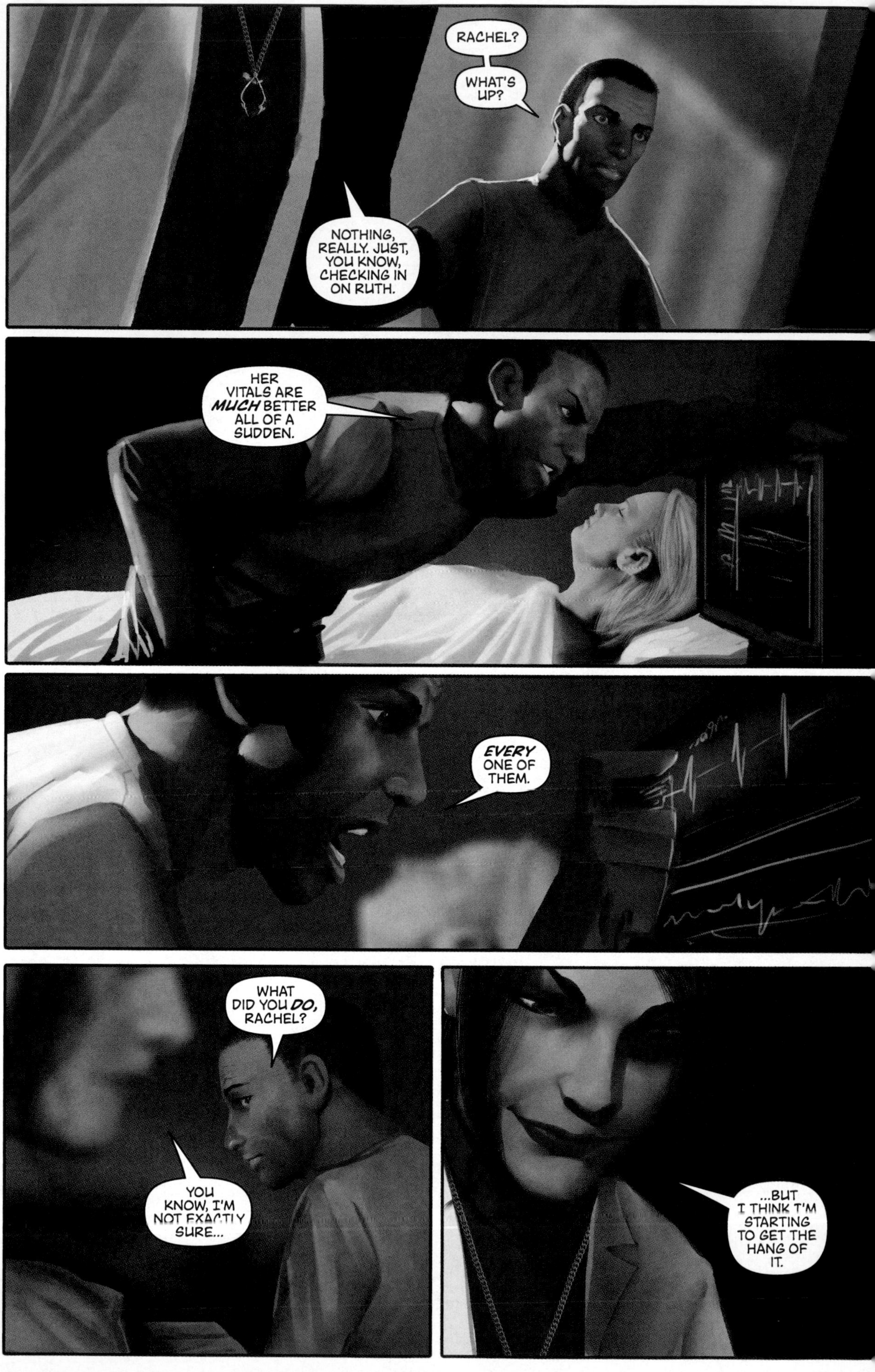

RACHEL?
WHAT'S UP?
NOTHING, REALLY. JUST, YOU KNOW, CHECKING IN ON RUTH.
HER VITALS ARE *MUCH* BETTER ALL OF A SUDDEN.
EVERY ONE OF THEM.
WHAT DID YOU *DO,* RACHEL?
YOU KNOW, I'M NOT EXACTLY SURE...
...BUT I THINK I'M STARTING TO GET THE HANG OF IT.

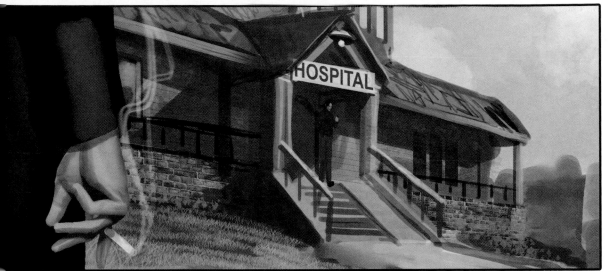

RACHEL...

...I'D LIKE TO STEAL A FEW MINUTES OF YOUR TIME, IF YOU DON'T MIND.

YOU *DO* TEND TO POP UP AT THE MOST UNEXPECTED TIMES, TOM JUDGE. WHAT CAN I DO FOR YOU THIS TIME?

I DON'T THINK YOU'VE MET MY ASSISTANT, *TILLY GRIMES.*

NO, I DON'T THINK SO, BUT SHE'LL FIT RIGHT IN AROUND HERE.

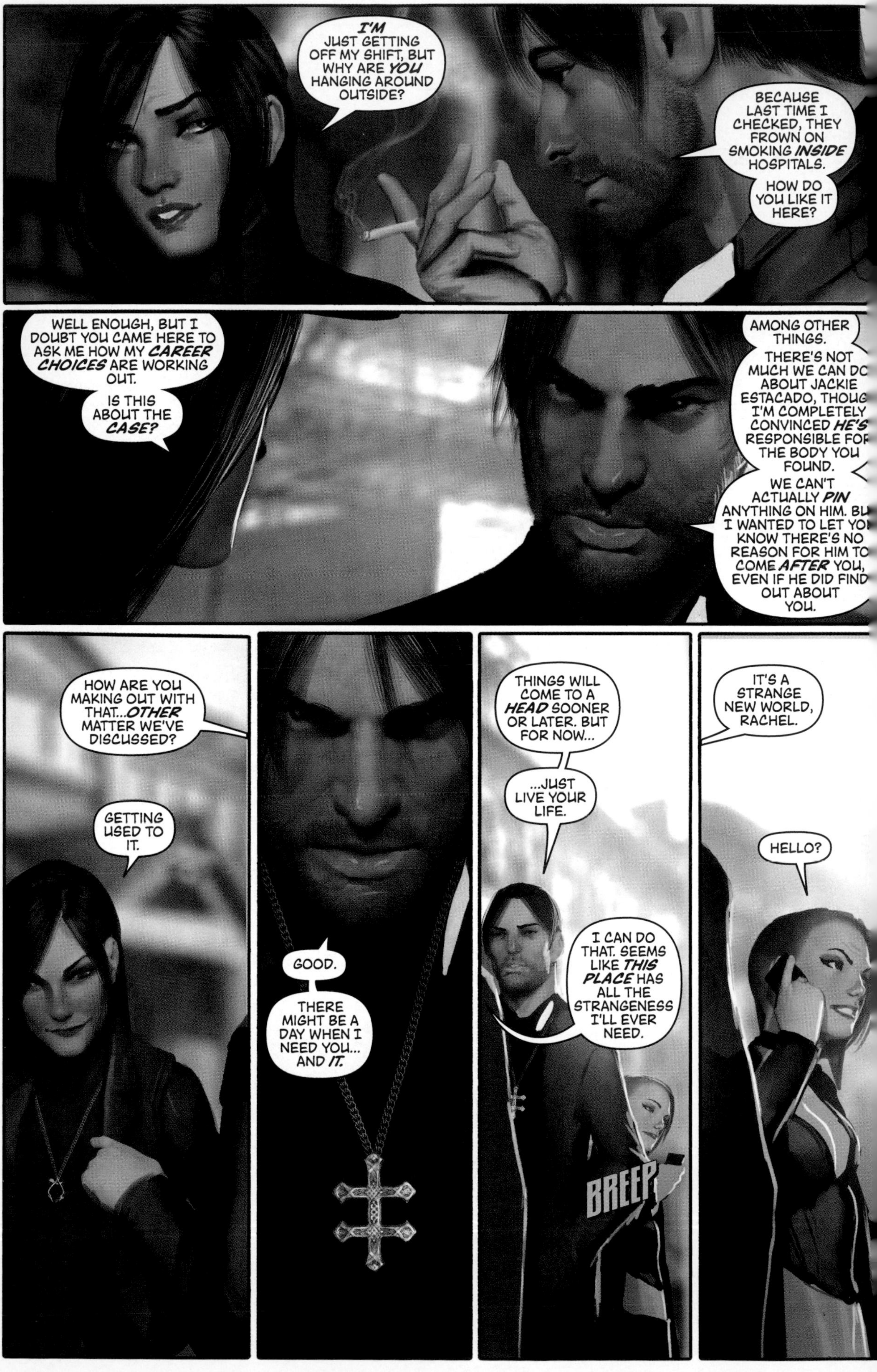
I'M JUST GETTING OFF MY SHIFT, BUT WHY ARE YOU HANGING AROUND OUTSIDE?
BECAUSE LAST TIME I CHECKED, THEY FROWN ON SMOKING INSIDE HOSPITALS.
HOW DO YOU LIKE IT HERE?
WELL ENOUGH, BUT I DOUBT YOU CAME HERE TO ASK ME HOW MY CAREER CHOICES ARE WORKING OUT.
IS THIS ABOUT THE CASE?
AMONG OTHER THINGS.
THERE'S NOT MUCH WE CAN DO ABOUT JACKIE ESTACADO, THOUGH I'M COMPLETELY CONVINCED HE'S RESPONSIBLE FOR THE BODY YOU FOUND.
WE CAN'T ACTUALLY PIN ANYTHING ON HIM. BUT I WANTED TO LET YOU KNOW THERE'S NO REASON FOR HIM TO COME AFTER YOU, EVEN IF HE DID FIND OUT ABOUT YOU.
HOW ARE YOU MAKING OUT WITH THAT...OTHER MATTER WE'VE DISCUSSED?
GETTING USED TO IT.
GOOD.
THERE MIGHT BE A DAY WHEN I NEED YOU... AND IT.
THINGS WILL COME TO A HEAD SOONER OR LATER. BUT FOR NOW...
...JUST LIVE YOUR LIFE.
I CAN DO THAT. SEEMS LIKE THIS PLACE HAS ALL THE STRANGENESS I'LL EVER NEED.
BREEP
IT'S A STRANGE NEW WORLD, RACHEL.
HELLO?

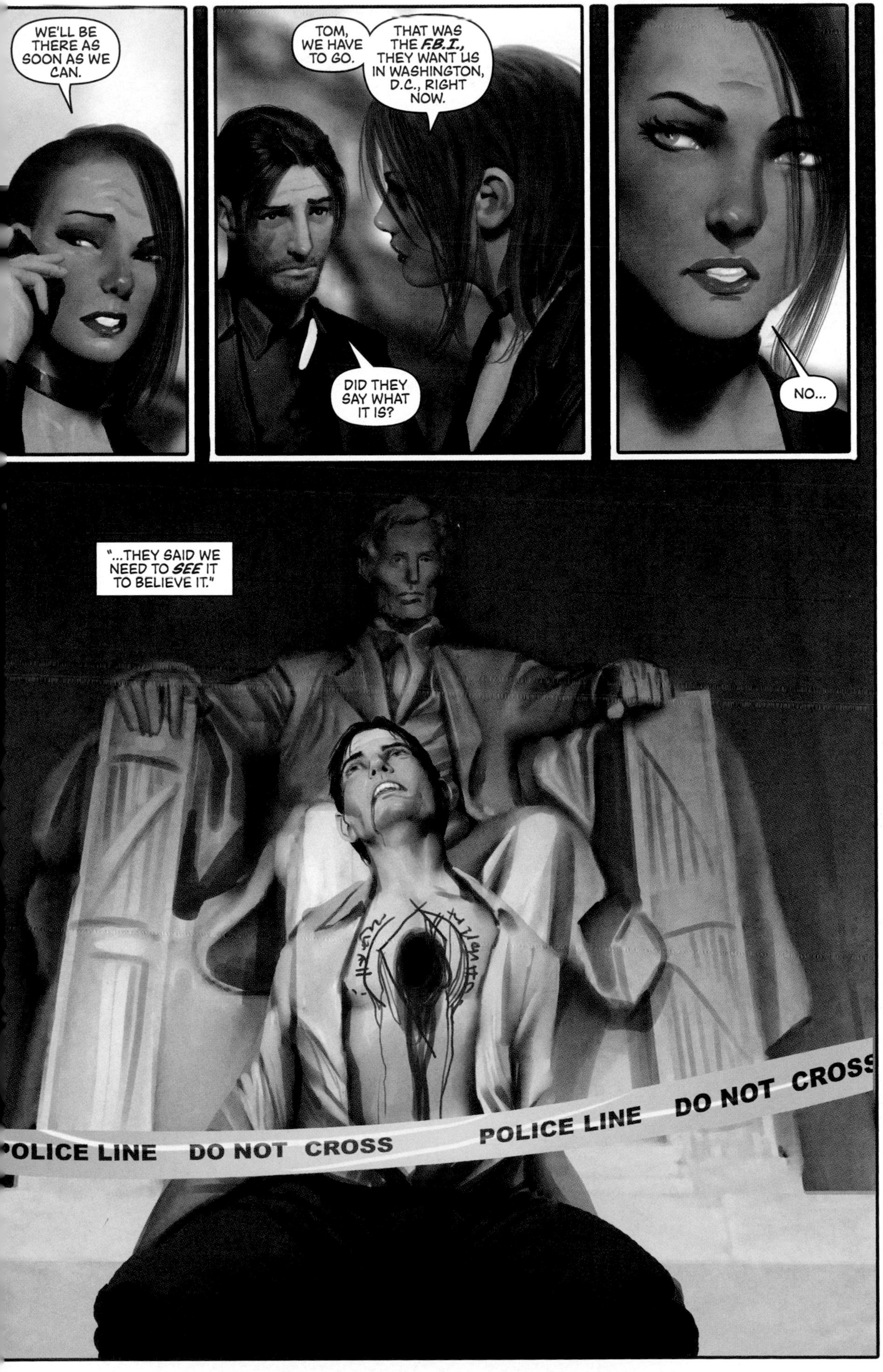
WE'LL BE THERE AS SOON AS WE CAN.
TOM, WE HAVE TO GO.
THAT WAS THE F.B.I., THEY WANT US IN WASHINGTON, D.C., RIGHT NOW.
DID THEY SAY WHAT IT IS?
NO...
"...THEY SAID WE NEED TO SEE IT TO BELIEVE IT."
POLICE LINE DO NOT CROSS
POLICE LINE DO NOT CROSS

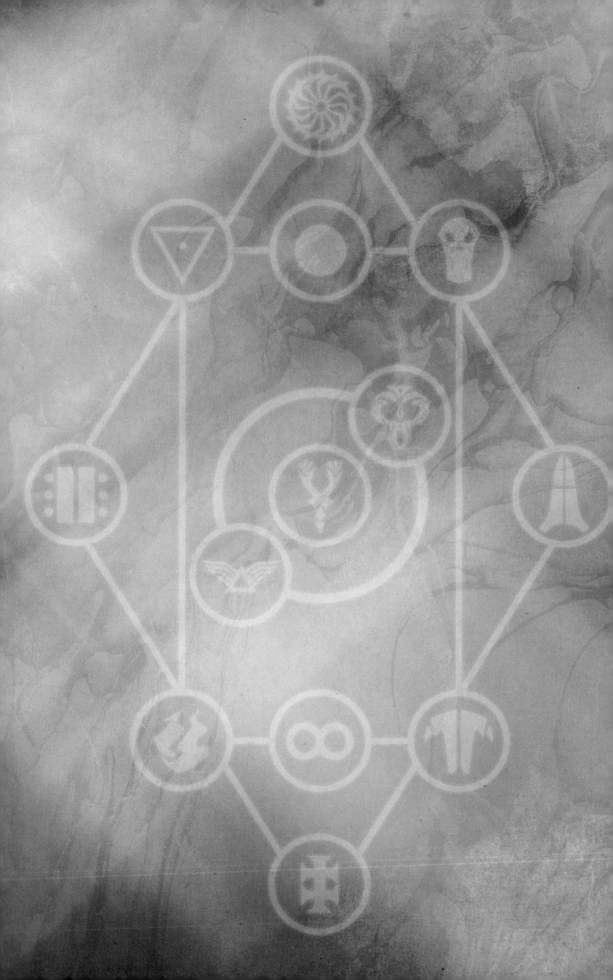

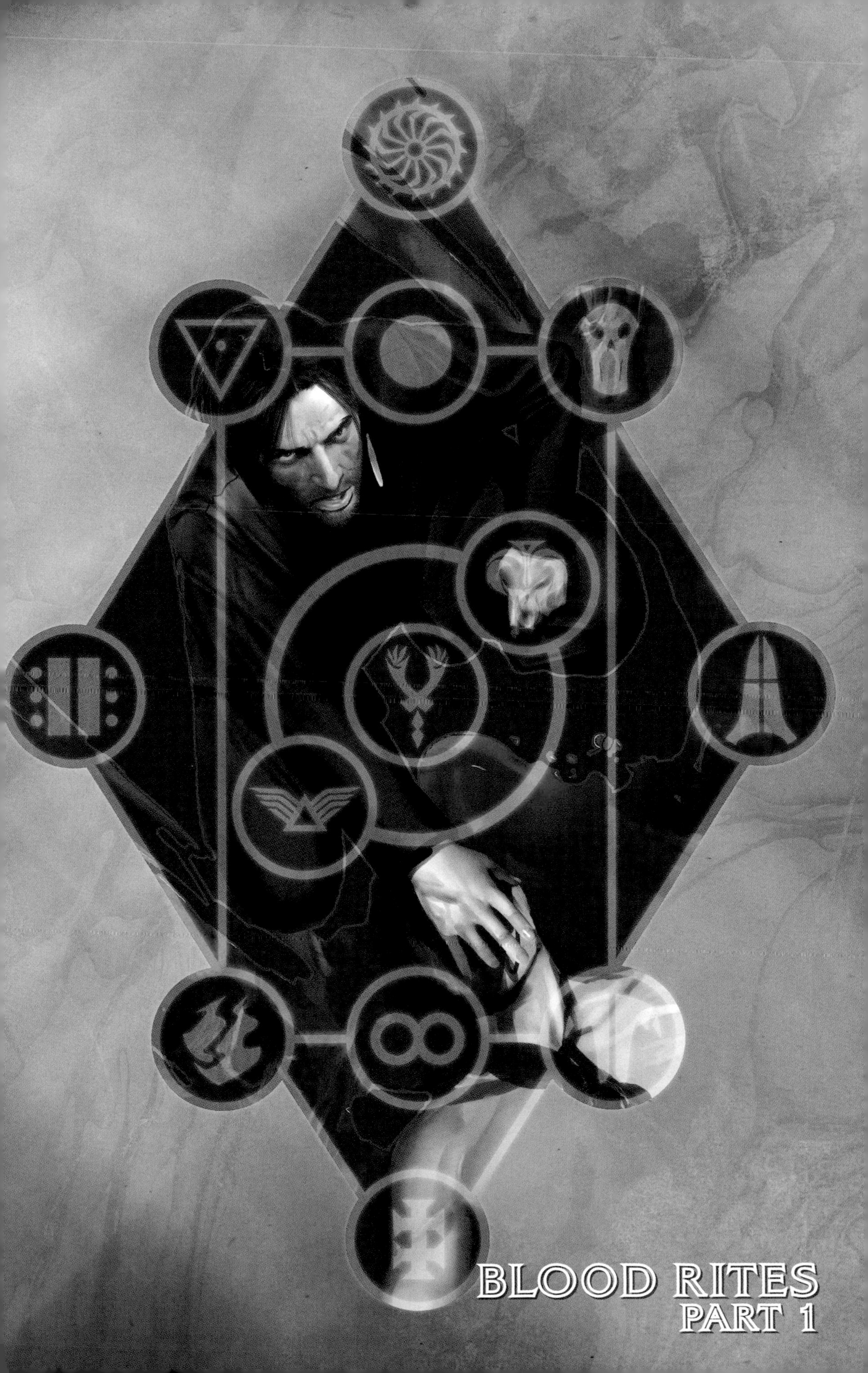
BLOOD RITES
PART 1

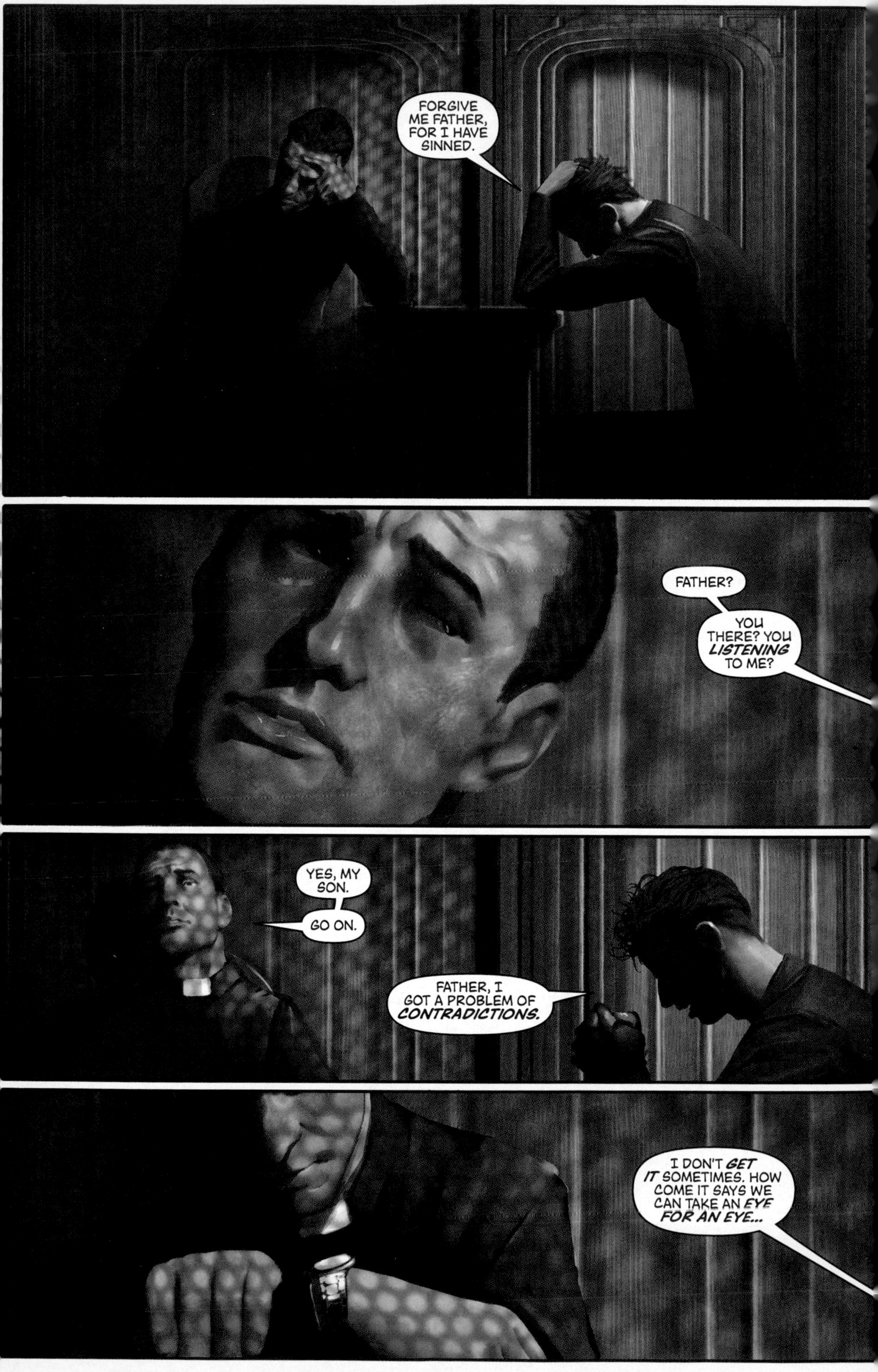
FORGIVE ME FATHER, FOR I HAVE SINNED.
FATHER?
YOU THERE? YOU *LISTENING* TO ME?
YES, MY SON.
GO ON.
FATHER, I GOT A PROBLEM OF *CONTRADICTIONS.*
I DON'T *GET IT* SOMETIMES. HOW COME IT SAYS WE CAN TAKE AN *EYE FOR AN EYE...*

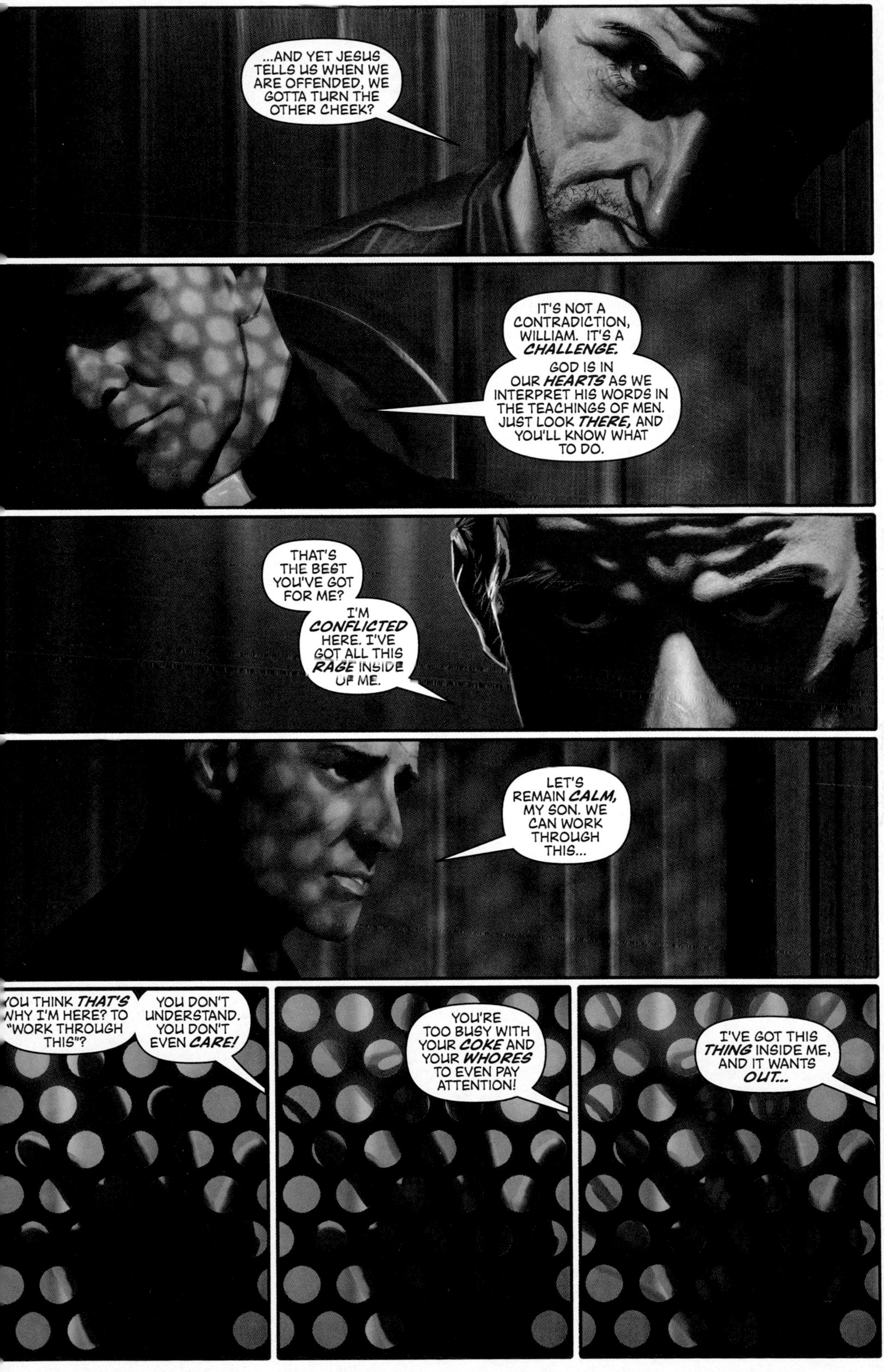
...AND YET JESUS TELLS US WHEN WE ARE OFFENDED, WE GOTTA TURN THE OTHER CHEEK?
IT'S NOT A CONTRADICTION, WILLIAM. IT'S A CHALLENGE.
GOD IS IN OUR HEARTS AS WE INTERPRET HIS WORDS IN THE TEACHINGS OF MEN. JUST LOOK THERE, AND YOU'LL KNOW WHAT TO DO.
THAT'S THE BEST YOU'VE GOT FOR ME?
I'M CONFLICTED HERE. I'VE GOT ALL THIS RAGE INSIDE OF ME.
LET'S REMAIN CALM, MY SON. WE CAN WORK THROUGH THIS...
YOU THINK THAT'S WHY I'M HERE? TO "WORK THROUGH THIS"?
YOU DON'T UNDERSTAND. YOU DON'T EVEN CARE!
YOU'RE TOO BUSY WITH YOUR COKE AND YOUR WHORES TO EVEN PAY ATTENTION!
I'VE GOT THIS THING INSIDE ME, AND IT WANTS OUT...

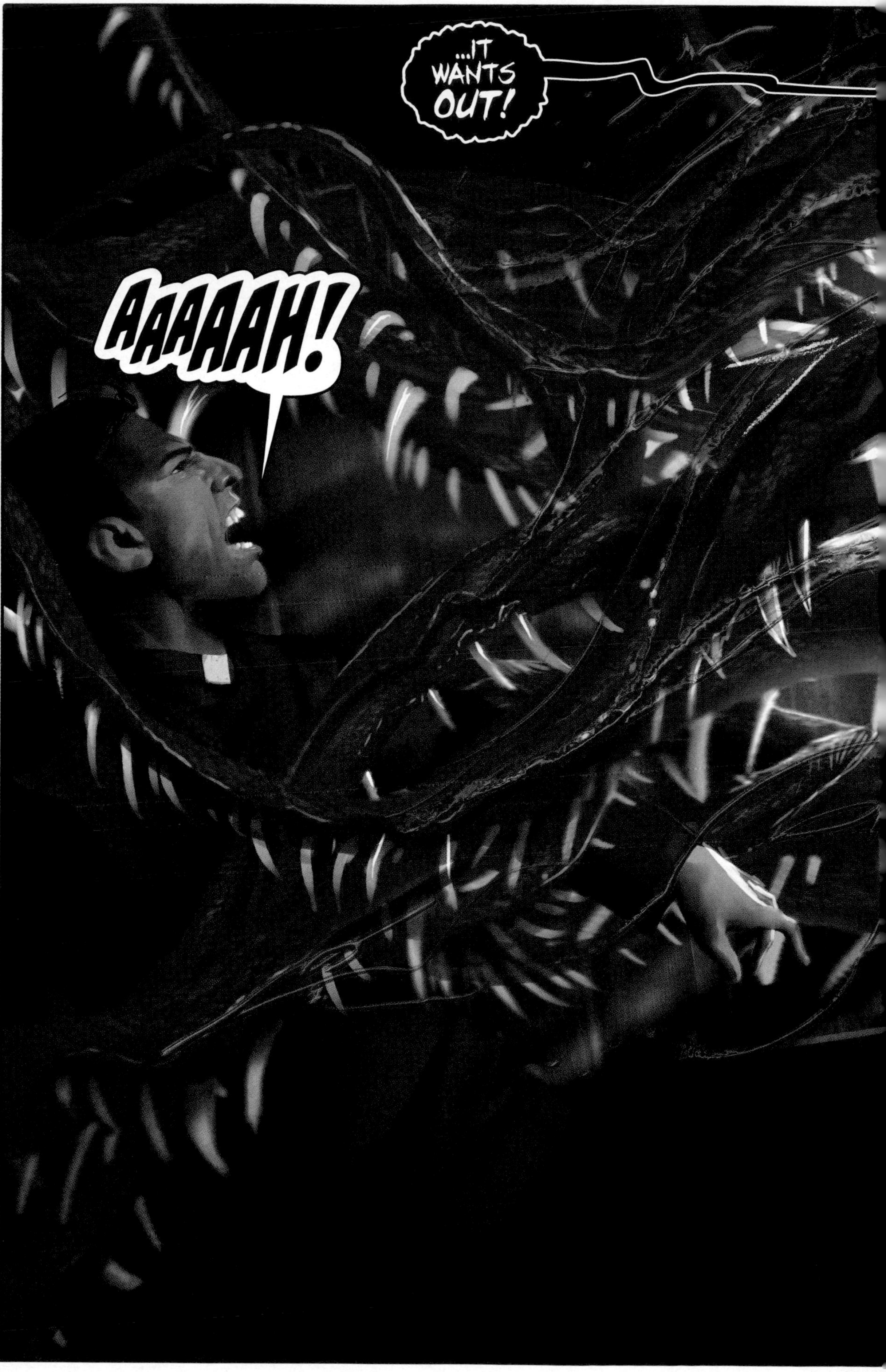
...IT WANTS OUT!
AAAAAH!

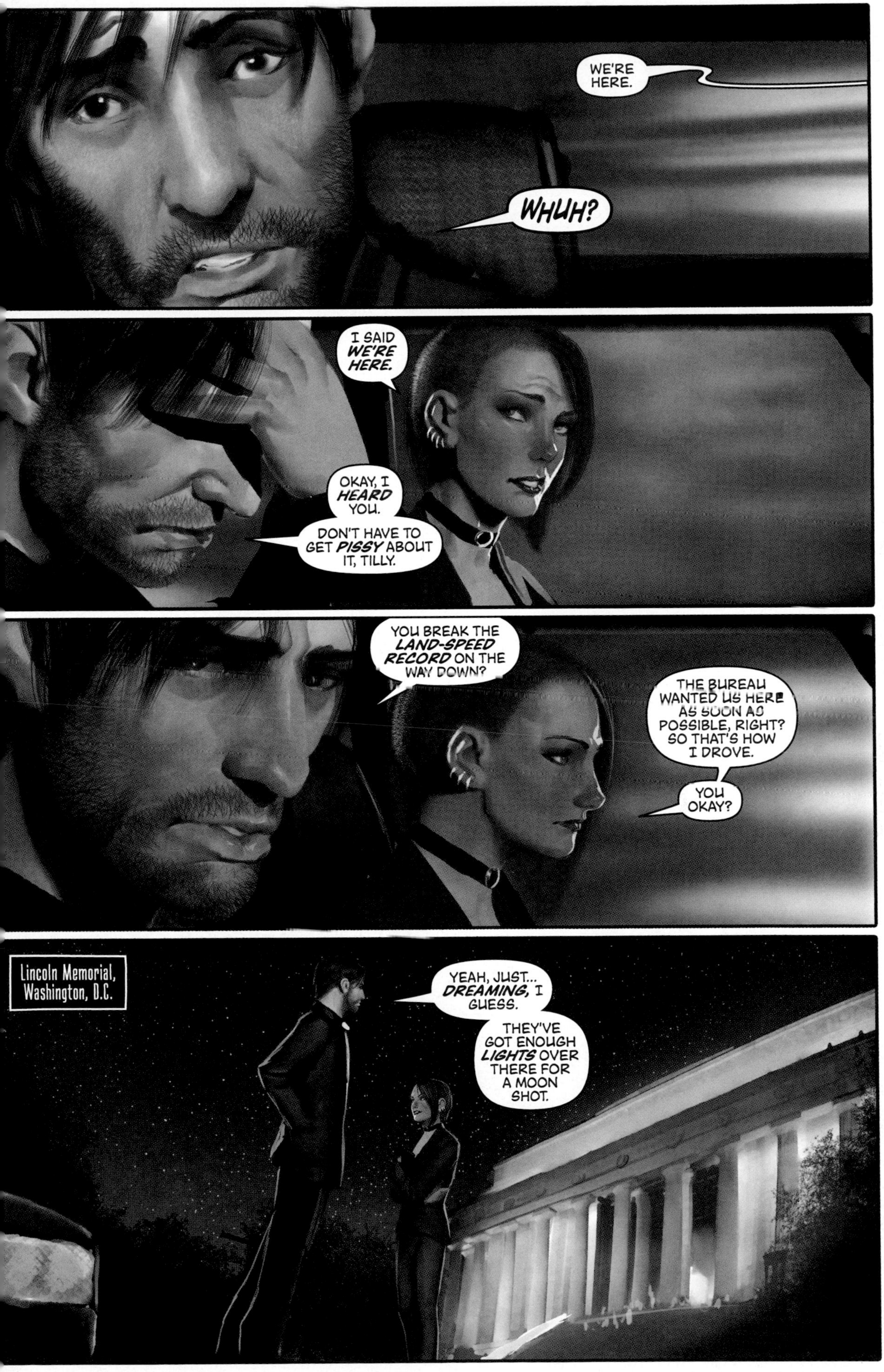
WE'RE HERE.
WHUH?
I SAID WE'RE HERE.
OKAY, I HEARD YOU.
DON'T HAVE TO GET PISSY ABOUT IT, TILLY.
YOU BREAK THE LAND-SPEED RECORD ON THE WAY DOWN?
THE BUREAU WANTED US HERE AS SOON AS POSSIBLE, RIGHT? SO THAT'S HOW I DROVE.
YOU OKAY?
Lincoln Memorial, Washington, D.C.
YEAH, JUST... DREAMING, I GUESS.
THEY'VE GOT ENOUGH LIGHTS OVER THERE FOR A MOON SHOT.

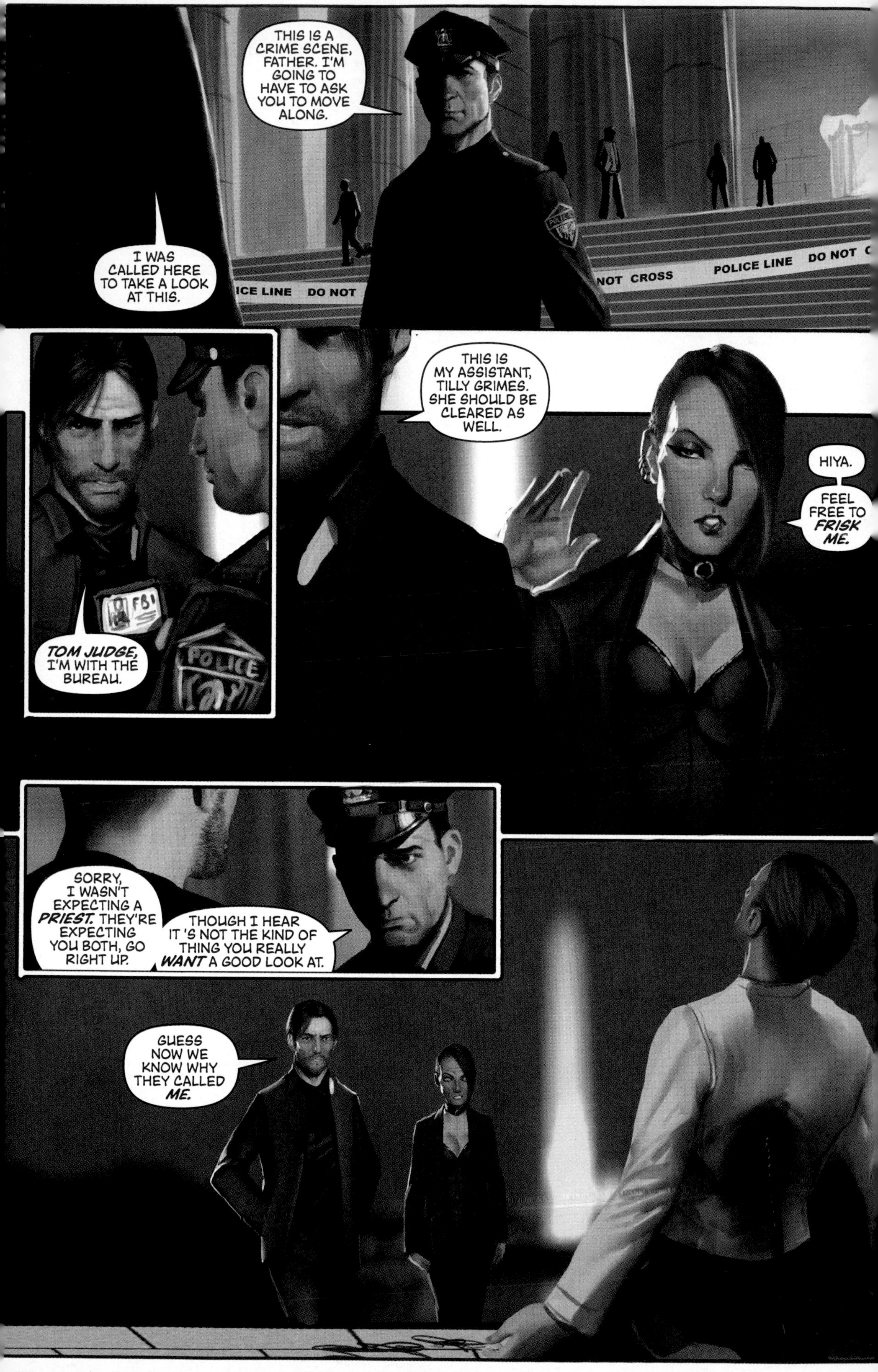
THIS IS A CRIME SCENE, FATHER. I'M GOING TO HAVE TO ASK YOU TO MOVE ALONG.
I WAS CALLED HERE TO TAKE A LOOK AT THIS.
POLICE LINE DO NOT CROSS
TOM JUDGE, I'M WITH THE BUREAU.
THIS IS MY ASSISTANT, TILLY GRIMES. SHE SHOULD BE CLEARED AS WELL.
HIYA.
FEEL FREE TO FRISK ME.
SORRY, I WASN'T EXPECTING A PRIEST. THEY'RE EXPECTING YOU BOTH, GO RIGHT UP.
THOUGH I HEAR IT'S NOT THE KIND OF THING YOU REALLY WANT A GOOD LOOK AT.
GUESS NOW WE KNOW WHY THEY CALLED ME.

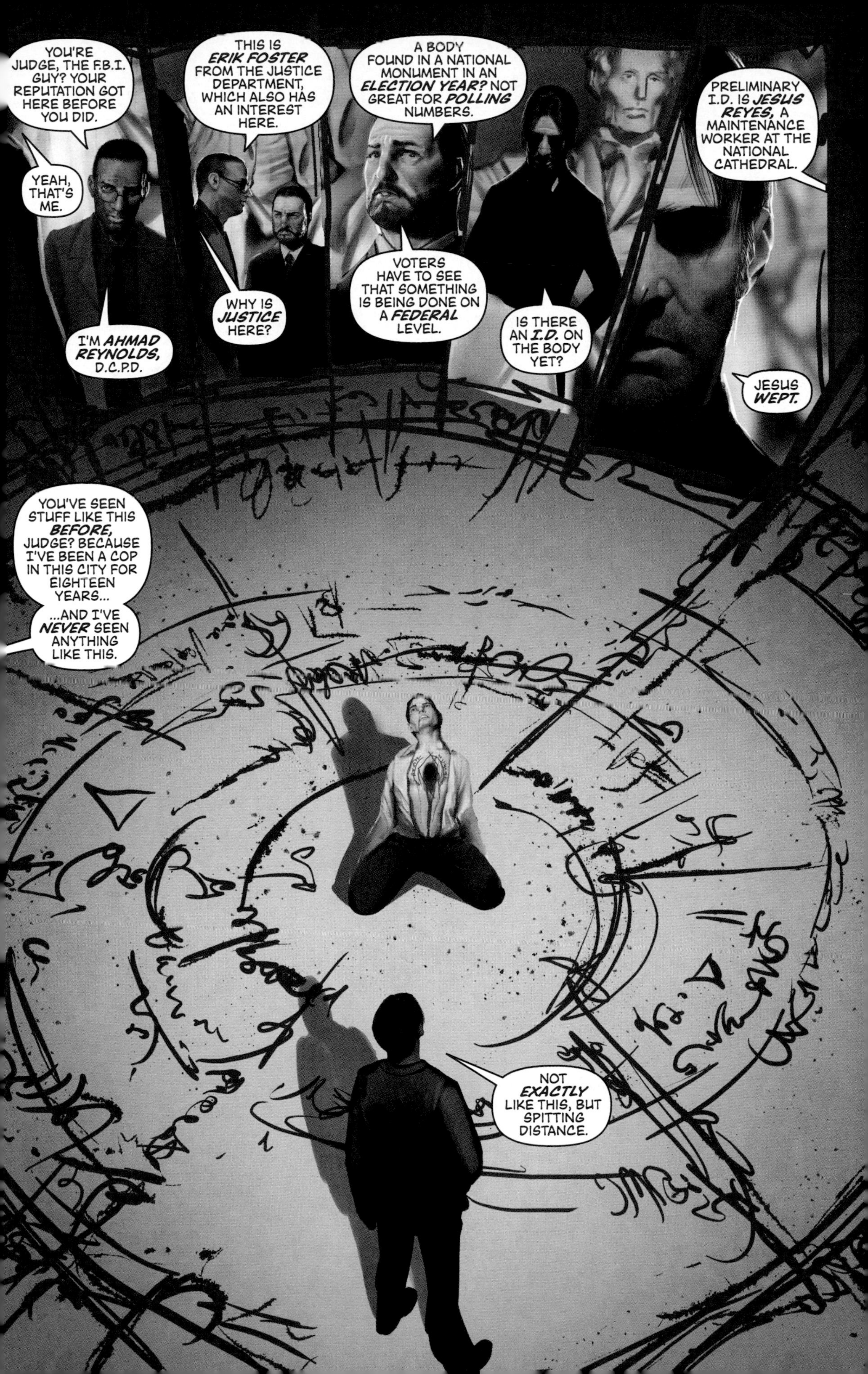

YOU'RE JUDGE, THE F.B.I. GUY? YOUR REPUTATION GOT HERE BEFORE YOU DID.
YEAH, THAT'S ME.
I'M AHMAD REYNOLDS, D.C.P.D.
THIS IS ERIK FOSTER FROM THE JUSTICE DEPARTMENT, WHICH ALSO HAS AN INTEREST HERE.
WHY IS JUSTICE HERE?
A BODY FOUND IN A NATIONAL MONUMENT IN AN ELECTION YEAR? NOT GREAT FOR POLLING NUMBERS.
VOTERS HAVE TO SEE THAT SOMETHING IS BEING DONE ON A FEDERAL LEVEL.
IS THERE AN I.D. ON THE BODY YET?
PRELIMINARY I.D. IS JESUS REYES, A MAINTENANCE WORKER AT THE NATIONAL CATHEDRAL.
JESUS WEPT.
YOU'VE SEEN STUFF LIKE THIS BEFORE, JUDGE? BECAUSE I'VE BEEN A COP IN THIS CITY FOR EIGHTEEN YEARS...
...AND I'VE NEVER SEEN ANYTHING LIKE THIS.
NOT EXACTLY LIKE THIS, BUT SPITTING DISTANCE.

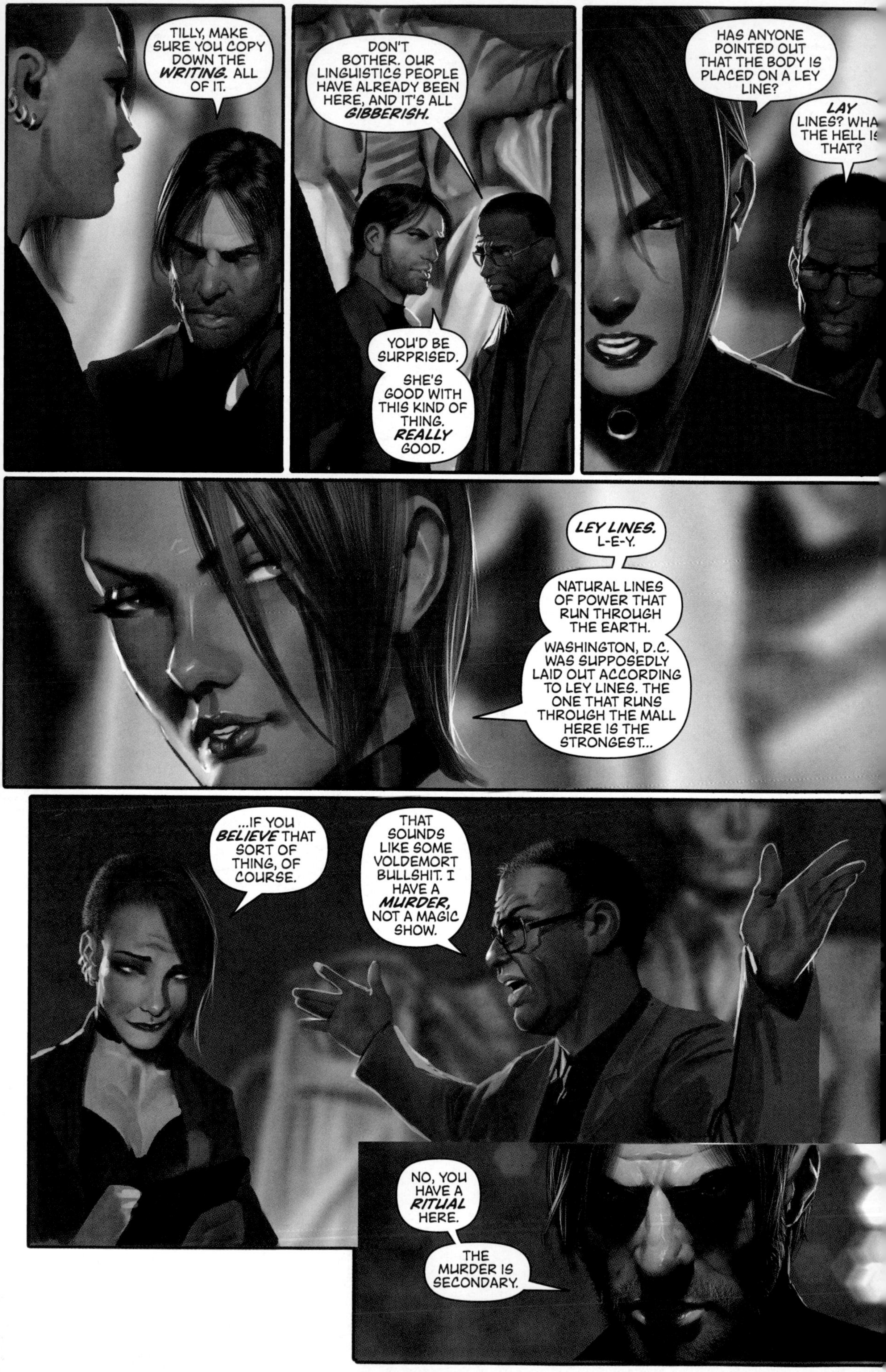

TILLY, MAKE SURE YOU COPY DOWN THE *WRITING.* ALL OF IT.
DON'T BOTHER. OUR LINGUISTICS PEOPLE HAVE ALREADY BEEN HERE, AND IT'S ALL *GIBBERISH.*
YOU'D BE SURPRISED.
SHE'S GOOD WITH THIS KIND OF THING. *REALLY* GOOD.
HAS ANYONE POINTED OUT THAT THE BODY IS PLACED ON A LEY LINE?
LAY LINES? WHA THE HELL I THAT?
LEY LINES. L-E-Y.
NATURAL LINES OF POWER THAT RUN THROUGH THE EARTH.
WASHINGTON, D.C. WAS SUPPOSEDLY LAID OUT ACCORDING TO LEY LINES. THE ONE THAT RUNS THROUGH THE MALL HERE IS THE STRONGEST...
...IF YOU *BELIEVE* THAT SORT OF THING, OF COURSE.
THAT SOUNDS LIKE SOME VOLDEMORT BULLSHIT. I HAVE A *MURDER,* NOT A MAGIC SHOW.
NO, YOU HAVE A *RITUAL* HERE.
THE MURDER IS SECONDARY.

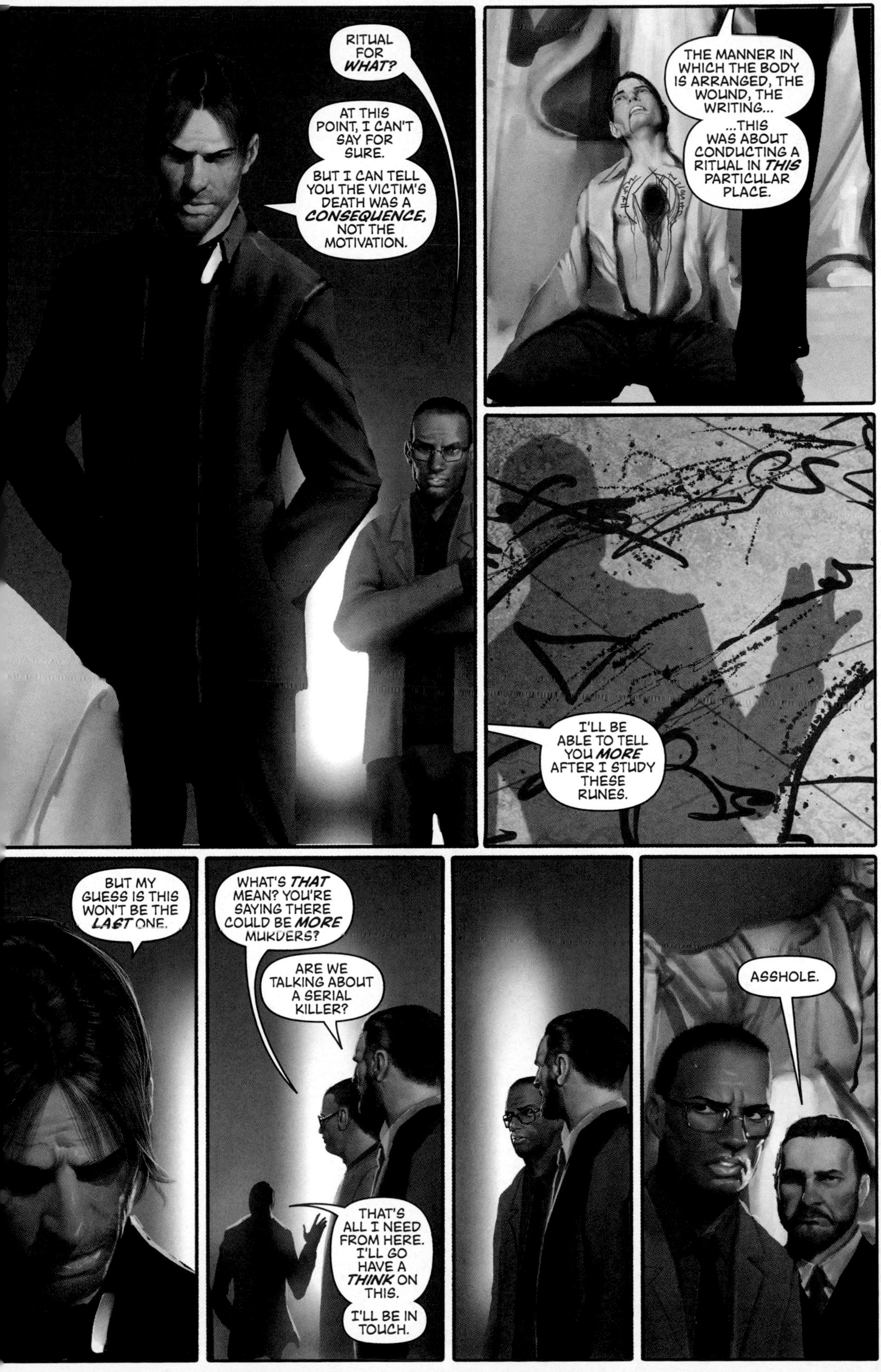
RITUAL FOR *WHAT?*
AT THIS POINT, I CAN'T SAY FOR SURE.
BUT I CAN TELL YOU THE VICTIM'S DEATH WAS A *CONSEQUENCE,* NOT THE MOTIVATION.
THE MANNER IN WHICH THE BODY IS ARRANGED, THE WOUND, THE WRITING...
...THIS WAS ABOUT CONDUCTING A RITUAL IN *THIS* PARTICULAR PLACE.
I'LL BE ABLE TO TELL YOU *MORE* AFTER I STUDY THESE RUNES.
BUT MY GUESS IS THIS WON'T BE THE *LAST* ONE.
WHAT'S *THAT* MEAN? YOU'RE SAYING THERE COULD BE *MORE* MURDERS?
ARE WE TALKING ABOUT A SERIAL KILLER?
THAT'S ALL I NEED FROM HERE. I'LL GO HAVE A *THINK* ON THIS.
I'LL BE IN TOUCH.
ASSHOLE.

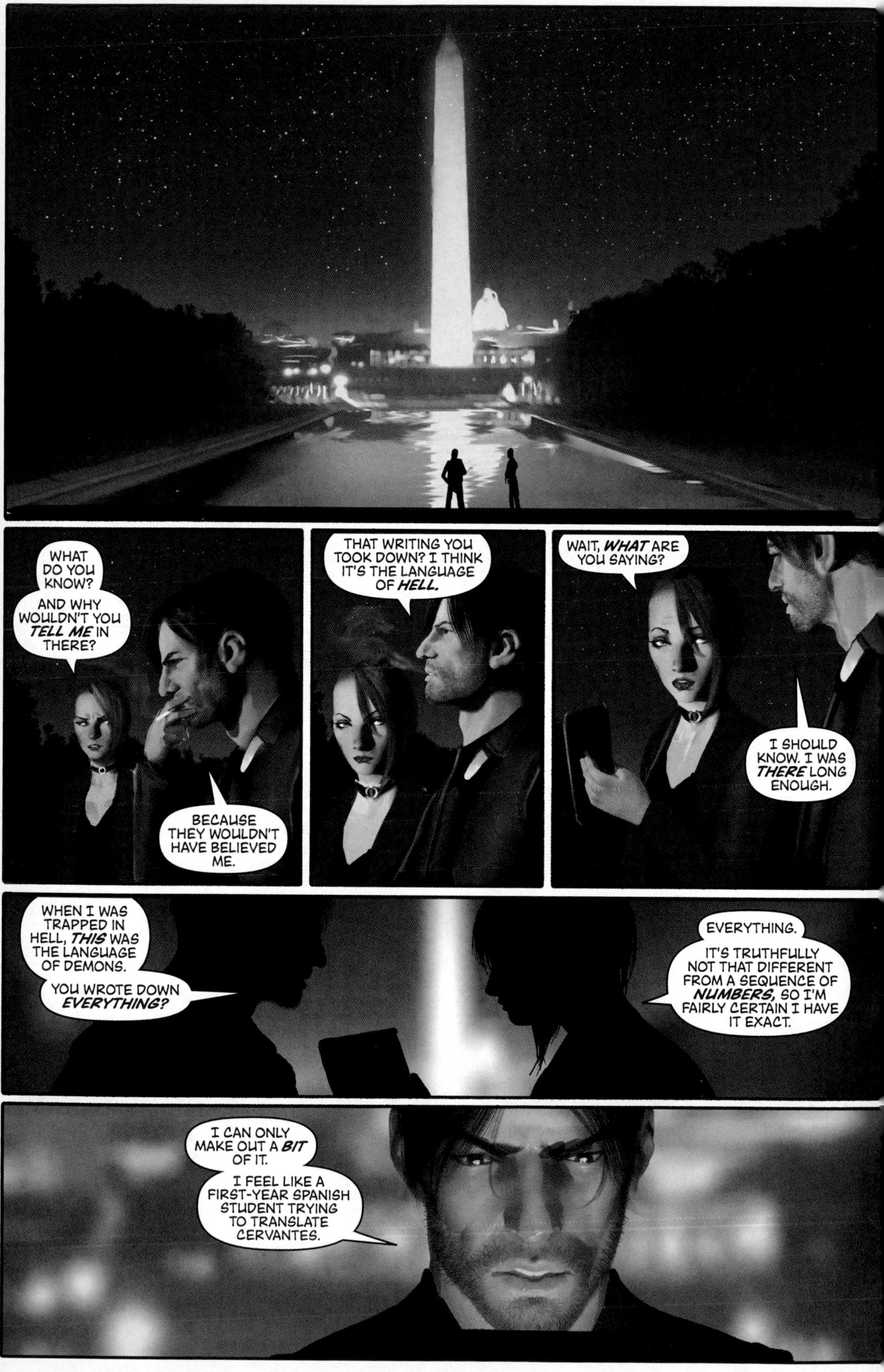

WHAT DO YOU KNOW?
AND WHY WOULDN'T YOU TELL ME IN THERE?
BECAUSE THEY WOULDN'T HAVE BELIEVED ME.
THAT WRITING YOU TOOK DOWN? I THINK IT'S THE LANGUAGE OF HELL.
WAIT, WHAT ARE YOU SAYING?
I SHOULD KNOW. I WAS THERE LONG ENOUGH.
WHEN I WAS TRAPPED IN HELL, THIS WAS THE LANGUAGE OF DEMONS.
YOU WROTE DOWN EVERYTHING?
EVERYTHING.
IT'S TRUTHFULLY NOT THAT DIFFERENT FROM A SEQUENCE OF NUMBERS, SO I'M FAIRLY CERTAIN I HAVE IT EXACT.
I CAN ONLY MAKE OUT A BIT OF IT.
I FEEL LIKE A FIRST-YEAR SPANISH STUDENT TRYING TO TRANSLATE CERVANTES.

BUT I'M SURE IT'S A *SUMMONING.*

LIKE A *RECIPE,* BUT THIS IS ONLY THE FIRST INGREDIENT.

THIS IS A PLACE OF POWER, FIGURATIVELY *AND* LITERALLY.

SOMEONE IS TRYING TO TAP INTO THAT POWER.

WE HAVE TO FIGURE OUT *WHO...*

...AND *WHY.*

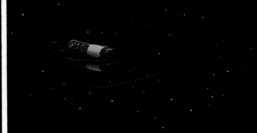

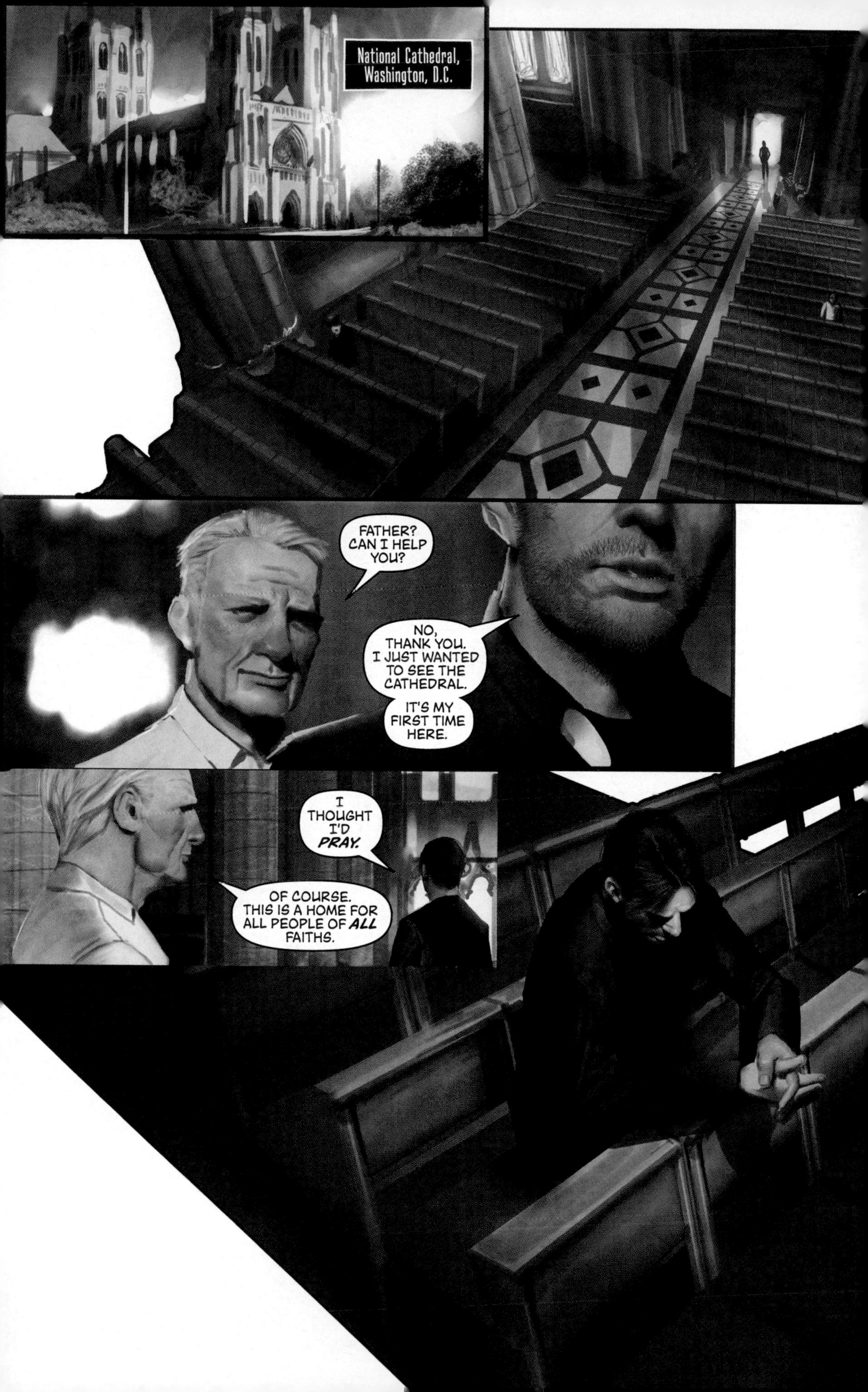
National Cathedral, Washington, D.C.
FATHER? CAN I HELP YOU?
NO, THANK YOU. I JUST WANTED TO SEE THE CATHEDRAL.
IT'S MY FIRST TIME HERE.
I THOUGHT I'D *PRAY.*
OF COURSE. THIS IS A HOME FOR ALL PEOPLE OF *ALL* FAITHS.

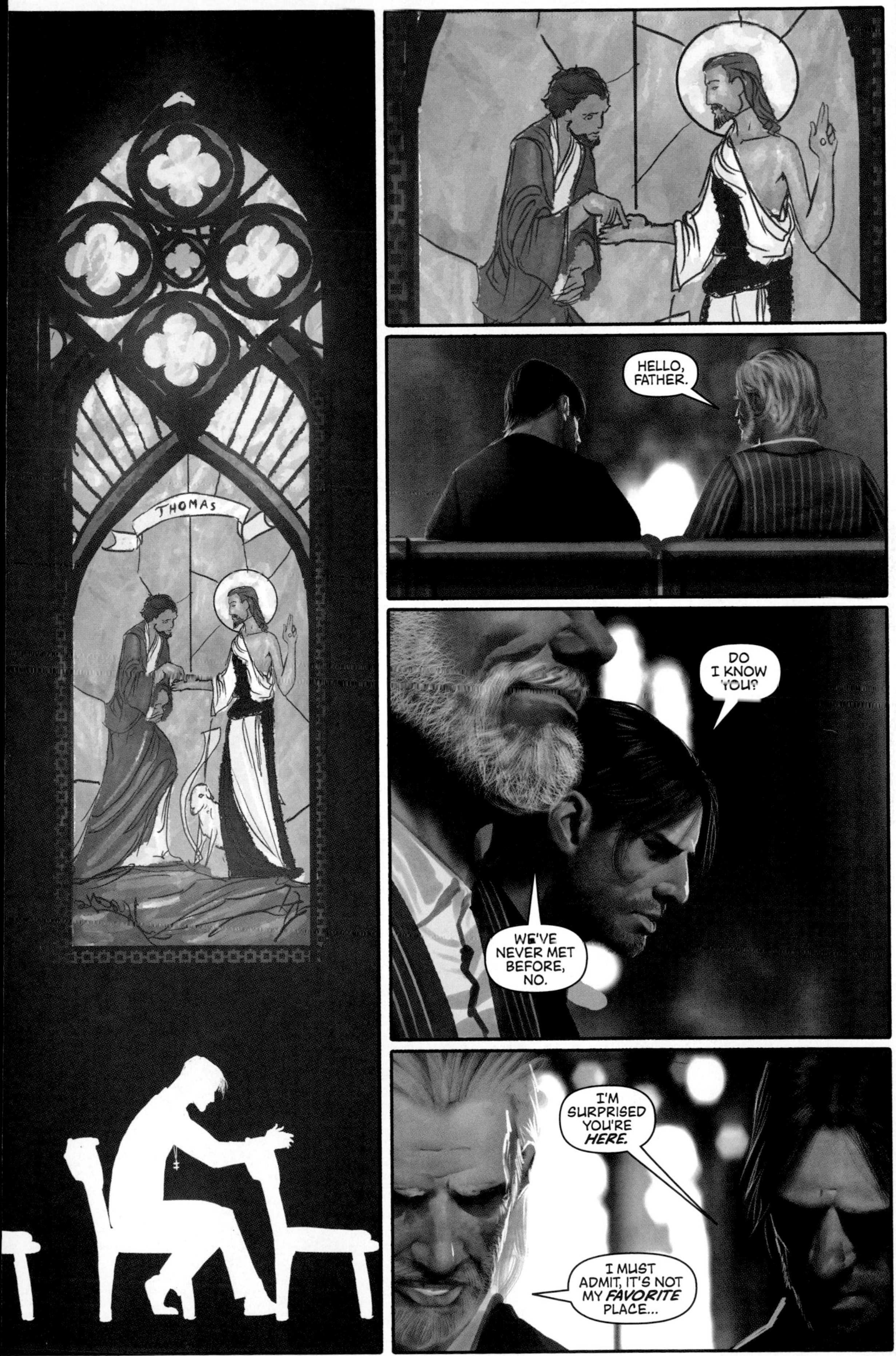
THOMAS
HELLO, FATHER.
DO I KNOW YOU?
WE'VE NEVER MET BEFORE, NO.
I'M SURPRISED YOU'RE *HERE.*
I MUST ADMIT, IT'S NOT MY *FAVORITE* PLACE...

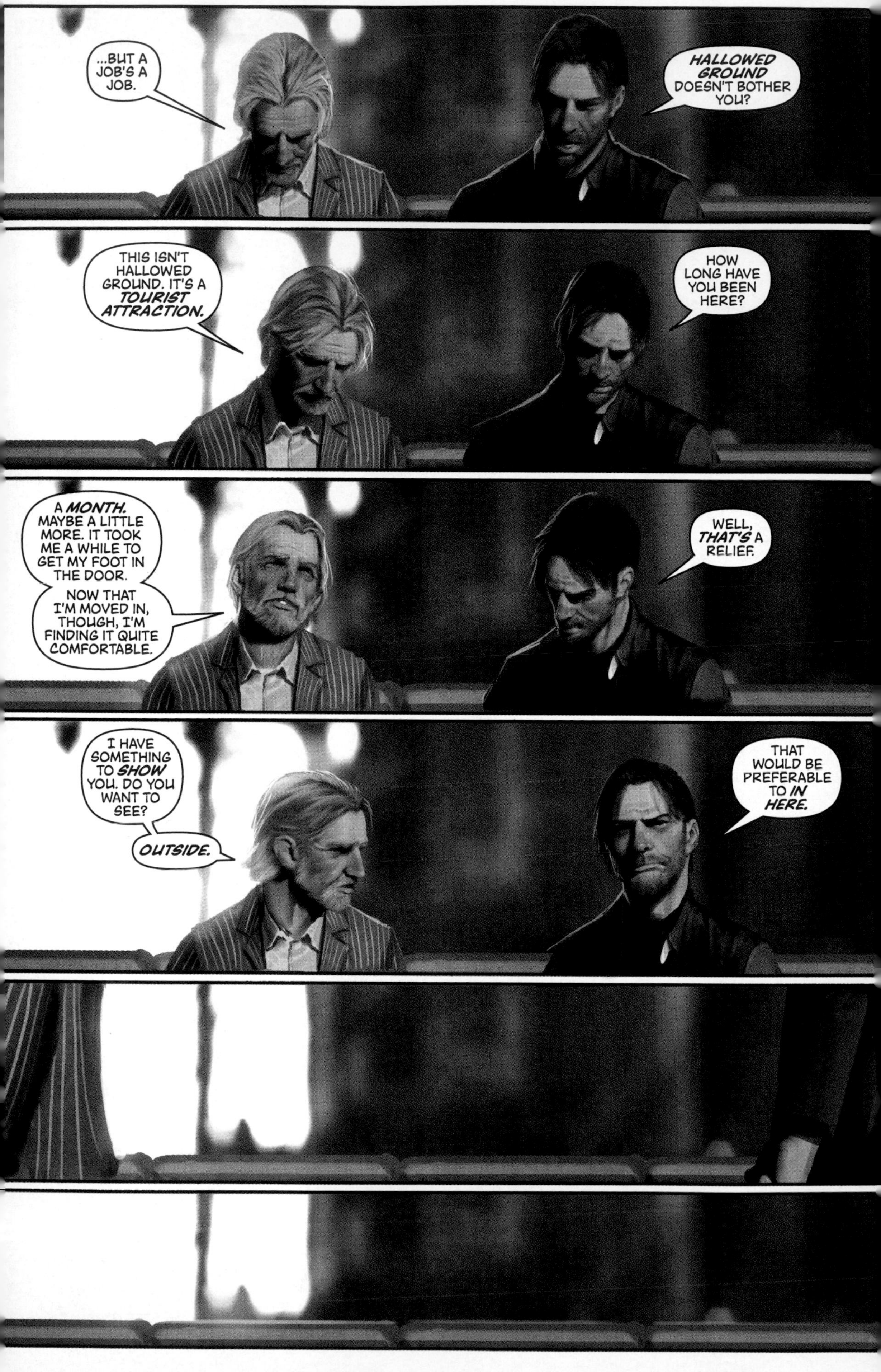

...BUT A JOB'S A JOB.
HALLOWED GROUND DOESN'T BOTHER YOU?
THIS ISN'T HALLOWED GROUND. IT'S A TOURIST ATTRACTION.
HOW LONG HAVE YOU BEEN HERE?
A MONTH. MAYBE A LITTLE MORE. IT TOOK ME A WHILE TO GET MY FOOT IN THE DOOR.
NOW THAT I'M MOVED IN, THOUGH, I'M FINDING IT QUITE COMFORTABLE.
WELL, THAT'S A RELIEF.
I HAVE SOMETHING TO SHOW YOU. DO YOU WANT TO SEE?
OUTSIDE.
THAT WOULD BE PREFERABLE TO IN HERE.

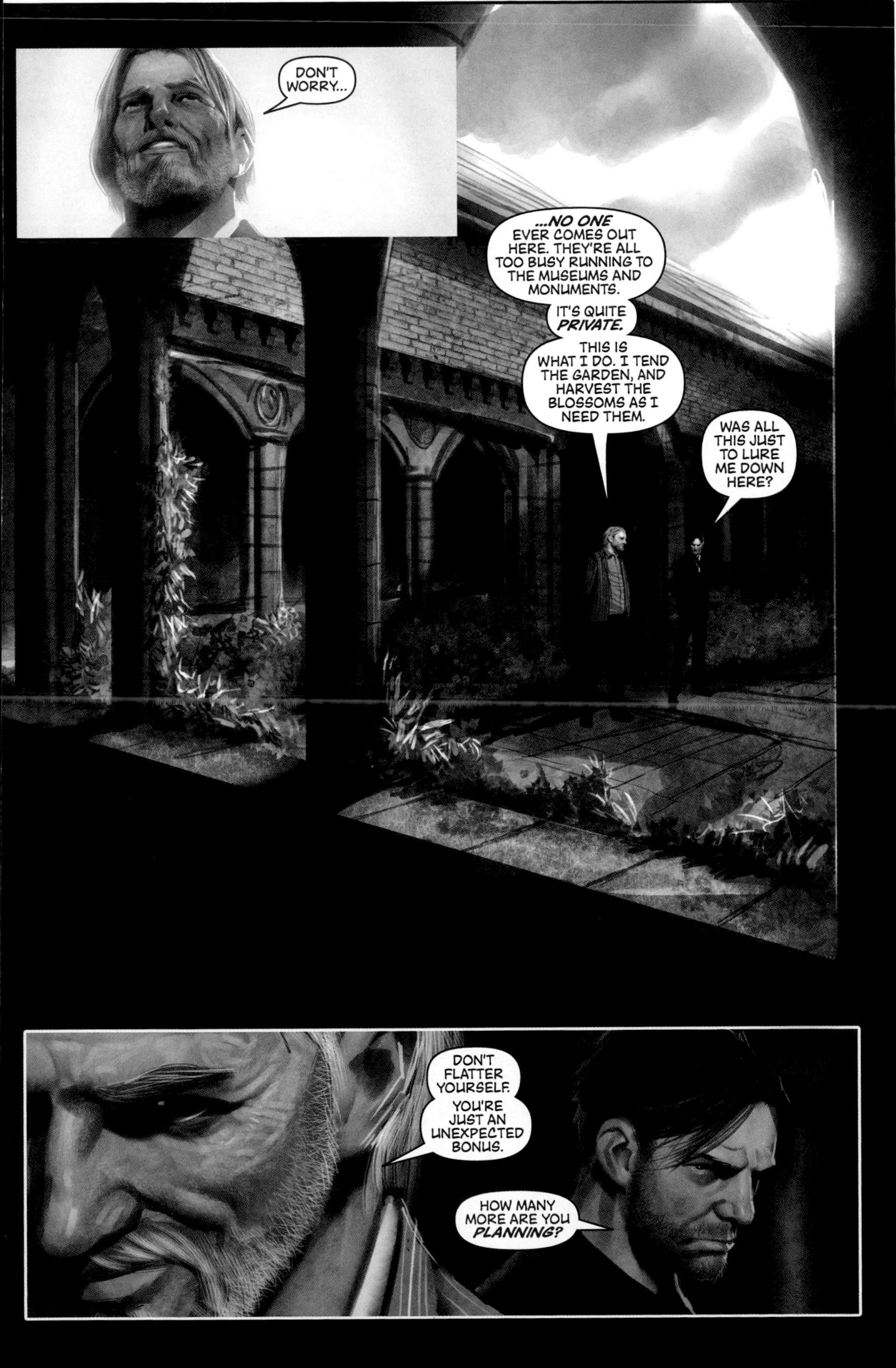
DON'T WORRY...
...NO ONE EVER COMES OUT HERE. THEY'RE ALL TOO BUSY RUNNING TO THE MUSEUMS AND MONUMENTS.
IT'S QUITE *PRIVATE.*
THIS IS WHAT I DO. I TEND THE GARDEN, AND HARVEST THE BLOSSOMS AS I NEED THEM.
WAS ALL THIS JUST TO LURE ME DOWN HERE?
DON'T FLATTER YOURSELF.
YOU'RE JUST AN UNEXPECTED BONUS.
HOW MANY MORE ARE YOU *PLANNING?*

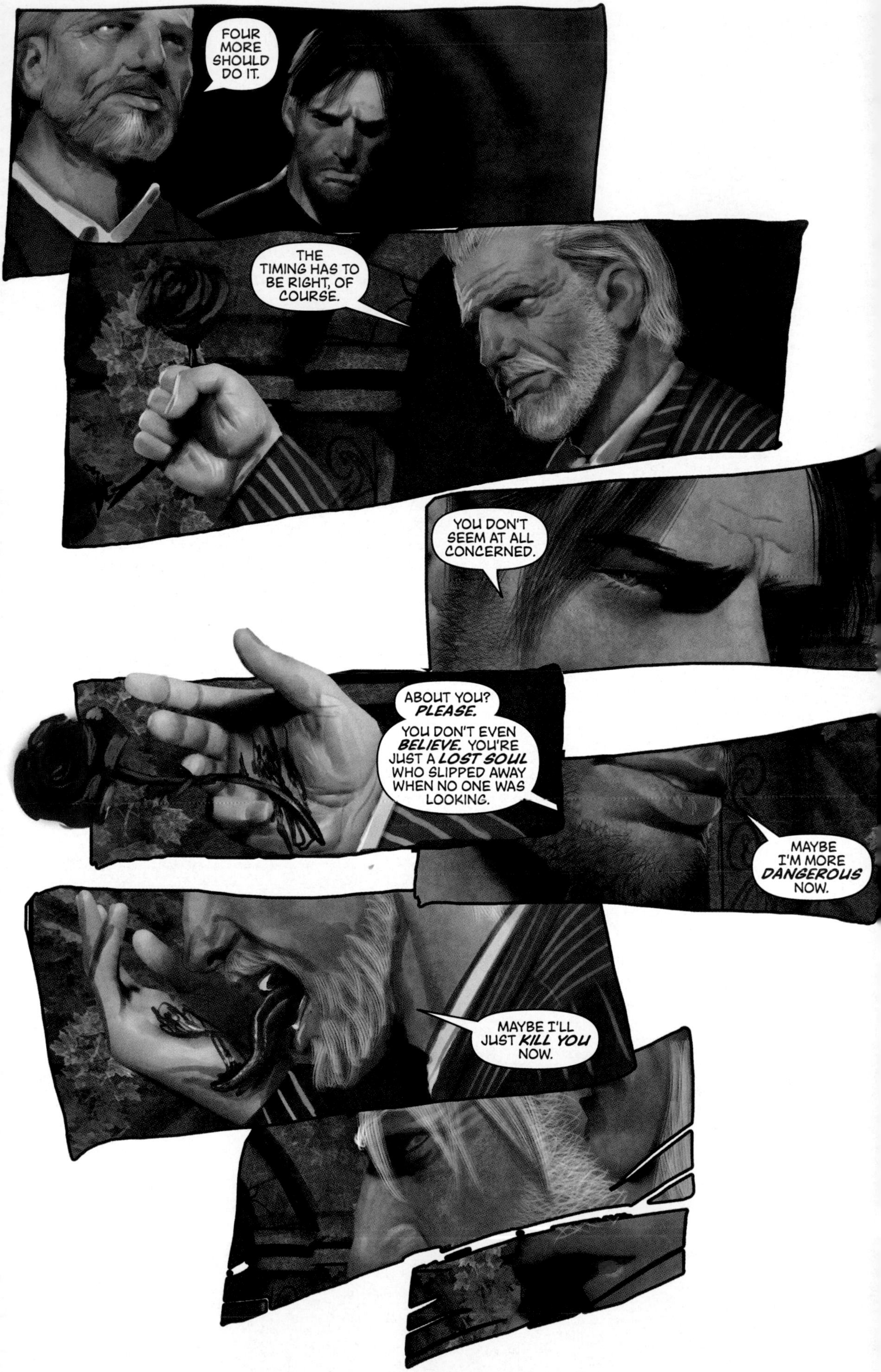
FOUR MORE SHOULD DO IT.
THE TIMING HAS TO BE RIGHT, OF COURSE.
YOU DON'T SEEM AT ALL CONCERNED.
ABOUT YOU? PLEASE.
YOU DON'T EVEN BELIEVE. YOU'RE JUST A LOST SOUL WHO SLIPPED AWAY WHEN NO ONE WAS LOOKING.
MAYBE I'M MORE DANGEROUS NOW.
MAYBE I'LL JUST KILL YOU NOW.

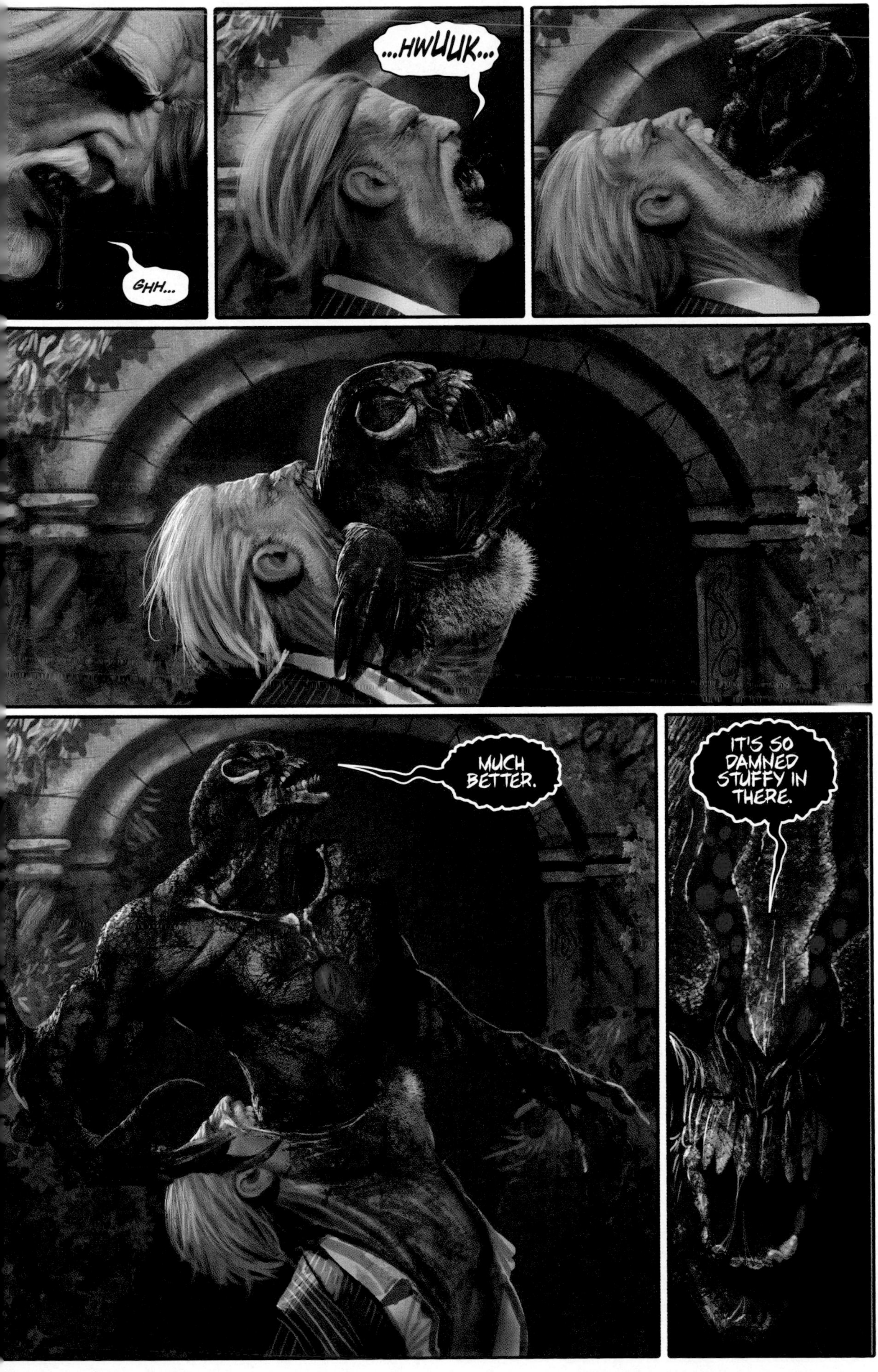
GHH...
...HWUUK...
MUCH BETTER.
IT'S SO DAMNED STUFFY IN THERE.

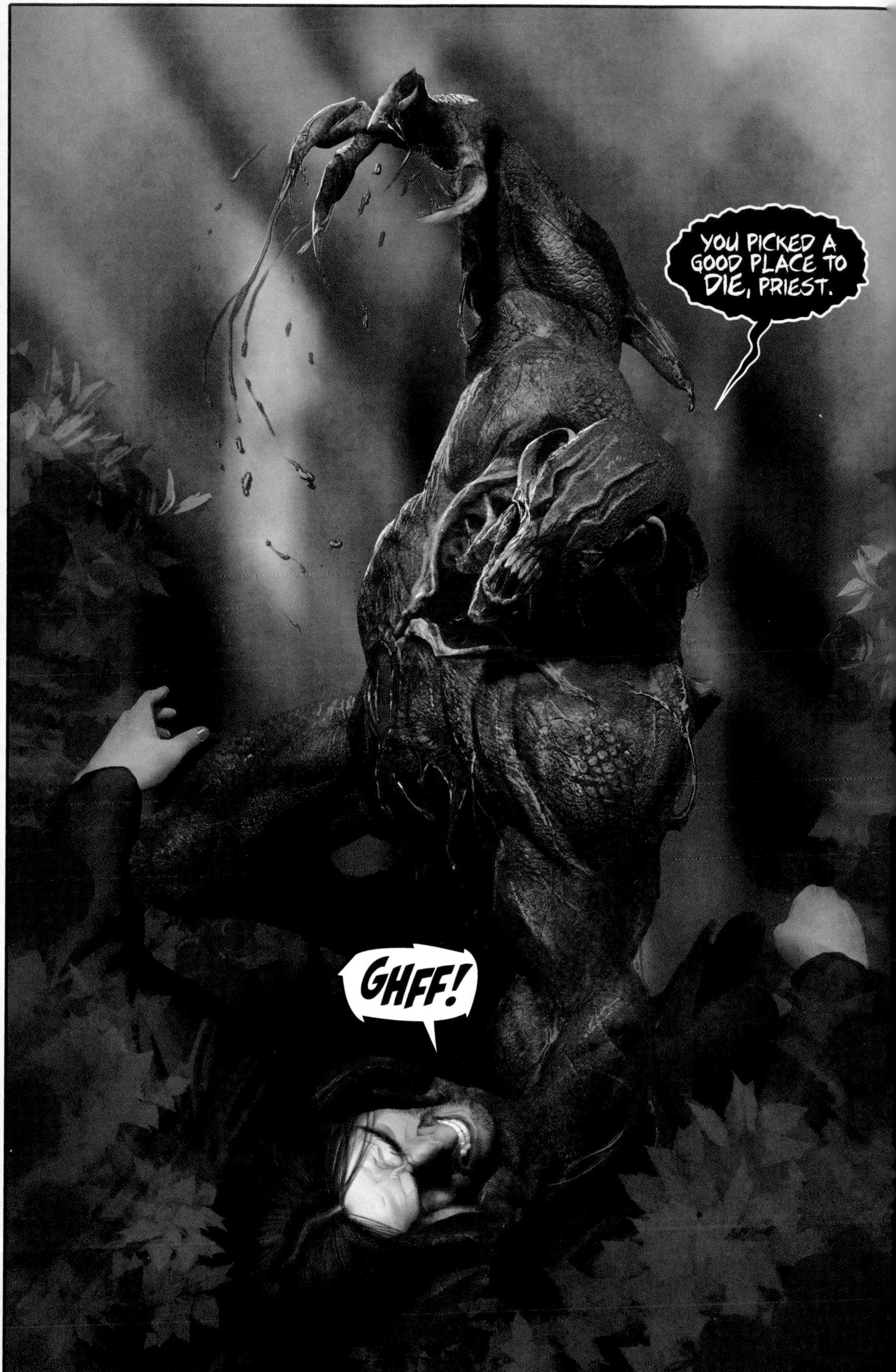
YOU PICKED A GOOD PLACE TO DIE, PRIEST.
GHFF!

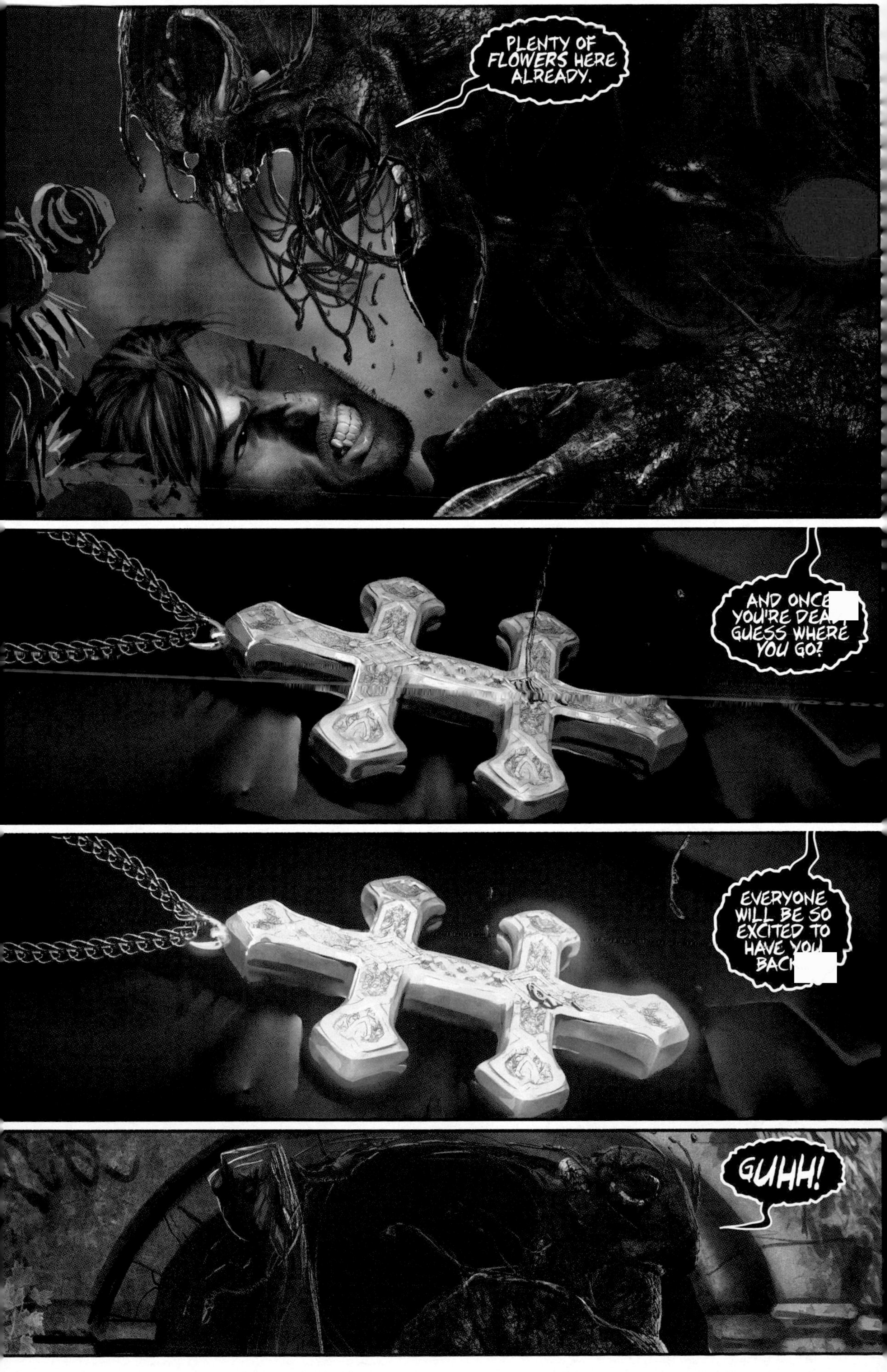
PLENTY OF FLOWERS HERE ALREADY.
AND ONCE YOU'RE DEA GUESS WHERE YOU GO?
EVERYONE WILL BE SO EXCITED TO HAVE YOU BAC
GUHH!

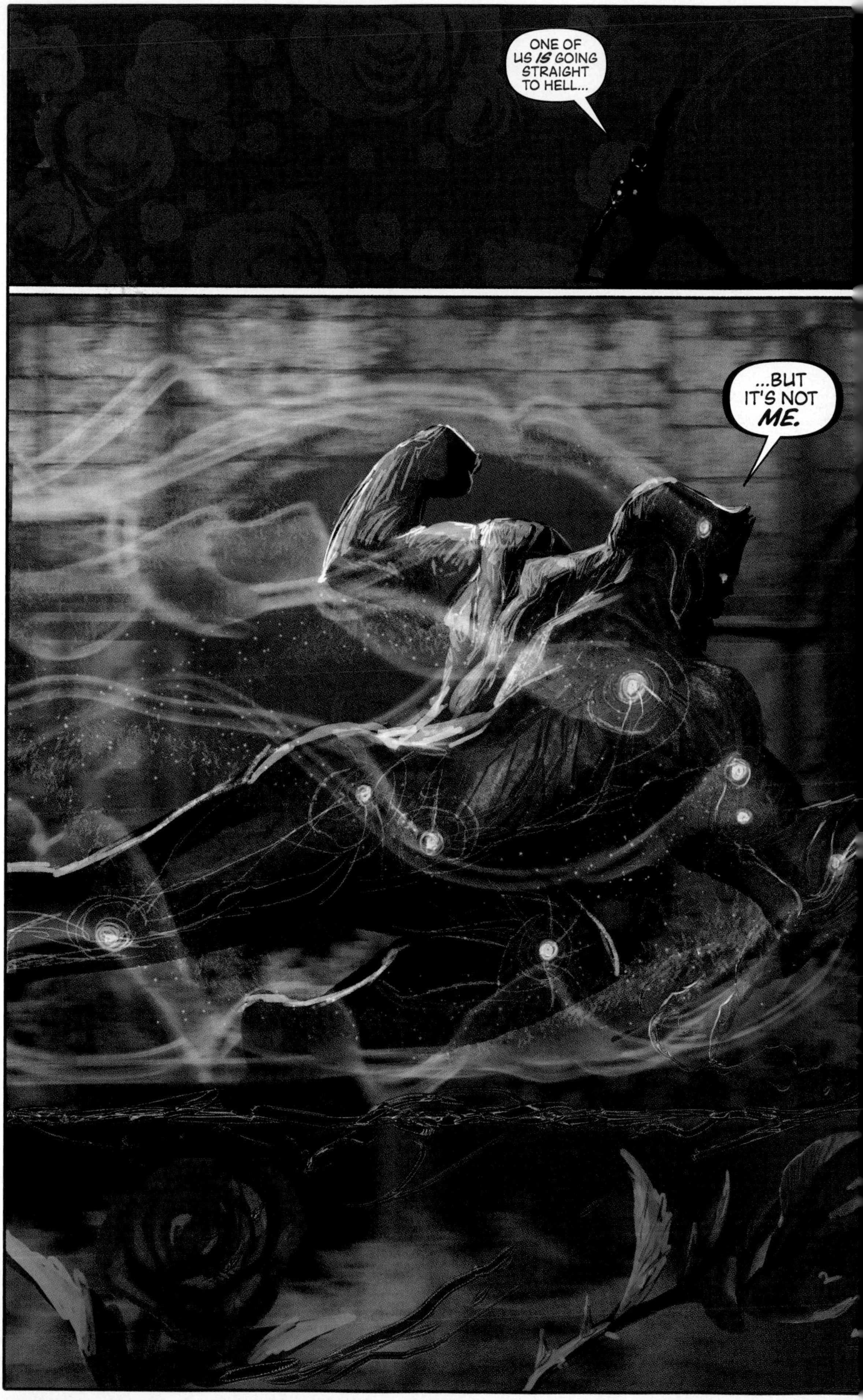
ONE OF US *IS* GOING STRAIGHT TO HELL...
...BUT IT'S NOT **ME.**

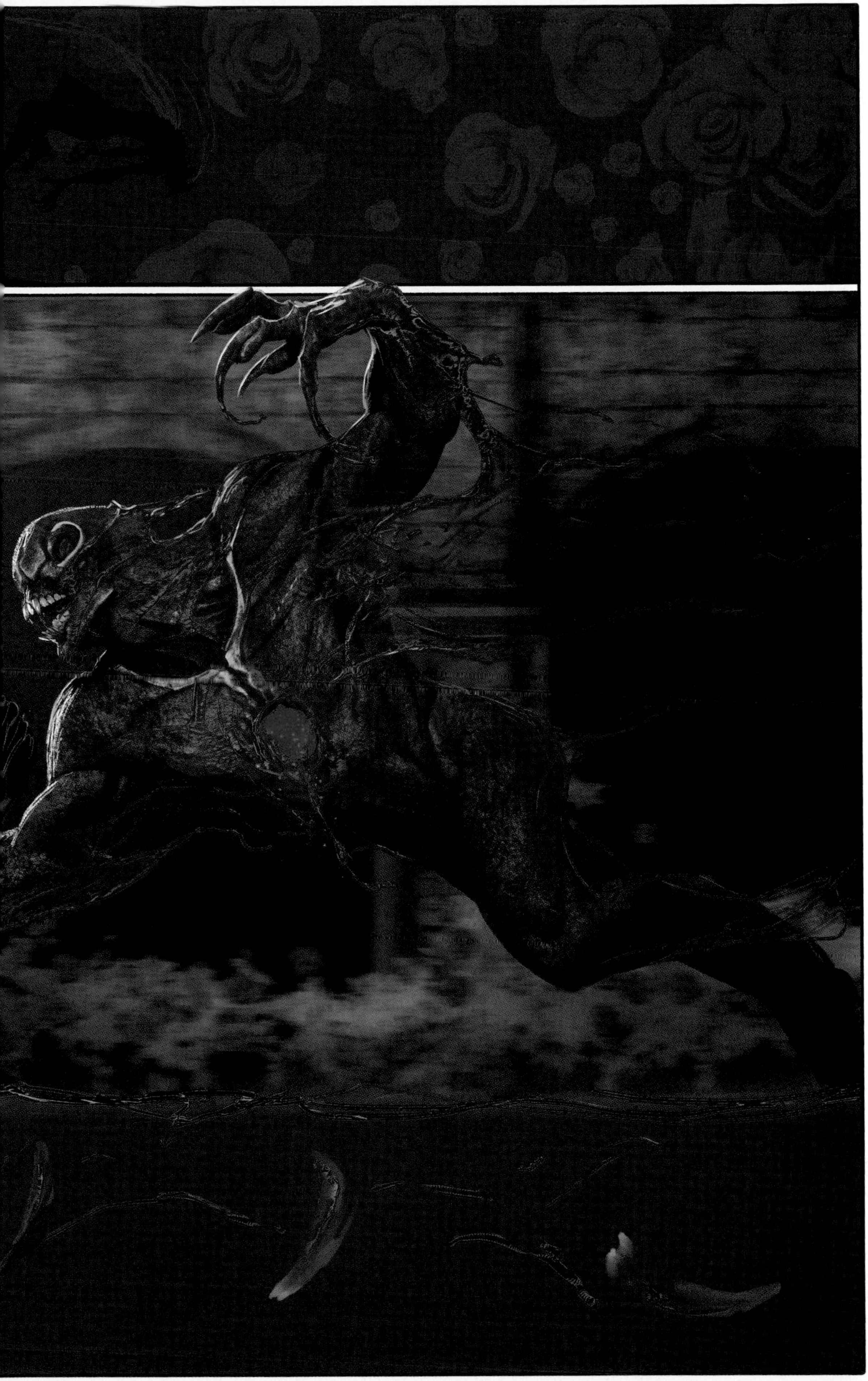

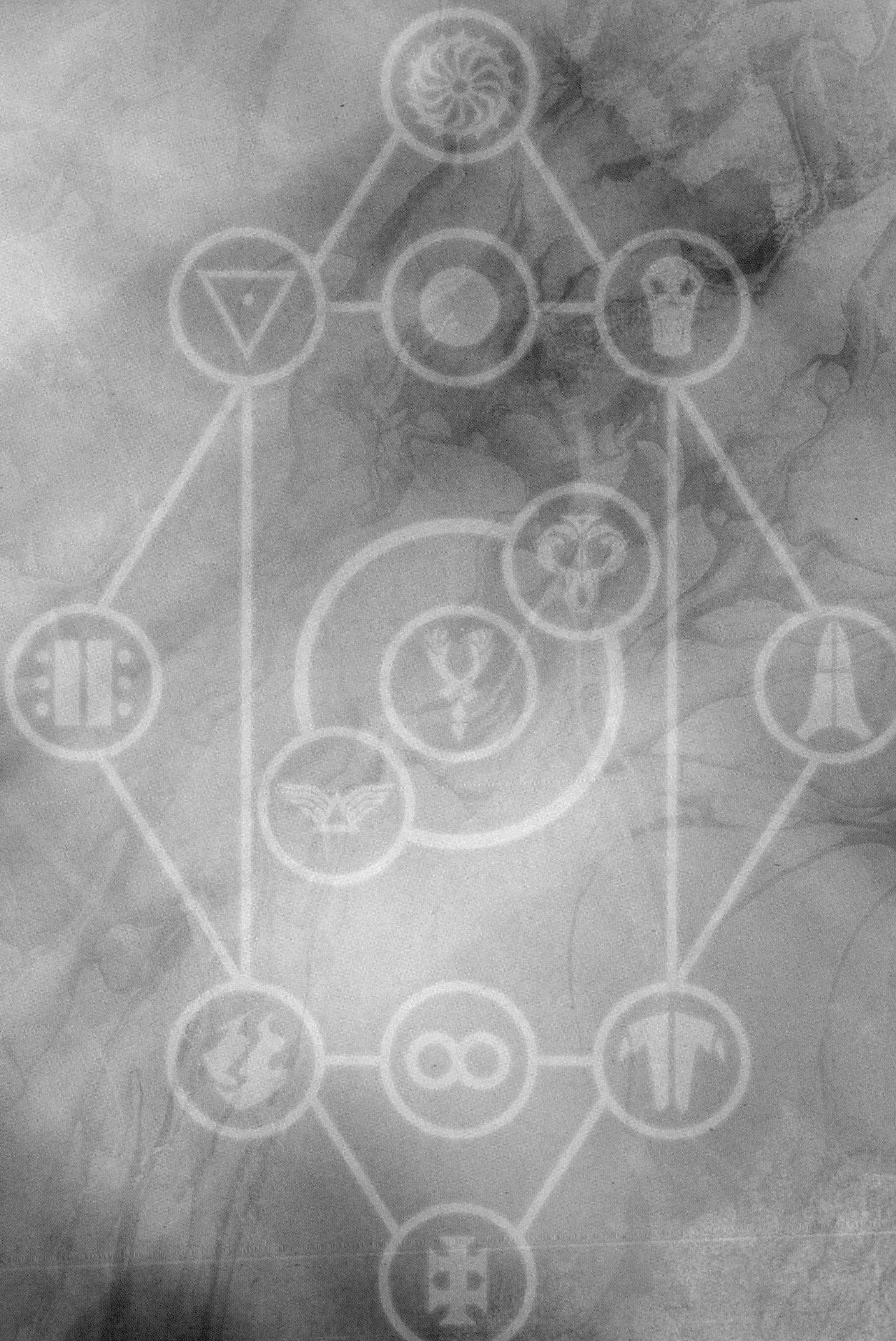

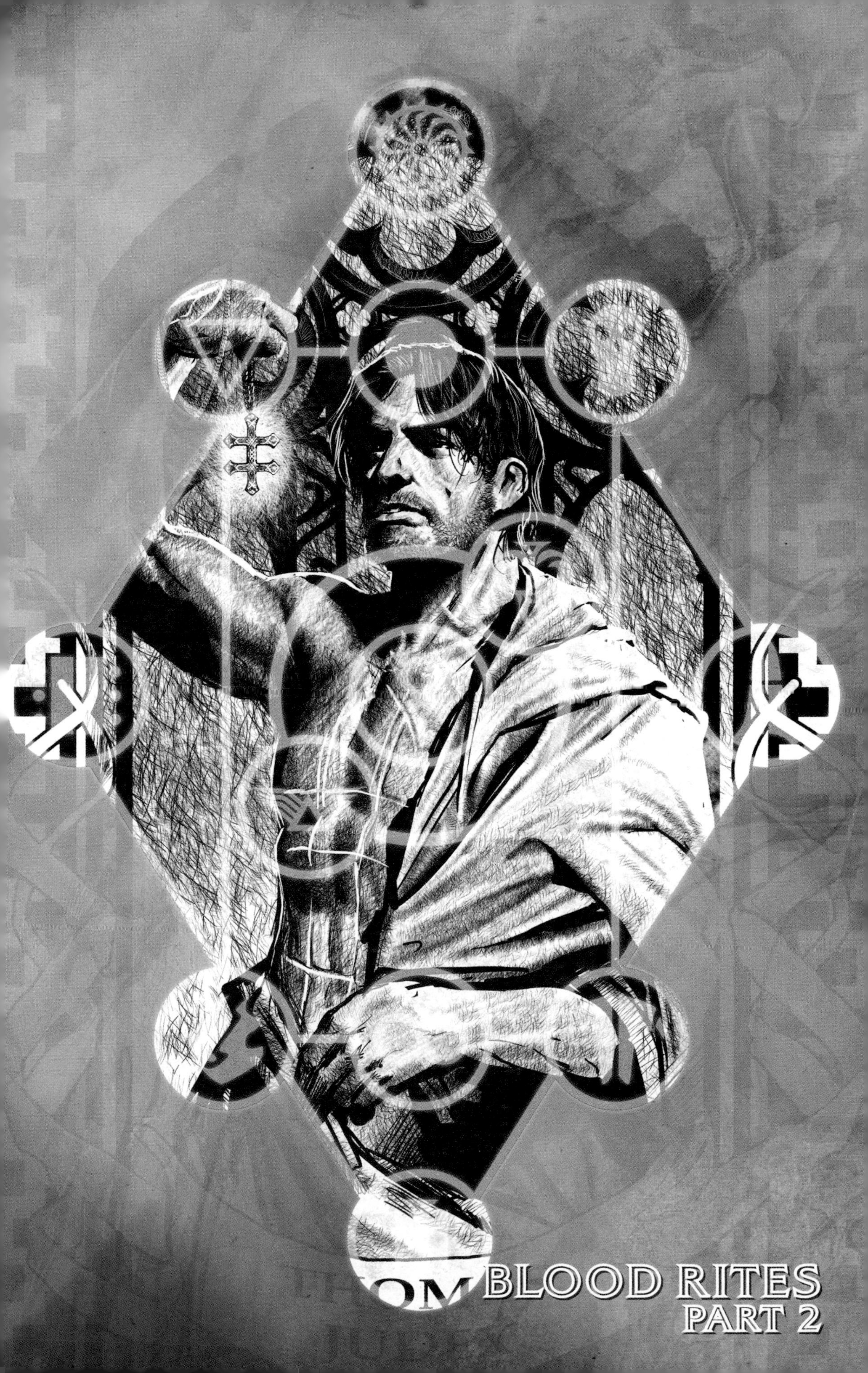
BLOOD RITES
PART 2

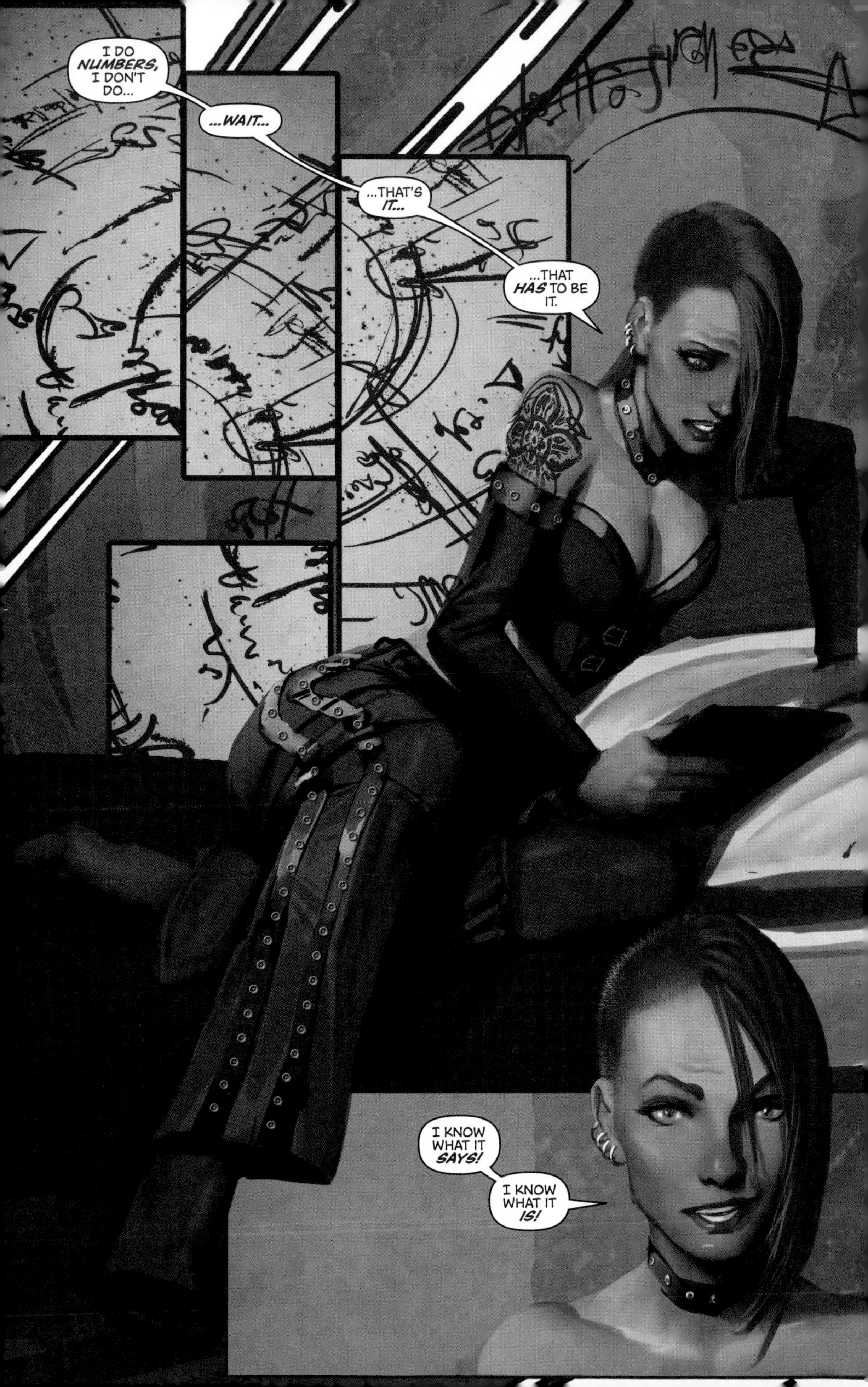
I DO NUMBERS, I DON'T DO...
...WAIT...
...THAT'S IT...
...THAT HAS TO BE IT.
I KNOW WHAT IT SAYS!
I KNOW WHAT IT IS!

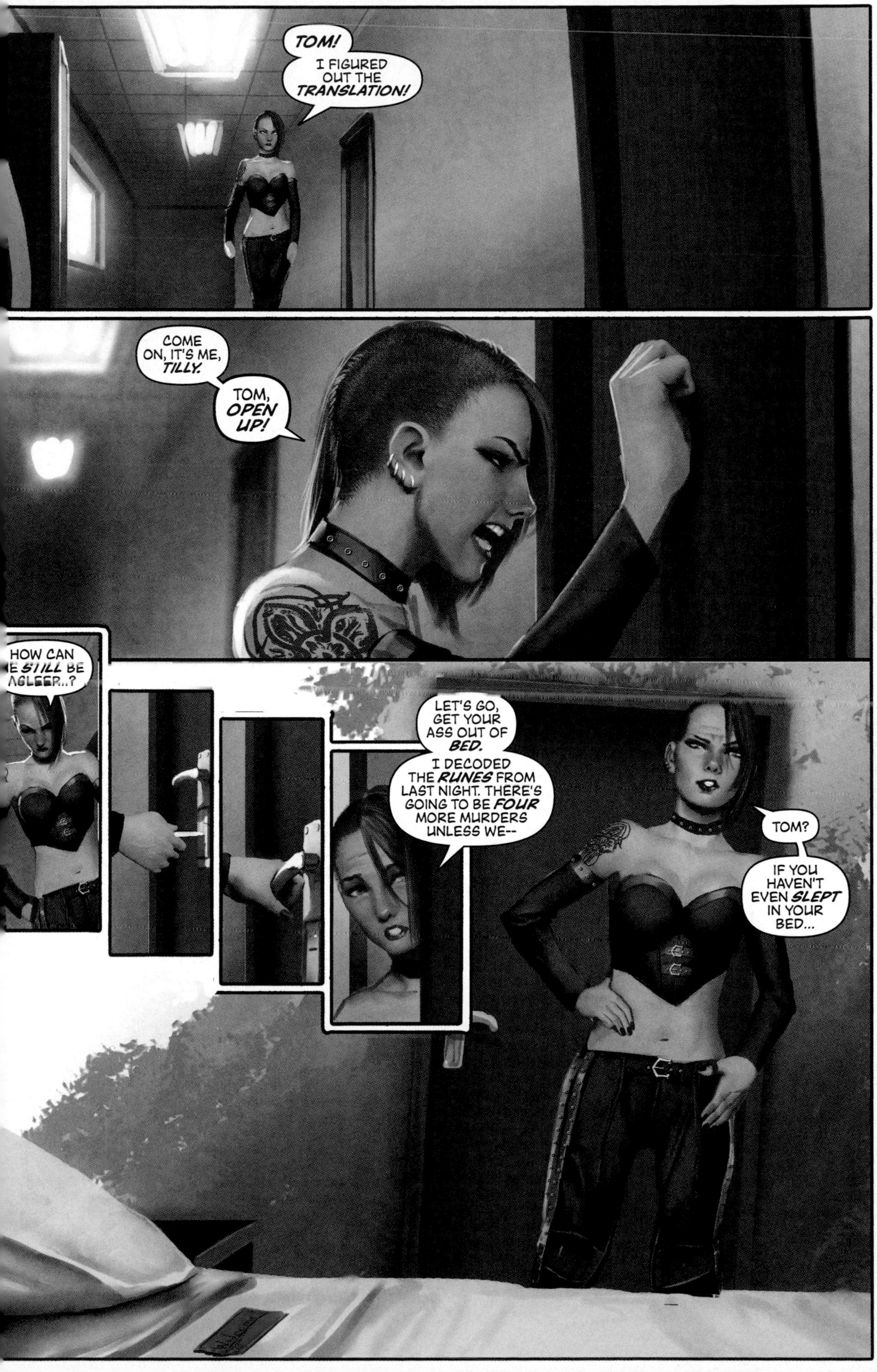
TOM!
I FIGURED OUT THE TRANSLATION!
COME ON, IT'S ME, TILLY.
TOM, OPEN UP!
HOW CAN E STILL BE ASLEEP...?
LET'S GO, GET YOUR ASS OUT OF BED.
I DECODED THE RUNES FROM LAST NIGHT. THERE'S GOING TO BE FOUR MORE MURDERS UNLESS WE--
TOM?
IF YOU HAVEN'T EVEN SLEPT IN YOUR BED...

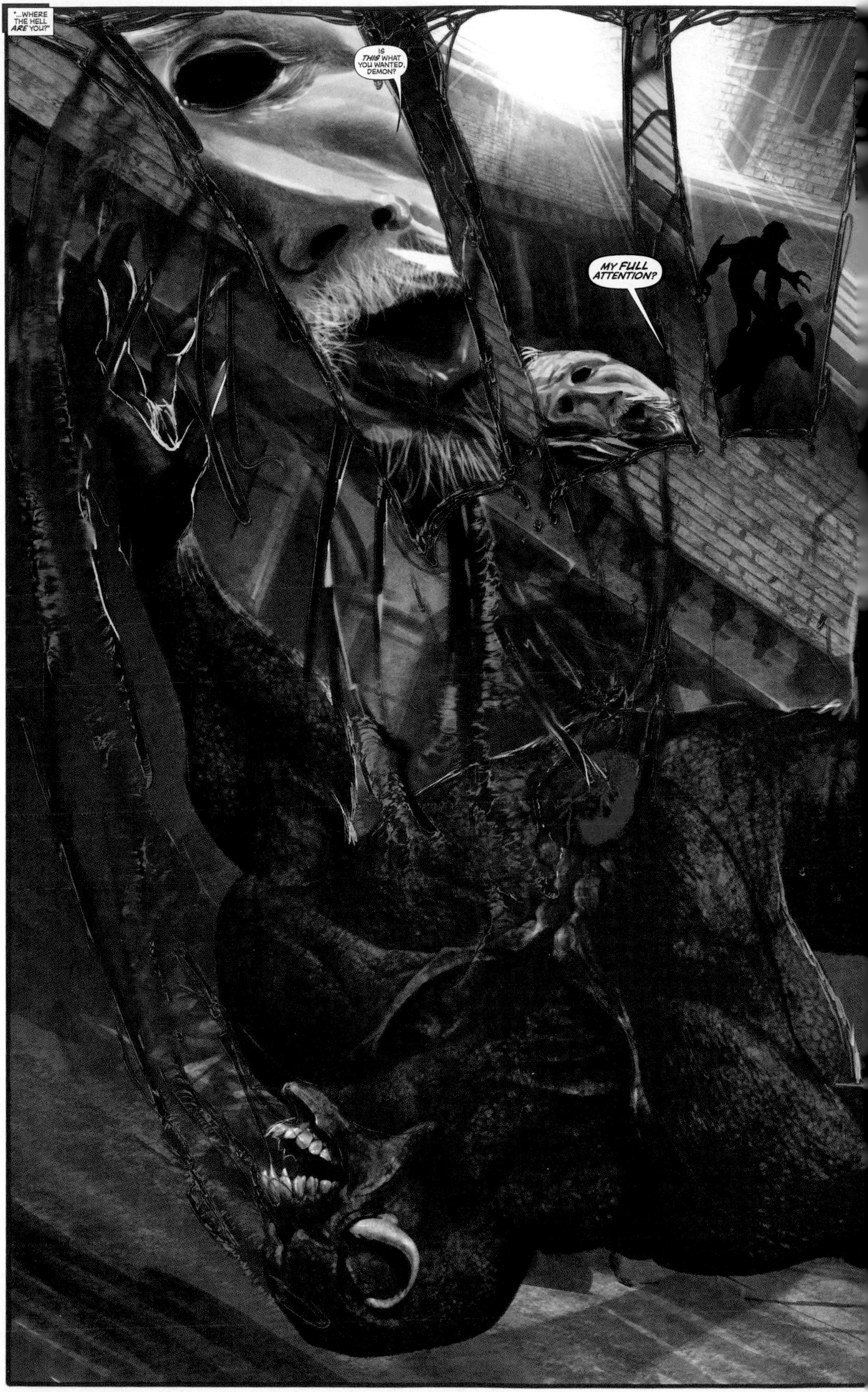
"...WHERE THE HELL ARE YOU?"
IS THIS WHAT YOU WANTED, DEMON?
MY FULL ATTENTION?

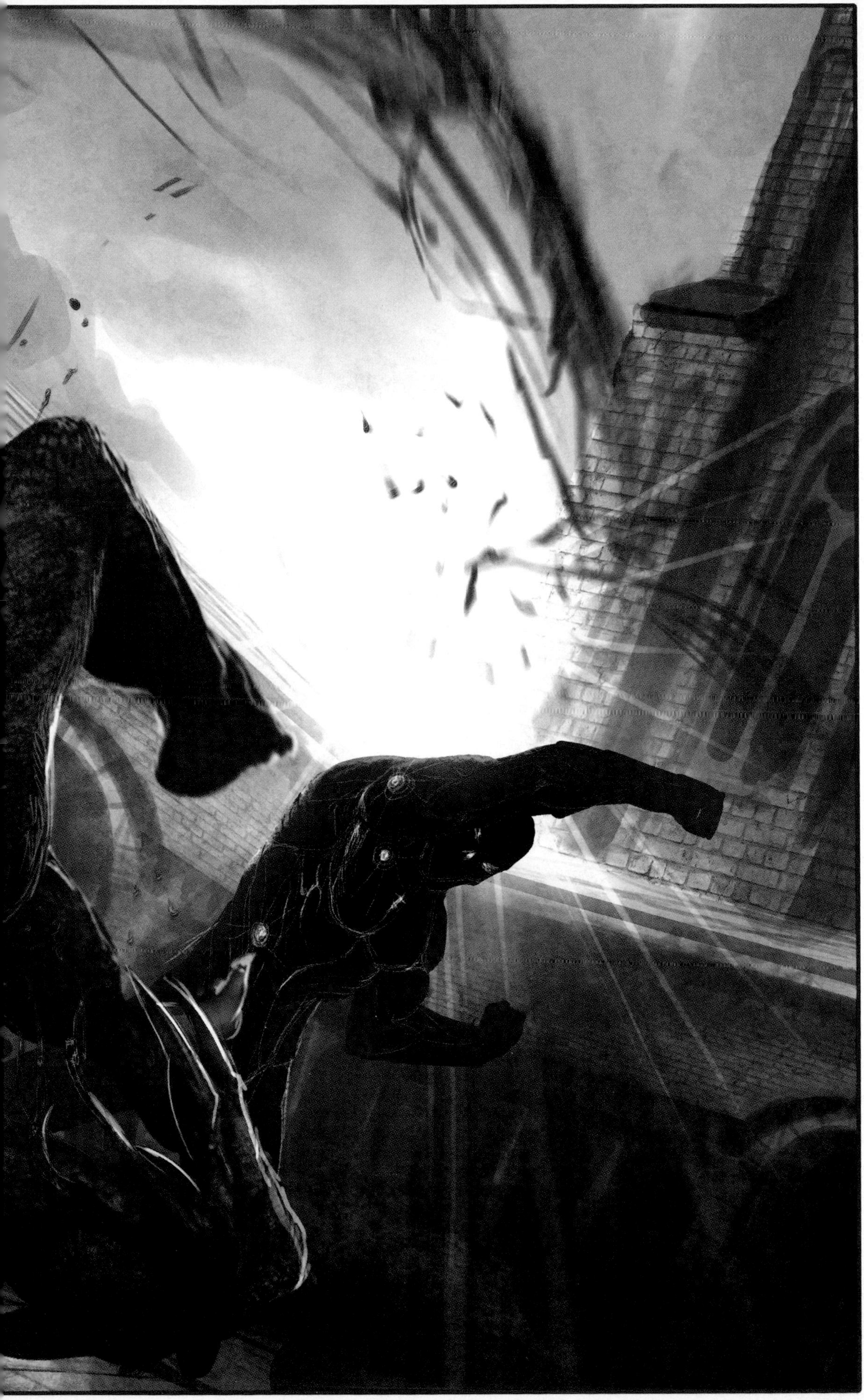

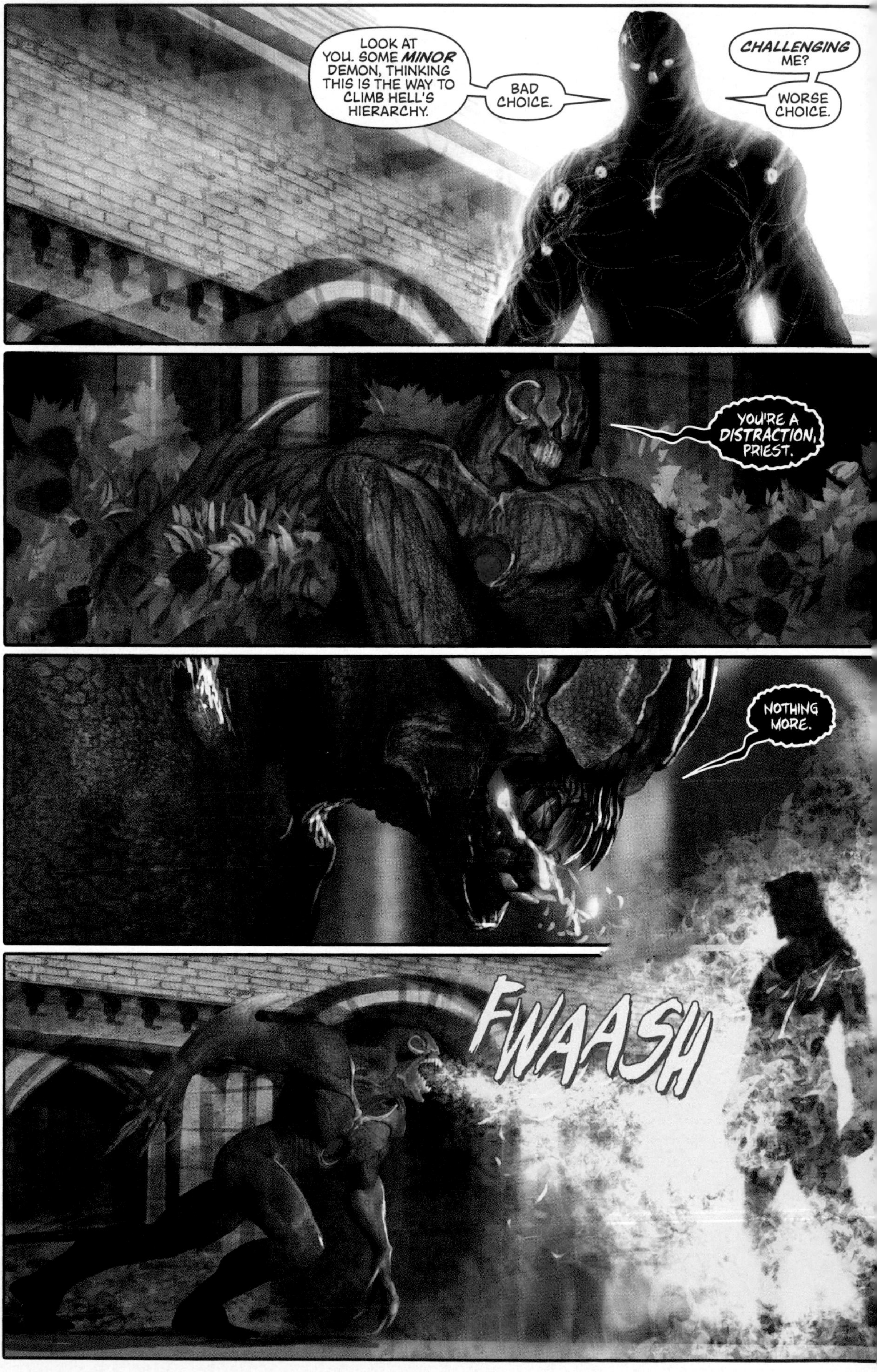
LOOK AT YOU. SOME *MINOR* DEMON, THINKING THIS IS THE WAY TO CLIMB HELL'S HIERARCHY.
BAD CHOICE.
CHALLENGING ME?
WORSE CHOICE.
YOU'RE A *DISTRACTION*, PRIEST.
NOTHING MORE.
FWAASH

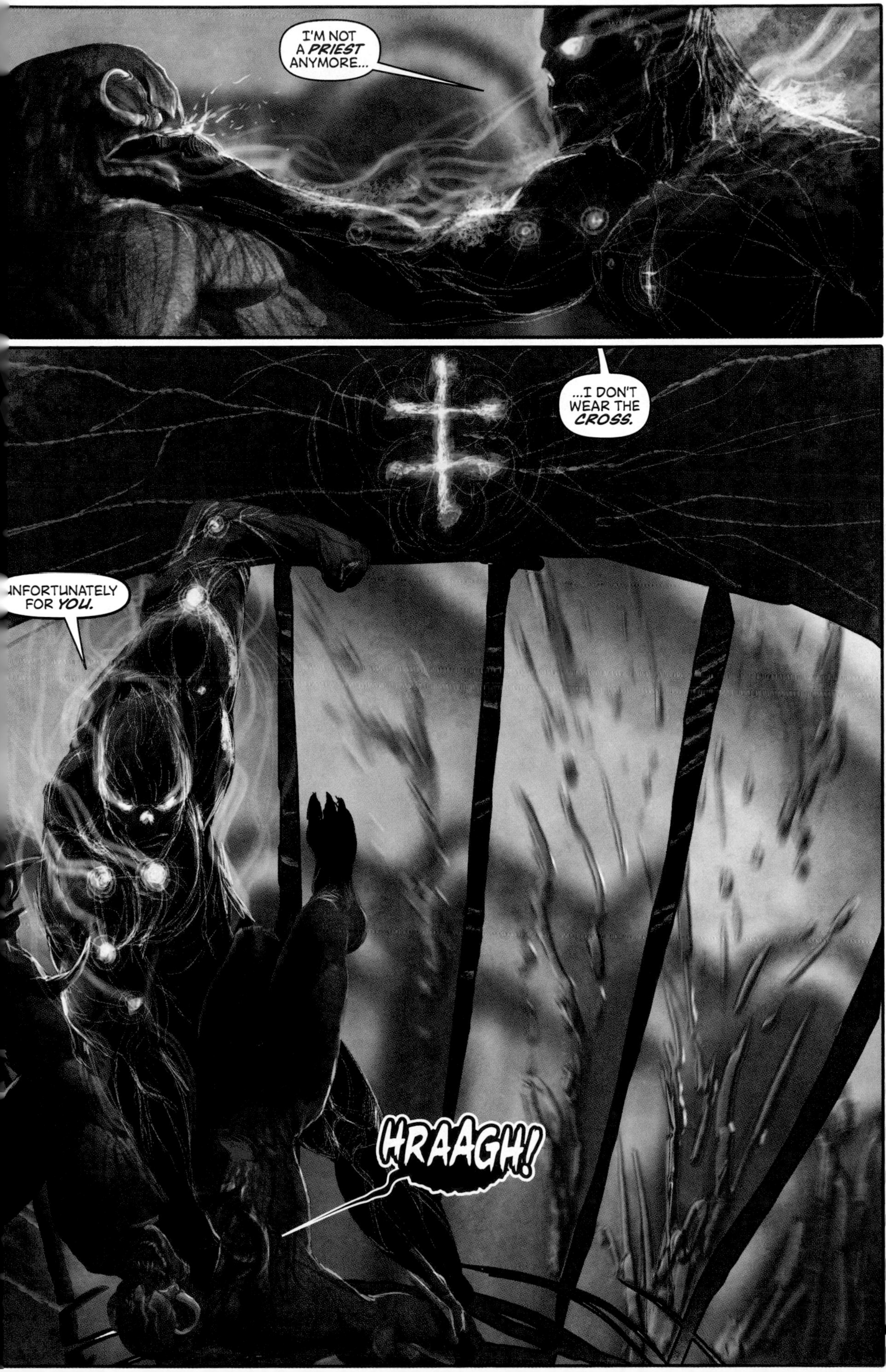
I'M NOT A PRIEST ANYMORE...
...I DON'T WEAR THE CROSS.
UNFORTUNATELY FOR YOU.
HRAAGH!

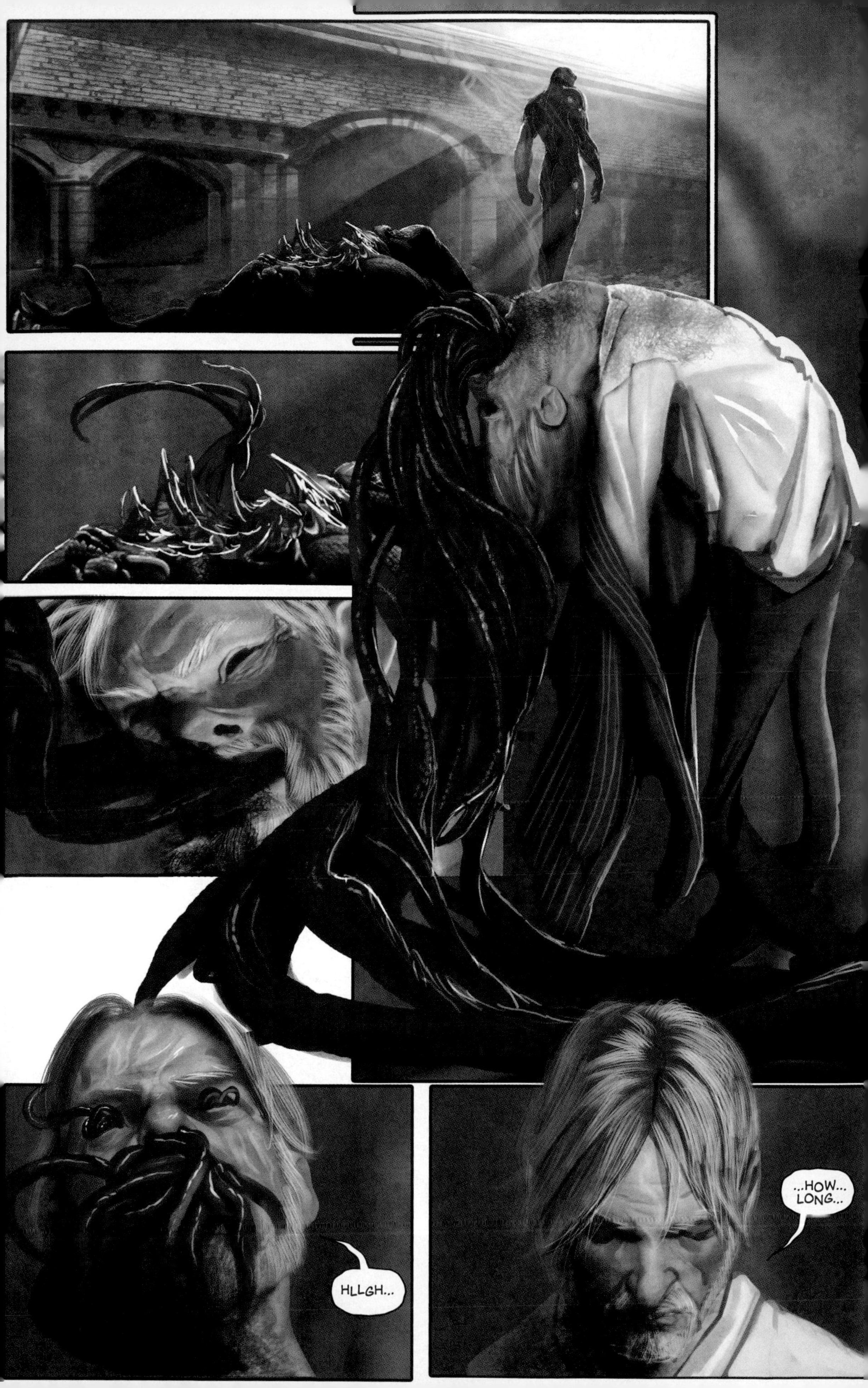
HLLGH...
...HOW... LONG...

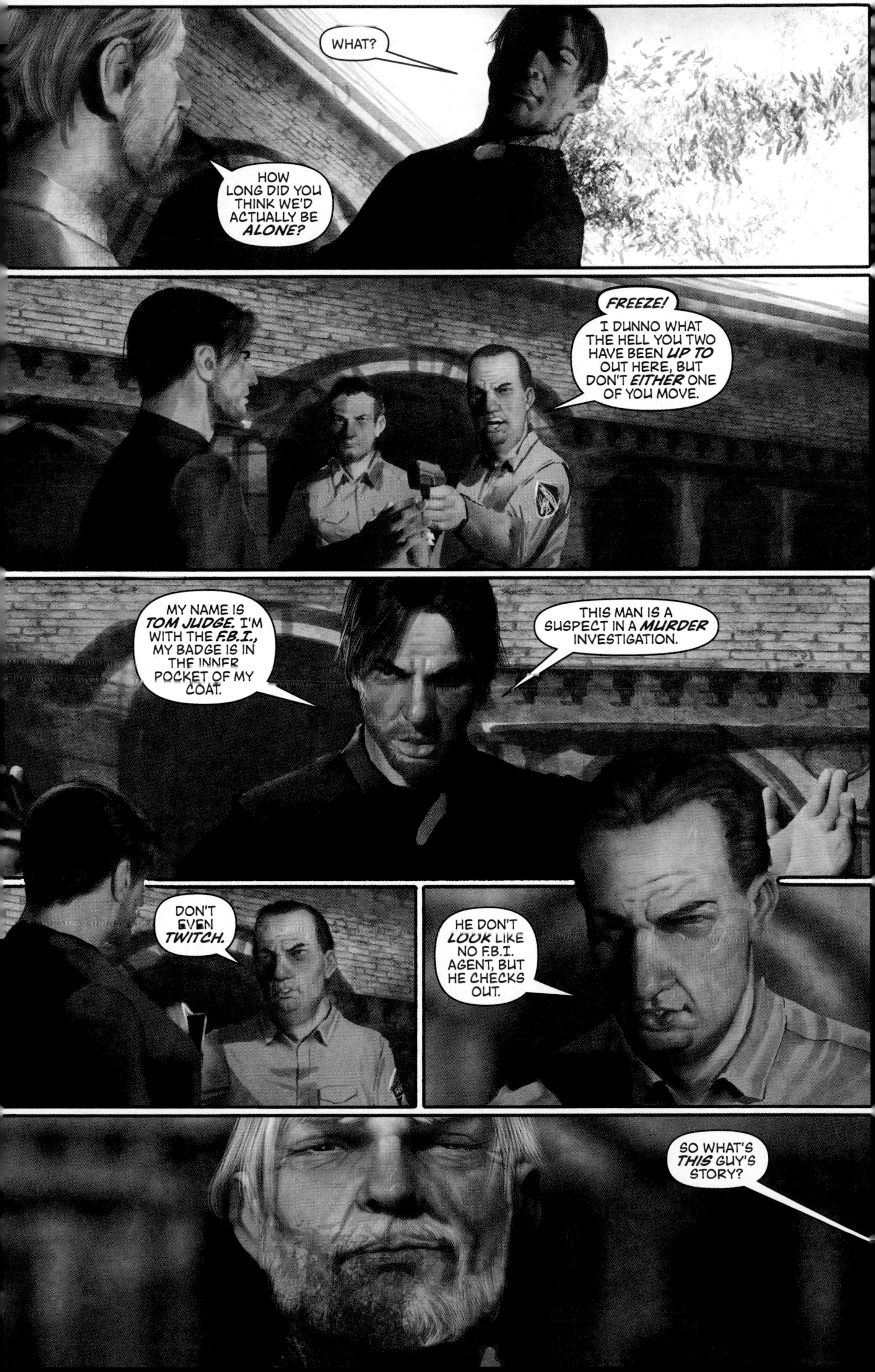
WHAT?
HOW LONG DID YOU THINK WE'D ACTUALLY BE ALONE?
FREEZE!
I DUNNO WHAT THE HELL YOU TWO HAVE BEEN UP TO OUT HERE, BUT DON'T EITHER ONE OF YOU MOVE.
MY NAME IS TOM JUDGE. I'M WITH THE F.B.I., MY BADGE IS IN THE INNER POCKET OF MY COAT.
THIS MAN IS A SUSPECT IN A MURDER INVESTIGATION.
DON'T EVEN TWITCH.
HE DON'T LOOK LIKE NO F.B.I. AGENT, BUT HE CHECKS OUT.
SO WHAT'S THIS GUY'S STORY?

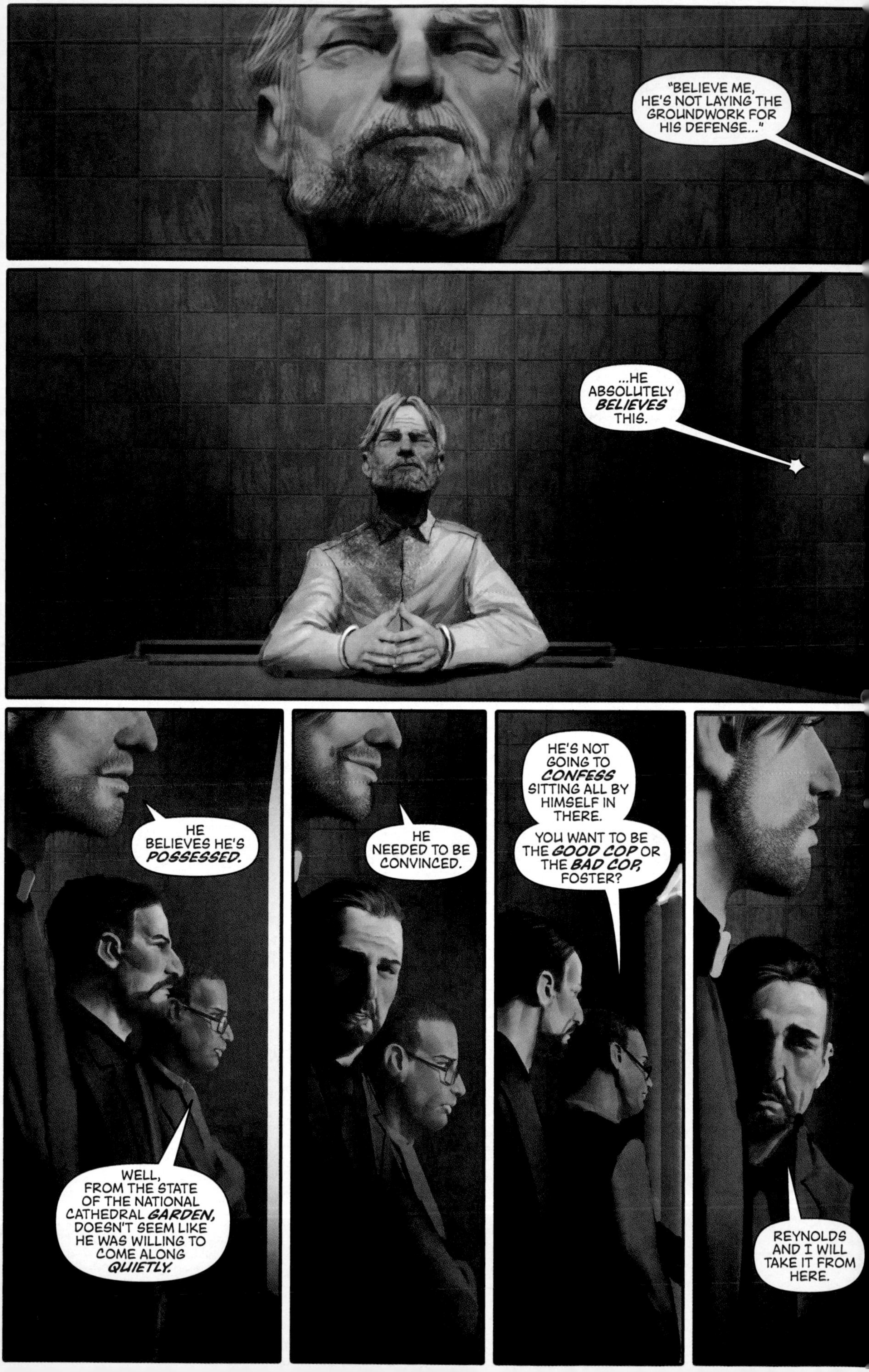
"BELIEVE ME, HE'S NOT LAYING THE GROUNDWORK FOR HIS DEFENSE..."
...HE ABSOLUTELY *BELIEVES* THIS.
HE BELIEVES HE'S *POSSESSED.*
WELL, FROM THE STATE OF THE NATIONAL CATHEDRAL *GARDEN,* DOESN'T SEEM LIKE HE WAS WILLING TO COME ALONG *QUIETLY.*
HE NEEDED TO BE CONVINCED.
HE'S NOT GOING TO *CONFESS* SITTING ALL BY HIMSELF IN THERE.
YOU WANT TO BE THE *GOOD COP* OR THE *BAD COP,* FOSTER?
REYNOLDS AND I WILL TAKE IT FROM HERE.

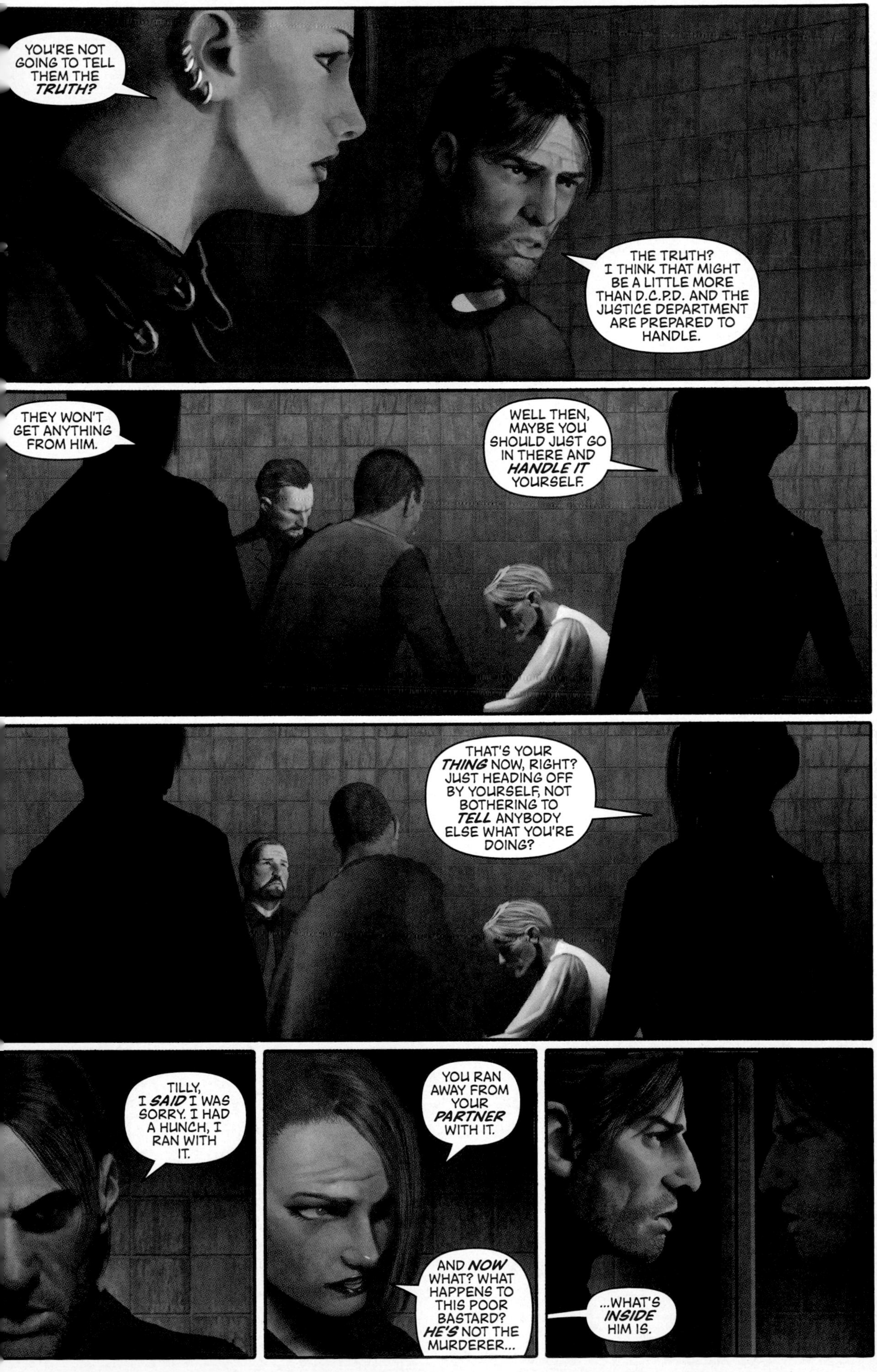
YOU'RE NOT GOING TO TELL THEM THE TRUTH?
THE TRUTH? I THINK THAT MIGHT BE A LITTLE MORE THAN D.C.P.D. AND THE JUSTICE DEPARTMENT ARE PREPARED TO HANDLE.
THEY WON'T GET ANYTHING FROM HIM.
WELL THEN, MAYBE YOU SHOULD JUST GO IN THERE AND HANDLE IT YOURSELF.
THAT'S YOUR THING NOW, RIGHT? JUST HEADING OFF BY YOURSELF, NOT BOTHERING TO TELL ANYBODY ELSE WHAT YOU'RE DOING?
TILLY, I SAID I WAS SORRY. I HAD A HUNCH, I RAN WITH IT.
YOU RAN AWAY FROM YOUR PARTNER WITH IT.
AND NOW WHAT? WHAT HAPPENS TO THIS POOR BASTARD? HE'S NOT THE MURDERER...
...WHAT'S INSIDE HIM IS.

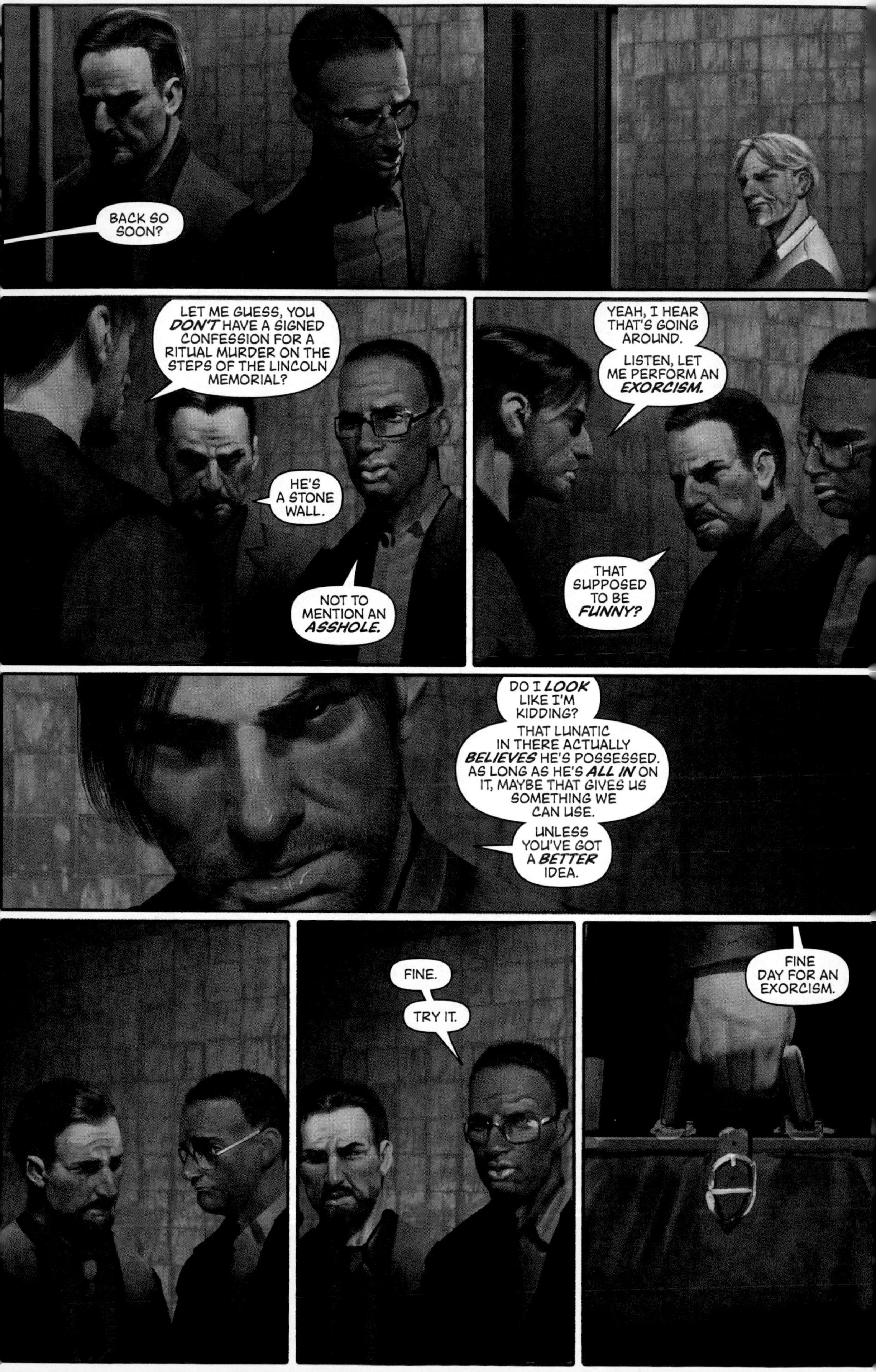
BACK SO SOON?
LET ME GUESS, YOU DON'T HAVE A SIGNED CONFESSION FOR A RITUAL MURDER ON THE STEPS OF THE LINCOLN MEMORIAL?
HE'S A STONE WALL.
NOT TO MENTION AN ASSHOLE.
YEAH, I HEAR THAT'S GOING AROUND.
LISTEN, LET ME PERFORM AN EXORCISM.
THAT SUPPOSED TO BE FUNNY?
DO I LOOK LIKE I'M KIDDING?
THAT LUNATIC IN THERE ACTUALLY BELIEVES HE'S POSSESSED. AS LONG AS HE'S ALL IN ON IT, MAYBE THAT GIVES US SOMETHING WE CAN USE.
UNLESS YOU'VE GOT A BETTER IDEA.
FINE.
TRY IT.
FINE DAY FOR AN EXORCISM.

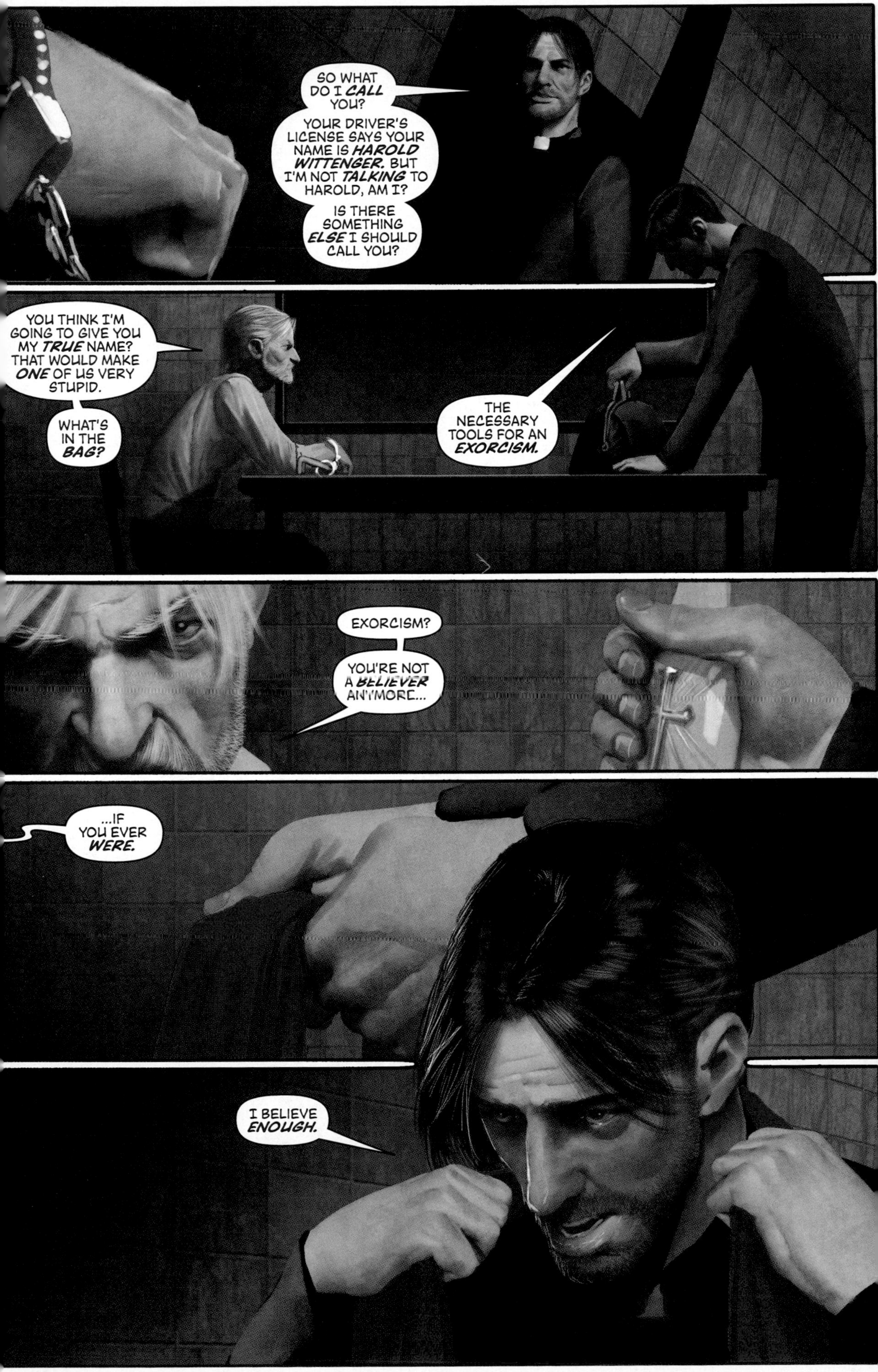
SO WHAT DO I CALL YOU?
YOUR DRIVER'S LICENSE SAYS YOUR NAME IS HAROLD WITTENGER. BUT I'M NOT TALKING TO HAROLD, AM I?
IS THERE SOMETHING ELSE I SHOULD CALL YOU?
YOU THINK I'M GOING TO GIVE YOU MY TRUE NAME? THAT WOULD MAKE ONE OF US VERY STUPID.
WHAT'S IN THE BAG?
THE NECESSARY TOOLS FOR AN EXORCISM.
EXORCISM?
YOU'RE NOT A BELIEVER ANYMORE...
...IF YOU EVER WERE.
I BELIEVE ENOUGH.

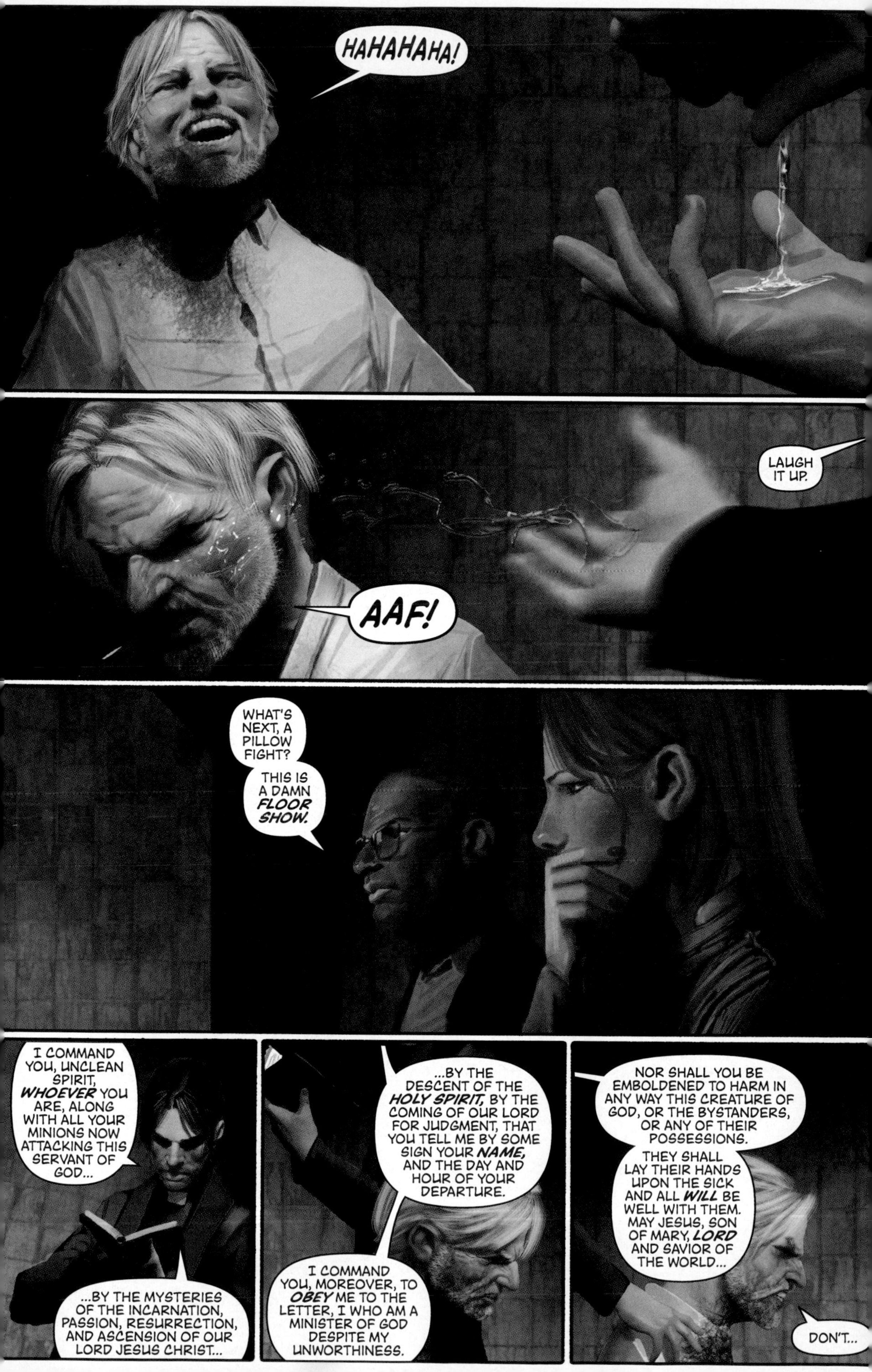
HAHAHAHA!
LAUGH IT UP.
AAF!
WHAT'S NEXT, A PILLOW FIGHT?
THIS IS A DAMN *FLOOR SHOW.*
I COMMAND YOU, UNCLEAN SPIRIT, *WHOEVER* YOU ARE, ALONG WITH ALL YOUR MINIONS NOW ATTACKING THIS SERVANT OF GOD...
...BY THE MYSTERIES OF THE INCARNATION, PASSION, RESURRECTION, AND ASCENSION OF OUR LORD JESUS CHRIST...
...BY THE DESCENT OF THE *HOLY SPIRIT,* BY THE COMING OF OUR LORD FOR JUDGMENT, THAT YOU TELL ME BY SOME SIGN YOUR *NAME,* AND THE DAY AND HOUR OF YOUR DEPARTURE.
I COMMAND YOU, MOREOVER, TO *OBEY* ME TO THE LETTER, I WHO AM A MINISTER OF GOD DESPITE MY UNWORTHINESS.
NOR SHALL YOU BE EMBOLDENED TO HARM IN ANY WAY THIS CREATURE OF GOD, OR THE BYSTANDERS, OR ANY OF THEIR POSSESSIONS.
THEY SHALL LAY THEIR HANDS UPON THE SICK AND ALL *WILL* BE WELL WITH THEM. MAY JESUS, SON OF MARY, *LORD* AND SAVIOR OF THE WORLD...
DON'T...

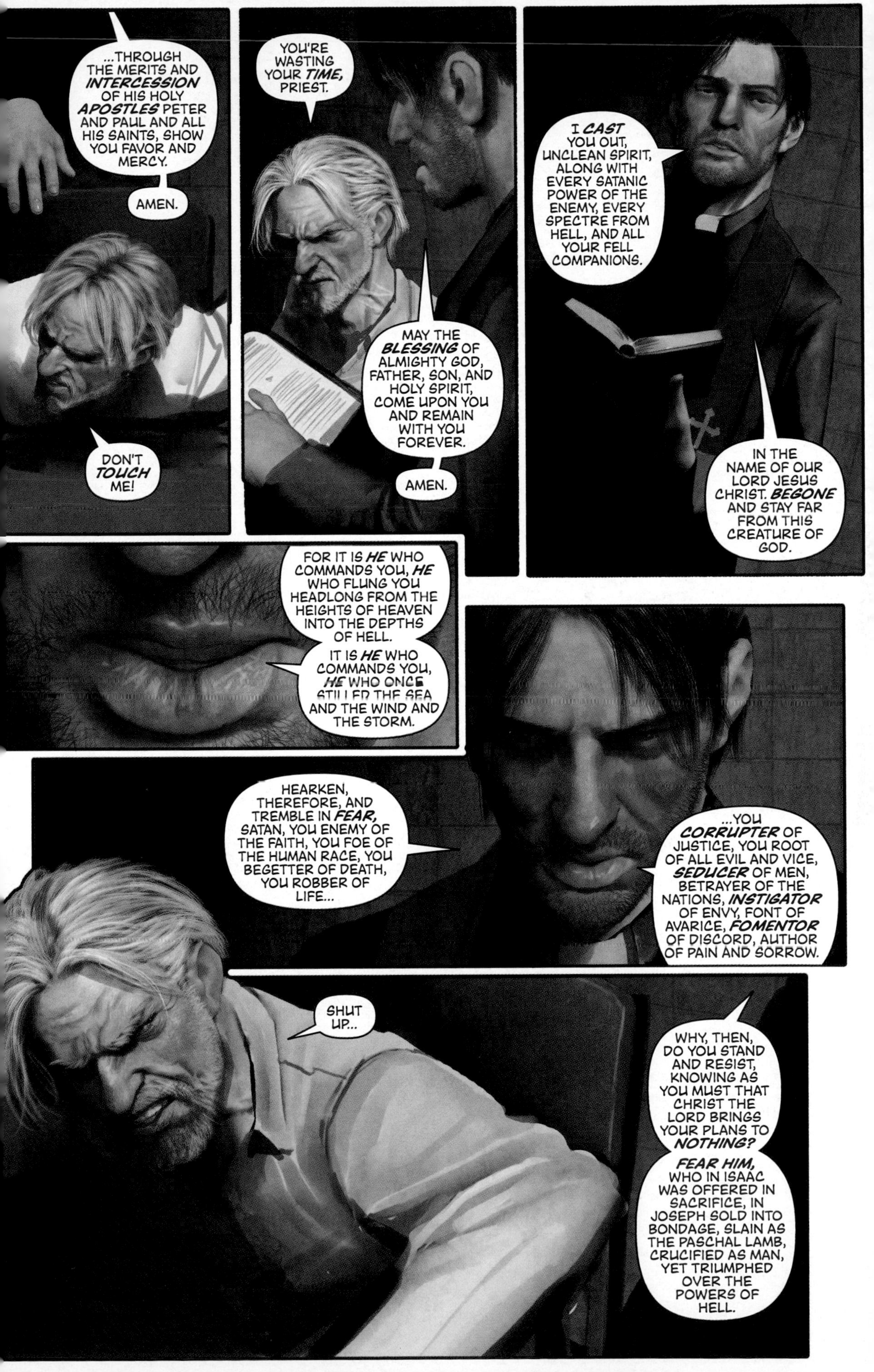
...THROUGH THE MERITS AND INTERCESSION OF HIS HOLY APOSTLES PETER AND PAUL AND ALL HIS SAINTS, SHOW YOU FAVOR AND MERCY.
AMEN.
DON'T TOUCH ME!
YOU'RE WASTING YOUR TIME, PRIEST.
MAY THE BLESSING OF ALMIGHTY GOD, FATHER, SON, AND HOLY SPIRIT, COME UPON YOU AND REMAIN WITH YOU FOREVER.
AMEN.
I CAST YOU OUT, UNCLEAN SPIRIT, ALONG WITH EVERY SATANIC POWER OF THE ENEMY, EVERY SPECTRE FROM HELL, AND ALL YOUR FELL COMPANIONS.
IN THE NAME OF OUR LORD JESUS CHRIST. BEGONE AND STAY FAR FROM THIS CREATURE OF GOD.
FOR IT IS HE WHO COMMANDS YOU, HE WHO FLUNG YOU HEADLONG FROM THE HEIGHTS OF HEAVEN INTO THE DEPTHS OF HELL.
IT IS HE WHO COMMANDS YOU, HE WHO ONCE STILLED THE SEA AND THE WIND AND THE STORM.
HEARKEN, THEREFORE, AND TREMBLE IN FEAR, SATAN, YOU ENEMY OF THE FAITH, YOU FOE OF THE HUMAN RACE, YOU BEGETTER OF DEATH, YOU ROBBER OF LIFE...
...YOU CORRUPTER OF JUSTICE, YOU ROOT OF ALL EVIL AND VICE, SEDUCER OF MEN, BETRAYER OF THE NATIONS, INSTIGATOR OF ENVY, FONT OF AVARICE, FOMENTOR OF DISCORD, AUTHOR OF PAIN AND SORROW.
SHUT UP...
WHY, THEN, DO YOU STAND AND RESIST, KNOWING AS YOU MUST THAT CHRIST THE LORD BRINGS YOUR PLANS TO NOTHING?
FEAR HIM, WHO IN ISAAC WAS OFFERED IN SACRIFICE, IN JOSEPH SOLD INTO BONDAGE, SLAIN AS THE PASCHAL LAMB, CRUCIFIED AS MAN, YET TRIUMPHED OVER THE POWERS OF HELL.

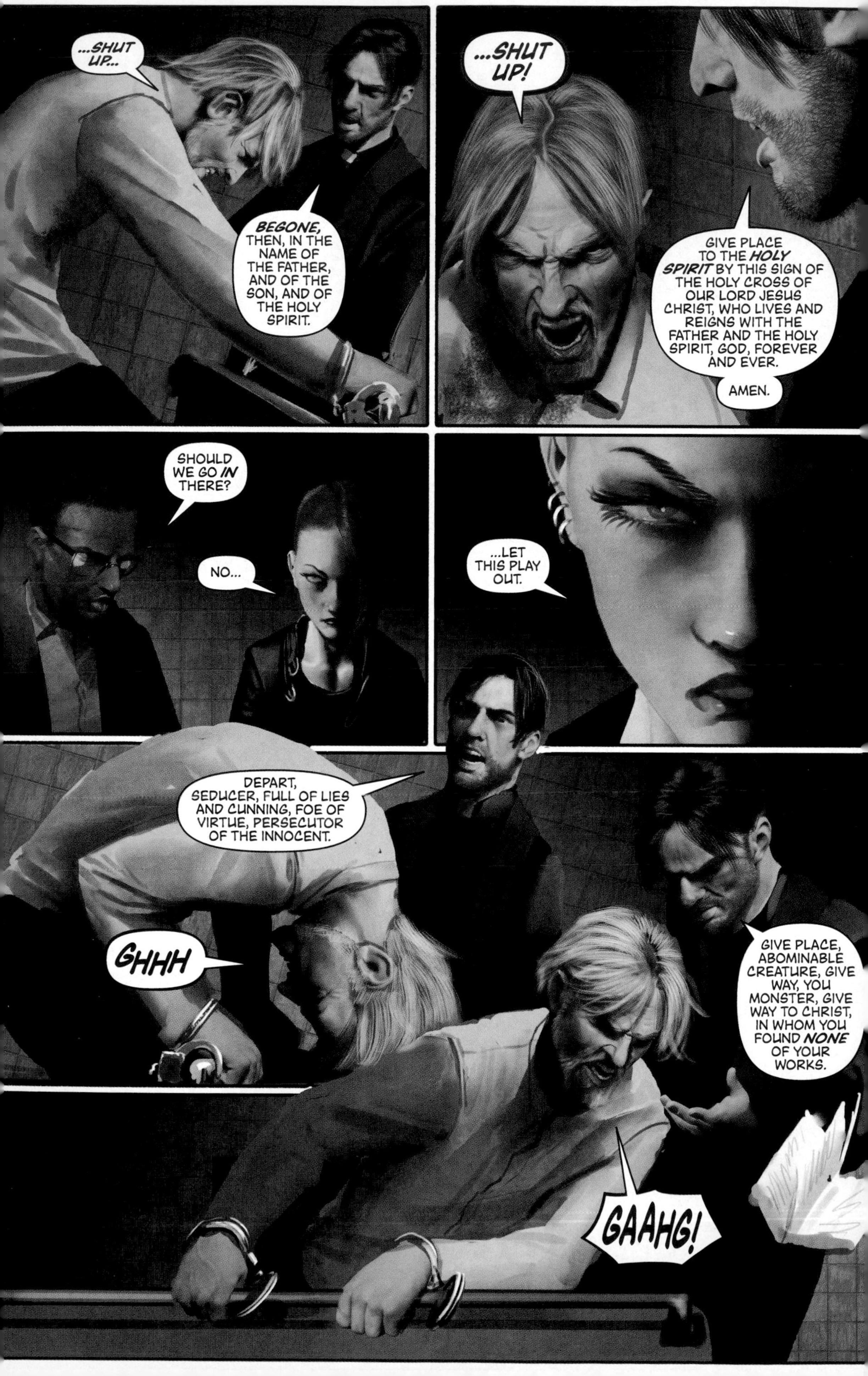
...SHUT UP...
BEGONE, THEN, IN THE NAME OF THE FATHER, AND OF THE SON, AND OF THE HOLY SPIRIT.
...SHUT UP!
GIVE PLACE TO THE HOLY SPIRIT BY THIS SIGN OF THE HOLY CROSS OF OUR LORD JESUS CHRIST, WHO LIVES AND REIGNS WITH THE FATHER AND THE HOLY SPIRIT, GOD, FOREVER AND EVER.
AMEN.
SHOULD WE GO IN THERE?
NO...
...LET THIS PLAY OUT.
DEPART, SEDUCER, FULL OF LIES AND CUNNING, FOE OF VIRTUE, PERSECUTOR OF THE INNOCENT.
GHHH
GIVE PLACE, ABOMINABLE CREATURE, GIVE WAY, YOU MONSTER, GIVE WAY TO CHRIST, IN WHOM YOU FOUND NONE OF YOUR WORKS.
GAAHG!

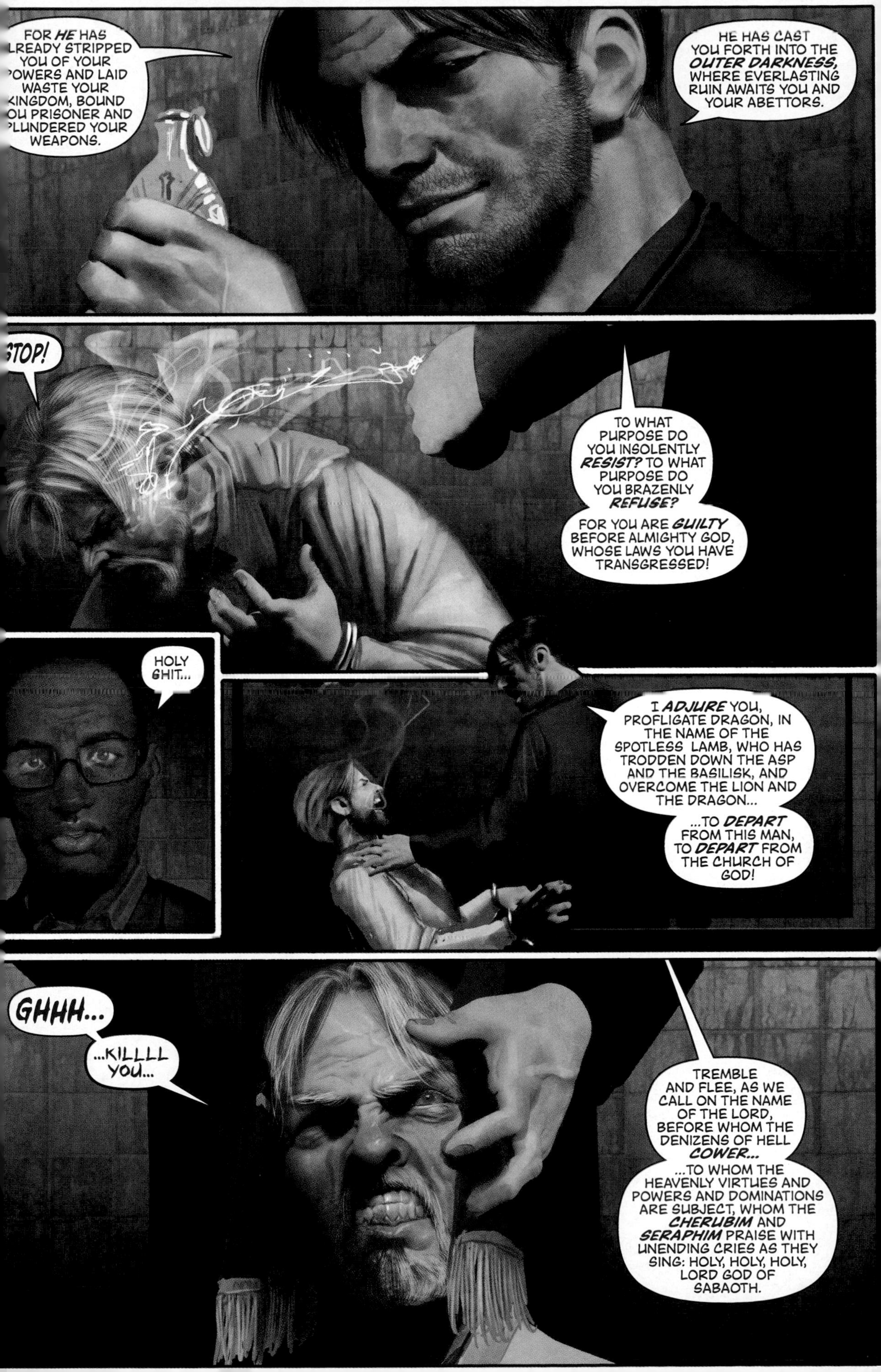
FOR HE HAS ALREADY STRIPPED YOU OF YOUR POWERS AND LAID WASTE YOUR KINGDOM, BOUND YOU PRISONER AND PLUNDERED YOUR WEAPONS.
HE HAS CAST YOU FORTH INTO THE OUTER DARKNESS, WHERE EVERLASTING RUIN AWAITS YOU AND YOUR ABETTORS.
STOP!
TO WHAT PURPOSE DO YOU INSOLENTLY RESIST? TO WHAT PURPOSE DO YOU BRAZENLY REFUSE?
FOR YOU ARE GUILTY BEFORE ALMIGHTY GOD, WHOSE LAWS YOU HAVE TRANSGRESSED!
HOLY SHIT...
I ADJURE YOU, PROFLIGATE DRAGON, IN THE NAME OF THE SPOTLESS LAMB, WHO HAS TRODDEN DOWN THE ASP AND THE BASILISK, AND OVERCOME THE LION AND THE DRAGON...
...TO DEPART FROM THIS MAN, TO DEPART FROM THE CHURCH OF GOD!
GHHH...
...KILLLL YOU...
TREMBLE AND FLEE, AS WE CALL ON THE NAME OF THE LORD, BEFORE WHOM THE DENIZENS OF HELL COWER...
...TO WHOM THE HEAVENLY VIRTUES AND POWERS AND DOMINATIONS ARE SUBJECT, WHOM THE CHERUBIM AND SERAPHIM PRAISE WITH UNENDING CRIES AS THEY SING: HOLY, HOLY, HOLY, LORD GOD OF SABAOTH.

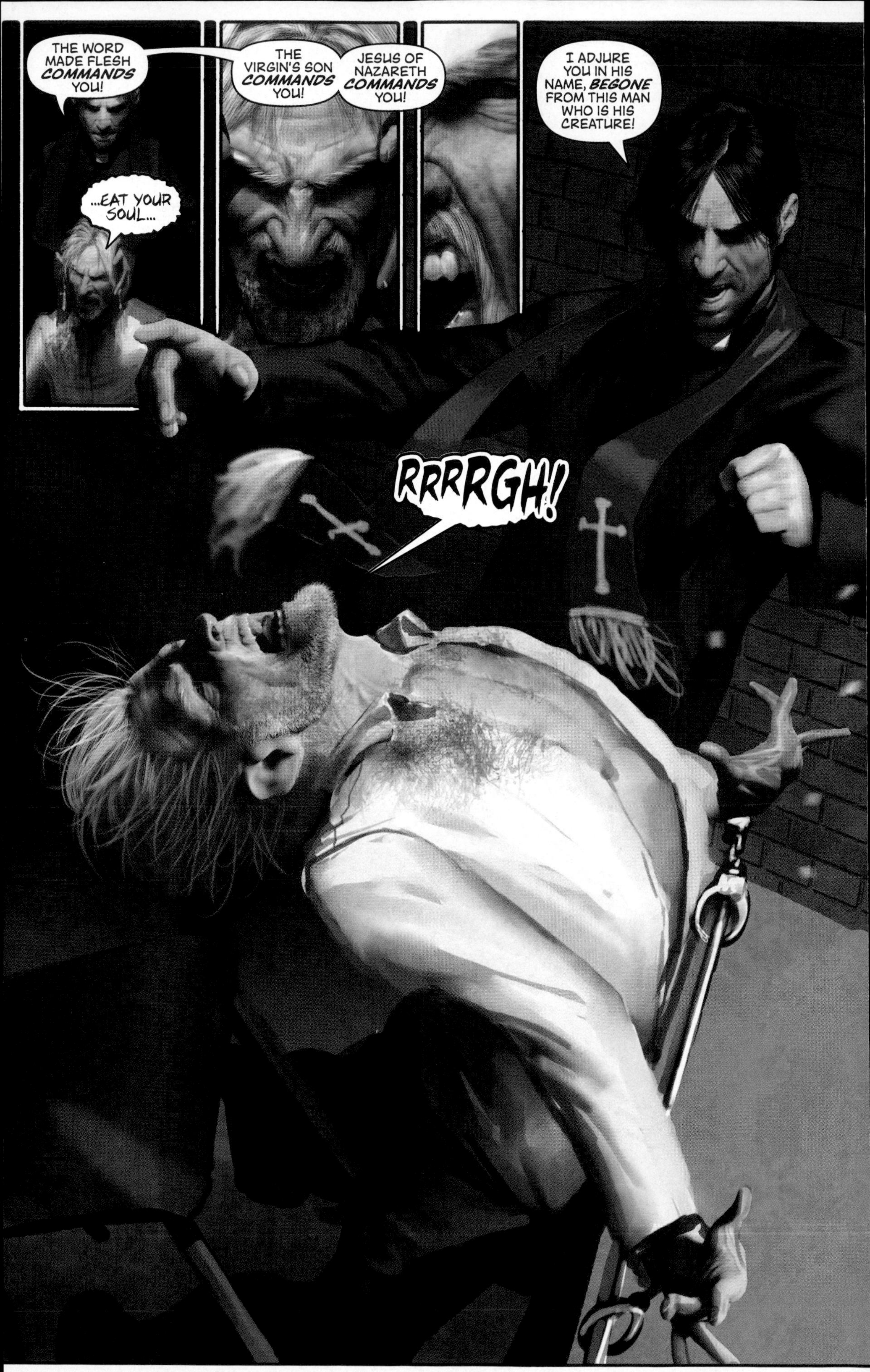
THE WORD MADE FLESH COMMANDS YOU!
...EAT YOUR SOUL...
THE VIRGIN'S SON COMMANDS YOU!
JESUS OF NAZARETH COMMANDS YOU!
I ADJURE YOU IN HIS NAME, BEGONE FROM THIS MAN WHO IS HIS CREATURE!
RRRRGH!

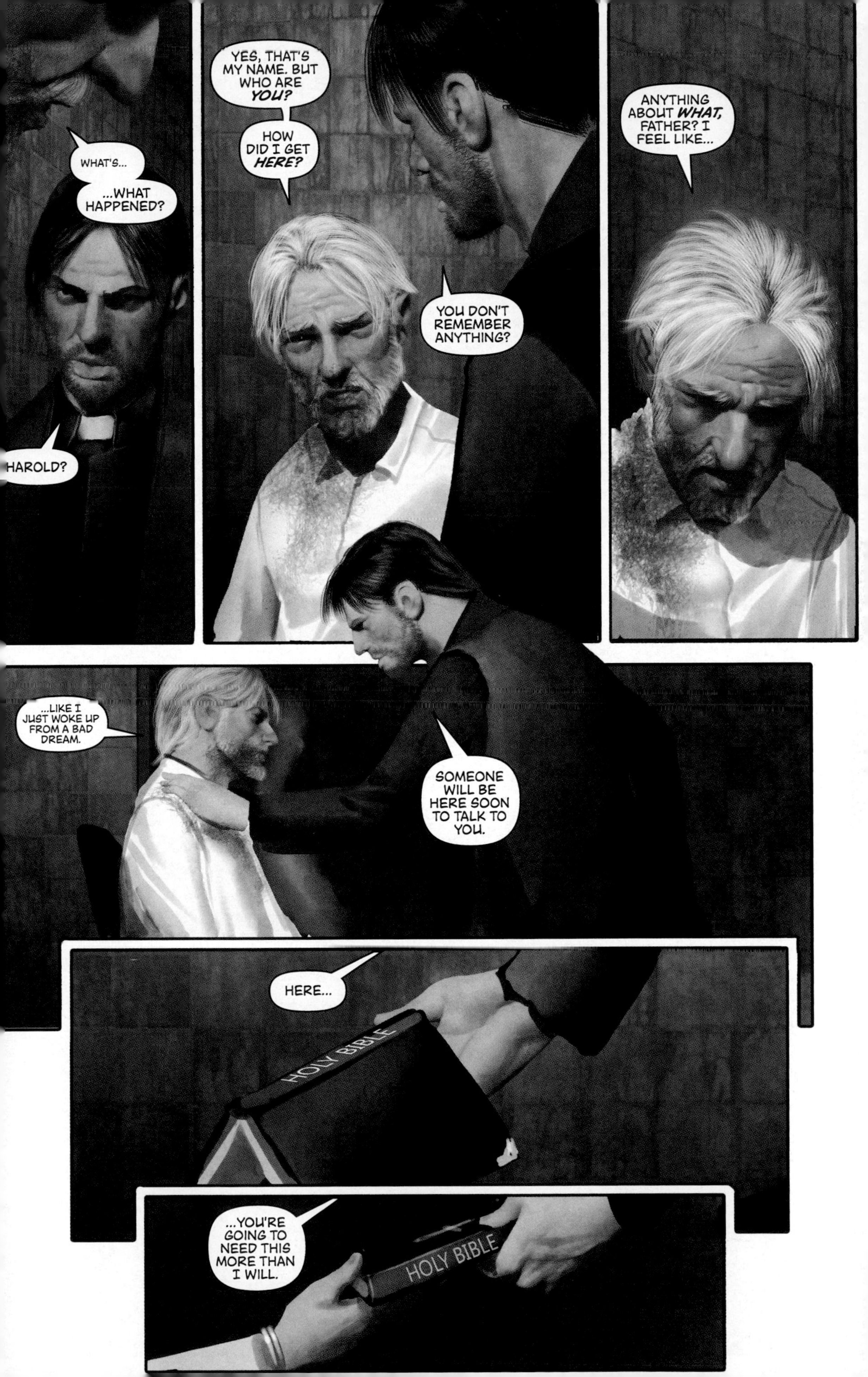

WHAT'S...
...WHAT HAPPENED?
HAROLD?
YES, THAT'S MY NAME. BUT WHO ARE *YOU?*
HOW DID I GET *HERE?*
YOU DON'T REMEMBER ANYTHING?
ANYTHING ABOUT *WHAT,* FATHER? I FEEL LIKE...
...LIKE I JUST WOKE UP FROM A BAD DREAM.
SOMEONE WILL BE HERE SOON TO TALK TO YOU.
HERE...
HOLY BIBLE
...YOU'RE GOING TO NEED THIS MORE THAN I WILL.
HOLY BIBLE

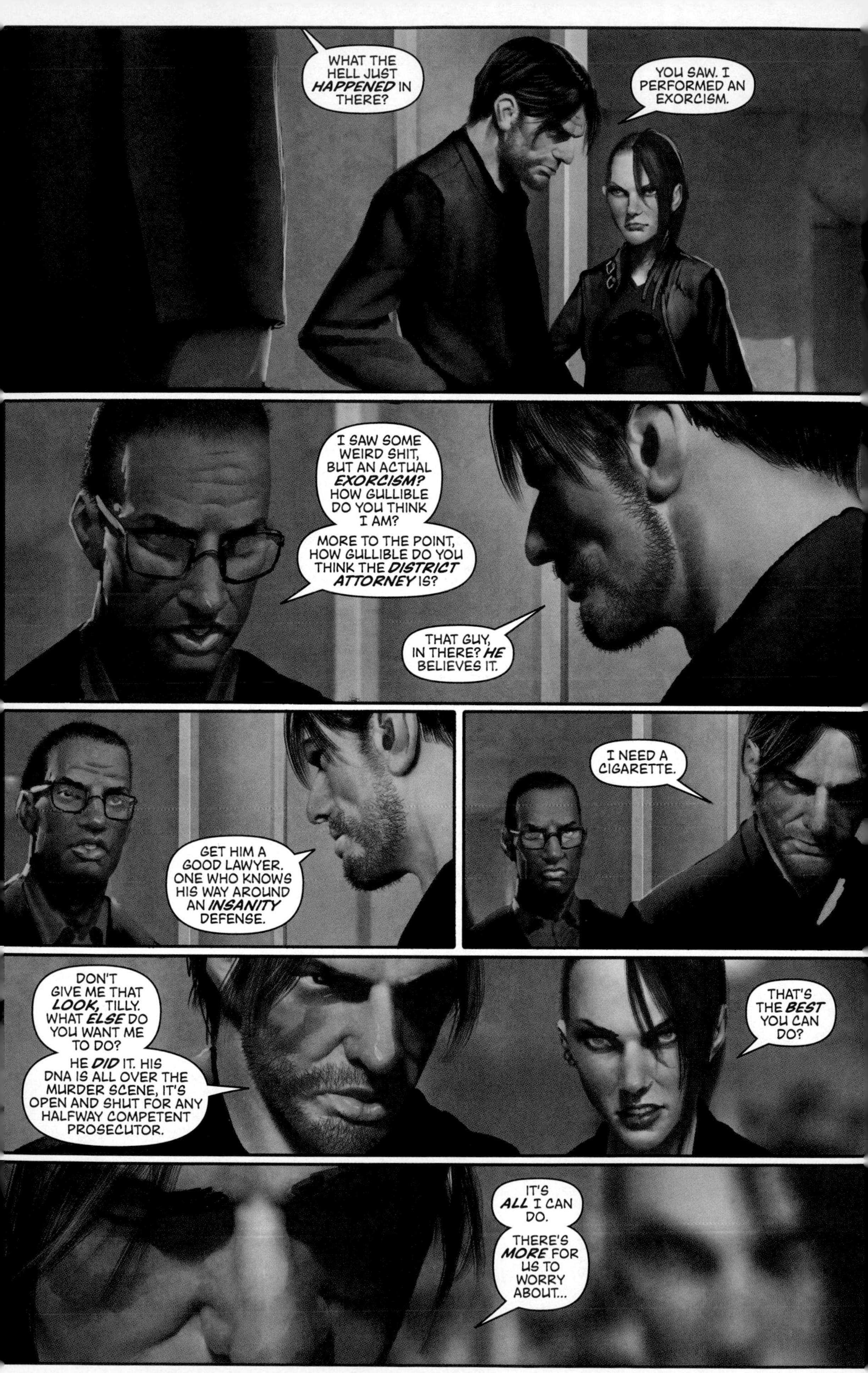
WHAT THE HELL JUST HAPPENED IN THERE?
YOU SAW. I PERFORMED AN EXORCISM.
I SAW SOME WEIRD SHIT, BUT AN ACTUAL EXORCISM? HOW GULLIBLE DO YOU THINK I AM?
MORE TO THE POINT, HOW GULLIBLE DO YOU THINK THE DISTRICT ATTORNEY IS?
THAT GUY, IN THERE? HE BELIEVES IT.
GET HIM A GOOD LAWYER. ONE WHO KNOWS HIS WAY AROUND AN INSANITY DEFENSE.
I NEED A CIGARETTE.
DON'T GIVE ME THAT LOOK, TILLY. WHAT ELSE DO YOU WANT ME TO DO?
HE DID IT. HIS DNA IS ALL OVER THE MURDER SCENE, IT'S OPEN AND SHUT FOR ANY HALFWAY COMPETENT PROSECUTOR.
THAT'S THE BEST YOU CAN DO?
IT'S ALL I CAN DO.
THERE'S MORE FOR US TO WORRY ABOUT...

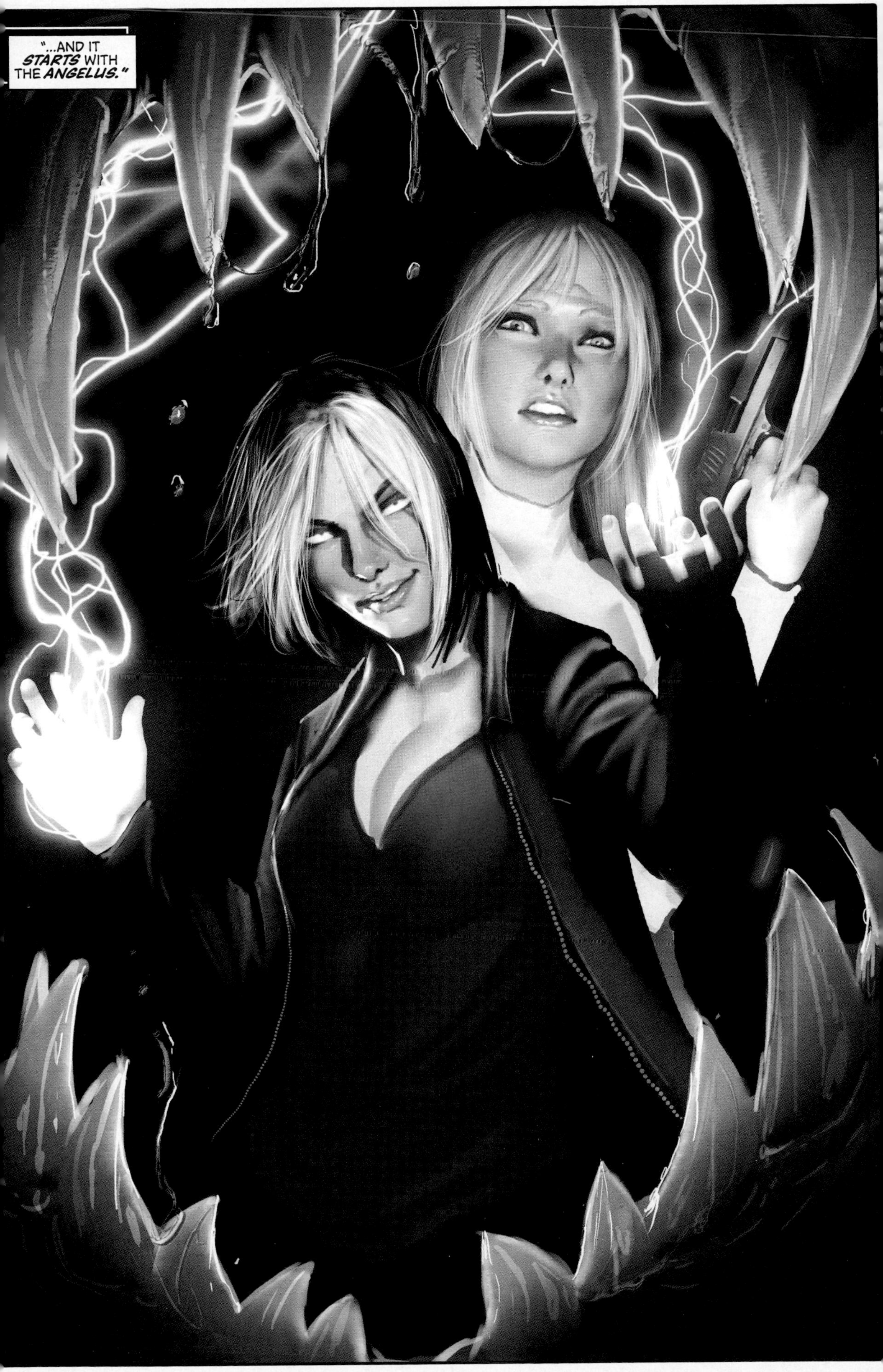
"...AND IT STARTS WITH THE ANGELUS."

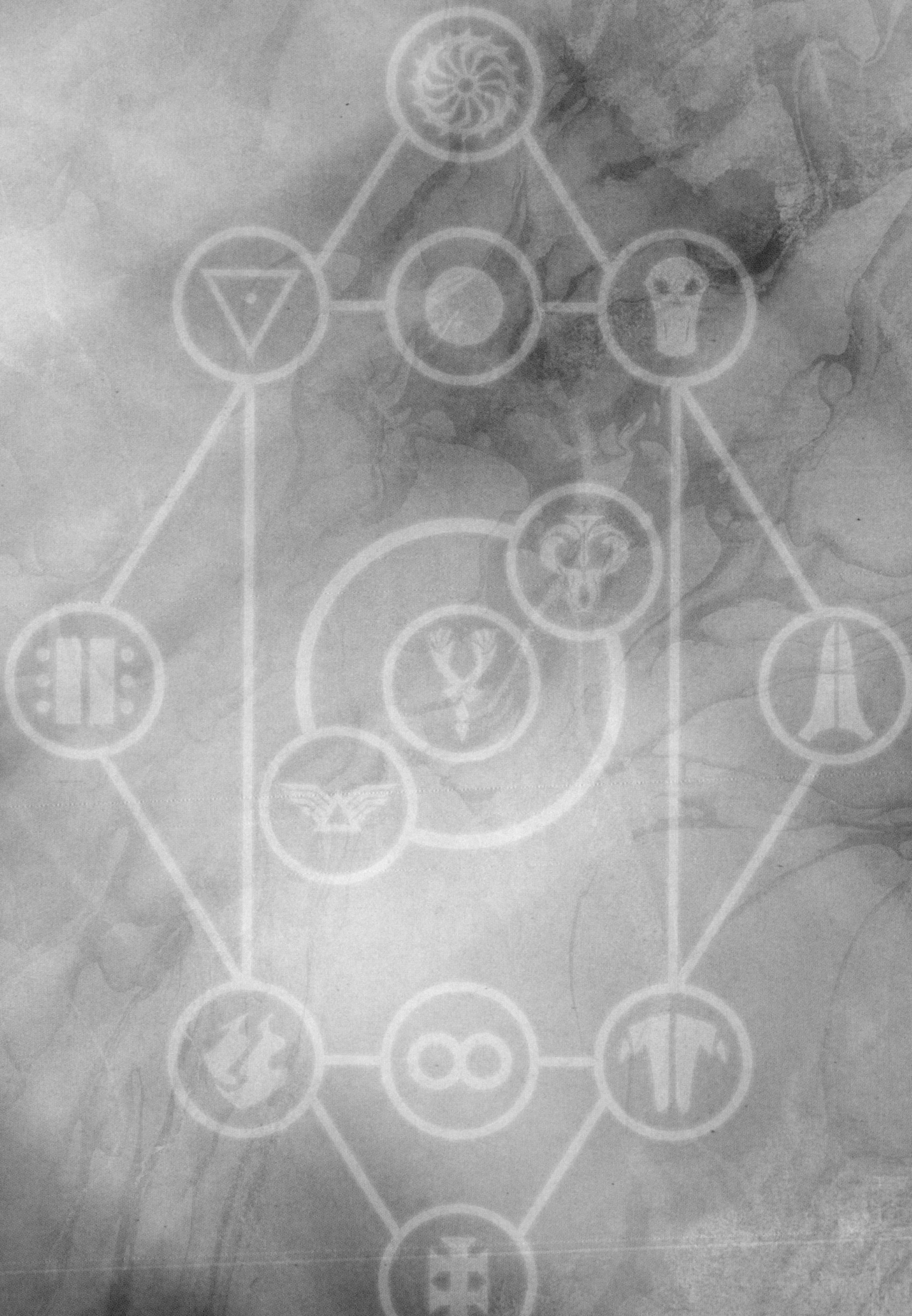

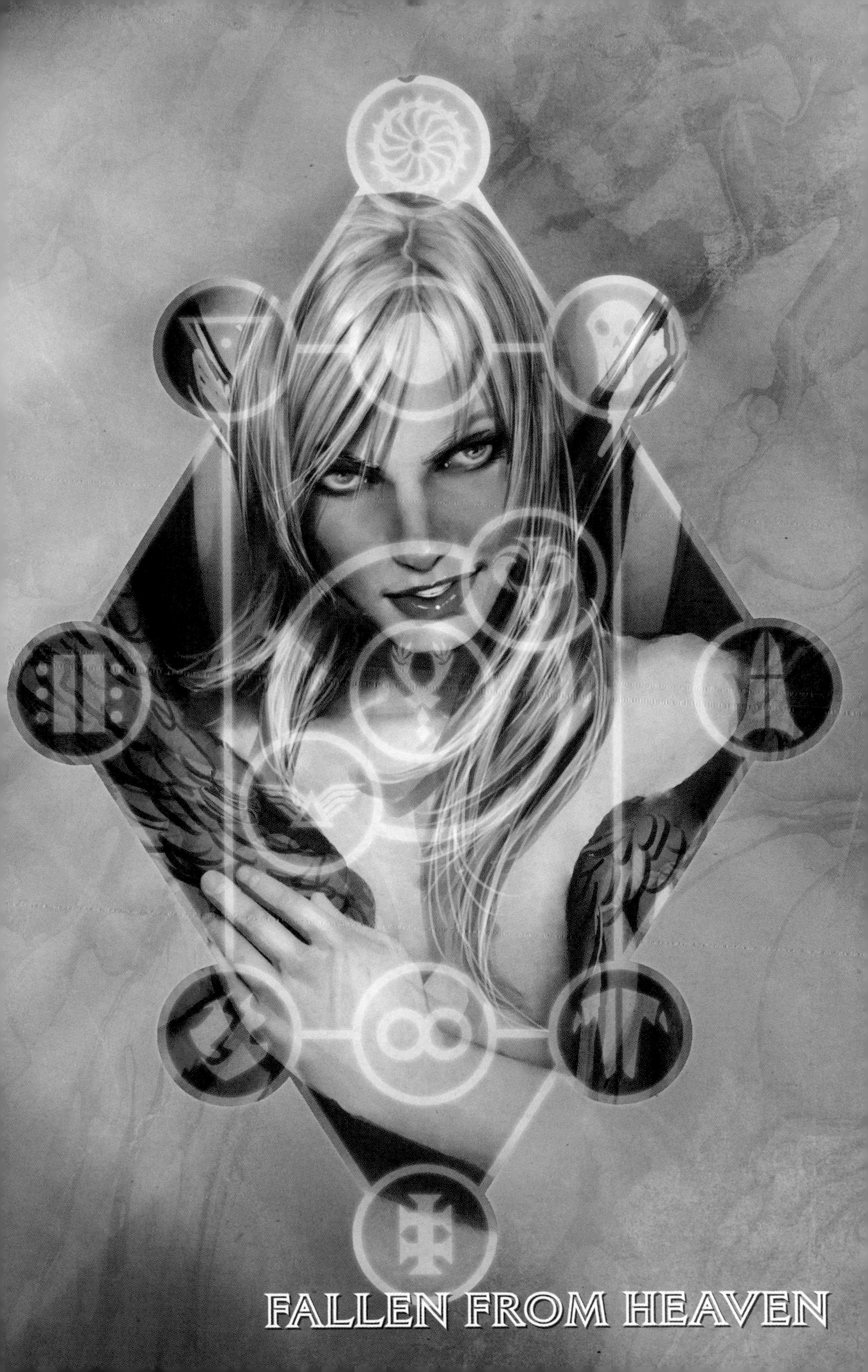
FALLEN FROM HEAVEN

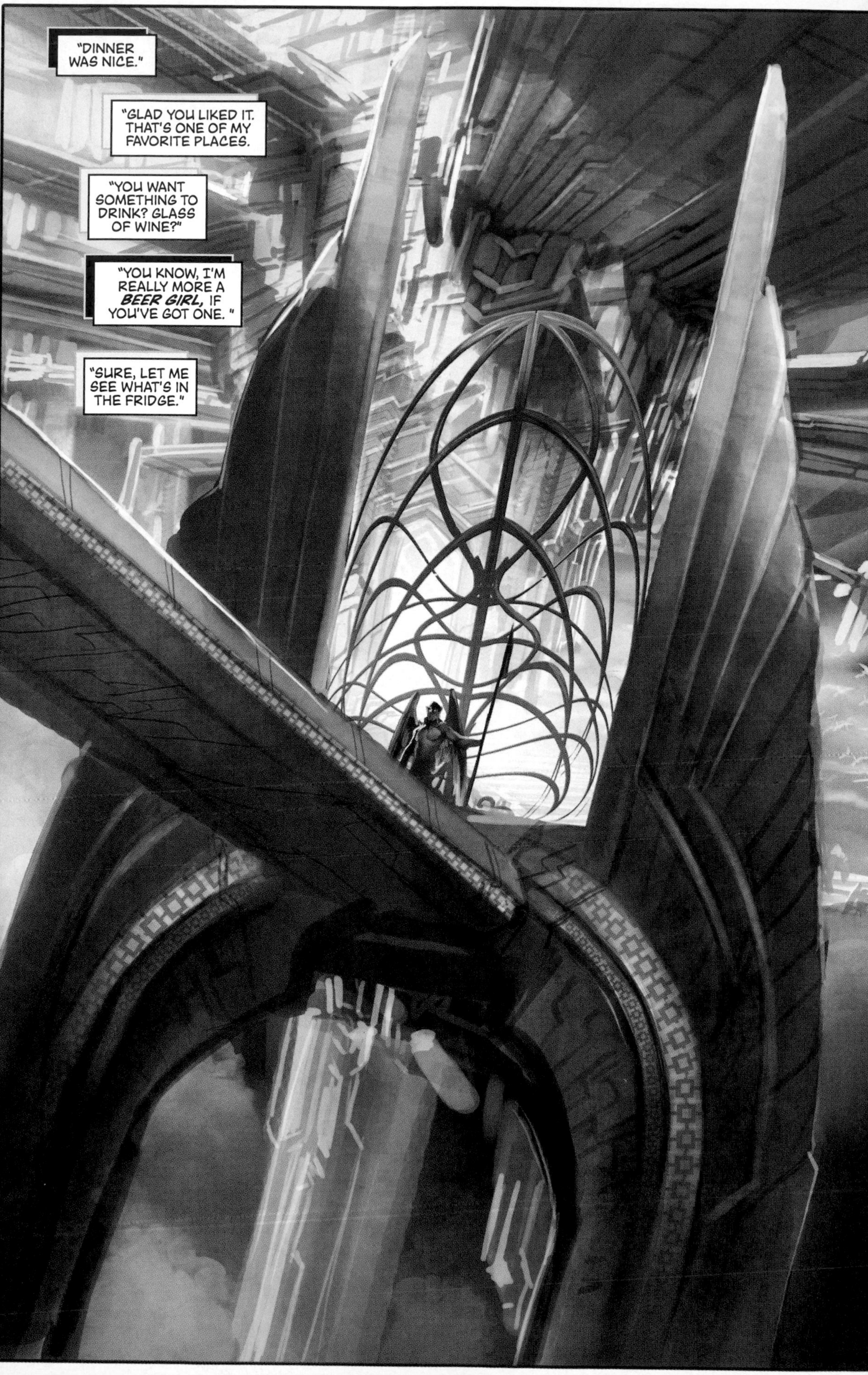
"DINNER WAS NICE."
"GLAD YOU LIKED IT. THAT'S ONE OF MY FAVORITE PLACES.
"YOU WANT SOMETHING TO DRINK? GLASS OF WINE?"
"YOU KNOW, I'M REALLY MORE A BEER GIRL, IF YOU'VE GOT ONE."
"SURE, LET ME SEE WHAT'S IN THE FRIDGE."

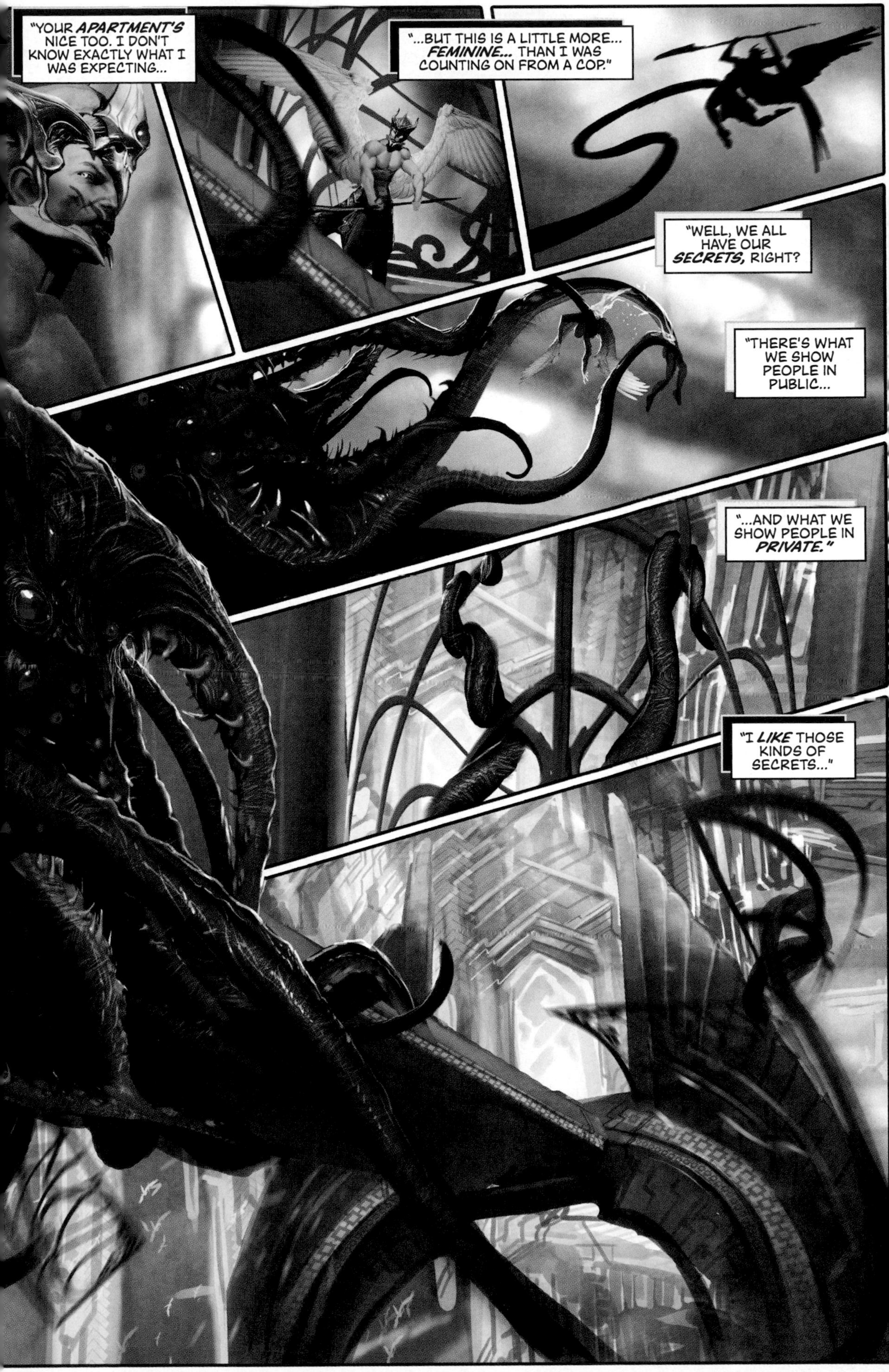
"YOUR APARTMENT'S NICE TOO. I DON'T KNOW EXACTLY WHAT I WAS EXPECTING...
"...BUT THIS IS A LITTLE MORE... FEMININE... THAN I WAS COUNTING ON FROM A COP."
"WELL, WE ALL HAVE OUR SECRETS, RIGHT?
"THERE'S WHAT WE SHOW PEOPLE IN PUBLIC...
"...AND WHAT WE SHOW PEOPLE IN PRIVATE."
"I LIKE THOSE KINDS OF SECRETS..."

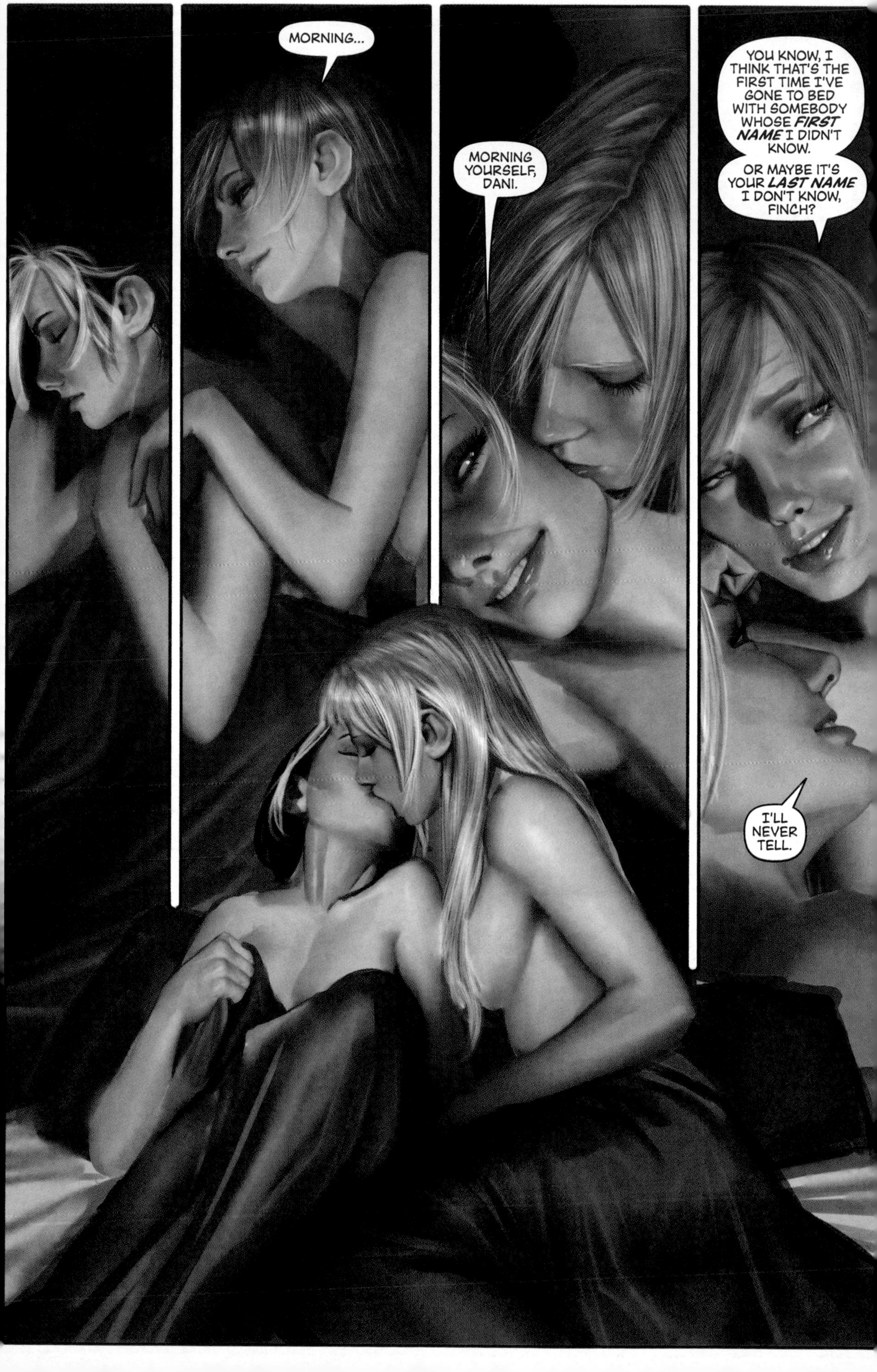
MORNING...
MORNING YOURSELF, DANI.
YOU KNOW, I THINK THAT'S THE FIRST TIME I'VE GONE TO BED WITH SOMEBODY WHOSE *FIRST NAME* I DIDN'T KNOW.
OR MAYBE IT'S YOUR *LAST NAME* I DON'T KNOW, FINCH?
I'LL NEVER TELL.

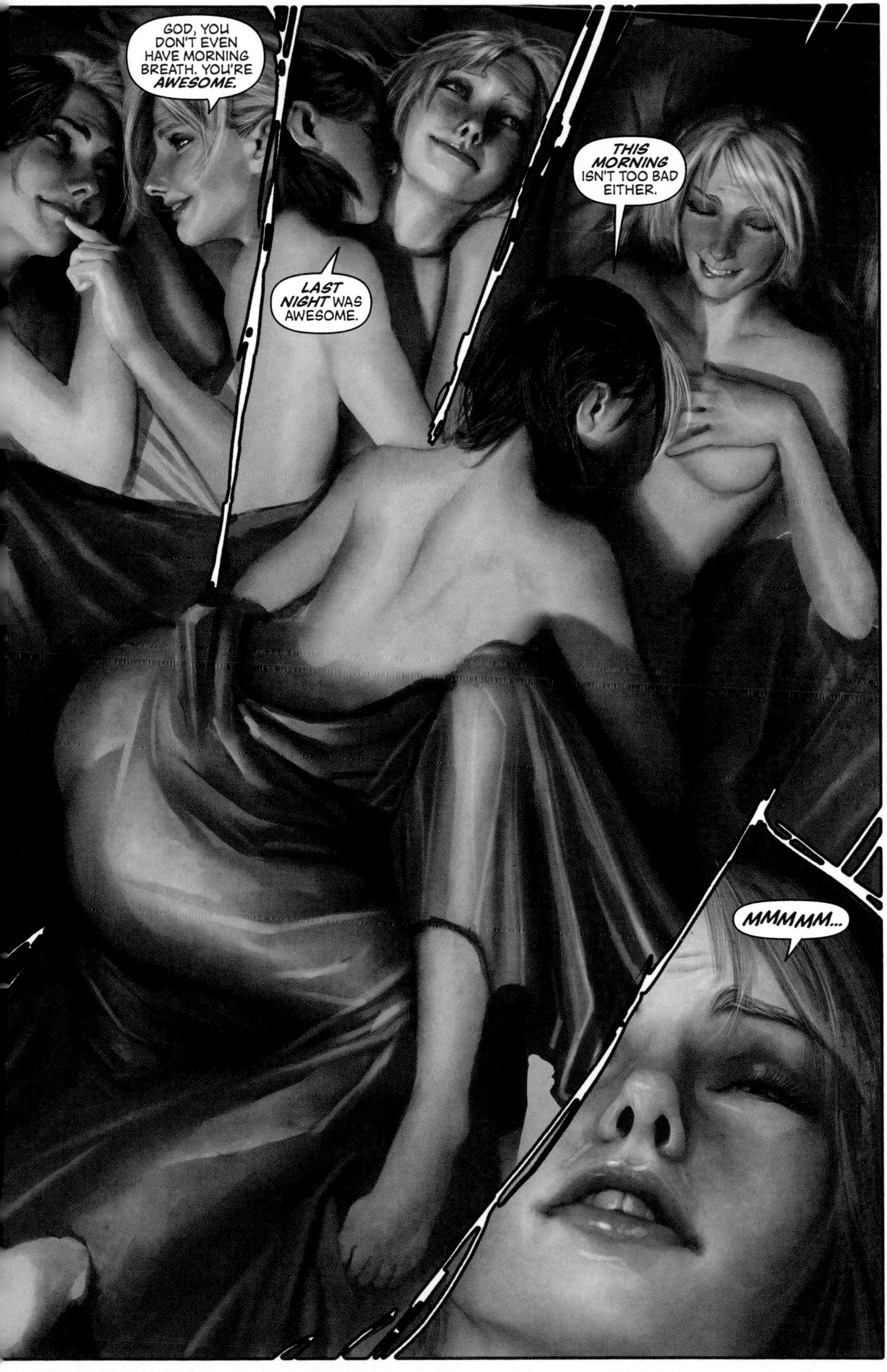

GOD, YOU DON'T EVEN HAVE MORNING BREATH. YOU'RE ***AWESOME.***
LAST NIGHT WAS AWESOME.
THIS MORNING ISN'T TOO BAD EITHER.
MMMMM...

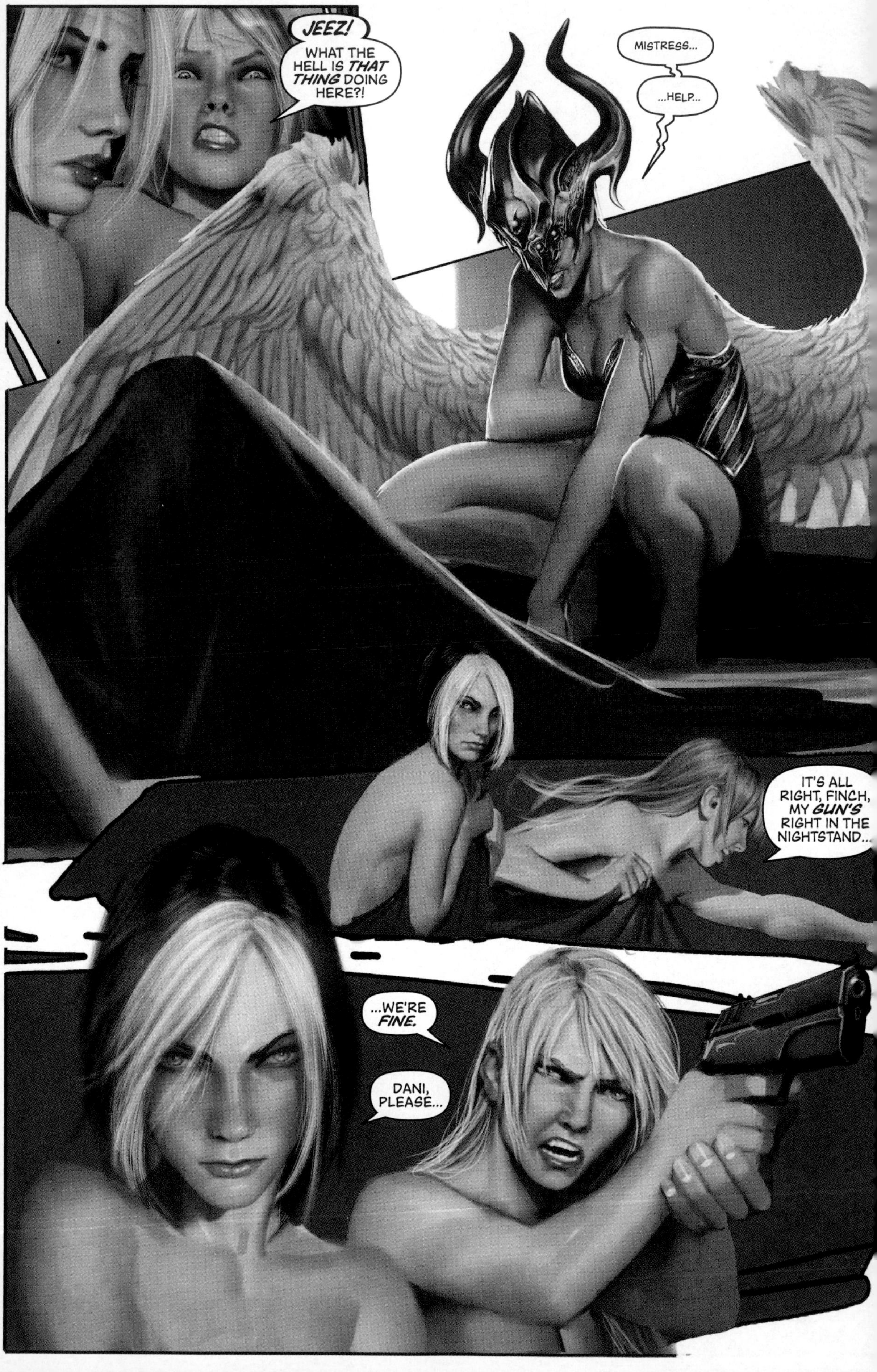
JEEZ! WHAT THE HELL IS THAT THING DOING HERE?!
MISTRESS...
...HELP...
IT'S ALL RIGHT, FINCH, MY GUN'S RIGHT IN THE NIGHTSTAND...
...WE'RE FINE.
DANI, PLEASE...

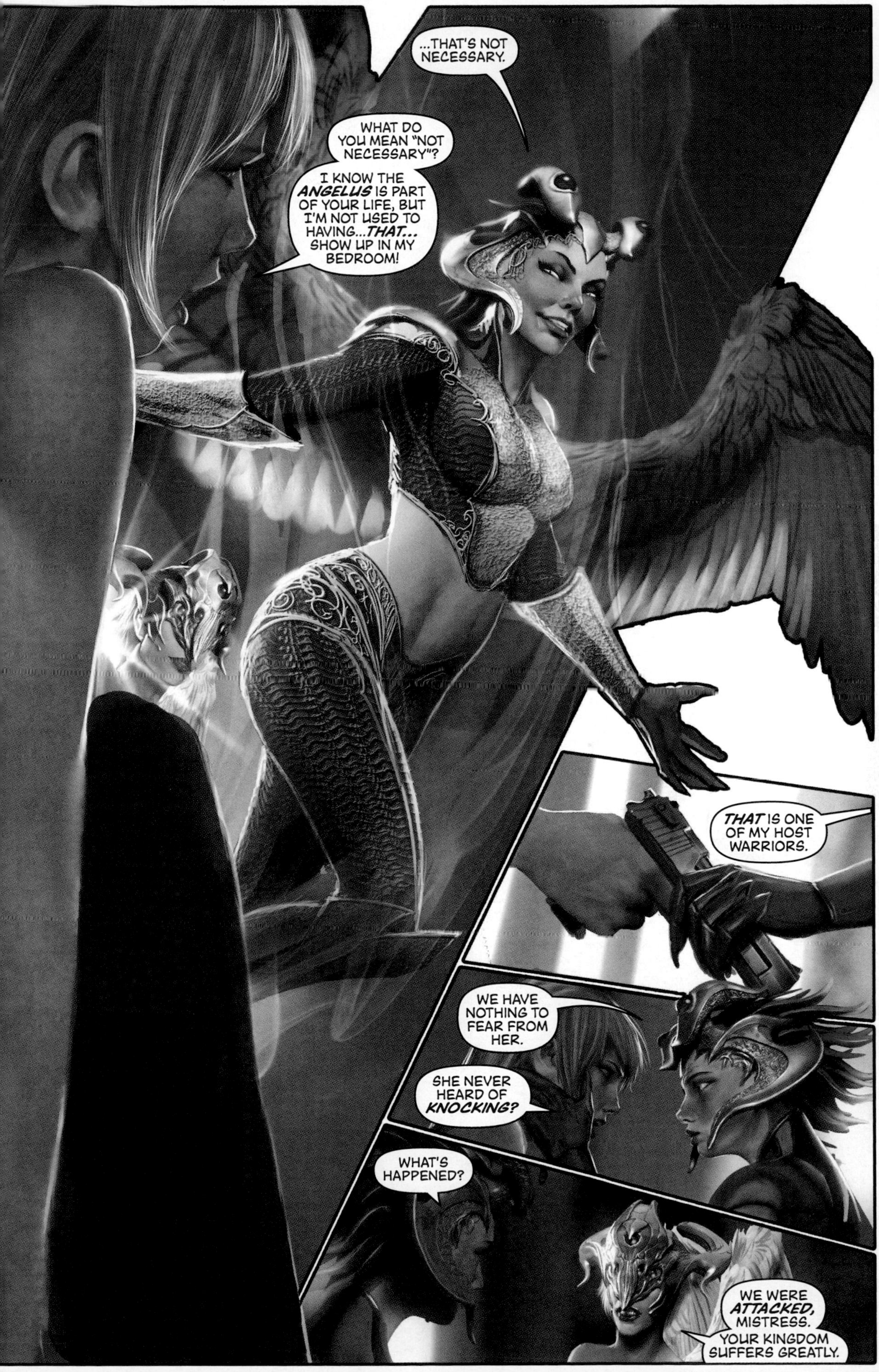
...THAT'S NOT NECESSARY.
WHAT DO YOU MEAN "NOT NECESSARY"?
I KNOW THE ANGELUS IS PART OF YOUR LIFE, BUT I'M NOT USED TO HAVING...THAT... SHOW UP IN MY BEDROOM!
THAT IS ONE OF MY HOST WARRIORS.
WE HAVE NOTHING TO FEAR FROM HER.
SHE NEVER HEARD OF KNOCKING?
WHAT'S HAPPENED?
WE WERE ATTACKED, MISTRESS.
YOUR KINGDOM SUFFERS GREATLY.

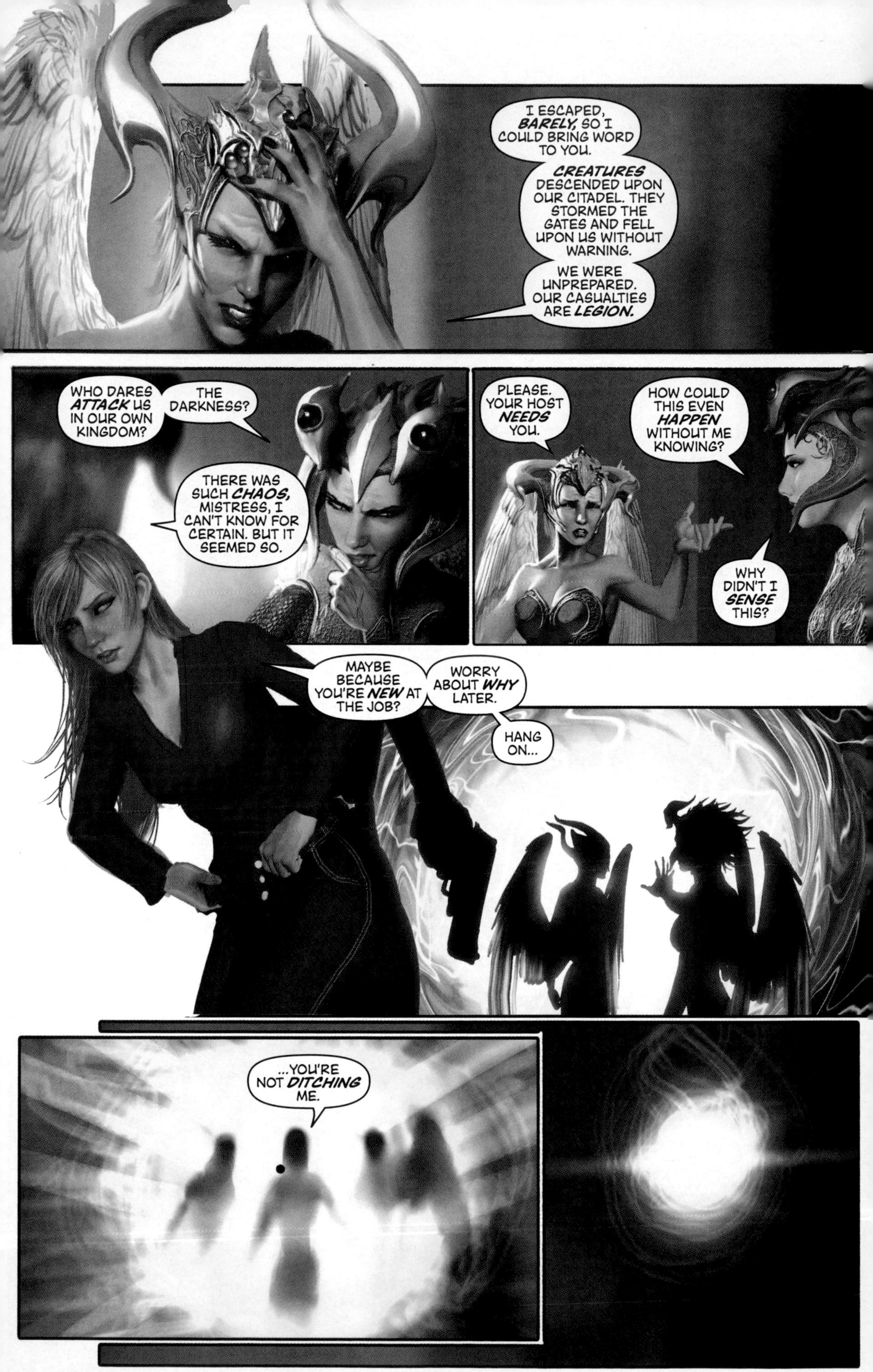
I ESCAPED, BARELY, SO I COULD BRING WORD TO YOU.
CREATURES DESCENDED UPON OUR CITADEL. THEY STORMED THE GATES AND FELL UPON US WITHOUT WARNING.
WE WERE UNPREPARED. OUR CASUALTIES ARE LEGION.
WHO DARES ATTACK US IN OUR OWN KINGDOM?
THE DARKNESS?
THERE WAS SUCH CHAOS, MISTRESS, I CAN'T KNOW FOR CERTAIN. BUT IT SEEMED SO.
PLEASE. YOUR HOST NEEDS YOU.
HOW COULD THIS EVEN HAPPEN WITHOUT ME KNOWING?
WHY DIDN'T I SENSE THIS?
MAYBE BECAUSE YOU'RE NEW AT THE JOB?
WORRY ABOUT WHY LATER.
HANG ON...
...YOU'RE NOT DITCHING ME.

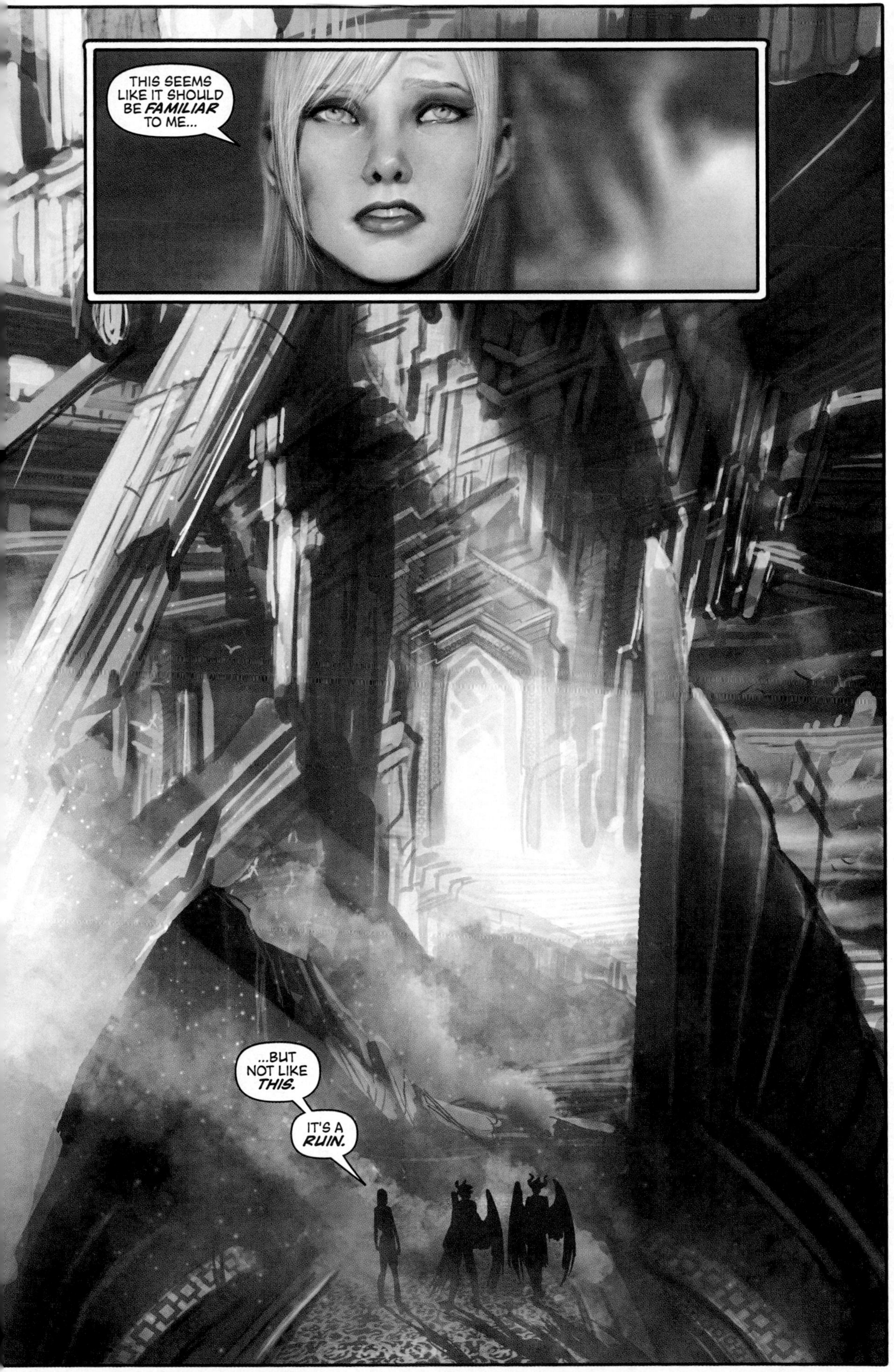
THIS SEEMS LIKE IT SHOULD BE *FAMILIAR* TO ME...
...BUT NOT LIKE *THIS.*
IT'S A *RUIN.*

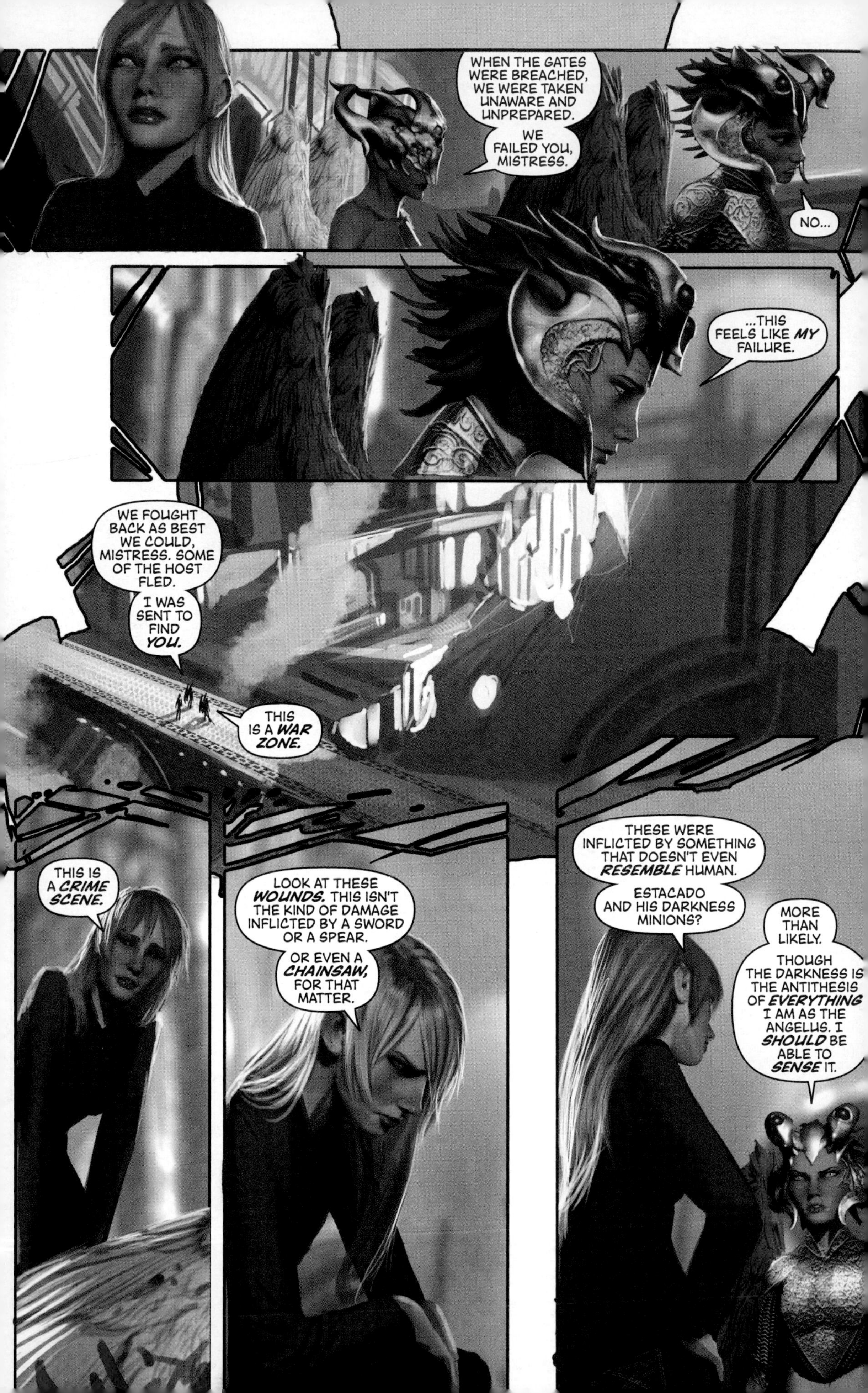
WHEN THE GATES WERE BREACHED, WE WERE TAKEN UNAWARE AND UNPREPARED.
WE FAILED YOU, MISTRESS.
NO...
...THIS FEELS LIKE *MY* FAILURE.
WE FOUGHT BACK AS BEST WE COULD, MISTRESS. SOME OF THE HOST FLED.
I WAS SENT TO FIND *YOU.*
THIS IS A *WAR ZONE.*
THIS IS A *CRIME SCENE.*
LOOK AT THESE *WOUNDS.* THIS ISN'T THE KIND OF DAMAGE INFLICTED BY A SWORD OR A SPEAR.
OR EVEN A *CHAINSAW,* FOR THAT MATTER.
THESE WERE INFLICTED BY SOMETHING THAT DOESN'T EVEN *RESEMBLE* HUMAN.
ESTACADO AND HIS DARKNESS MINIONS?
MORE THAN LIKELY.
THOUGH THE DARKNESS IS THE ANTITHESIS OF *EVERYTHING* I AM AS THE ANGELUS. I *SHOULD* BE ABLE TO *SENSE* IT.

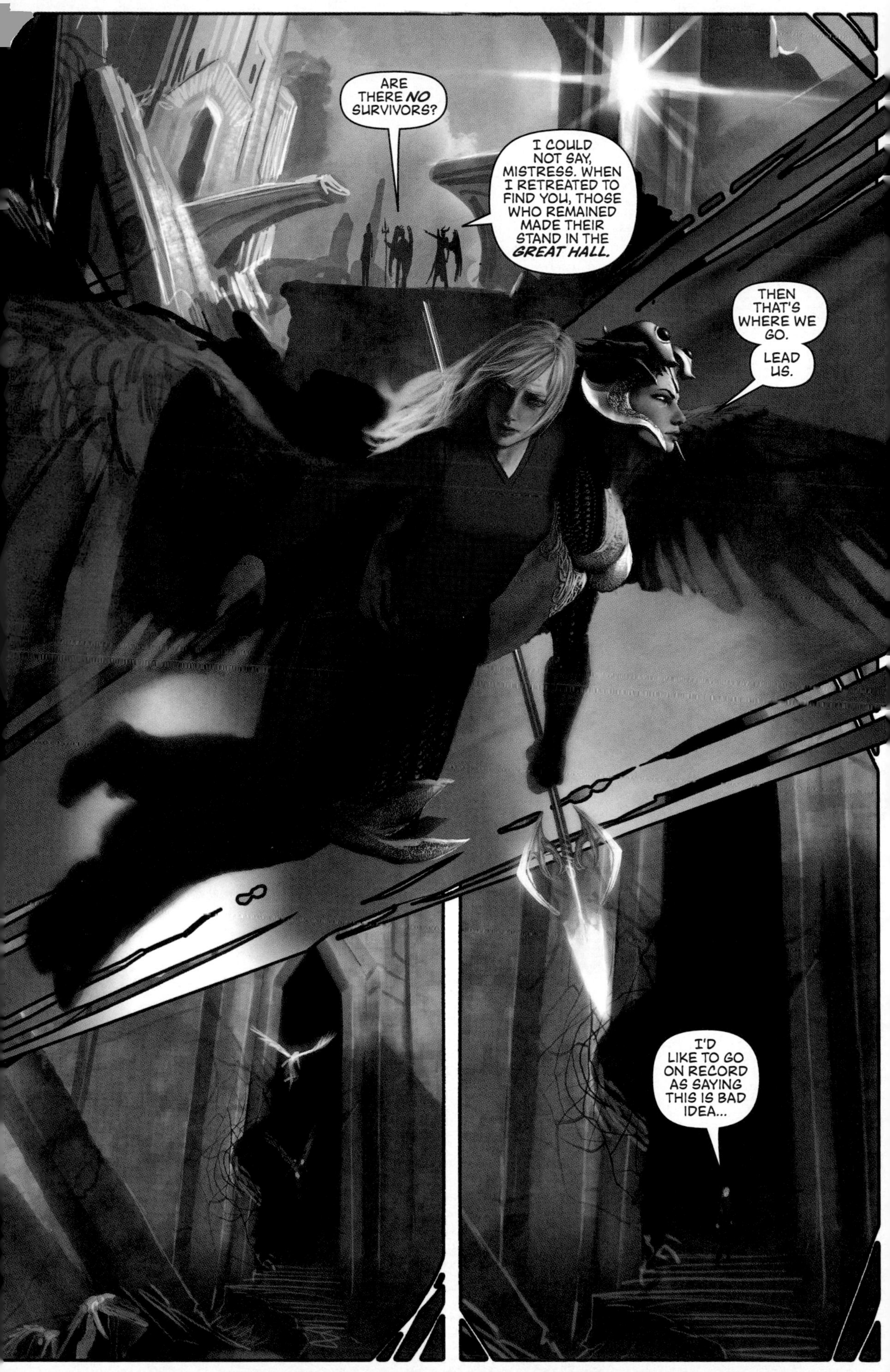
ARE THERE NO SURVIVORS?
I COULD NOT SAY, MISTRESS. WHEN I RETREATED TO FIND YOU, THOSE WHO REMAINED MADE THEIR STAND IN THE GREAT HALL.
THEN THAT'S WHERE WE GO.
LEAD US.
I'D LIKE TO GO ON RECORD AS SAYING THIS IS BAD IDEA...

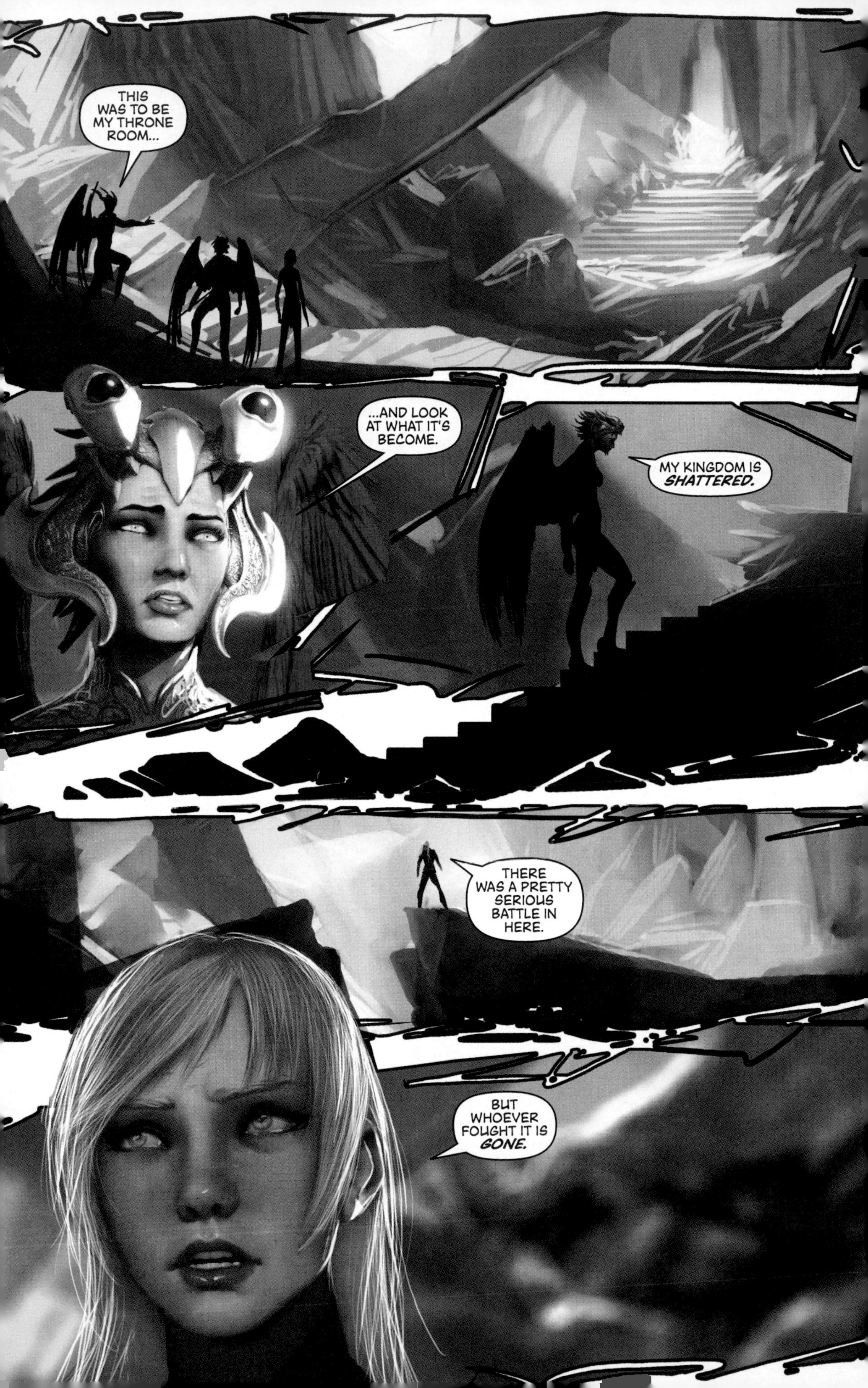
THIS WAS TO BE MY THRONE ROOM...
...AND LOOK AT WHAT IT'S BECOME.
MY KINGDOM IS *SHATTERED.*
THERE WAS A PRETTY SERIOUS BATTLE IN HERE.
BUT WHOEVER FOUGHT IT IS *GONE.*

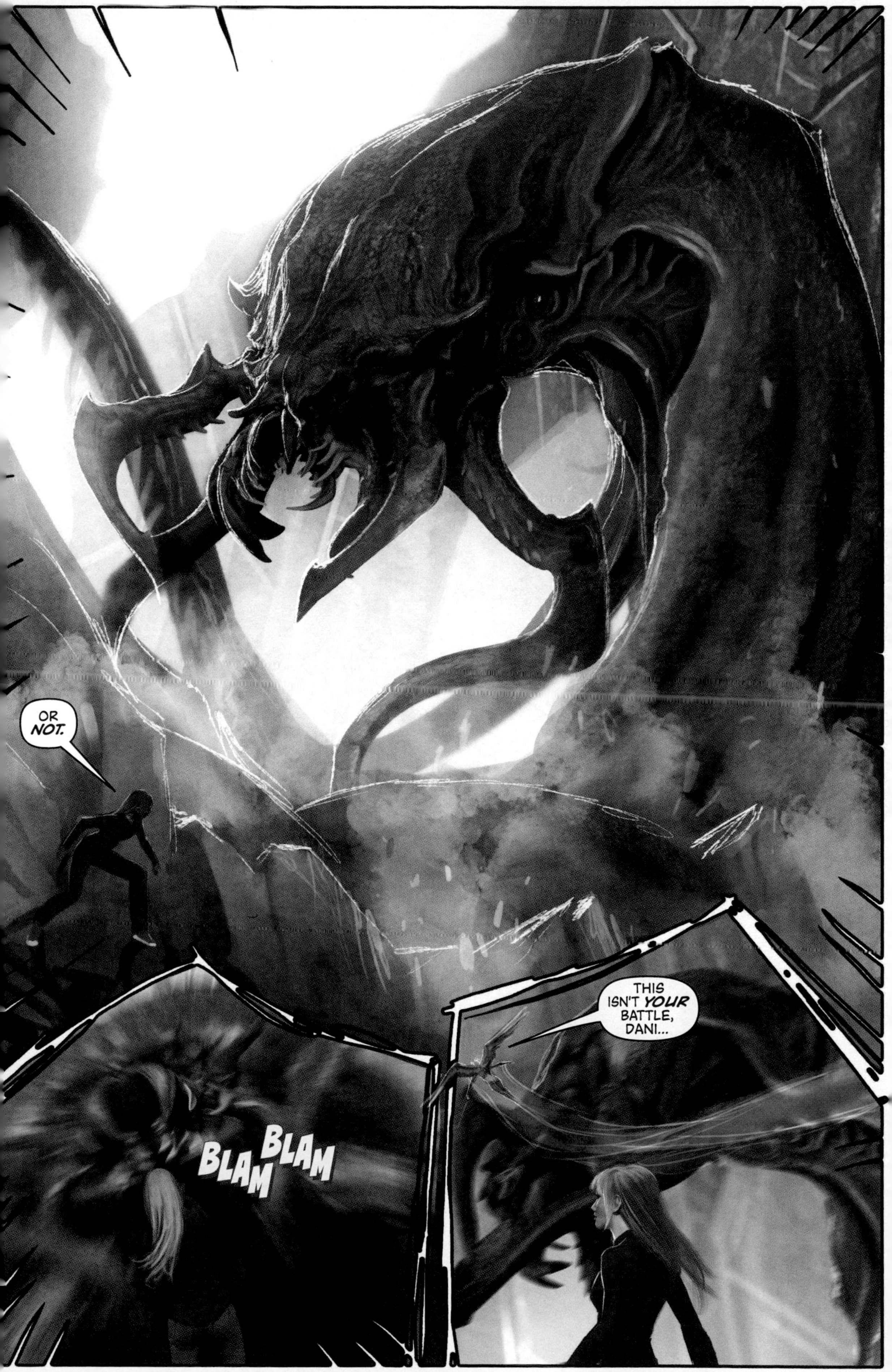
OR NOT.
BLAM BLAM
THIS ISN'T YOUR BATTLE, DANI...

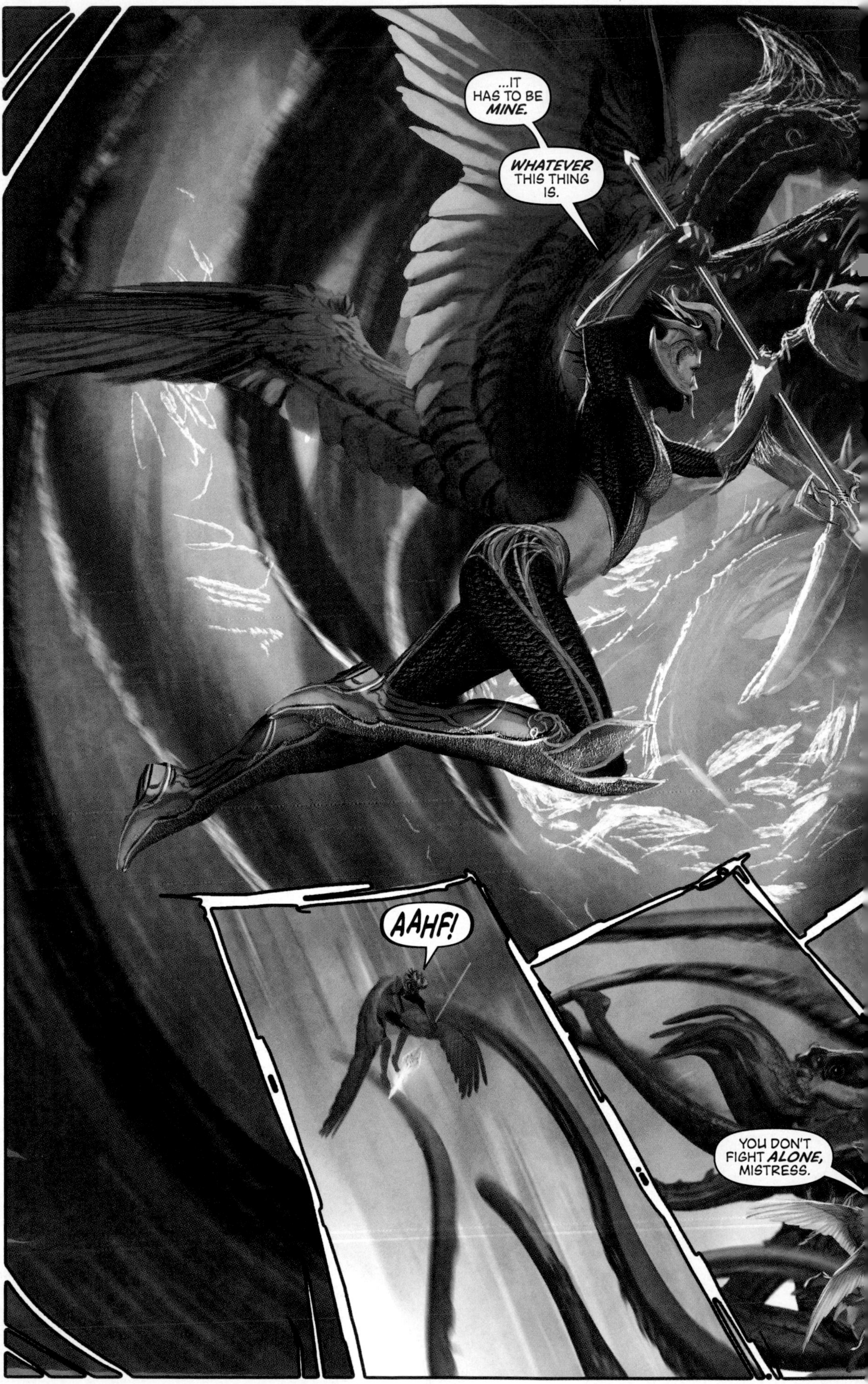
...IT HAS TO BE *MINE.*
WHATEVER THIS THING IS.
AAHF!
YOU DON'T FIGHT *ALONE,* MISTRESS.

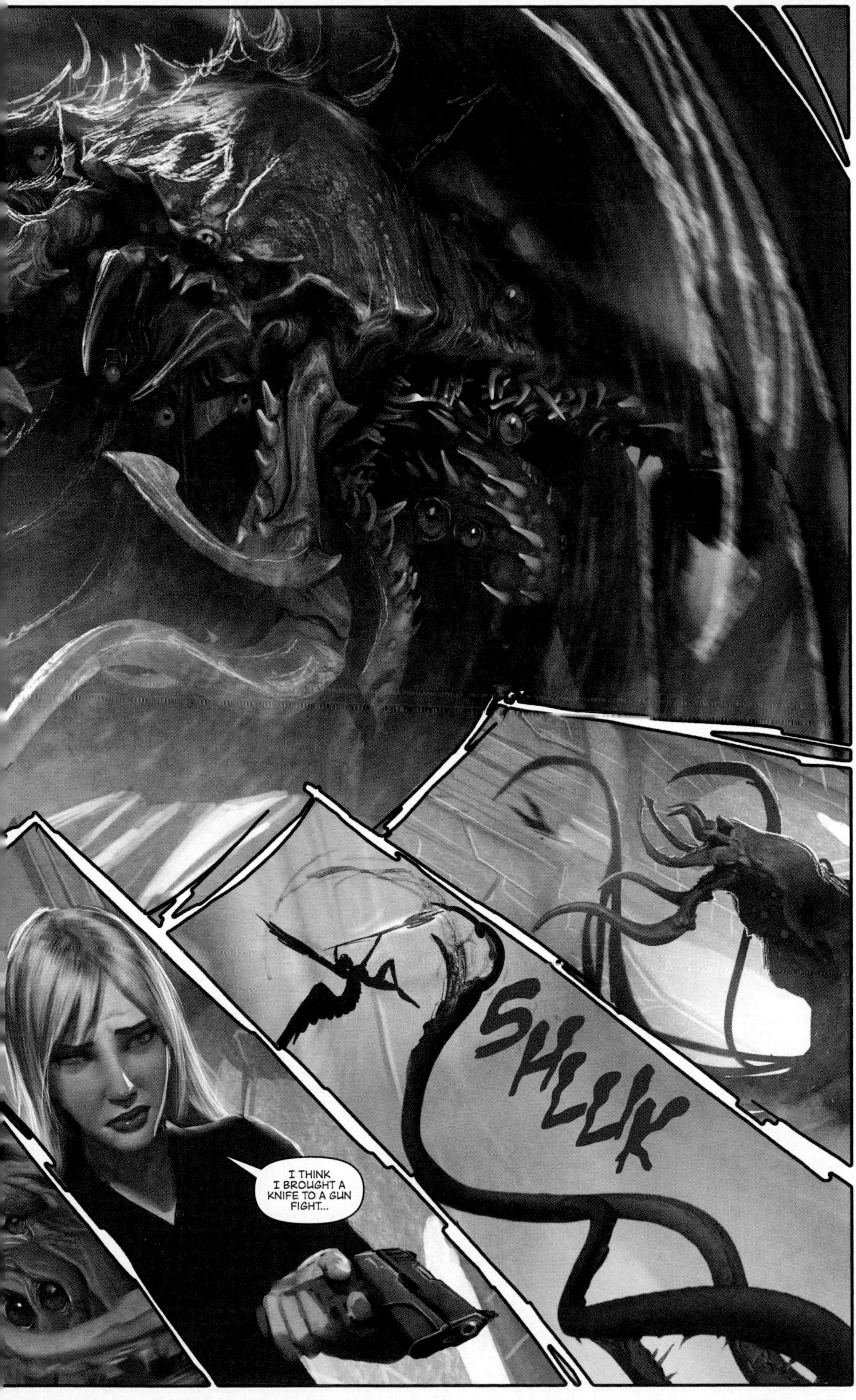
SHLUK
I THINK I BROUGHT A KNIFE TO A GUN FIGHT...

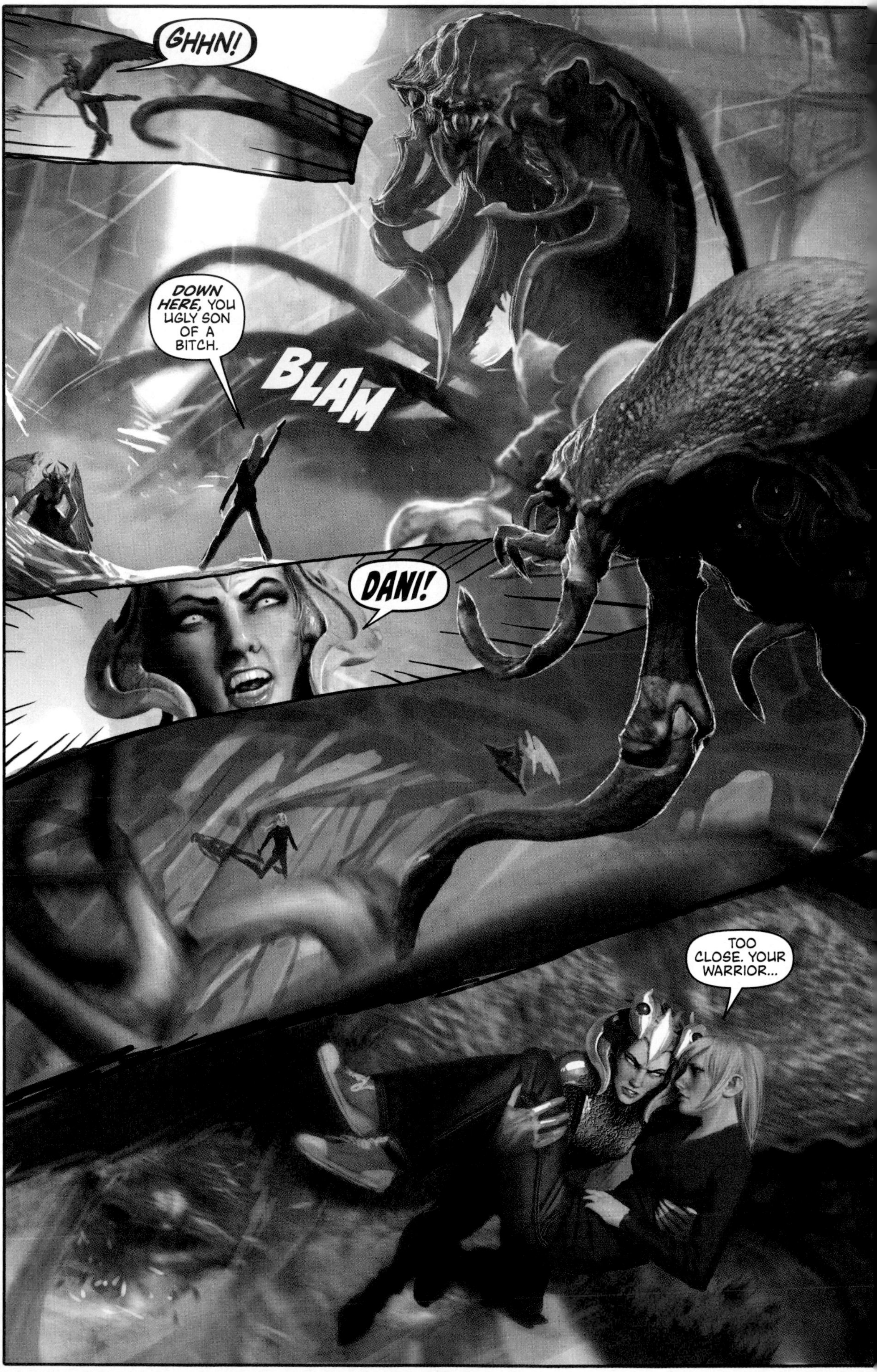
GHHN!
DOWN HERE, YOU UGLY SON OF A BITCH.
BLAM
DANI!
TOO CLOSE. YOUR WARRIOR...

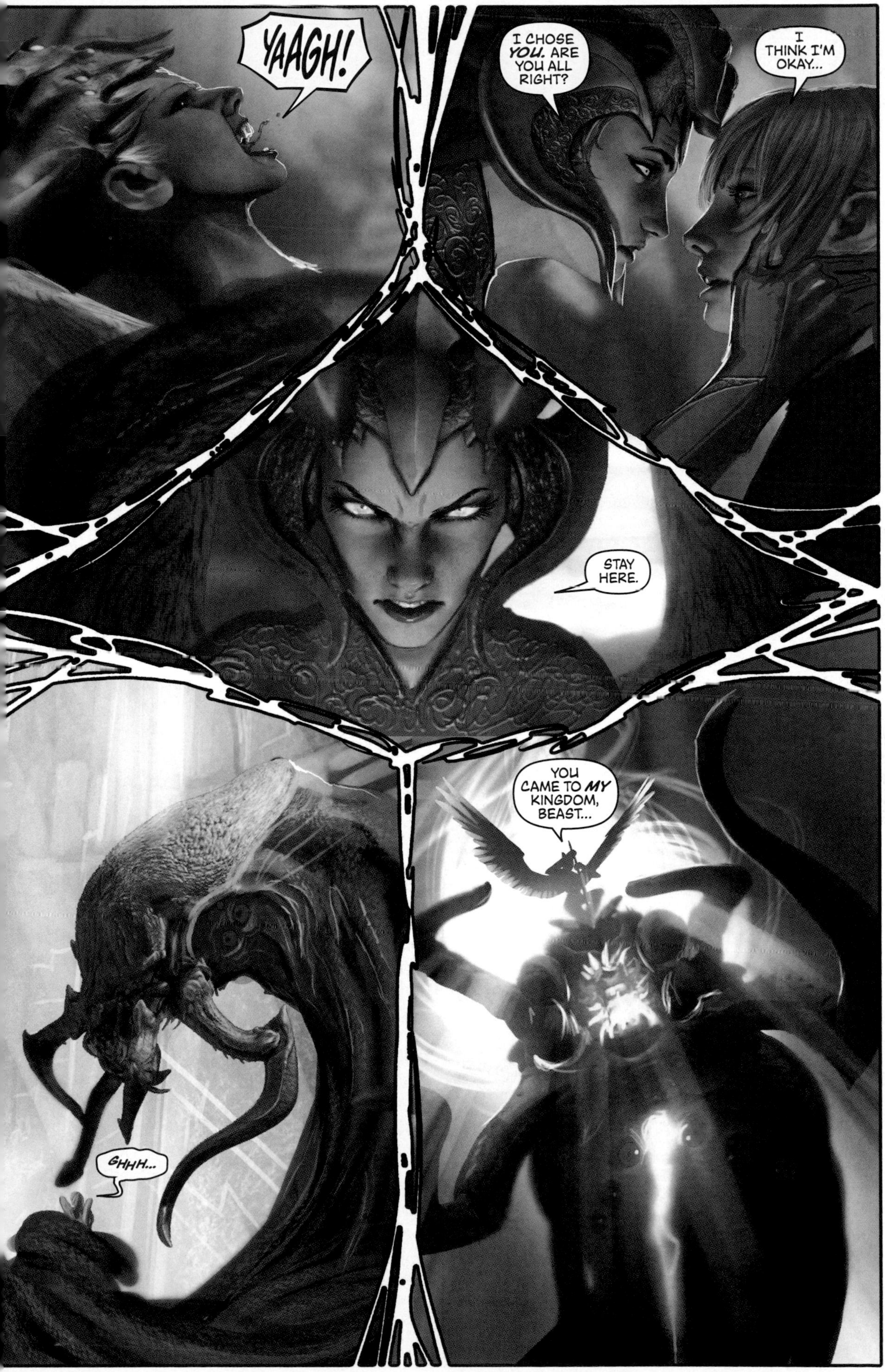
YAAGH!
I CHOSE YOU. ARE YOU ALL RIGHT?
I THINK I'M OKAY...
STAY HERE.
GHHH...
YOU CAME TO MY KINGDOM, BEAST...

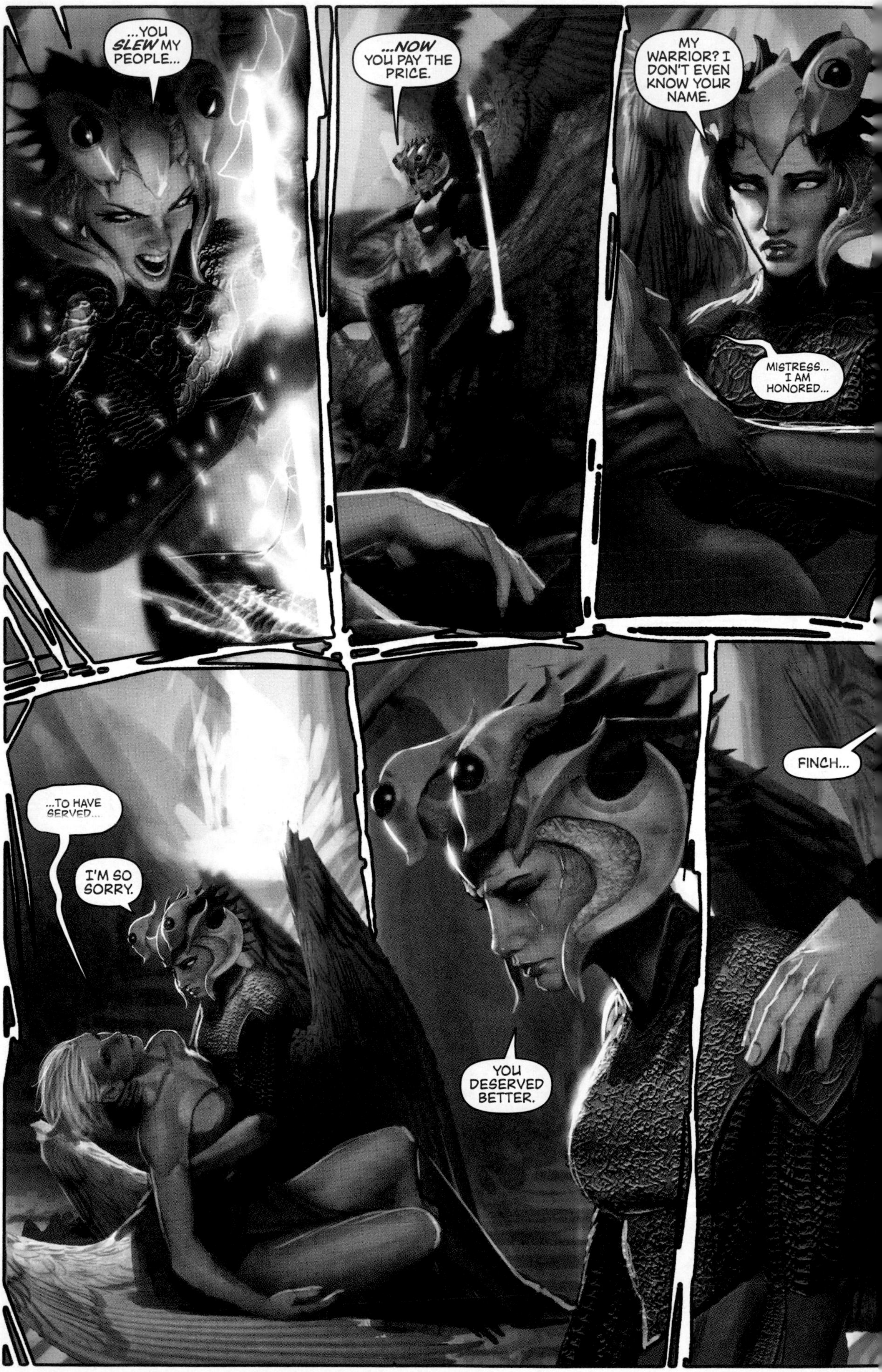
...YOU SLEW MY PEOPLE...
...NOW YOU PAY THE PRICE.
MY WARRIOR? I DON'T EVEN KNOW YOUR NAME.
MISTRESS... I AM HONORED...
...TO HAVE SERVED...
I'M SO SORRY.
YOU DESERVED BETTER.
FINCH...

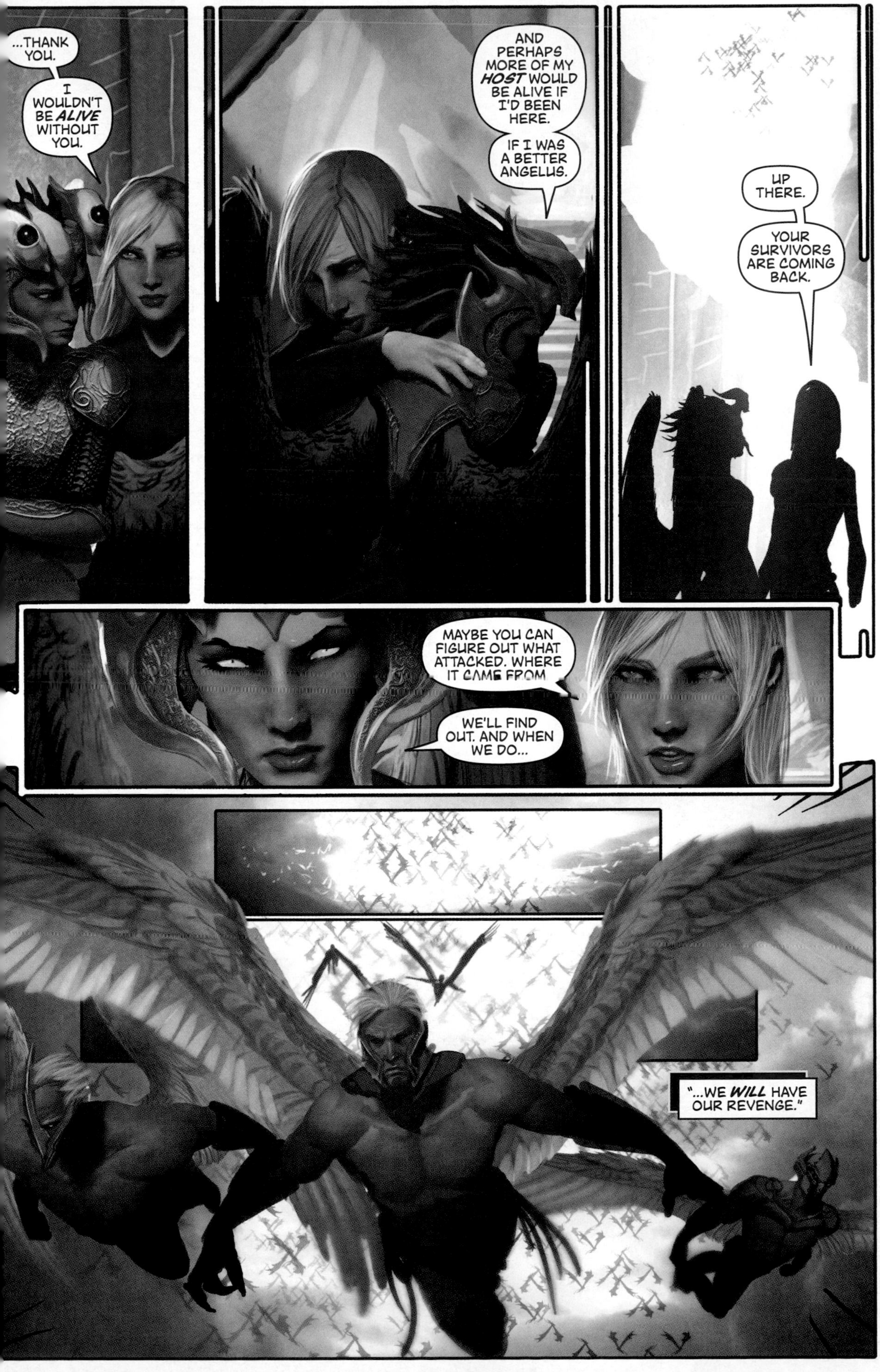
...THANK YOU.
I WOULDN'T BE *ALIVE* WITHOUT YOU.
AND PERHAPS MORE OF MY ***HOST*** WOULD BE ALIVE IF I'D BEEN HERE.
IF I WAS A BETTER ANGELUS.
UP THERE.
YOUR SURVIVORS ARE COMING BACK.
MAYBE YOU CAN FIGURE OUT WHAT ATTACKED. WHERE IT CAME FROM
WE'LL FIND OUT. AND WHEN WE DO...
"...WE ***WILL*** HAVE OUR REVENGE."

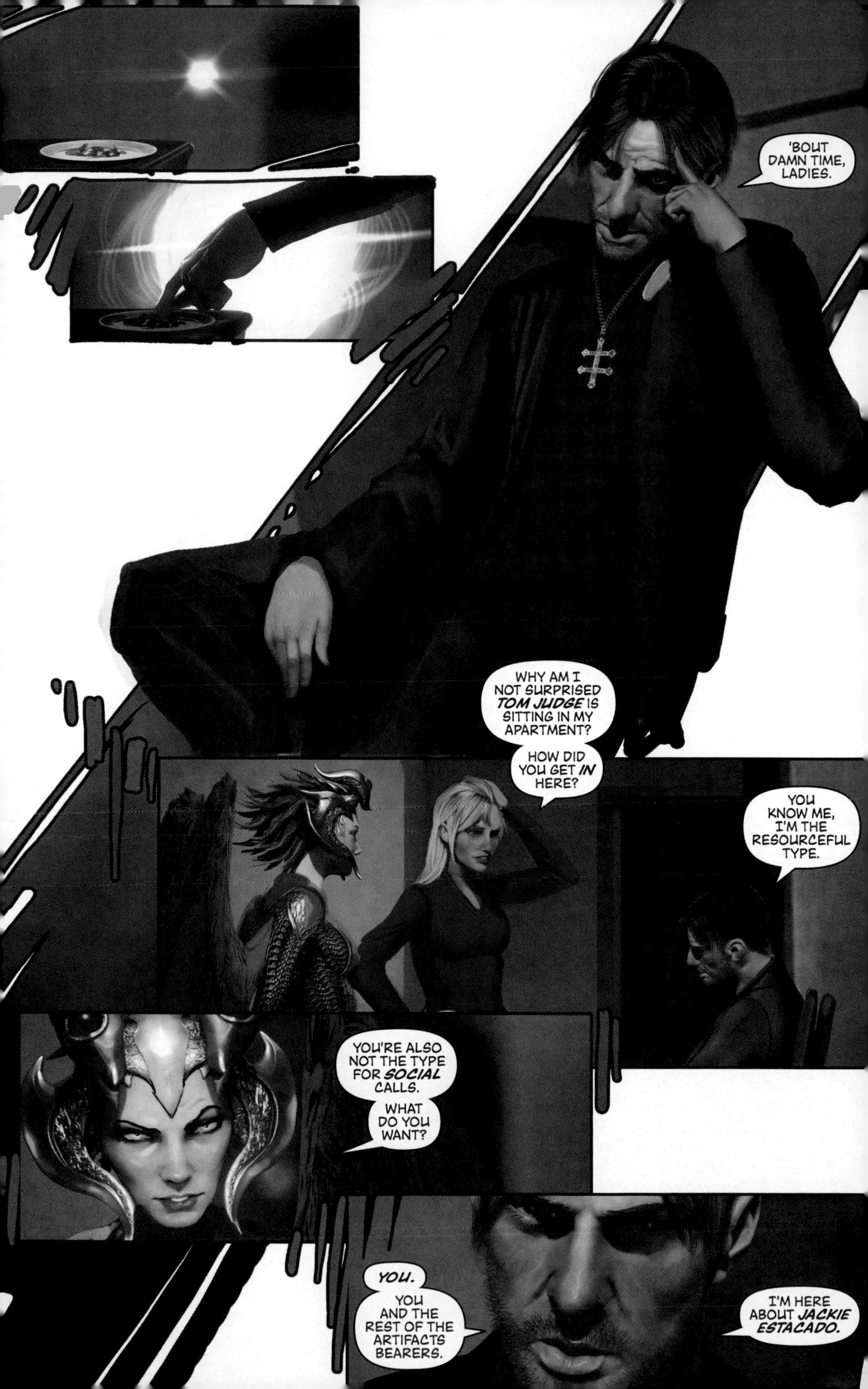
'BOUT DAMN TIME, LADIES.
WHY AM I NOT SURPRISED *TOM JUDGE* IS SITTING IN MY APARTMENT?
HOW DID YOU GET *IN* HERE?
YOU KNOW ME, I'M THE RESOURCEFUL TYPE.
YOU'RE ALSO NOT THE TYPE FOR *SOCIAL* CALLS.
WHAT DO YOU WANT?
I'M HERE ABOUT *JACKIE ESTACADO.*
YOU.
YOU AND THE REST OF THE ARTIFACTS BEARERS.

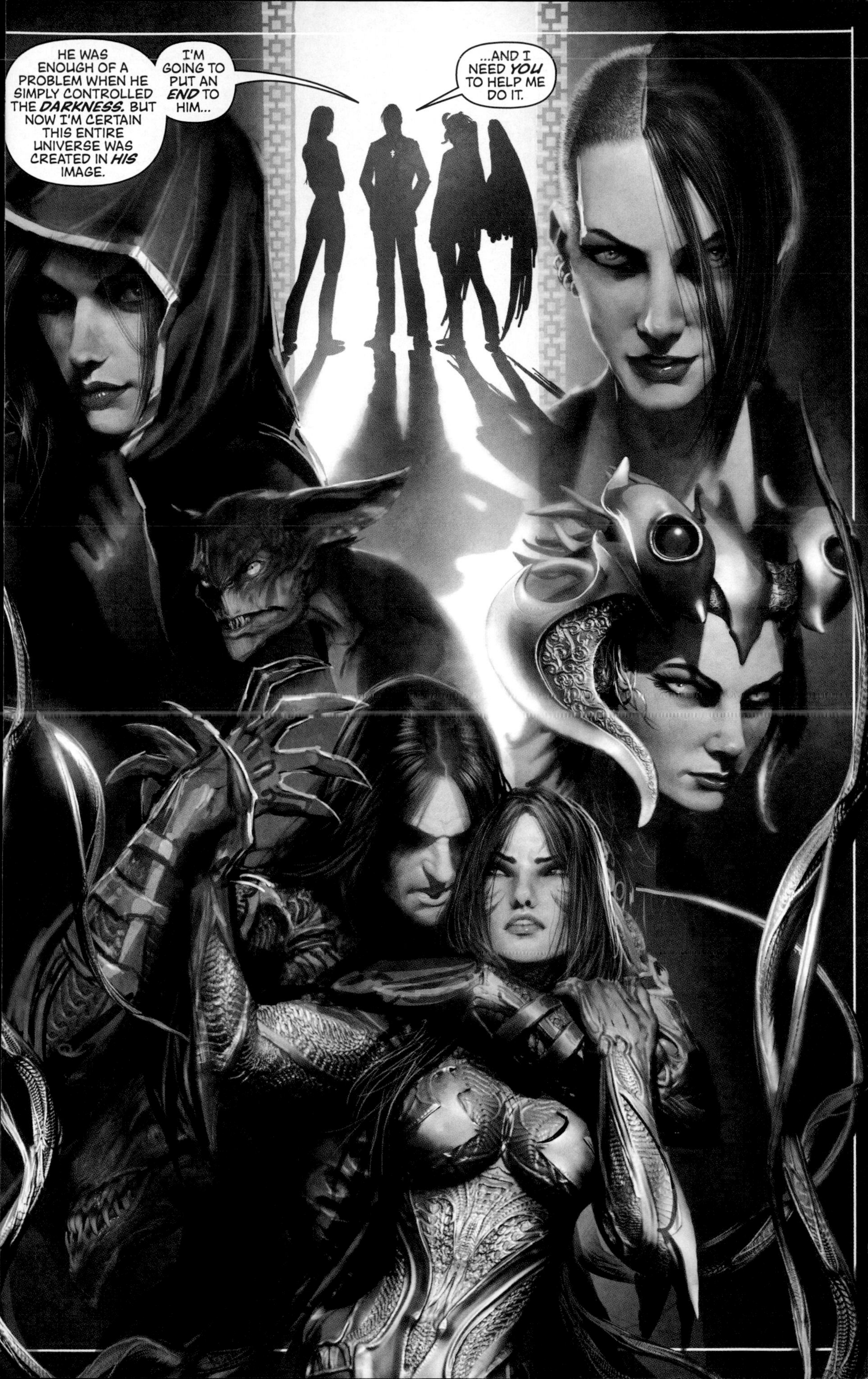

HE WAS ENOUGH OF A PROBLEM WHEN HE SIMPLY CONTROLLED THE *DARKNESS.* BUT NOW I'M CERTAIN THIS ENTIRE UNIVERSE WAS CREATED IN *HIS* IMAGE.
I'M GOING TO PUT AN *END* TO HIM...
...AND I NEED *YOU* TO HELP ME DO IT.

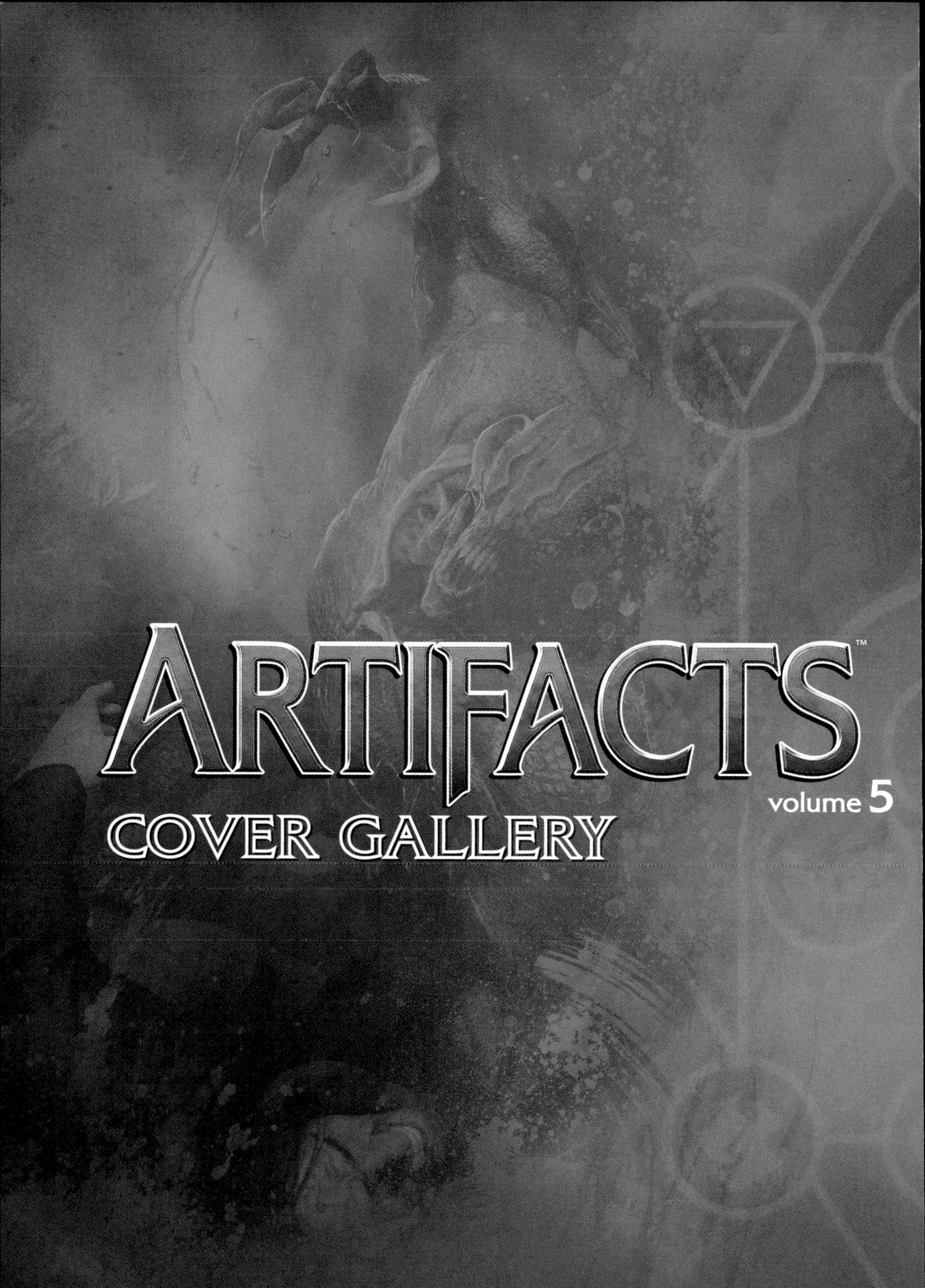

ARTIFACTS™ volume 5
COVER GALLERY

Artifacts issue #19, cover B, San Diego Comic Con Variant, art by: **Michael Broussard & Sunny Gho**

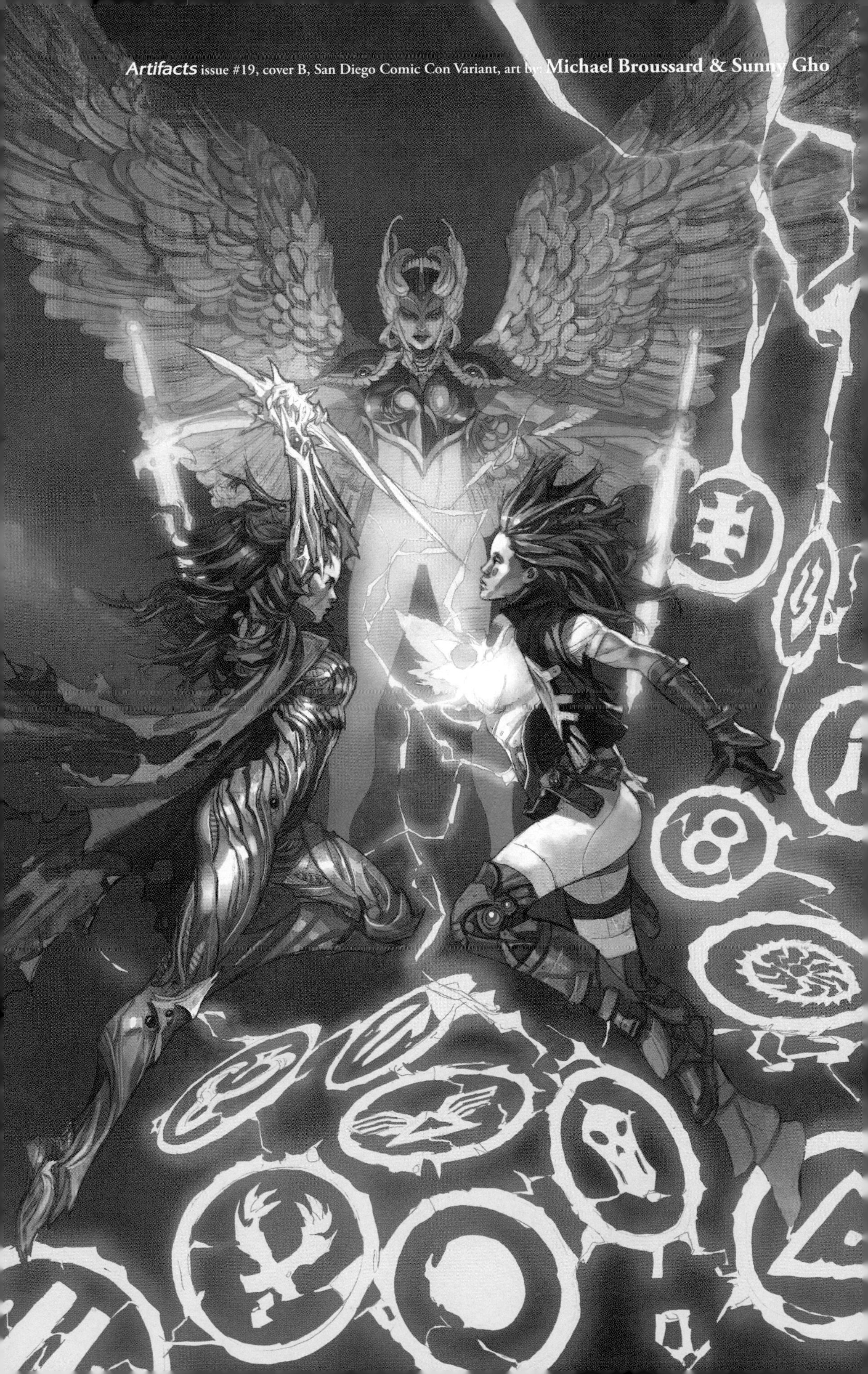

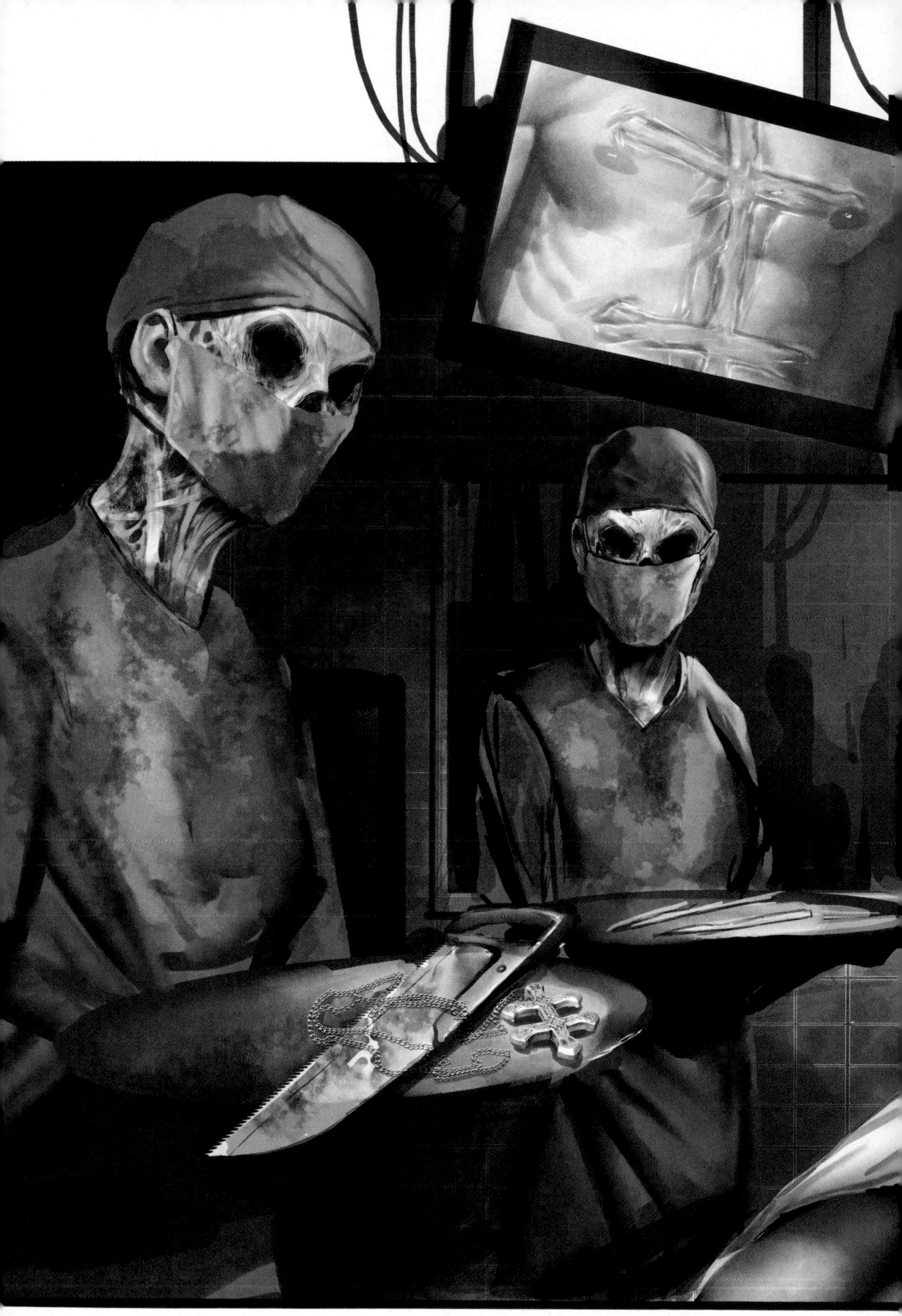

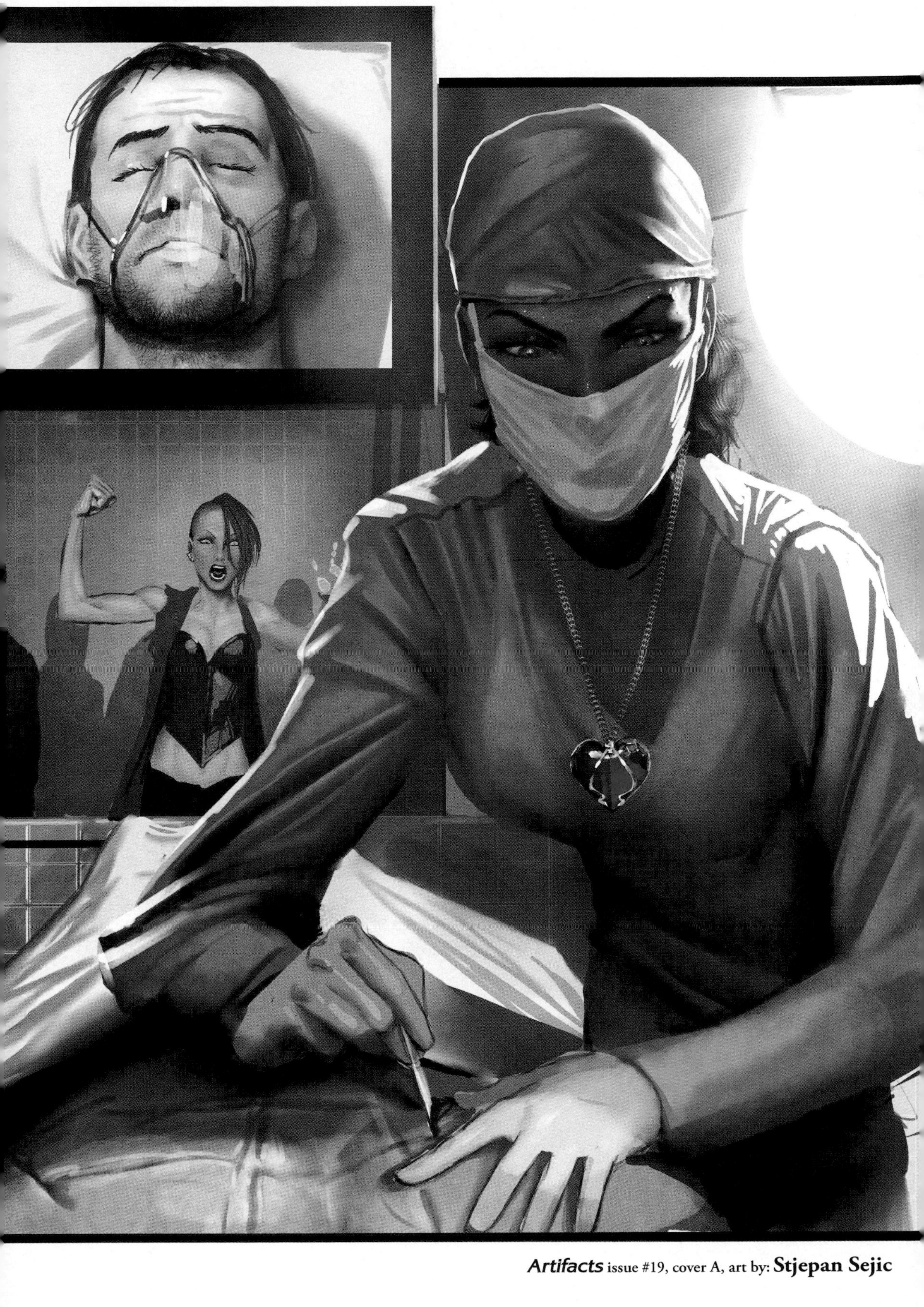

Artifacts issue #19, cover A, art by: **Stjepan Sejic**

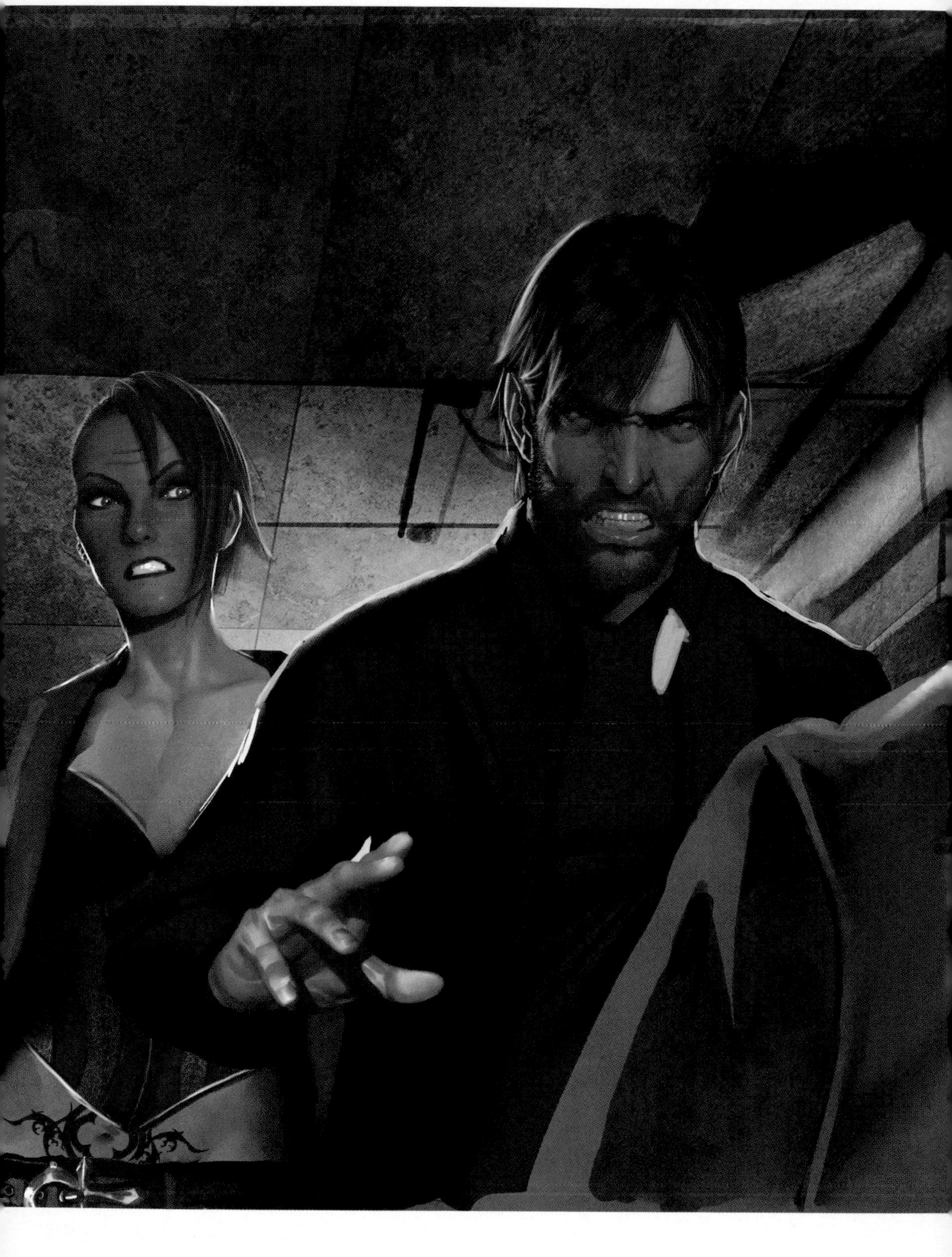

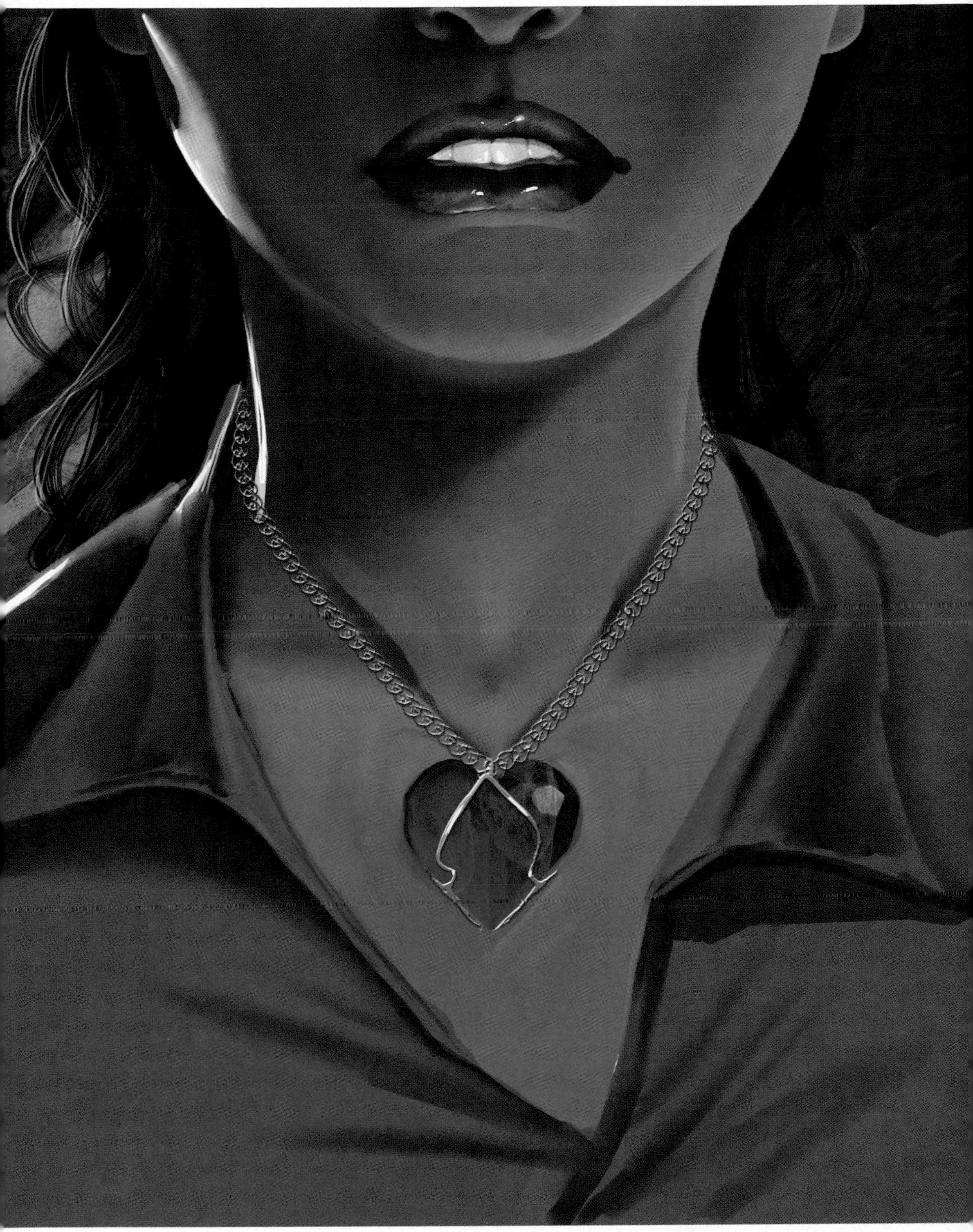

Artifacts issue #21, cover A, art by: **Stjepan Sejic**

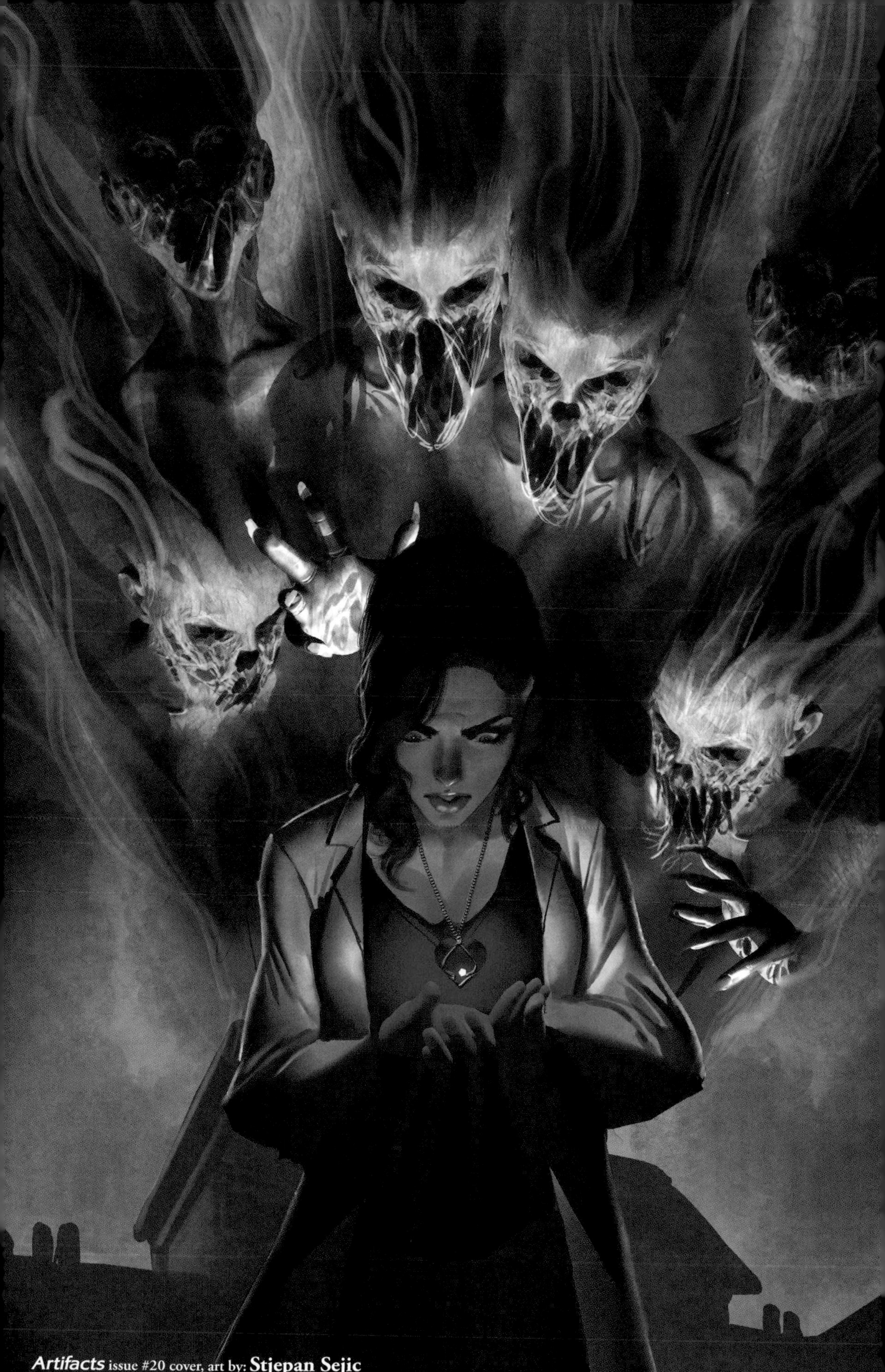

Artifacts issue #20 cover, art by: **Stjepan Sejic**

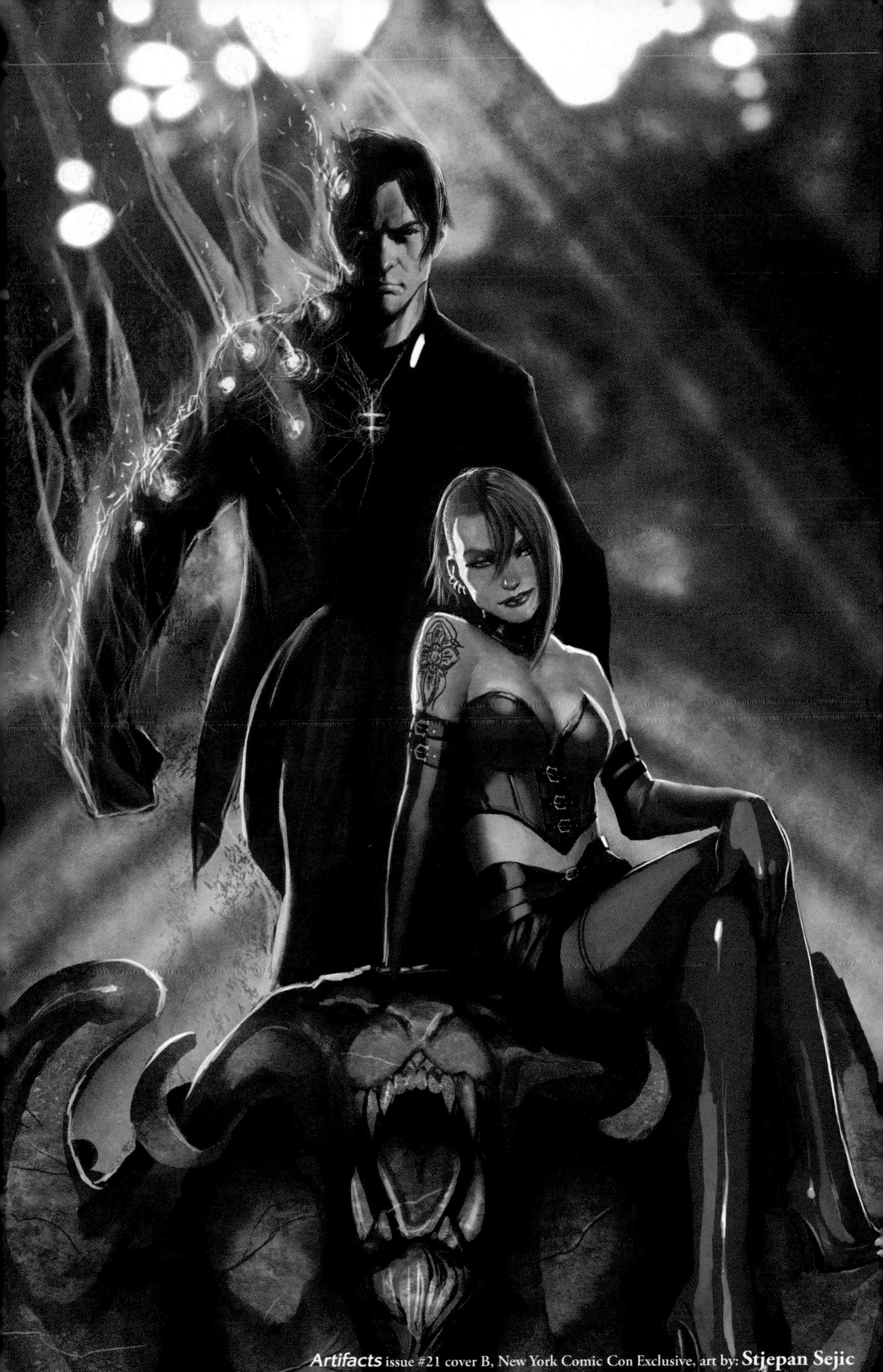

Artifacts issue #21 cover B, New York Comic Con Exclusive, art by: **Stjepan Sejic**

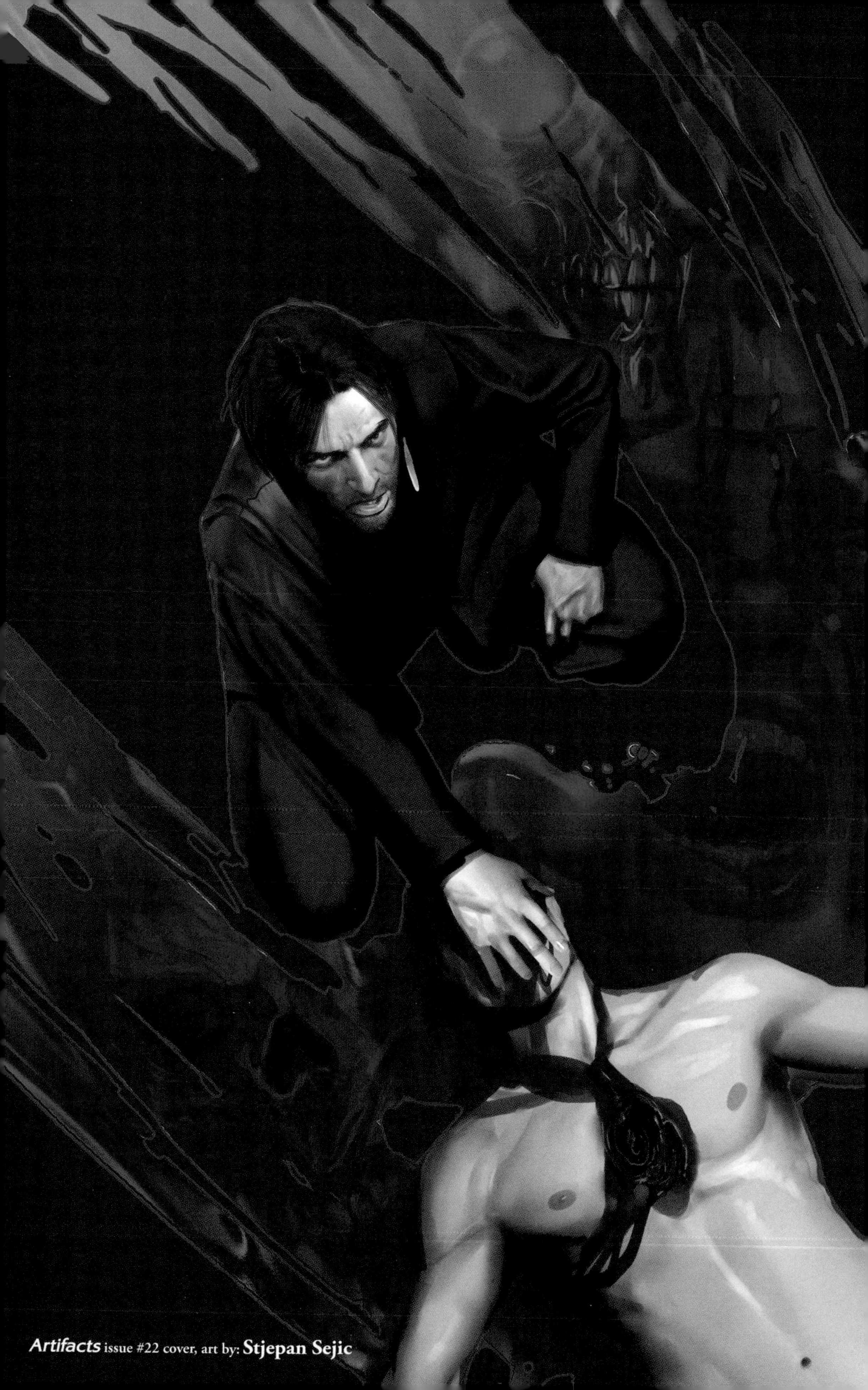

Artifacts issue #22 cover, art by: **Stjepan Sejic**

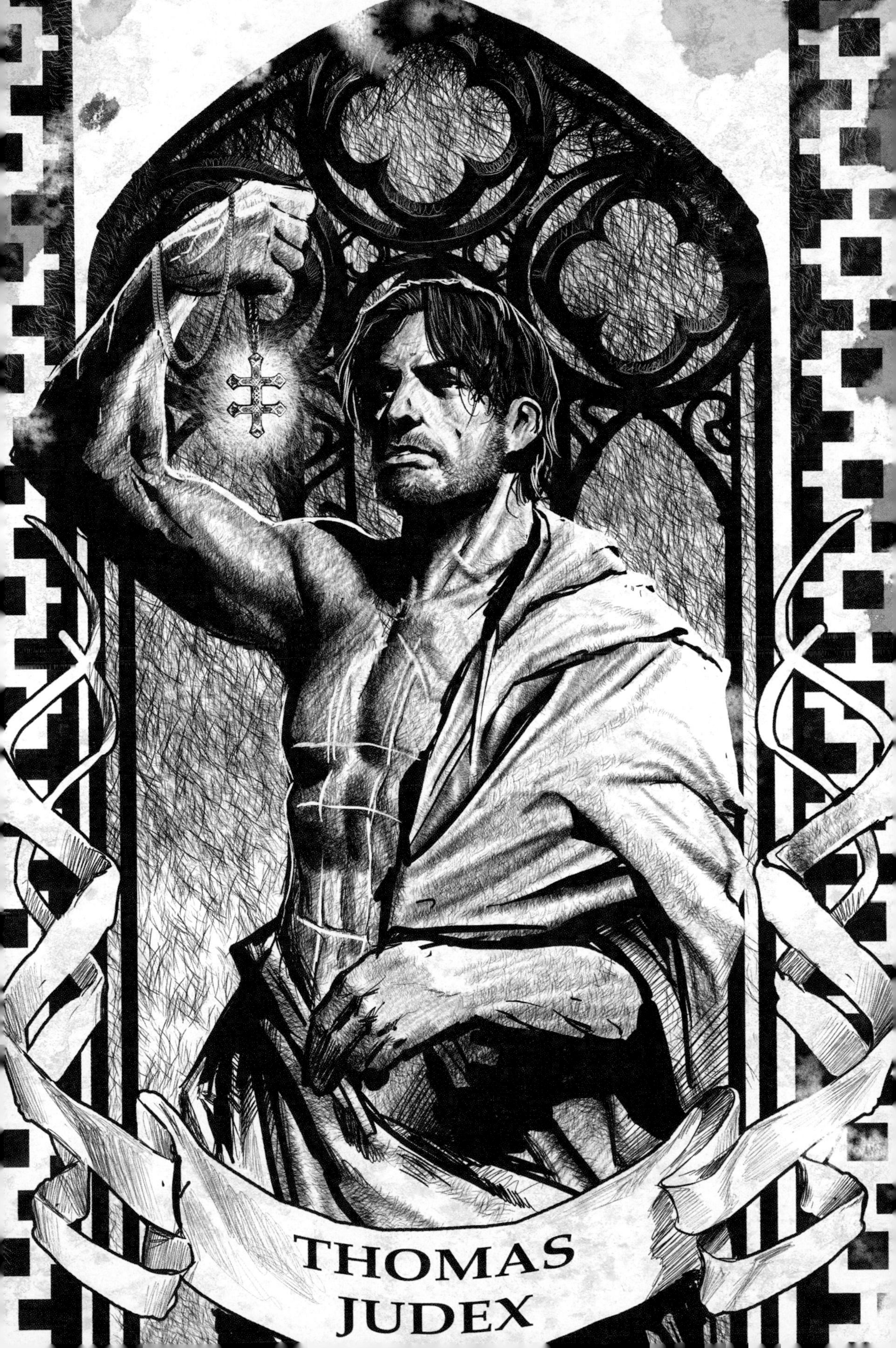
THOMAS
JUDEX

Artifacts issue #23 cover, art by: Stjepan Sejic

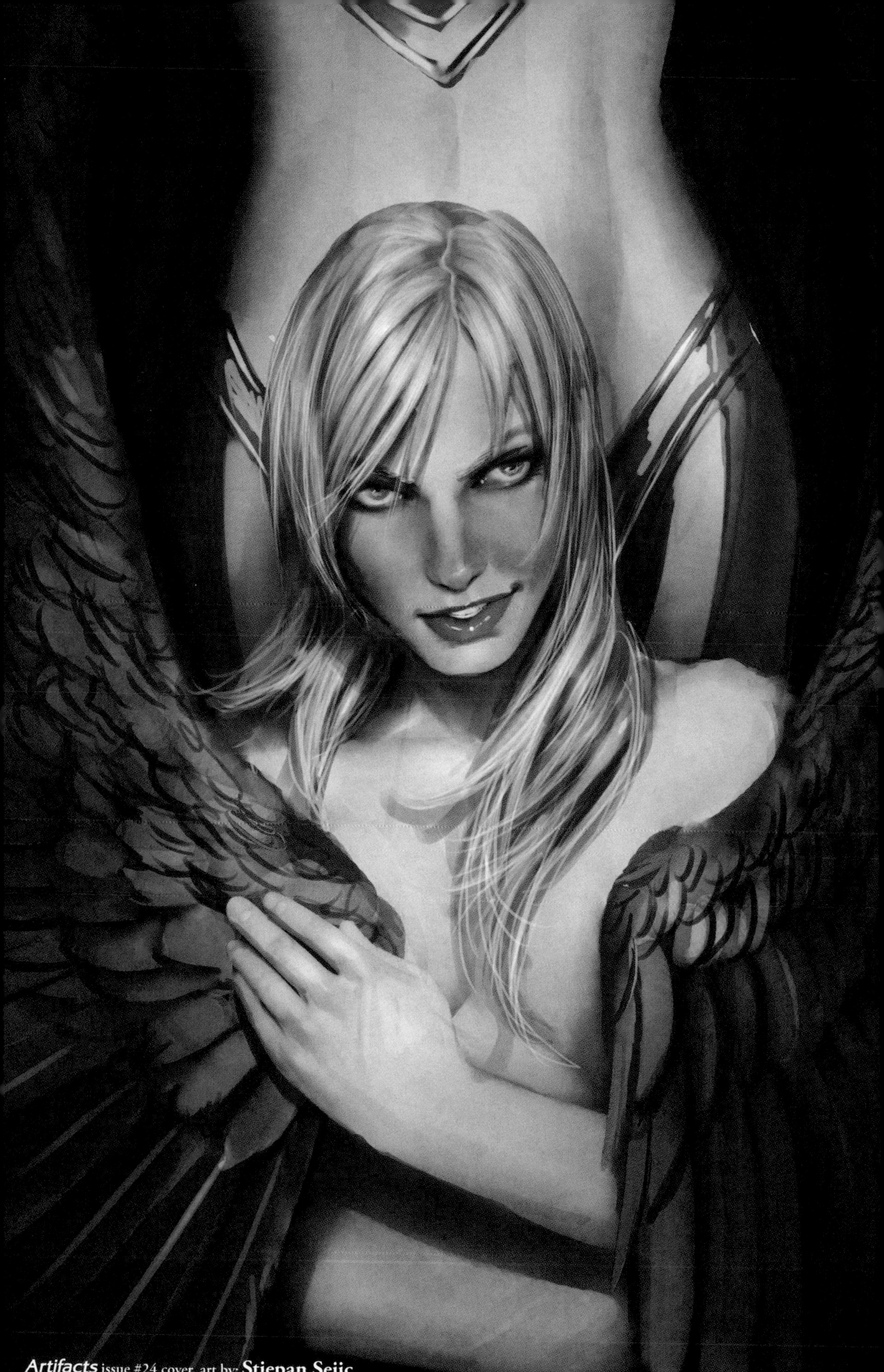

Artifacts issue #24 cover, art by: **Stjepan Sejic**

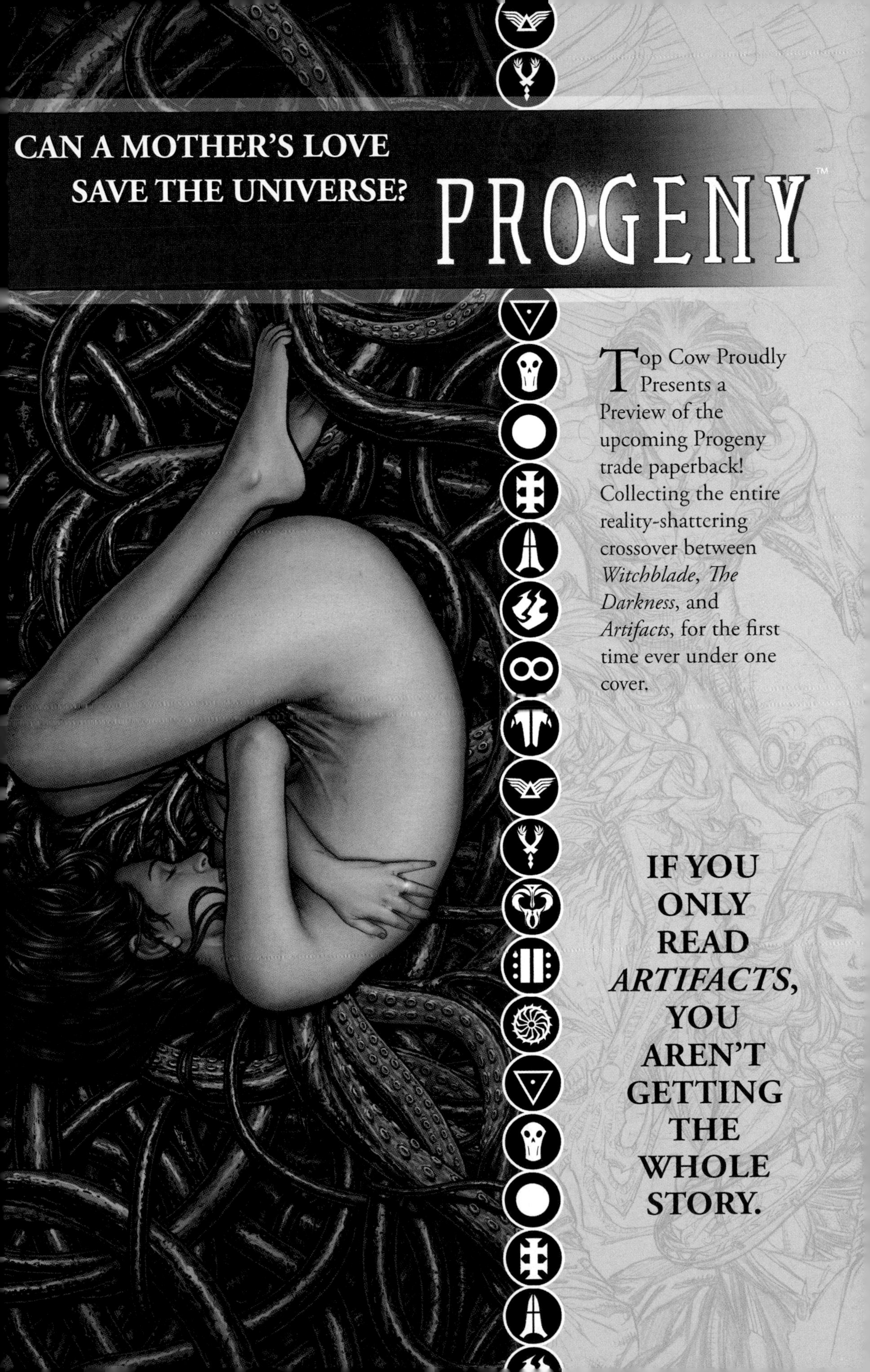
CAN A MOTHER'S LOVE
SAVE THE UNIVERSE?
PROGENY™
Top Cow Proudly Presents a Preview of the upcoming Progeny trade paperback! Collecting the entire reality-shattering crossover between *Witchblade*, *The Darkness*, and *Artifacts*, for the first time ever under one cover.
IF YOU ONLY READ *ARTIFACTS*, YOU AREN'T GETTING THE WHOLE STORY.

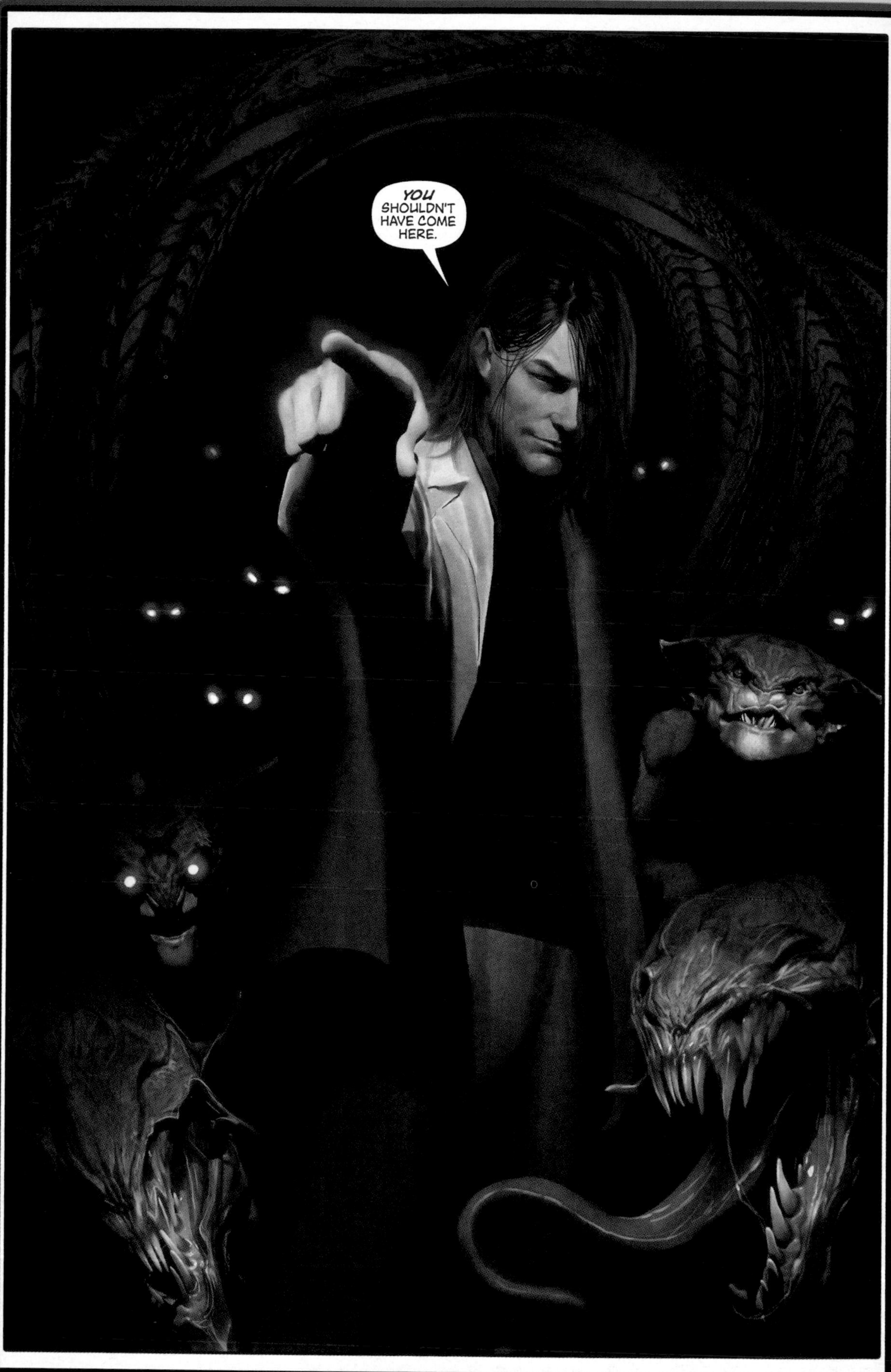
YOU SHOULDN'T HAVE COME HERE.

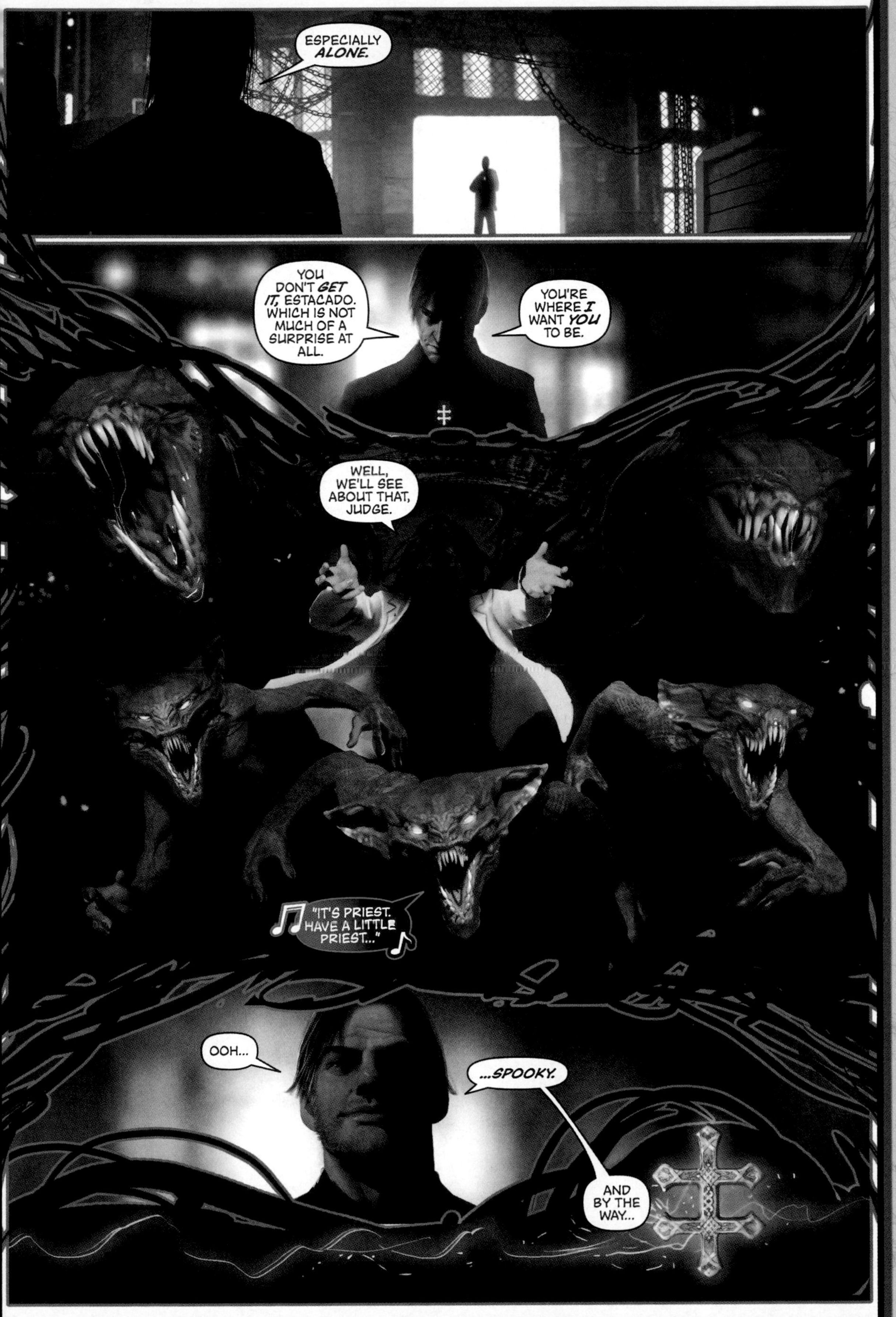
ESPECIALLY ALONE.
YOU DON'T GET IT, ESTACADO. WHICH IS NOT MUCH OF A SURPRISE AT ALL.
YOU'RE WHERE I WANT YOU TO BE.
WELL, WE'LL SEE ABOUT THAT, JUDGE.
"IT'S PRIEST. HAVE A LITTLE PRIEST..."
OOH...
...SPOOKY.
AND BY THE WAY...

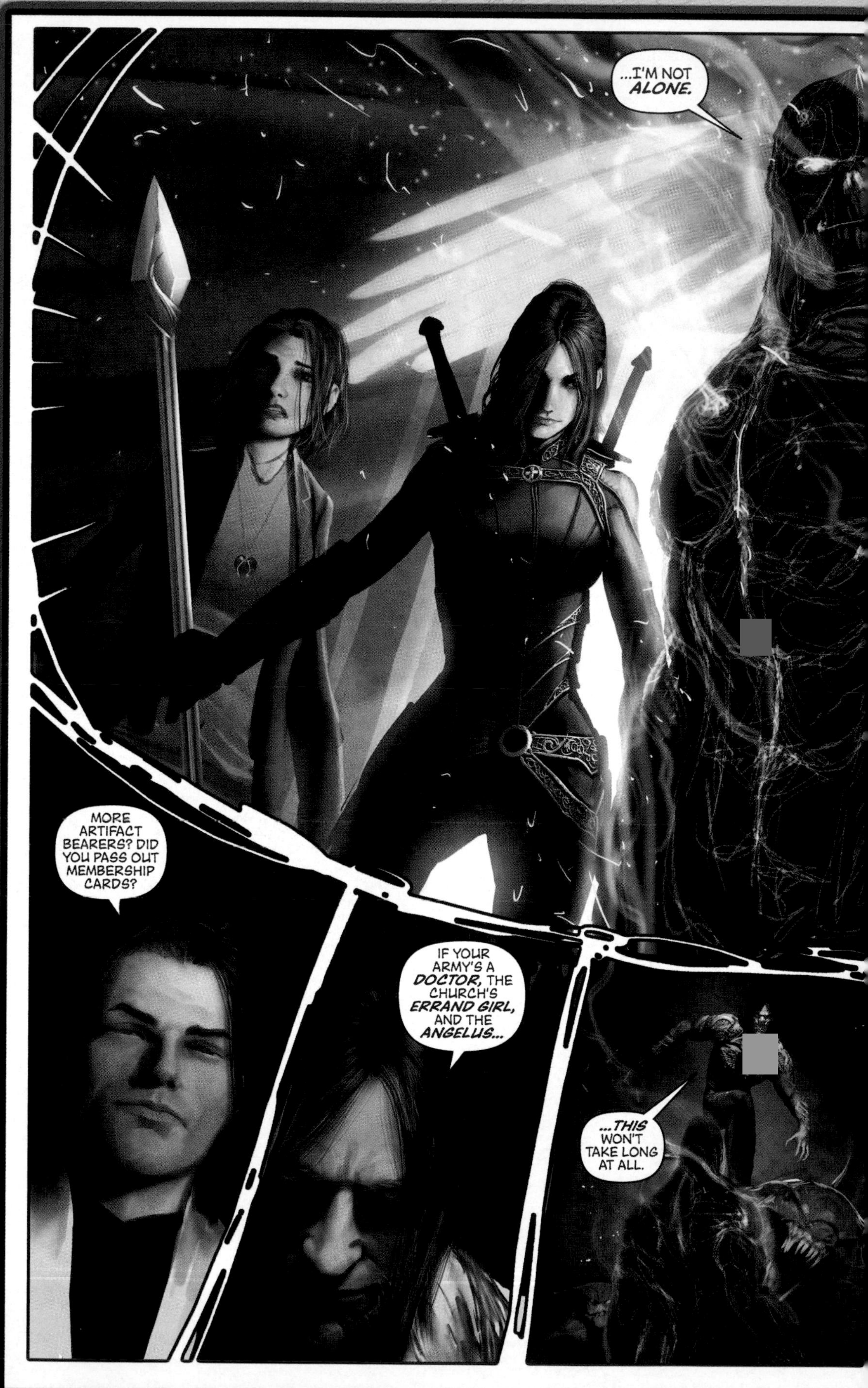
...I'M NOT ALONE.
MORE ARTIFACT BEARERS? DID YOU PASS OUT MEMBERSHIP CARDS?
IF YOUR ARMY'S A DOCTOR, THE CHURCH'S ERRAND GIRL, AND THE ANGELUS...
...THIS WON'T TAKE LONG AT ALL.

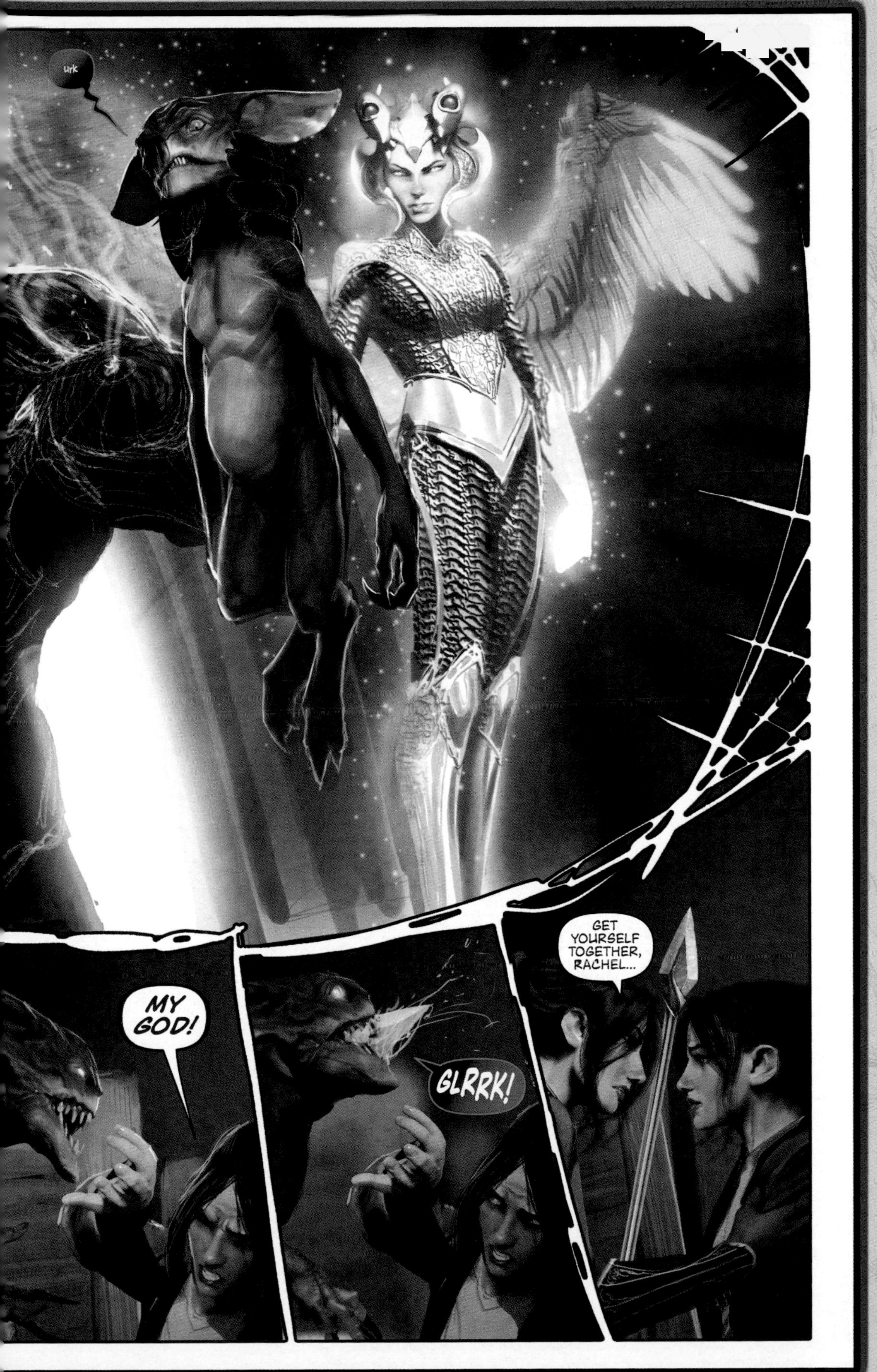
urk
MY GOD!
GLRRK!
GET YOURSELF TOGETHER, RACHEL...

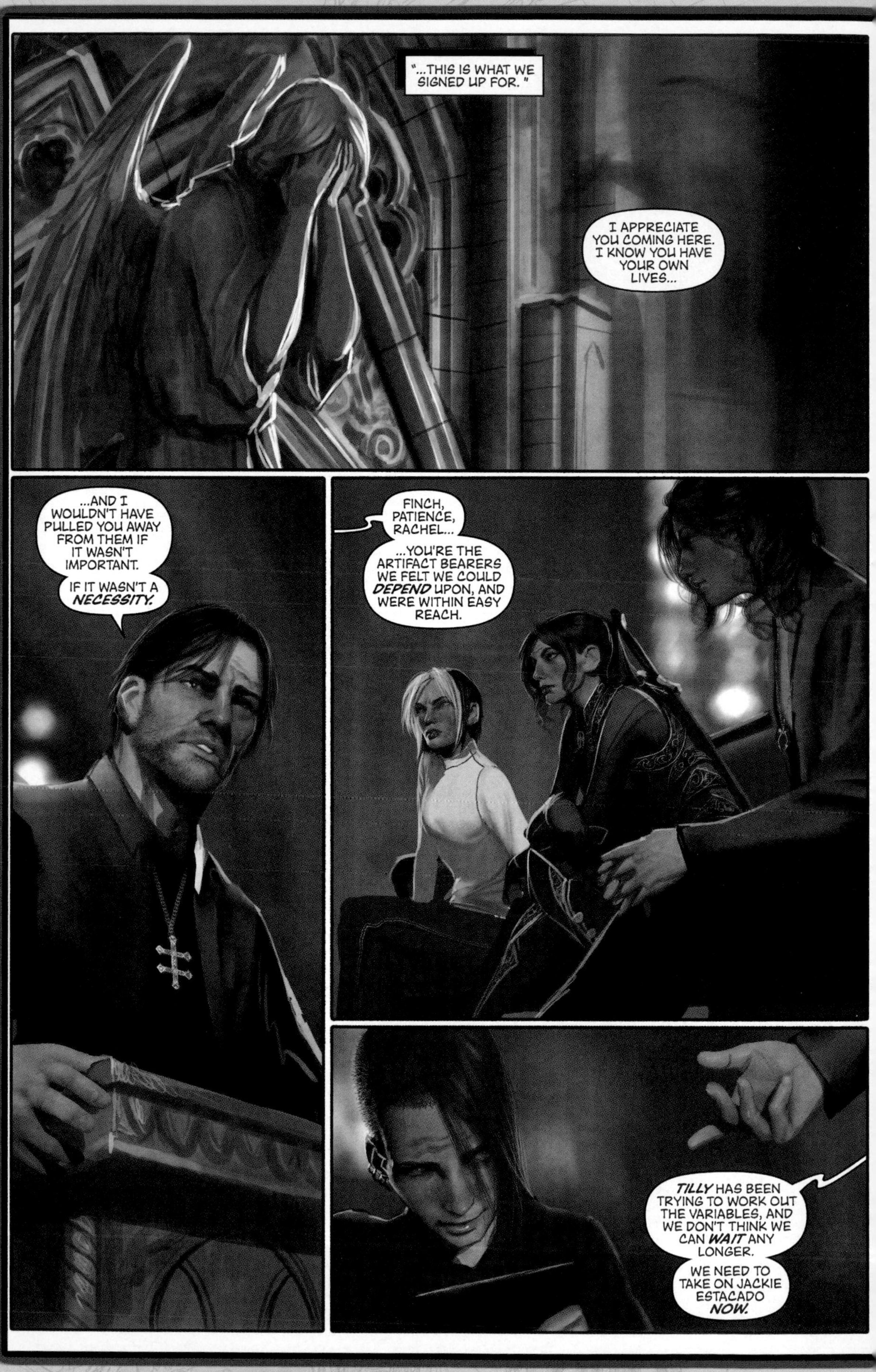
"...THIS IS WHAT WE SIGNED UP FOR."
I APPRECIATE YOU COMING HERE. I KNOW YOU HAVE YOUR OWN LIVES...
...AND I WOULDN'T HAVE PULLED YOU AWAY FROM THEM IF IT WASN'T IMPORTANT.
IF IT WASN'T A *NECESSITY.*
FINCH, PATIENCE, RACHEL...
...YOU'RE THE ARTIFACT BEARERS WE FELT WE COULD *DEPEND* UPON, AND WERE WITHIN EASY REACH.
TILLY HAS BEEN TRYING TO WORK OUT THE VARIABLES, AND WE DON'T THINK WE CAN *WAIT* ANY LONGER.
WE NEED TO TAKE ON JACKIE ESTACADO *NOW.*

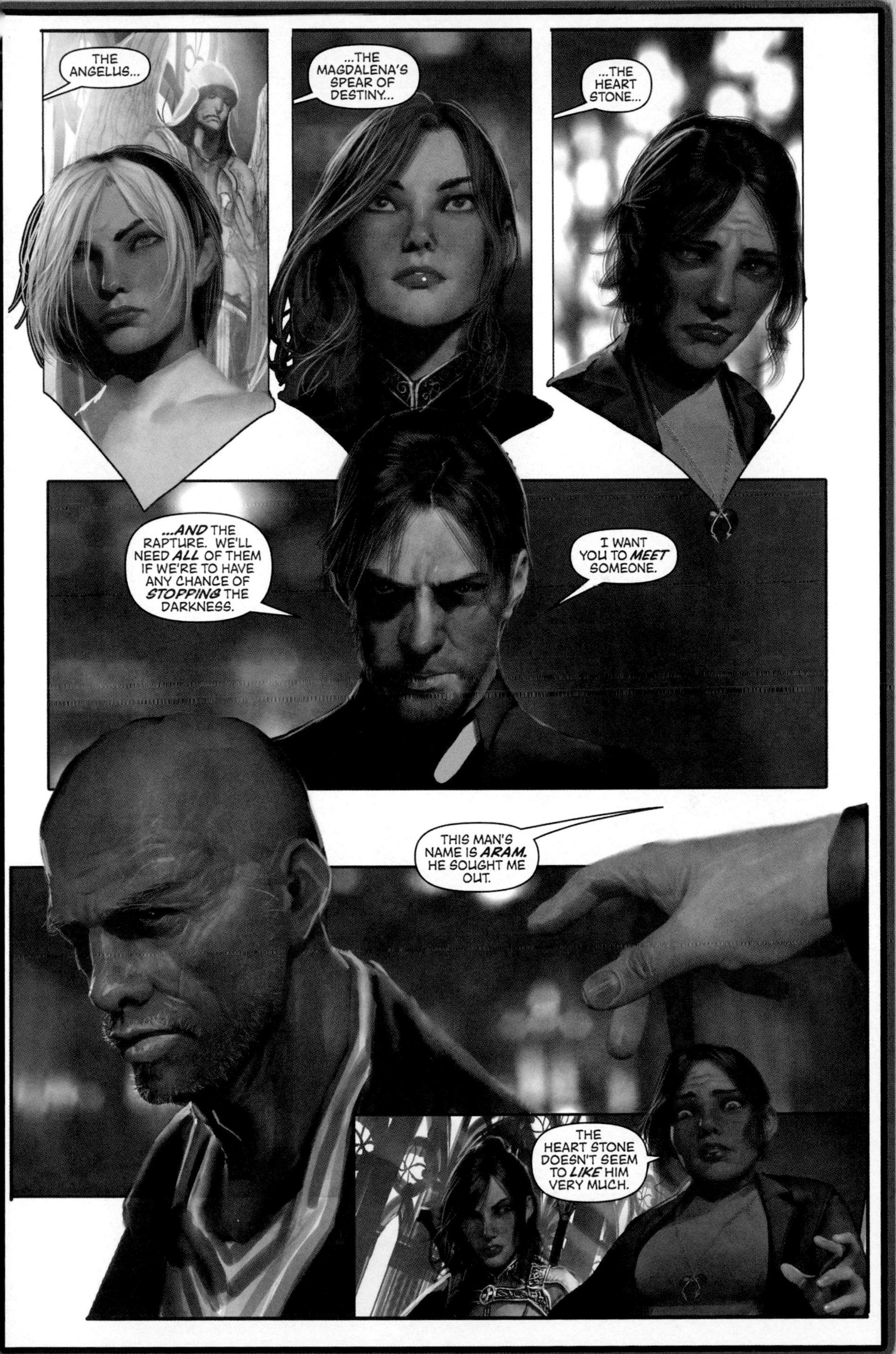
THE ANGELUS...
...THE MAGDALENA'S SPEAR OF DESTINY...
...THE HEART STONE...
...AND THE RAPTURE. WE'LL NEED ALL OF THEM IF WE'RE TO HAVE ANY CHANCE OF STOPPING THE DARKNESS.
I WANT YOU TO MEET SOMEONE.
THIS MAN'S NAME IS ARAM. HE SOUGHT ME OUT.
THE HEART STONE DOESN'T SEEM TO LIKE HIM VERY MUCH.

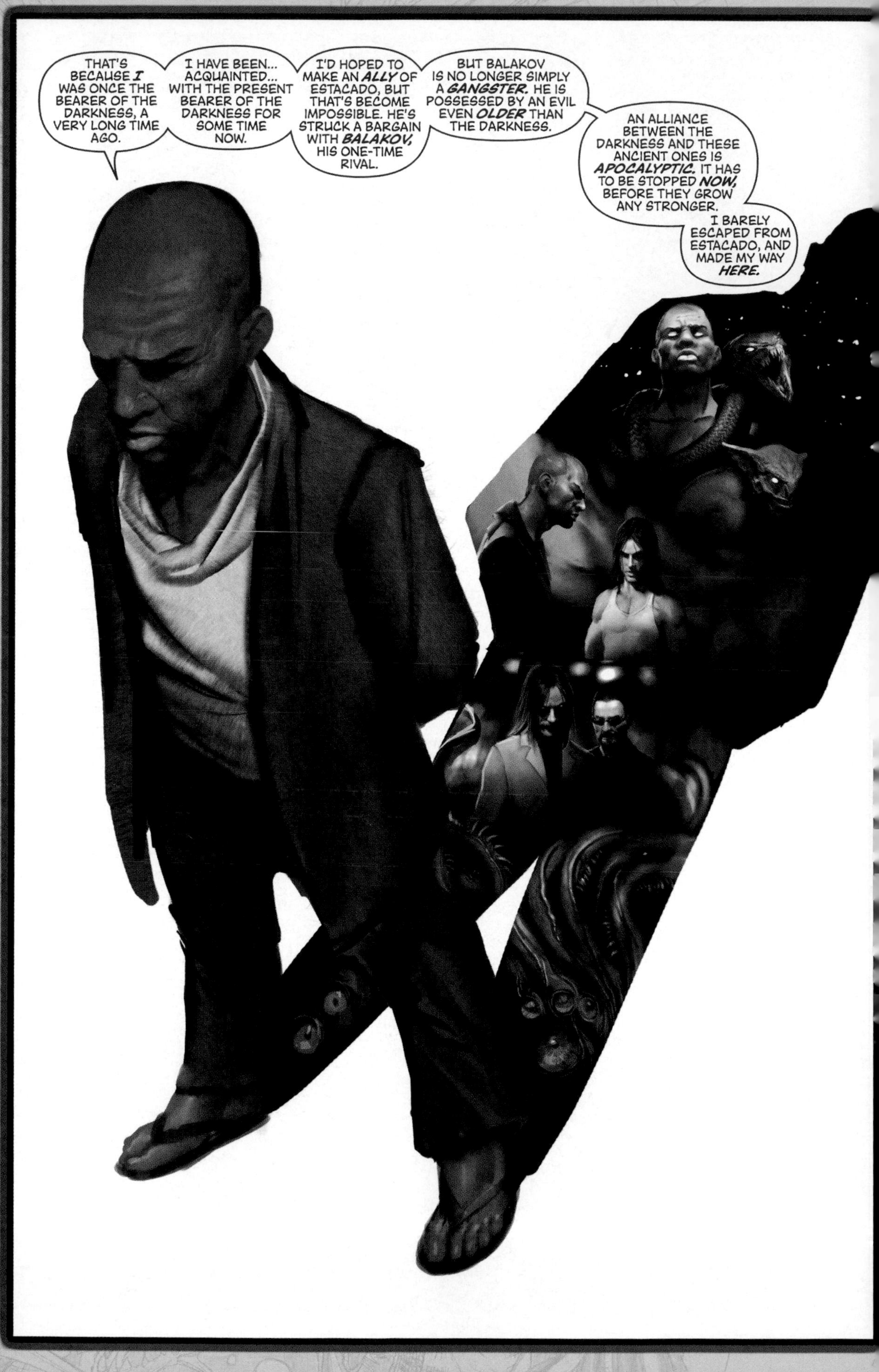
THAT'S BECAUSE *I* WAS ONCE THE BEARER OF THE DARKNESS, A VERY LONG TIME AGO.
I HAVE BEEN... ACQUAINTED... WITH THE PRESENT BEARER OF THE DARKNESS FOR SOME TIME NOW.
I'D HOPED TO MAKE AN *ALLY* OF ESTACADO, BUT THAT'S BECOME IMPOSSIBLE. HE'S STRUCK A BARGAIN WITH *BALAKOV,* HIS ONE-TIME RIVAL.
BUT BALAKOV IS NO LONGER SIMPLY A *GANGSTER.* HE IS POSSESSED BY AN EVIL EVEN *OLDER* THAN THE DARKNESS.
AN ALLIANCE BETWEEN THE DARKNESS AND THESE ANCIENT ONES IS *APOCALYPTIC.* IT HAS TO BE STOPPED *NOW,* BEFORE THEY GROW ANY STRONGER.
I BARELY ESCAPED FROM ESTACADO, AND MADE MY WAY *HERE.*

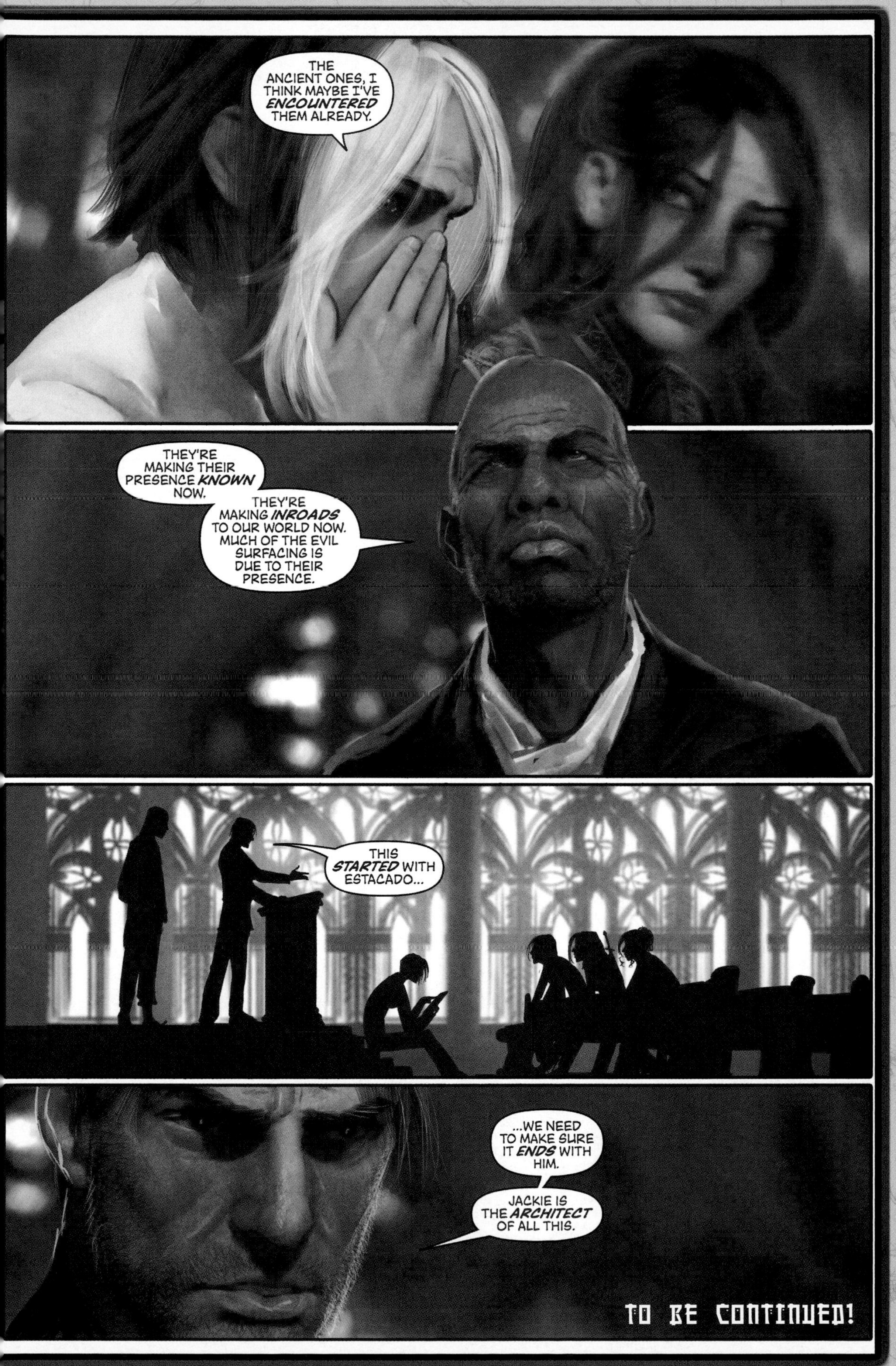
THE ANCIENT ONES, I THINK MAYBE I'VE ENCOUNTERED THEM ALREADY.
THEY'RE MAKING THEIR PRESENCE KNOWN NOW.
THEY'RE MAKING INROADS TO OUR WORLD NOW. MUCH OF THE EVIL SURFACING IS DUE TO THEIR PRESENCE.
THIS STARTED WITH ESTACADO...
...WE NEED TO MAKE SURE IT ENDS WITH HIM.
JACKIE IS THE ARCHITECT OF ALL THIS.
TO BE CONTINUED!

TOP COW UNIVERSE

ORIGINS

Witchblade: Origins Vol. 1-3

The Darkness: Origins Vol. 1-4

The Magdalena Origins: Vol. 1-2

Tom Judge: The Rapture Vol. 1

Necromancer Vol. 1

FIRST BORN

Witchblade Vol. 1-8

Artifacts Origins: First Born

ACCURSED

The Darkness: Accursed Vol. 1-7

Broken Trinity Vol. 1-2

The Magdalena Vol. 1-2

REDEMPTION

Witchblade: Redemption Vol. 1-4

ARTIFACTS

Angelus Vol. 1

Artifacts Vol. 1-3

REBIRTH

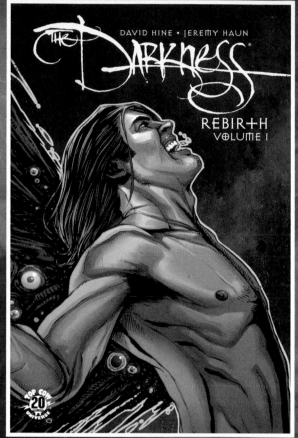

WITCHBLADE: REBIRTH VOL.1

written by: **TIM SEELEY**
art by: **DIEGO BERNARD**

No gun. No badge. No backup.
No problem.

In the wake of Top Cow's REBIRTH, Sara Pezzini has relocated from New York to Chicago and struggles to adapt to being a private detective. Pezzini quickly discovers that a change of scenery and occupation hasn't changed one thing... the Witchblade is still a magnet for the supernatural. Quickly drawn into a conflict between two mystical gangs, she must once again balance her responsibility as bearer of the Witchblade with her personal life.

collects issues #151-#155

(ISBN: 978-1-60706-532-6)

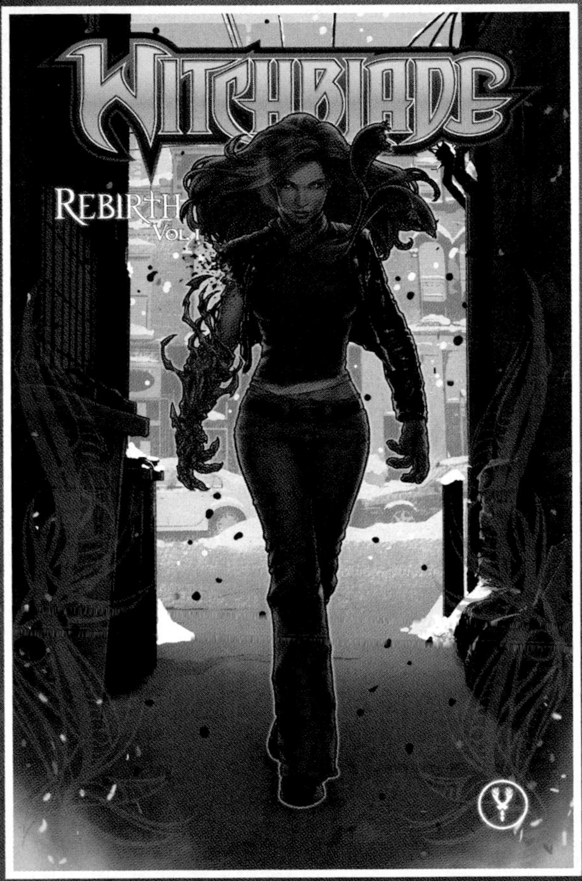
WITCHBLADE
REBIRTH
VOL. 1

WITCHBLADE: REBIRTH VOL.2

written by: **TIM SEELEY**
art by: **DIEGO BERNARD**

THE REBIRTH OF WITCHBLADE CONTINUES!

The upstart creative team of TIM SEELEY (HACK/SLASH, BLOODSTRIKE) and DIEGO BERNARD (The Man With No Name) continues their hot run on Top Cow's flagship title! Even as Sara Pezzini tries to settle into her new life in Chicago, the Witchblade's talent for seeking out weirdness pulls her into bizarre case after bizarre case. This volume sees Pezzini dealing with mercenary mana-hunters, spirit realms, fantastical steampunk warriors, and the most distilled embodiment of evil she's ever encountered. And that's before the local cops and corrupt political system complicates her life...?

collects issues #156-#160

(ISBN: 978-1-60706-637-8)

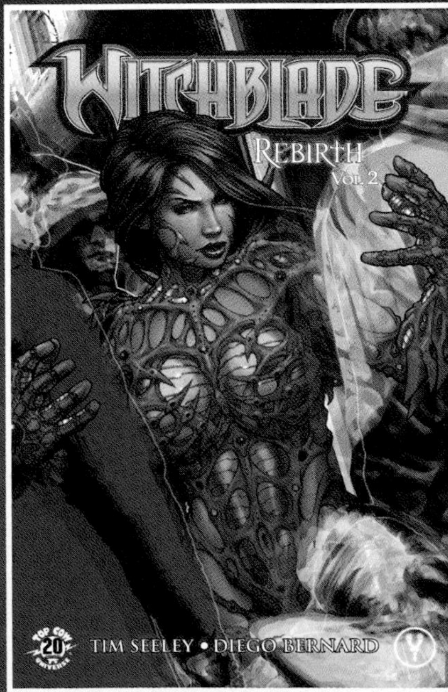
WITCHBLADE
REBIRTH
VOL. 2
TIM SEELEY • DIEGO BERNARD

MORE ARTIFACTS READING

ARTIFACTS
volume 4
REBIRTH
Ron Marz • Stjepan Sejic

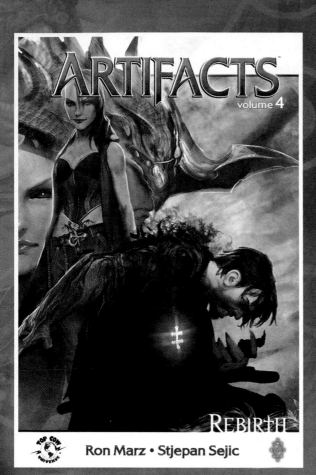

ARTIFACTS, VOL.4

written by: **RON MARZ**
art by: **STJEPAN SEJIC**

LONGTIME WITCHBLADE TEAM RON MARZ & STJEPAN SEJIC RESHAPE THE TOP COW UNIVERSE!

In this introductory-priced volume, the longtime *WITCHBLADE* team of RON MARZ and STJEPAN SEJIC unveil the new shape of the Top Cow Universe. Former priest and current FBI profiler, Tom Judge, can't shake the feeling that something is horribly and inherently wrong with the world. He blames it on past trauma, but a new investigation of gangland violence linked to mobster Jackie Estacado will reveal he may very well be right... and setting things right may destroy everything.

collects issues #14-#18

(ISBN: 978-1-60706-562-3)

Ron Marz • Michael Broussard
ARTIFACTS
volume 1

ARTIFACTS, VOL.1

written by: **RON MARZ**
art by: **MICHAEL BROUSSARD**

(ISBN: 978-1-60706-201-1)

Ron Marz • Whilce Portacio
ARTIFACTS
volume 2

ARTIFACTS, VOL.2

written by: **RON MARZ**
art by: **WHILCE PORTACIO**

(ISBN: 978-1-60706-211-0)

Ron Marz • Jeremy Haun • Dale Keown
ARTIFACTS
volume 3

ARTIFACTS, VOL.3

written by: **RON MARZ**
art by: **JEREMY HAUN & DALE KEOWN**

(ISBN: 978-1-60706-425-1)